World Heritage and Sustainable Development

In 2015, the General Assembly of State Parties to the World Heritage Convention passed a ground-breaking Sustainable Development policy that seeks to bring the World Heritage system into line with the UN's sustainable development agenda (UNESCO 2015). *World Heritage and Sustainable Development* provides a broad overview of the process that brought about the new policy and the implications of its enactment.

The book is divided into four parts. Part I puts the policy in its historical and theoretical context, and Part II offers an analysis of the four policy dimensions on which the policy is based – environmental sustainability, inclusive social development, inclusive economic development and the fostering of peace and security. Part III presents perspectives from IUCN, ICOMOS and ICCROM – the three Advisory Bodies to the World Heritage Committee, and Part IV offers 'case study' perspectives on the practical implications of the policy. Contributions come from a wide range of experienced heritage professionals and practitioners who offer both 'inside' perspectives on the evolution of the policy and 'outside' perspectives on its implications. Combined, they present and analyse the main ideas, debates and implications of the policy change.

This book is key reading for all heritage professionals interested in developing a better understanding of the new Sustainable Development policy. It is also essential reading for scholars and students working in the area.

Peter Bille Larsen is a lecturer at the University of Lucerne, Switzerland. He is a Danish anthropologist who works on the intersection between conservation and social equity concerns. He has worked closely with the Advisory Bodies and the World Heritage Centre.

William Logan is an Emeritus Professor at Deakin University, Australia. He is a fellow of the Academy of Social Sciences in Australia and formerly a member of the Heritage Council of Victoria. He is a member of the editorial board of the *International Journal of Heritage Studies* and co-editor of *A Companion to Heritage Studies* (2015) and the 'Key Issues in Cultural Heritage' book series.

Key Issues in Cultural Heritage

Series Editors: William Logan and Laurajane Smith

Also in the series

For more information about this series, please visit: www.routledge.com/Key-Issues-in-Cultural-Heritage/book-series/KICH

World Heritage and Sustainable Development

New Directions in World Heritage Management

Edited by Peter Bille Larsen and William Logan

Routledge
Taylor & Francis Group

LONDON AND NEW YORK

First published 2018
by Routledge
2 Park Square, Milton Park, Abingdon, Oxon OX14 4RN

and by Routledge
711 Third Avenue, New York, NY 10017

Routledge is an imprint of the Taylor & Francis Group, an informa business

British Library Cataloguing-in-Publication Data
A catalogue record for this book is available from the British Library

Library of Congress Cataloging-in-Publication Data
A catalog record has been requested for this book

ISBN: 978-1-138-09139-9 (hbk)
ISBN: 978-1-138-09140-5 (pbk)
ISBN: 978-1-315-10804-9 (ebk)

Typeset in Times New Roman
by Apex CoVantage, LLC

MIX
Paper from
responsible sources
FSC   FSC™ C013985
www.fsc.org

Printed in the United Kingdom
by Henry Ling Limited

Contents

Illustrations

Figures

Tables

Contributors

Patricia Alberth is a World Heritage Specialist with extensive experience at the UNESCO World Heritage Centre and the UNESCO Regional Bureau for Culture in Asia and the Pacific. Since 2013, she heads the World Heritage Office of the City of Bamberg. She holds degrees in International Business (BA) and World Heritage Studies (MSc).

Tim Badman is the Director of the World Heritage Programme at the International Union for Conservation of Nature (IUCN). Prior to joining IUCN in 2007, he worked in local government in Dorset County Council (UK) as Environment Policy Manager. He originally qualified in geology and countryside management and has worked extensively on World Heritage, protected areas, coastal zone management and geological heritage.

Dina Ishak Bakhoum is an engineer and art historian specializing in cultural heritage conservation, management and capacity building. She collaborates with the American Research Center in Egypt, the Aga Khan Trust for Culture, UNESCO, ICOMOS and other institutions. She also lectures on related topics at a number of universities.

Giovanni Boccardi is an architect conservator and has been a UNESCO staff member for more than 20 years. As Focal Point for sustainable development and disaster risk reduction within the UNESCO Culture Sector until 2015, he spearheaded the development of a policy for the integration of a sustainable development perspective within the World Heritage Convention into the processes of the World Heritage Convention.

Luisa De Marco, architect and PhD in conservation of architectural monuments and landscape, has been working at the Ministry of Cultural Properties, Activities and Tourism in Italy since 2000. She is the appointed Resident Adviser in a European Union-funded Twinning Project on Cultural Heritage between Italy and the Republic of Moldova (2017–2019). She has been an ICOMOS World Heritage Adviser since 2009.

Susan Denyer, FSA, is a World Heritage Adviser at ICOMOS (International Council on Monuments and Sites) and also the Secretary of ICOMOS-UK.

She has worked for the National Trust, in museums and as lecturer, including six years in East and West Africa, and has been the Chair of BASIN, an international network for low-cost housing. She has published widely on cultural landscapes and is an occasional lecturer at various universities.

Stefan Disko is an ethnologist whose professional life has focused on working with indigenous organizations on human rights issues, mostly in the context of the United Nations. He holds a master's in World Heritage studies and serves as a consultant to the International Work Group for Indigenous Affairs (IWGIA) on issues related to the World Heritage Convention.

Duong Bich Hanh provided support to the capacity building and management of the eight World Heritage sites in Viet Nam during the period of 2009–2016. She is especially interested in linking World Heritage with local communities and finding ways for World Heritage to play a greater role in Viet Nam's sustainable development. Hanh is currently the Chief of the Culture Unit at the UNESCO Bangkok Office.

Regina Durighello, art historian, is in charge of the World Heritage Monitoring and Advisory Unit at ICOMOS International Secretariat.

Jyoti Hosagrahar is the Director of the Division of Creativity in UNESCO's Culture Sector. She directs the implementation of two major culture conventions and leads the integration of culture in the 2030 Agenda for Sustainable Development. Before joining UNESCO, she was a professor at Columbia University, New York; UNESCO Chair at Srishti Institute of Art, Design and Technology in Bangalore; and Founder-Director of Sustainable Urbanism International, a Bangalore NGO.

Juan Luis Isaza Londoño is an architect who has held numerous positions in public and private heritage organizations in Colombia, including Director of Heritage at the Ministry of Culture of Colombia. He is currently Director of Cultural Heritage Management, Fundación Ferrocarril de Antioquia, Medellín. He consults at the international level and has been an invited professor at national and foreign universities.

Muhammad Juma is a Director of Urban and Rural Planning in Zanzibar. He worked at the Stone Town Conservation and Development Authority and as an in-house consultant at UNESCO World Heritage Centre in Paris. Dr Muhammad represents the United Republic of Tanzania at the World Heritage Committee and is working on articulating cultural and heritage values on spatial planning.

Sophia Labadi is a Senior Lecturer and co-Director of the Centre for Heritage at the University of Kent (UK) and regularly acts as consultant for international organizations on cultural heritage issues. She is the author of *UNESCO, Cultural Heritage, and Outstanding Universal Value* (Altamira Press, 2013), as well as the co-editor with William Logan of *Urban Heritage, Development, and Sustainability* (Routledge, 2015).

Peter Bille Larsen, anthropologist and lecturer at the University of Lucerne, works on the intersection between conservation and social equity in the fields of heritage, human rights, biodiversity and the anthropology of international organizations. He has also worked closely with the Advisory Bodies and the World Heritage Centre.

William Logan is an Emeritus Professor at Deakin University, Melbourne, and fellow of the Academy of Social Sciences in Australia. He was formerly UNESCO Chair of Heritage and Urbanism, a member of the Heritage Council of Victoria and president of Australia ICOMOS. He is co-editor of the Routledge 'Key Issues in Cultural Heritage' book series and the *Wiley-Blackwell Companion to Heritage Studies*.

Nguyen Viet Cuong is a PhD candidate at Ha Noi University of Culture. His research focuses on the implementation of the World Heritage Convention in the context of Viet Nam. Cuong is chief of the Relics and Monuments Management Division, Department of Cultural Heritage, Ministry of Culture, Sports and Tourism of Vietnam and a member of the Vietnamese delegation to World Heritage Committee meetings.

Max Ooft is a Policy Officer at the Bureau of VIDS, the Association of Indigenous Village Leaders in Suriname, doing policy and advocacy work, strategic planning, program and project design and implementation and providing hands-on support to indigenous communities. He has been involved in various indigenous peoples' policy development processes of various UN agencies.

Elena Osipova joined the IUCN World Heritage Program in August 2012 and currently holds the position of Monitoring Officer. Elena coordinates the IUCN World Heritage Outlook initiative and is responsible for monitoring the state of conservation of natural and mixed World Heritage sites in Latin America and the Caribbean, Eastern Europe and Oceania. She also coordinates the Program's work on benefits and ecosystem services provided by natural sites.

Christian Ost is a Professor of Economics and former Dean of ICHEC Brussels Management School. He has been a visiting lecturer at the Raymond Lemaire International Centre for Conservation at KU Leuven, the Ecole Nationale Supérieure d'Architecture at Paris-Belleville and the Burgundy School of Business and a scholar-in-residence at the Getty Conservation Institute (2008–2009). He sits on the Advisory Board of Global Heritage Fund and the ICOMOS International Economics Scientific Committee (Chairman 2000–2005).

Pham Thi Thanh Huong is a Culture Specialist at UNESCO Ha Noi. She also serves as a board member of the Global Public Use Planning Consortium that promotes a holistic approach in heritage planning and management. She holds a master's degree in public policy, media and communications and a bachelor's degree in international economics and politics. Her research areas of interest include heritage studies, cultural tourism and creative industries.

Lindsay Scott received her MSc in Sustainable Heritage from University College London before working with Giovanni Boccardi on Disaster Preparedness and Sustainable Development at UNESCO's World Heritage Centre in Paris. Prior to UCL, she managed an expedition to Everest Base Camp, where she highlighted the effects of climate change on the world's melting glaciers and Nepal's natural heritage.

César Augusto Velandia Silva has a PhD in geography and is an architect, researcher and consultant based at the University of Ibagué, Colombia. He worked as coordinator of the Cultural Landscape of the Coffee of Colombia in the Ministry of Culture of Colombia (2012–2015). He currently develops research projects on cultural landscapes in the region of Tolima, Colombia.

Jane Thompson is an architect and a qualified project manager working to improve the management and conservation of cultural heritage. She brings together more than two decades of site experience with international-level research, policy work and capacity development initiatives. She is a senior advisor to the Italian Ministry of Culture.

Tran Thi Thu Thuy is a National Program Officer in the UNESCO Ha Noi Office, where she oversees the implementation of cultural projects on creative industries, responsible tourism and sustainable management of natural and cultural heritage. She also acts as the country representative in Viet Nam for the Public Use Planning Consortium. Thuy has a master's degree in Public Management from the Université Libre de Bruxelles.

Gamini Wijesuriya is an architect and archaeologist with a 40-year career focused on conserving and managing heritage. Until December 2017, he was a staff member of ICCROM, where his work involved organizing variety of international capacity development activities, research, policy and providing advisory service to the World Heritage Committee as part of ICCROM's official mandate. He has many publications to his credit.

Ege Yıldırım is an urban planner specializing in heritage conservation and management with 20 years of experience working in Turkey and internationally. She has been based in Istanbul since 2013 as an independent consultant/instructor for various municipalities and universities. Dr Yıldırım is currently the ICOMOS Focal Point for the Sustainable Development Goals and Heritage Site Manager of the Historic Guild Town of Mudurnu.

Zhou Jian is an established scholar in the field of cultural heritage and urban regeneration. Besides regular teaching and research in Tongji University, China, he also takes responsibilities as the Secretary-General of UNESCO WHITRAP and plays important roles in several distinguished academic societies. His recent research focuses on local mechanisms in heritage management, participatory approach of conservation and sustainable community development.

Acknowledgments

We would like to thank Giovanni Boccardi for the intellectual energy in getting the process of drafting the World Heritage and Sustainable Development policy up and running, for selecting the working group, guiding the group's discussions in Cottbus, Ninh Binh and electronically, and encouraging the publication of this book.

We are grateful to the many contributors who were ready to develop their drafting notes, workshop presentations and thoughts into the more systematic reflections about heritage and sustainable development found in their chapters in the book. We thank them for being willing to do this work on top of their regular commitments and across different languages and time zones.

We would also like to thank the German and Vietnamese authorities for hosting the initial collective discussions, thus creating the basis for sustainable development as a field of dialogue. Our hope with the book is to call for the deepening of this conversation. We therefore also thank the book series co-editors and Routledge for their support in seeing that this book reaches a wide readership.

Series editors' foreword

The interdisciplinary field of Heritage Studies is now well established in many parts of the world. It differs from earlier scholarly and professional activities that focused narrowly on the architectural or archaeological preservation of monuments and sites. Such work remains important, especially as modernization and globalization lead to new developments that threaten natural environments, archaeological sites, historic urban landscapes, traditional buildings and arts, crafts and other forms of intangible heritage. But they are subsumed within the new field that sees 'heritage' as a social and political construct encompassing all those places, artefacts and cultural expressions inherited from the past that, because they are seen to reflect and validate our identity as nations, communities, families and even individuals, are worthy of some form of respect and protection.

Heritage results from a selection process, often government-initiated and supported by official regulation; it is not the same as history, although this, too, has its own elements of selectivity. Heritage can be used in positive ways to give a sense of community to disparate groups and individuals or to create jobs in cultural industries, including museums and cultural tourism. It can be actively used by governments and communities to foster respect for cultural and social diversity, and to challenge prejudice and misrecognition. But it can also be used by governments in less benign ways, to reshape public attitudes in line with undemocratic political agendas or even to rally people against their neighbours in civil and international wars, ethnic cleansing and genocide. In this way, there is a real connection between heritage, social justice and human rights.

Heritage protection does not depend alone on top-down interventions by governments and global heritage organizations or the expert actions of heritage industry professionals but must involve local communities and other communities of interest. It is critical that the values and practices of communities, together with traditional management systems where such exist, are understood, respected and incorporated in management plans and policy documents so that this allows communities to enjoy a sense of 'ownership' of the heritage that underpins their cultural identity and take a leading role in sustaining it into the future.

This series of books canvasses the key issues dealt with in the new Heritage Studies. It seeks to identify key interdisciplinary debates within the field and to explore how they impact on the practices not only of heritage conservation and management but also the processes of production, consumption and engagement with heritage in its many and varied forms.

William Logan
Laurajane Smith

Part I

Historical, theoretical and institutional frameworks

Chapter 1

Policy-making at the World Heritage-sustainable development interface

Introductory remarks

William Logan and Peter Bille Larsen

The world is at a crucial point, faced as it is with daunting sustainability challenges ranging from climate change and resource depletion to growing social inequalities and massively destructive military conflicts. Twenty-five years have passed since the United Nations (UN) adopted its *Framework Convention on Climate Change* (UN 1992a), yet the latest monitoring continues to show increased global warming. Other global statistics are equally dramatic. The Living Planet Index shows that species abundance declined by 58 per cent between 1970 and 2012 (WWF 2016). In the 2012, the wealthiest one per cent held 18 per cent of total household wealth, six times as much as the mere three per cent held by the 40 per cent poorest (Keeley 2015: 3). Armed conflict, war and polarization continue to destroy people and places, destabilizing large parts of the world and triggering refugee streams and misery.

As outlined below, there have been efforts to bring sustainability to the forefront of international, national and local debate and policy making since the 1980s. Yet, have three decades of sustainability policy-making as the means to peace and prosperity, to put things bluntly, failed or simply been dwarfed by other priorities? Belief in economic growth as the development mantra largely continues unabated, and, despite ever more detailed global agreements and international standards to promote social equity, inclusion and environmental sustainability, much obviously remains to be done.

What does the fact that the globe is moving beyond its carrying capacity mean for efforts to hold on to remnants from the past, particularly places of heritage value to nations and local communities and to the World Heritage system? From an environmental perspective, the risks of planetary collapse seem overwhelming. The theoretical and practical implications may also appear daunting and well beyond the capability of individual heritage site managers or even a country's leading policy makers to formulate an effective response.

The UN has certainly tried, at least on paper. Its latest attempts to chart a global roadmap and a post-2015 sustainable development agenda are laid out in key documents such as *Transforming Our World: The 2030 Agenda for Sustainable Development* (UNGA 2015) as well as the Paris Agreement on Climate Change (UN 2015). As a member of the UN family of institutions, UNESCO has a responsibility to promote this agenda and to ensure that all of its programs adhere to sustainable development principles. This includes its programs relating to the safeguarding of heritage under its various Conventions – heritage places (UNESCO 1972), underwater heritage (UNESCO 2001), intangible heritage (UNESCO 2003) and cultural expressions (UNESCO 2005). Documentary heritage is also included under the Memory of the World program established in 1992 (UNESCO 2017a). UNESCO's heritage project offers a privileged perspective allowing us to rethink and, ideally, integrate, the sustainability of heritage from multiple perspectives.

Until recently, the question challenging the minds of those working within UNESCO's flagship World Heritage program was whether or not it was expected to play a major part in promoting the sustainable development agenda. Earlier UN agreements had, in effect, only given scant recognition of the linkage between heritage, development and sustainability. The 1992 *Rio Declaration on Environment and Development*, for instance, made no reference to heritage at all (UN 1992b). Agenda 21 promoted World Heritage sites as part of a call for the establishment and expansion of protected area systems in forest areas (United Nations 1992c) and alluded to cultural heritage only once in a sentence essentially relating to tourism.

Even the World Heritage Committee's 'reflection on the future of the Convention' in 2008 appeared to be a lost opportunity to broaden the scope of World Heritage system ambitions. This reflection was considered timely as the Convention approached its 40th anniversary and the World Heritage List its 1,000th inscription. The resultant *Vision and Strategic Action Plan, 2012–2022* was adopted by the General Assembly of State Parties to the Convention in 2011. The plan identified six goals:

1   The Outstanding Universal Value (OUV) of World Heritage sites is maintained;
2   The World Heritage List is a credible selection of the world's most outstanding cultural and natural heritage;
3   Heritage protection and conservation considers present and future environmental, societal and economic needs;
4   World Heritage maintains or enhances its brand quality;
5   The Committee can address policy and strategic issues;
6   Decisions of statutory meetings are informed and effectively implemented.

This sought to make the system run more efficiently and effectively, but it also clearly reasserted the primacy within the Convention of protecting and conserving the OUV of those places deemed by the Committee to possess it. From a sustainability perspective, Goal 3 looked somewhat more promising. Yet, the plan aimed at only a single outcome under that goal: 'Increased consideration of sustainable development through connecting conservation to communities'. No elaboration was provided, nor was any mention made of other societal needs such as inclusive economic and social development or human rights, which increasing numbers of academics and practitioners were seeing as inextricably connected to heritage conservation and sustainable development.

The plan was a disappointment to many working within the system, especially given that the Committee and its secretariat, the World Heritage Centre, had a strong record of taking on board new ideas, generating discussions and promoting systemic change. Examples include the introduction of the Cultural Landscape category (1992), the Nara Document on Authenticity that highlighted the intangible aspects of World Heritage sites (1994) and the Historic Urban Landscape approach (2011). The Committee's 2011 strategic plan did, however, see itself as 'a living document' to be considered in conjunction with other UNESCO documents such as the *Strategy for Reducing Risks at World Heritage Properties* (UNESCO 2007a), the *Policy Document on the Impacts of Climate Change on World Heritage Properties* (UNESCO 2007b) and the *World Heritage Strategy for Capacity Building* (UNESCO 2011b). The policy intention to address wider sustainability concerns beyond a narrow heritage scope was clear, yet it hardly covered the full range of social, economic and environmental challenges. The global momentum to address these has since then grown not least through the process of preparing for and adopting the UN Sustainable Development Goals.

The focus of the debate has also bifurcated. Initially, the concern was inward-looking, focusing on the sustainability of the heritage places and safeguarding practices within the World Heritage system itself. This first concern led, among other things, to a growing acceptance that the meaningful engagement of local communities and indigenous peoples in the identification and management of the places for which they have traditionally been custodians provides the best guarantee for the survival of traditional heritage sites. In the meantime, a second, outward-looking perspective that heritage principles and practice could and should contribute to wider social, cultural and environmental sustainability has emerged. Questions to be answered include whether World Heritage sites are merely islands of protection and attributes of nostalgia in wider seas of environmental and cultural degradation? If the policy ambition, indeed, is to contribute beyond heritage conservation narrowly defined, then what impact could the 1,071 World Heritage sites in 167 countries make towards overcoming the sustainability challenges facing local communities, nations and the world at large? Furthermore, how would such a contribution be made – by policy or through rhetoric and persuasion (Logan 2017)?

Some answers came in November 2015 when a potentially ground-breaking event took place at the General Assembly of the State Parties to the World Heritage Convention. This was the adoption of a new *Policy on the Integration of a Sustainable Development Perspective into the Processes of the World Heritage Convention* (hereafter World Heritage and Sustainable Development Policy) (UNESCO 2015). The policy aims to bring the World Heritage system into line with the UN's sustainable development agenda and refers to all World Heritage processes, including nominations and inscriptions, site conservation, management and interpretation and State of Conservation reports and other forms of monitoring. This also potentially concerns heritage sites more generally because of the ways in which the global heritage discourse often filters down to national and local heritage systems.

The policy has enormous potential ramifications because of the way it conceptualizes and specifies the meaning of sustainable development. It draws on the conceptual framework adopted in discussions leading to the UN's post-2015 development agenda and the report *Realizing the Future We Want for All* (UNTT 2012). This sees the achievement of sustainable development as being dependent on three overarching principles and four main sets of factors. The overarching principles are human rights, equality and long-term sustainability. The four main sets of factors concern environmental sustainability, inclusive social development, inclusive economic development and the fostering of peace and security. While adopting this UN conceptualization, the policy also adapts it to World Heritage-specific terminology and mechanisms with objectives that respond to the key challenges faced in implementing the Convention.

The policy calls on State Parties not only to protect the OUV of World Heritage properties, but also to 'recognise and promote the properties' inherent potential to contribute to all dimensions of sustainable development … [and to] ensure that their conservation and management strategies are aligned with broader sustainable development objectives'. Note that the World Heritage and Sustainable Development policy is binding on all State Parties.

Note, too, that while the working group was developing its draft policy for World Heritage, however, a parallel policy development was occurring under the Intangible Convention 2003 (UNESCO 2003), again by an international, multicultural and multidisciplinary team. A draft policy was prepared entitled 'Safeguarding intangible cultural heritage and sustainable development at the national level'. This is being inserted into the *Operational Directives for the implementation of the Convention for the Safeguarding of the Intangible Heritage* (UNESCO 2016b) following its endorsement by the Intergovernmental Committee for the Safeguarding of the Intangible Cultural Heritage in December 2015 and the General Assembly of State Parties to the Convention at its sixth session in June 2016.

A determined effort was made to ensure consistency between the two policy statements. This collaboration was another step towards overcoming the unfortunate separation of heritage place and intangible heritage management under two separate conventions (Logan 2017). There is at least a growing understanding in the expert community of the way all these matters need to cohere and be assessed together. The task will be to bring other heritage professionals and stakeholders into this understanding.

This volume

In this volume, we trace the evolution of the debate leading up to the drafting and approval of UNESCO's 2015 policy and to explore what the multifaceted character of sustainable development means for the implementation of the World Heritage Convention. We also seek to show that beneath the consensual language of sustainability, potential contradictions and conflicts are ever present (Neumayer 2013). These may be found within seemingly neutral discussions around value and economic gain to the multiple uses of the term 'local development'. The hope of World Heritage conservation as good *per se* followed by an ever-growing multiplier of positive spin-offs such as poverty reduction, wealth generation, environmental conservation and world peace has its clear limits. In response, a less loaded discussion is now needed.

A typology of heritage-sustainable development intersections

In seeking to clarify the issues at stake, it is useful to consider four different perspectives on the heritage conservation-sustainable development linkage. This typology is by no means exhaustive, but presented here to stimulate discussion.

The first perspective – *sustainable heritage* – principally reflects an inward-looking perspective concerned with whether or to what extent heritage itself is being sustained for new generations. This, in many respects, refers to the core of the heritage project. As we saw with the World Heritage Committee's reflection on the future of the Convention, this is at times expressed as a concern not to lose track of the core conservation purpose. This perspective is sometimes staunchly defended by practitioners who view the sustainable development discourse as carrying the risk of diluting the main conservation mission.

The second perspective – *heritage vs. sustainable development* – builds on the age-old opposition between heritage and development, each seen as a threat to the other. It suggests that the sustainable development concept offers no solution to this potential conflict but, rather, runs the risk of green-washing potential threats to heritage in the guise of sustainability. This may emerge, for example, in discussions about how to reconcile restoration vs. using new building materials, or solar panels or windmills set up in the name of sustainability in heritage places.

The third approach – *sustainable development for heritage* – is about adapting development paths to the needs and requirement of heritage conservation. It may involve the celebration of heritage targets in sustainability development policy, as recently witnessed in the context of the SDGs. It may also involve arguments in support of development investments and trade-offs in order to generate societal, political and financial support for heritage.

The fourth approach – *heritage for sustainable development* – shares the characteristics of the first perspective in terms of considering OUV protection as the main mission. Yet it specifically adds arguments about the contributions of heritage can make to solving wider sustainability challenges. 'No sustainable development without culture', UNESCO and like-minded organizations have argued. This is where debates about the contribution of heritage conservation to the UN's post-2015 development agenda, climate change mitigation and *Realizing the Future We Want for All* fit in.

Such a diversity of notions is found across the heritage field. This partly reflects the elasticity of both underlying concepts, partly the embedded nature of discussions as well as the highly diverse heritage contexts. Sustainable development may be identified as a need, a threat, a solution or even an objective of heritage. This flexibility may lead to a productive creativity and an ability to adapt to local situations. Yet, there is also a potential risk of confusion leading to an inadequate basis for the types of collective action necessary to address the sustainability challenges of our times.

Consequently, clarification of the concepts and their interlinkage was a fundamental aspect of the process of drafting the UNESCO World Heritage and Sustainability policy. Support for considering the linkage between the World Heritage Convention, heritage conservation and sustainable development was initially given at the World Heritage Committee's 34th session in Brasilia in 2010. At the 38th session in Doha in 2014, the Committee requested the World Heritage Centre, with the support of the Advisory Bodies, to convene a small international working group to develop a proposal for a policy to integrate sustainable development into the processes of the World Heritage Convention.

The volume brings together many of those who were involved in drafting the policy – an international team of heritage policy thinkers and site managers and practitioners with hands-on experience of World Heritage issues. The volume thereby conforms with the ambition of the 'Key Issue in Cultural Heritage' series to recognize that ideas about heritage are tied to diverse heritage practices, geographical settings and different philosophical perspectives. In this case, those who had responsibility to lead the working group discussions on specific sections of the policy have developed their ideas into chapter format.

The three Advisory Bodies named in the Convention – the International Union for the Conservation of Nature (IUCN), the International Council on Monuments and Sites (ICOMOS) and the International Centre for the Study of the Preservation and Restoration of Cultural Property (ICCROM) – were represented in the working group and here in the volume outline their institutional perspectives. The site managers, in turn, tie the discussions and the policy perspectives back to their specific World Heritage places. Together, the chapters provide an analytical account of major sustainable development challenges and how new approaches are being or might be conceived in the World Heritage arena.

The volume has four parts. *Part I* traces the evolution of the debate about the heritage/sustainable development linkage and the steps taken towards the adoption of the World Heritage and Sustainable Development policy in November 2015. Giovanni Boccardi from the World Heritage Centre was charged with setting up the drafting group and coordinated its discussions across 2014–2015 in Cottbus, Germany, and Ninh Binh, Vietnam, as well as electronically. In Chapter 2, writing with colleague Lindsay Scott, Boccardi provides a 'view from the inside' of the process leading to the adoption of the policy. This is followed by a background literature review by Sophia Labadi of the historical, theoretical and international considerations on culture, heritage and (sustainable) development (Chapter 3). Both chapters highlight conflicting perspectives and the need for better understanding of the forces at work in a theoretically sound and practically useful policy approach.

Part II comprises six chapters analysing the four policy dimensions identified by the UN and framing the new UNESCO policy – that is, environmental sustainability, inclusive social development, inclusive economic development and the fostering of peace and security. It also explores the three overarching sets of principles relating to human rights, equality and sustainability (UN Task Team 2012). The different dimensions and principles are interlinked and overlapping. Equality, one of the overarching principles (ibid: 25), for example, is addressed in the chapters on social inclusion, human rights, indigenous peoples and gender. Sustainability runs across all chapters, whereas human rights have a dedicated chapter in the policy.

Environmental sustainability

Environmental sustainability, as a key dimension, concerns matters such as 'ensuring a stable climate, stopping ocean acidification, preventing land degradation and unsustainable water use, sustainably managing natural resources and protecting the natural resources base, including biodiversity' (UN Task Team 2012: 27). On the one hand, it addresses how heritage may be at greater risk from environmental concerns such as natural disasters or climate change. On the other hand, it concerns how heritage conservation can contribute towards environmental sustainability. The IUCN chapter by Elena Osipova et al., which is described below, particularly addresses this dimension with a focus on natural heritage sites as well as a broader outlook on environmental sustainability across all types of World Heritage properties.

Inclusive economic development

Rethinking sustainability will require challenging the economy in multiple ways. Are win-win scenarios possible where new heritage commodities both serve economic and conservation purposes? Or is the push for economic value a Trojan horse potentially hollowing out heritage conservation from within through commodification and problematic trade-offs? The World Heritage context demonstrates the problematic nature of certain strands of mainstream economics in the sustainability field, as Christian Ost's Chapter 4 shows. A policy agenda on inclusive economies, in turn, recognizes heritage as an uneven playing field. It thereby potentially challenges basic assumptions about the risks and opportunities involved with certain neoliberal strands of value creation. Questions of inclusion concern whether a given World Heritage space is accessible, who is in control of it and whether, in economic terms, it promotes locally driven businesses, livelihoods and economies.

Inclusive social development

The concrete meaning and significance of equitable conservation, social inclusion and even the category of indigenous peoples have a long history of being renegotiated and contested in specific contexts. The use of the community concept in the World Heritage field has been notoriously vague prompting critique, yet also offered openings for more pro-active engagement. Chapter 5 by Jyoti Hosagrahar opens up this field of enquiry and action stressing the centrality of participation enhancing opportunities, access to resources, voice and respect for human rights. She underlines the importance reducing inequalities, including their structural causes, prompting World Heritage practice to be far more sensitive and responsive to social complexity.

Gender equality has long been an international goal, yet it illustrates more than most issues the complexity of making progress. In Chapter 6, Sophia Labadi underlines how current practice falls short of incorporating gender concerns. It is thus in need, she argues, of an even clearer policy framework to tackle the power issues and amend core World Heritage mechanisms, such as nomination formats, if they are to fully reflect and respond more effectively to gender concerns.

In their contribution, Chapter 7, Stefan Disko and Max Ooft describe the new path the World Heritage community has embarked upon in relation to indigenous peoples. While the authors were not directly involved in the policy process, both have been instrumental in convening indigenous peoples' and advocacy organizations on the topic of indigenous peoples rights and World Heritage (Disko and Tugendhat 2014). Their chapter recognizes the World Heritage Sustainable Development policy as a milestone in terms of indigenous peoples' rights, yet also call for urgent changes in the Operational Guidelines to secure mandatory action in new nominations as well as existing sites.

In Chapter 8, Peter Bille Larsen asks whether the explicit human rights language offers the long-awaited reform and redress of the social deficit or, conversely, will remain empty words that simply allow heritage to be reproduced as usual? If the World Heritage and Sustainable Development policy asks State Parties to uphold, respect and contribute to the implementation of the full range of international human rights standards (Sinding-Larsen and Larsen 2017; Larsen 2018), Larsen here emphasizes major challenges and opportunities in terms of reworking the uneven playing field, high levels of uncertainty and an urgent need to put in place practical social safeguards.

Peace and security

The possibilities for sustainable development and the sustainability of the world's cultural and natural heritage may be rapidly undermined by war, civil conflict and other forms of violence including terrorist attacks on civilians. Since the World Heritage Convention is an integral part of UNESCO's constitutional mandate to build bridges towards peace and security, it follows that the World Heritage Committee and

State Parties to the Convention should ensure that the processes established under the Convention are used to promote the achievement and maintenance of peace and security both between and within State Parties. In Chapter 9, William Logan elaborates on these assertions, now embedded in UNESCO's new World Heritage and Sustainable Development policy. He considers what such ambitions might mean for heritage practice within the World Heritage system, including nominations to the World Heritage List and site management, as well as for national and local systems more generally. His chapter concludes with a reality check, asking how seriously will the policy be applied, given UNESCO's status as an intergovernmental organization and the State Parties' determination to put their own national interests first.

Part III comprises chapters from each of the Advisory Bodies that were named in the 1972 World Heritage Convention. That there are three is a reflection of another of the great debates in the World Heritage field – here about the relationship between 'natural' and 'cultural' forms of heritage (Larsen and Wijesuriya 2015). While it may not be the case today, at the time the Convention was formulated, the two forms were seen as largely separate. Thus, the IUCN advises on natural heritage and takes the lead on mixed sites; ICOMOS advises on cultural heritage places and takes the lead on cultural landscapes, whereas ICCROM has a broader mandate of advising on, training in and conducting research into the conservation of all forms of cultural heritage, including museum collections. Each Advisory Body has pursued the sustainable development issue in relation to its own responsibilities.

The IUCN has historically had a key role to play in the very articulation of sustainability in the last quarter of the twentieth century, as Elena Osipova, Tim Badman and Peter Bille Larsen outline in Chapter 10. Focussing on the environmental dimension of the Sustainable Development policy, natural heritage sites often offer high-level protection for globally significant ecosystems that are important well beyond immediate site boundaries, indeed, critically important for the health of the planet as a whole. During roughly the same period as IUCN, ICOMOS began undertaking its own discussions about sustainability as outlined by Luisa de Marco, Susan Denyer, Regina Durighello and Ege Yıldırım in Chapter 11. The steady shift in ICCROM's position from 'sustaining heritage' to 'heritage sustaining broader societal wellbeing and benefits' as explained by Jane Thompson and Gamini Wijesuriya in Chapter 12 is another example. Each Advisory Body has a rich institutional history of debate and of developing its own approaches. Such institutional trajectories are not merely historically significant, but also point to how changing policy debates often involved separate conversations. Still, within the last five years there has been growing inter-agency cooperation in the fields of rights-based approaches, nature-culture interlinkages as well as capacity building. Furthermore, Advisory Bodies meetings and action planning processes are increasingly centred on sustainability issues. This provides some hope for the future about a more concerted agenda.

Part IV comprises a series of case studies written by site managers and other heritage officers who participated in one or both of the Cottbus and Ninh Binh working group meetings. Their presence in those meetings helped to ensure that the policy reflected the kinds of concerns that have emerged through decades of World Heritage implementation. This is important precisely because it departs from sustainability as consensual mainstream or global discourse, alone, to also recognize and prompt attention to real-life problems and opportunities specifically experienced in the World Heritage context and at the site level.

Heritage practice has, it must be recognized, developed over the years both globally and within the various states in a fractured way. While, on paper, there is consensus around certain principles, such as the need for effective management, what this means in practice may differ substantially. This is also true in relation to the way sustainability has been understood. National officials, site managers and practitioners may agree to the necessity of sustainable development, yet have very different understandings of the concept. Differences may be driven by special features of the sites for which they are responsible or result from sectoral perspectives. In the intergovernmental arena, such fracturing is further deepened by instrumental politics seeking to promote nominations or avoid 'in danger' listing. While this may be considered a challenge to the holistic ambition underscoring the new policy, such fractures do serve as a reality check in terms of ongoing practice.

Key questions taken up by these case study chapters include: What does the new policy mean for managing particular World Heritage sites? What particular positions have been taken to address critical debates about inclusion, exclusion, social justice and why? Does the policy give strength to the argument that heritage policies should not be implemented at the expense or to the detriment of concerned communities? What immediately strikes the reader of these case studies is the combined intensity and diversity of sustainability. The issues and challenges are clearly not uniform, yet all demonstrate complex processes of dialogue, decision-making and solution-building with a wide range of actors. If studies at times portray heritage management as fixed systems, the emphasis on change and transformation instead draws attention to domestic, negotiated and home-grown processes of tying heritage management into local socio-economic and political systems.

In Chapter 13, Dina Ishak Bakhoum, an Egyptian heritage specialist, takes Cairo as her case study. She explains how the field of cultural heritage conservation and management in Cairo has been technically orientated with an emphasis on the scientific, historic and artistic values of heritage. From the late 1990s, however, a new genre of projects emerged that linked culture with development and stressed its socio-economic components. This approach was gradually recognized by official agencies, although, Bakhoum argues, the sustainability of such initiatives requires the ongoing support and participation of stakeholders both from the government and the business field.

Chapter 14 provides a European case study that has addressed a similar sustainability concern and found its own set of answers. This is the 'Town of Bamberg' in Germany, written by Patricia Alberth, head of Bamberg's World Heritage Office. The Bamberg experience illustrates how heritage brings a particular perspective to the development equation. Countering the loss of gardening traditions and land use, the Market Gardener's district was embraced and enhanced by the municipality, an approach that has empowered the gardeners and promoted economic opportunity and quality jobs for community residents.

Juan Luis Isaza Londoño and César Augusto Velandia Silva deal, in Chapter 15, with sustainable development and nature-culture linkages in the 'Coffee Cultural Landscape of Colombia'. This World Heritage is the largest productive cultural landscape in Latin America and an exceptional example of a living, continuous and productive agricultural landscape reflecting a tradition of small-scale coffee production and adaptation to the steep mountains of the Colombian Cordilleras. Isaza and Velandia outline the distinctive culture based on collective work in coffee production and the evolving associative processes passed down through generations. They show how these collective efforts relate to the economic and social well-being of the coffee farmers and other inhabitants of the property and also make possible the environmental sustainability of coffee production in this living Columbian cultural landscape.

Chapter 16 focuses on Vietnam, a country which in a couple of decades has embraced World Heritage. The case study by Duong Bich Hanh, Tran Thi Thu Thuy, Pham Thi Thanh Huong and Nguyen Viet Cuong brings together a comprehensive reflection on sustainable development by cultural heritage specialists and officials in Vietnam, including the UNESCO Hanoi Office. Building on the motto 'conservation for development, development for conservation', the chapter describes the achievements made in the heritage field as well as pointing to new sustainability challenges such as the risks associated with the attitude of some stakeholders that World Heritage inscription primarily serves as a means for economic development, particularly through tourism.

In Chapter 17, Muhammad Juma, Director of Urban and Rural Planning in Zanzibar, describes the changing conservation thinking and practices over time in his island territory. He provides a fascinating account of how new conservation approaches, such as the Historic Urban Landscape, can facilitate local processes to link urban conservation, heritage management and urban planning. Drawing on the challenges experienced in the buffer of the 'Stone Town of Zanzibar' World Heritage site, where a pilot project called Ng'ambo Tuitakayo was initiated in 2015, Juma outlines the steps taken to influence inclusive social and economic development, to enhance resilience and to improve environmental sustainability.

Chapter 18 provides a case study from China written by Zhou Jian, a heritage scholar based at Tongji University. It deals with the reconstruction of the Xijie Historic Quarter following the disastrous earthquake in 2008. Zhou outlines the various elements of the project such as heritage conservation, housing improvement and tourism development. Despite the constraints of current national policies on land use and housing, the prevailing top-down approach of urban conservation in China and the hesitation some residents had in participating, there are, according to Zhou, numerous valuable lessons for future project implementation. These revolve mostly around the use of a cooperative implementation approach that included active community participation in policy design.

Challenges

The case study chapters show there is much to learn from paying attention to the insights of site managers in relation to challenges facing the formulation and implementation of policies and practices that benefit both heritage and sustainable development. The following section looks at a number of other challenges confronting this endeavour at a more systemic level.

Heritage and growth

The prominence of economic growth in the World Heritage system in general, and the World Heritage and Sustainable Development policy in particular, deserves special attention. Inscriptions are often show-cased as contributing to 'steady economic growth' (see, for instance, UNESCO 2017b). While the World Heritage Committee in specific cases has been ready to challenge development investments when they jeopardize OUV (see UNESCO 2007c:184–186), there are no indications that it would be ready to forego major growth opportunities for the sake of distant sustainability targets. Dwindling public budgets for heritage, *realpolitik* and willingness to accommodate economic activities may, however, not only undermine heritage values *per se*, but also raise wider sustainability concerns. Has the time come for change?

For some observers, World Heritage is too intimately tied to contemporary consumption patterns, mass tourism and the concentration of capital, accelerating inequalities and creating sustainability problems in the first place. For others, World Heritage sites offer unprecedented resources and commitment for resolving longstanding poverty, heritage protection needs and bridging social divides. For the latter, World Heritage could – at least – serve to demonstrate that a more sustainable alternative *is* possible. The idea sounds attractive, but is it wishful thinking?

Lately, the World Heritage system has turned from opposing development imperatives and profit-based investments to a more 'win-win' language. The World Heritage system has shifted since the 1990s towards a 'values approach' to heritage management, particularly for cultural properties – an approach that allows some new development within and around inscribed properties as long as the OUV is safeguarded. Heritage, we are now told, is not a problem but a resource for economic growth (UN 2011; Logan 2017). Indeed, UNESCO ran a conference in Hue, Vietnam, in April 2000 on this very topic: 'Preserving Urban Heritage as a Vector for Development'. The introduction to a UNESCO Bangkok World Heritage study asserts that 'heritage preservation is not an obstacle to economic growth, in fact, it is a critical element of sustainable socio-economic development'(UNESCO Bangkok, n.d.). The *Huangzhou Declaration* (UNESCO 2013) put culture 'at the heart of sustainable development' but, in what some might see as part of a longstanding Asian viewpoint (Logan 2016), qualified its position by affirming that 'one size does not fit all and that different cultural perspectives will result in different paths to development'.

When the *Hoi An Declaration on the Conservation of Historic Districts in Asia* was revised in June 2017, the change of its title to the *Hoi An Declaration on Urban Heritage Conservation and Development in Asia* was emblematic of the increased emphasis on the economic value of heritage to be found throughout the World Heritage system. However, as Duong Binh Hanh et al. demonstrate in their Vietnam case study in this volume, this shift signals not only the agility of heritage professionals to defend heritage as a component of development, but it also gives rise to new dilemmas. These include the need to reinforce heritage regulations as well as strengthen the authority and capacity of the site managers who deal with complex situations of compromise and trade-offs on a daily basis. What would help site managers, they argue, are tools and good models of effective management practices such as those ensuring the implementation of a rights-based approach, effective community participation, public-private partnerships, stakeholder engagement and conflict resolution.

To what extent is it realistic to expect World Heritage to deliver alternatives to the planetary obsession with growth? This has not been clear and opinions have been and are still divided in some quarters, particularly in academic circles. Somewhat paradoxically, the global aspiration to sustain World Heritage for future generations very often triggers a process of massive transformation in social, economic and environmental terms. In many respects, places and people are never quite the same again (and not necessarily more sustainable) once properties are recognized as World Heritage. One might conclude, if somewhat provocatively, that the evidence currently points more in the direction of heritage properties becoming islands of intensive growth, tourism and elite consumption, rather than alternative spaces of de-growth, social empowerment and inclusion. Whereas experimentation with sustainable production and consumption may be on the increase within World Heritage sites, it remains the exception in a market place fuelled by stimulating more rather than less consumption.

Revising the operational guidelines

The successful passage of the policy through the General Assembly and World Heritage Committee was something of a surprise to some members of the international working group who drafted the policy. Many feared the ambitious agenda might backfire. Similar fears were also expressed when the first steps were taken to promote a rights-based approach within the World Heritage system. There, too, it was thought that being too direct in seeking change might be counter-productive and that the most that might be hoped for in the short term would be some tweaking of the Operational Guidelines (Logan 2012: 241). We need to know whether and what proposed changes are adopted by the World Heritage Committee before an assessment of what the policy will really mean for heritage practice can be made.

However, the optimists in the working group won the day and the policy was approved, thereby establishing a common framework of principles and aspirational goals for all the relevant dimensions of sustainable development, which is a major step forward for UNESCO and its World Heritage program. Even so, the policy still has some way to go before it begins to impact on practice. In the public policy field, policies generally reflect the highest level of decision-making, whereas the design of guidelines represents the weaker, technical dimension of rolling out of decisions (Larsen 2013). In the World Heritage system, the opposite is true. While there have been attempts to clarify policy adopted by the Committee, the Operational Guidelines constitute the *de facto* core policy document. The crucial work of implementing the policy through the adoption of revised Operational Guidelines and other mechanisms has therefore still to be undertaken. What changes to the Operational Guidelines would be needed? How difficult will it be to make the necessary changes? Is there still a possibility that its potential may be dissipated?

Nervousness now applies to the prospects for quick changes to the wording of the Operational Guidelines. As Boccardi and Scott note in their chapter, the World Heritage Committee at its 35th Session in Paris in 2011 decided that the Operational Guidelines should be 'restricted to operational guidance, and that a new document "Policy Guidelines" [should] be developed as a means to capture the range of policies that the Committee and the General Assembly adopt'. This new Policy Guidelines are only advancing slowly, equally affecting efforts to accommodate the World Heritage and Sustainable Development policy. Meanwhile, time is ticking, and it is urgent that far more resolute action is taken with regard to the UNESCO's 2015 sustainability commitments.

Time for a game changer?

Such challenges prompt even further questions about the actual significance of the World Heritage and Sustainable Development policy. Will it merely remain in the soon dusty archives of well-intentioned aspirations, or does it actually have real implications for both existing and new sites? Certain topics and windows of immediate win-win opportunities are likely to be more eagerly pursued than others. Apart from some planning attempts, single-case advances and surgical changes in the reporting formats, much remains to be fleshed out. Much follow-up action appears to depend on additional funding and capacity building. Current sustainability targets thus appear as mere aspirations rather than an obligatory framework for delivery. There has been very limited talk about responsibility and accountability to deliver on the sustainable development targets, not least if it would require the Committee to seriously challenge a State Party. It is, for example, currently unlikely, a part from a few exceptions, to expect the Committee to confront a State Party on peace and human rights violations, as we argue in our individual chapters in this volume. This would arguably also require a consistent approach from the Committee, something currently lacking in a highly uneven playing field.

What are some of the questions this might raise? As the system moves from ignoring human rights to promoting their realization, when should a management system be considered compatible with international standards? How should the Committee, in turn, deal with contentious or unresolved human rights records? In the light of current climate change dynamics, what should be the targets in terms of carbon emissions for the World Heritage field? Is a zero-emission agenda for site designation and management possible? Are climate change resilient pathways addressing both mitigation and adaptation for all World Heritage sites realistic in the near future (Denton et al. 2014)? How to deal with trade-offs between other heritage values and alternative developments?

Answers to these and many other questions will depend on the willingness to translate policy into real decisions when it comes to nominations, danger listing and the adoption of specific operational guidelines. Yet, perhaps more importantly, it will depend on whether the policy is translated into a shared political project shared across regions, rather than being dependent on individual country initiatives.

From politicization to sustainability politics?

The next stage of operationalizing the principles and goals raises the immediate challenge of the distinct form of politicization that has occurred within the World Heritage system over the past 20 years and the difficulty of achieving reform. State Parties are as vigorous as ever in asserting their national sovereignty, some even back-tracking on compliance with World Heritage standards to put their own state interests first. Members of delegations to the World Heritage Committee are now more likely to be career diplomats than heritage professionals and to form strategic alliances to achieve decisions that meet their national interests (Meskell and Brumann 2015: 35). Based on her analyses of World Heritage Committee interventions and voting patterns, Meskell (2014) identified pacting between the 'BRICS' (Brazil, Russia, India, China and South Africa), but, as the study of Australia's behaviour in relation to Kathmandu and Kakadu shows, developed Western State Parties will also engage in pacting if it is in their national political and economic interests (Logan 2013).

Can such pacting be mobilized to raise the bar in terms of standards for delivery on sustainability targets rather than merely serve individual States Party interests? Given the scale of global challenges, a shift from current trends of inwards-looking politicization towards progressive sustainability politics is warranted. While recent history points in the opposite direction, one could cautiously hope, or actively lobby for, for strong Committee decision-making in this regard. This could also involve the Committee establishing a group of sustainability pioneers ready to move forward with the implementation of the World Heritage and Sustainable Development policy in a more proactive manner. Such pioneers might spearhead efforts to undertake sustainability reviews, raise the bar in terms of performance indicators and pioneer more transparent and accountable engagement. If they are unlikely to make a difference alone, they may pave the way for alternative practices – and eventually for a truly ambitious sustainability agenda – to emerge. In the end, however, much will depend on how seriously UNESCO and the State Parties to the World Heritage Convention take the policy and its implementation – and this is the biggest question of all.

References

Denton, F. et al. (2014). 'Climate-resilient pathways: Adaptation, mitigation, and sustainable development', in C. B. Field et al. (eds), *Climate Change 2014: Impacts, Adaptation, and Vulnerability, Part A: Global and Sectoral Aspects: Contribution of Working Group II to the Fifth Assessment Report of the Intergovernmental Panel on Climate Change*. Cambridge: Cambridge University Press.

Disko, S. and Tugendhat, H. (2014). *World Heritage Sites and Indigenous Peoples' Rights*. Copenhagen: IWGIA.

Keeley, B. (2015). *Income Inequality: The Gap between Rich and Poor*. Paris: OECD.

Larsen, P. B. (2013). 'The politics of technicality: Guidance culture in environmental governance and the international sphere', in B. Müller (ed), *The Gloss of Harmony: The Politics of Policy Making in Multilateral Organisations*. London: Pluto Press.

Larsen, P. B. (2018). *World Heritage and Human Rights: Lessons from the Asia Pacific and the Global Arena*. London: Earthscan/Routledge.

Larsen, P. B. and Wijesuriya, G. (2015). 'Nature: Culture interlinkages in World Heritage: Bridging the gap', *World Heritage*, 75, 4–15.

Logan, W. (2012). 'Cultural diversity, cultural heritage and human rights: Towards heritage management as human rights-based cultural practice', *International Journal of Heritage Studies*, 18(3), 231–244.

Logan, W. (2013). 'Australia, Indigenous Peoples and World Heritage from Kakadu to Cape York: State party behaviour under the World Heritage Convention', *Journal of Social Archaeology*, 13(2), 153–176.

Logan, W. (2016). 'Collective cultural rights in Asia: Recognition and reinforcement', in A. Jakubowski (ed), *Cultural Rights as Collective Rights: An International Law Perspective*. Leiden and Boston: Brill Nijhoff.

Logan, W. (2017). 'UNESCO Heritage-speak: Words, syntax and rhetoric', in C. Antons and W. Logan (eds), *Intellectual Property, Cultural Property and Intangible Cultural Heritage*. London: Routledge.

Meskell, L. M. (2014). 'States of conservation: Protection, politics and pacting within UNESCO's World Heritage Committee', *Anthropological Quarterly*, 87(1), 267–292.

Meskell, L. M. and Brumann, C. (2015). 'UNESCO and new world orders', in L. Meskell (ed), *Global Heritage: A Reader*. Chichester, UK: Wiley Blackwell.

Neumayer, E. (2013). *Weak versus Strong Sustainability: Exploring the Limits of Two Opposing Paradigms*. Cheltenham: Edward Elgar.

Sinding-Larsen, A. and Larsen, P. B. (eds) (2017). *Our Common Dignity Initiative: Rights-Based Approaches in World Heritage: Taking Stock and Looking Forward, Advisory Body Activities between 2011 and 2016*. An Advisory Body Report. Oslo, Norway: ICOMOS.

UNESCO (1972). *Convention Concerning the Protection of the World Cultural and Natural Heritage* (World Heritage Convention) (online). Available at: http://whc.unesco.org/archive/convention-en.pdf (accessed 20 November 2017).

UNESCO (2001). *Convention on the Protection of the Underwater Cultural Heritage* (online). Available at: http://unesdoc.unesco.org/images/0012/001246/124687e.pdf#page=56 (accessed 20 November 2017).

UNESCO (2003). *Convention for the Safeguarding of the Intangible Cultural Heritage.* (Intangible Heritage Convention) (online). Available at: http://unesdoc.unesco.org/images/0013/001325/132540e.pdf (accessed 20 November 2017).

UNESCO (2005). *Convention on the Protection and Promotion of the Diversity of Cultural Expressions* (online). Available at: http://unesdoc.unesco.org/images/0014/001429/142919e.pdf (accessed 20 November 2017).

UNESCO (2007a). *Strategy for Reducing Risks at World Heritage Properties* (online). Available at: http://whc.unesco.org/archive/2007/whc07-31com-72e.pdf (accessed 20 November 2017).

UNESCO (2007b). *Policy Document on the Impacts of Climate Change on World Heritage Properties* (online). Available at: http://whc.unesco.org/en/CC-policy-document/ (accessed 20 November 2017).

UNESCO (2007c). *World Heritage: Challenges for the Millennium.* Paris: UNESCO.

UNESCO (2011a). *Strategic Action Plan for the Implementation of the World Heritage Convention 2012–2022* (online). Available at: http://whc.unesco.org/archive/2011/whc11-18ga-11-en.pdf (accessed 20 November 2017).

UNESCO (2011b). *World Heritage Strategy for Capacity Building* (online). Available at: http://whc.unesco.org/archive/2011/whc11-35com-9Be.pdf (accessed 20 November 2017).

UNESCO (2013). *The Huangzhou Declaration: Placing Culture at the Heart of Sustainable Development Policies* (online). Available at: www.unesco.org/fileadmin/MULTIMEDIA/HQ/CLT/images/FinalHangzhouDeclaration20130517.pdf (accessed 7 December 2017).

UNESCO (2015). *Policy Document for the Integration of a Sustainable Development Perspective into the Processes of the World Heritage Convention* (online). Available at: http://whc.unesco.org/en/sustainabledevelopment/ (accessed 29 August 2017).

UNESCO (2016a). *Operational Guidelines for the Implementation of the World Heritage Convention* Document WHC.16/01 (online). Available at: http://whc.unesco.org/en/guidelines (accessed 27 August 2017).

UNESCO (2016b). *Operational Directives for the Implementation of the Convention for the Safeguarding of the Intangible Heritage* (online). Available at: https://ich.unesco.org/en/directives (accessed 20 November 2017).

UNESCO (2017a). *Memory of the World* (online). Available at: https://en.unesco.org/programme/mow (accessed 20 November 2017).

UNESCO (2017b). *Examples of the Convention at Work* (online). Available at: http://whc.unesco.org/en/casestudies/ (accessed 5 December 2017).

UNESCO (n.d.). *An Introduction to World Heritage* (Bangkok: Asia and Pacific Regional Bureau for Education) (online). Available at: www.unescobkk.org/fileadmin/user_upload/news/doc/World_Heritage_Convention_Introduction.pdf (accessed 3 October 2017).

United Nations (UN) (1992a). *UN Framework Convention on Climate Change* (online). Available at: https://unfccc.int/resource/docs/convkp/conveng.pdf (accessed 20 November 2017).

United Nations (UN) (1992b). *The Rio Declaration on Environment and Development* (online). Available at: www.un-documents.net/rio-dec.htm (accessed 20 November 2017).

United Nations (UN) (1992c). *Agenda 21: United Nations Conference on Environment and Development, Rio de Janerio, Brazil, 3 to 14 June 1992* (online). Available at: https://sustainabledevelopment.un.org/content/documents/Agenda21.pdf (accessed 20 November 2017).

United Nations (UN) (2011). *Culture and Development: Report of the Director-General of the United Nations Educational, Scientific and Cultural Organization.* General Assembly

A/66/187 (online). Available at: www.unesco.or.kr/eng/front/programmes/links/2_Note bySecretary_General.pdf (accessed 6 December 2017).

United Nations (UN) (2015). *Paris Agreement [on Climate Change]* (online). Available at:http://unfccc.int/files/essential_background/convention/application/pdf/english_paris_agreement.pdf (accessed 20 November 2017).

United Nations General Assembly (UNGA) (2015). *Transforming Our World: The 2030 Agenda for Sustainable Development*. Document A/RES/70/1 (online). Available at: www.un.org/ga/search/view_doc.asp?symbol=A/RES/70/1&Lang=E (accessed 20 September 2017).

United Nations Task Team on the Post-2015 UN Development Agenda (UNTT) (2012). *Realizing the Future We Want for All* (Report to the Secretary-General) (online). Available at: www.un.org/millenniumgoals/pdf/Post_2015_UNTTreport.pdf (accessed 20 September 2017).

World Wildlife Fund (WWF) (2016). *Living Planet Report 2016: Risk and Resilience in a New Era*. Gland: WWF International.

Chapter 2

A view from the inside

An account of the process leading to the adoption of the policy for the integration of a sustainable development perspective within the World Heritage Convention[1]

Giovanni Boccardi and Lindsay Scott

The adoption in 2015 of a policy that aims to integrate a sustainable development perspective into the processes of the World Heritage Convention (UNESCO 2015a) was a significant step for the heritage conservation field and will inevitably have a lasting impact.[2] This decision was the product of a path that had been laid out by international bodies and heritage workers over decades. From site managers who had faced conflicting interests, at times leading them to make controversial decisions, from the increasing dangers of climate change and natural disasters affecting sites and from the growing importance of sustainable development principles within the UN community, the adoption of the policy was the natural and necessary next step in the evolution of World Heritage practice. Its goal was to define a baseline to help heritage managers understand and approach heritage with a more holistic view, resulting in positive advances for the planet, the people, the economy and heritage together. While its unanimous adoption represented a landmark achievement, the sometimes-challenging process of how it came into being gives insight into the reality of what the integration of these two fields – World Heritage and sustainable development – means. As with any document addressing large numbers of people or organizations, the creation of this policy was not without obstacles and limitations. Understanding the progress that led to the creation of the original policy proposal and the perspectives of the actors involved helps to contextualize the final text of the policy now adopted. Knowing how and why decisions were made can also aid those preparing for any possible implementation in the future.

Sustainable development gains importance

After sustainable development was first introduced as a notion in the Brundtland Report *Our Common Future* (United Nations World Commission on Environment and Development 1987), it took considerable time for the World Heritage community to consider its relevance to the Convention. The word 'sustainable' first appeared in the 1994 edition of the *Operational Guidelines for the Implementation of the World Heritage Convention* (UNESCO 2016b) (hereafter the Operational Guidelines), in connection to the newly introduced concept of cultural landscapes, which were recognized as often reflecting 'specific techniques of sustainable land-use' worthy of protection and 'helpful in maintaining biological diversity'. It was only in 2002, however, that the reciprocal relationship between heritage and sustainable development was officially recognized for the first time in the Budapest Declaration adopted by the Committee on the thirtieth anniversary of the Convention (UNESCO 2002).[3] In 2007, with Decision 31 COM 13A (WHC 2007), the Committee recalled the Budapest Declaration, adding 'communities' as the fifth strategic objective for implementation of the World Heritage Convention. 'Communities' was termed 'the fifth C' because it was to sit alongside credibility, conservation, capacity-building and communication. This was a significant turning point in opening the doors for sustainable development as it affirmed that the wellbeing of the concerned communities, including both present and future generations, was the ultimate goal of conservation.

Over the following years, and despite the lack of an agreed-upon definition, the terms 'sustainable development' and 'communities' were increasingly used in the context of World Heritage, mainly in relation to individual state of conservation reports and nomination files. Notwithstanding these advances, the Convention remained – in its policies and procedures – mainly focused on the protection of the attributes of Outstanding Universal Value (OUV), the key requirement for the inscription of sites on the World Heritage List. All other aspects related to social, economic and environmental dimensions of sustainable development were considered in World Heritage only insofar as they constituted a threat to the OUV of a given listed property, not as objectives of the Convention in their own right.

It was only in 2009, in beginning the reflection leading to the fortieth anniversary of the Convention, which was to take place in 2012, at the same time as the Rio+20 UN Conference on Sustainable Development, that the Committee deemed it necessary to launch a deeper reflection on what sustainable development actually meant in relation to World Heritage conservation. A first expert meeting was thus organized, which took place in Paraty, Brazil from 29 to 31 March 2010. This resulted in a report and Action Plan that were considered by the Committee at its 34th Session in 2010 (UNESCO 2010).

The Paraty Meeting emphasized how the protection of heritage, as an attribute of natural and cultural diversity, played a fundamental role in fostering strong communities, supporting the physical and spiritual wellbeing of its individuals and promoting mutual understanding and peace. It recognized also how, through a variety of goods and services and as a storehouse of knowledge, a well-protected World Heritage property very often contributed directly to livelihoods and sustainable development across all of its dimensions. In this respect, the experts in the Meeting noted that the great potential of World Heritage, and heritage in general, for contributing to sustainable development was still not sufficiently recognized.

At the same time, the Paraty Meeting noted how unsustainable development was perhaps the most significant threat to heritage conservation, both in developing and developed countries. It argued, in this respect, that sustainable development was a development that also took into account the need to conserve the heritage, while – conversely – a sustainable conservation of the heritage would take into account and integrate a concern for the social, economic and environmental dimension of development. The Meeting concluded therefore, that the possible conflict between conservation and development should have been resolved through a balanced compromise that would take into account all legitimate interests while reconciling global and local values. To this end, the Paraty Meeting called for the introduction, within the framework of the Convention, of policies and procedures that, together with maintaining the OUV of properties through the protection of their heritage attributes, would make the contribution to sustainable development an explicit and intentional objective of World Heritage conservation.

Based on the results of the Paraty Meeting, the Committee, at its 34th Session in Brasilia, 2010, agreed 'that it would be desirable to further consider, in the implementation of the Convention, policies and procedures that maintain the Outstanding Universal Value of properties, and also contribute to sustainable development' (Decision 34 COM 5D) (WHC 2010) and requested a further consultative meeting on the matter. This took place from 5 to 8 February 2012 at Ouro Preto, also in Brazil, and made significant progress in clarifying the terms of the relationship between World Heritage, conservation and sustainable development. In their conclusions, the participants in the Ouro Preto meeting recognized that

> with changing demographics, growing inequalities and diminishing resources, the goals and objectives of heritage conservation must be seen in the context of a greater system of social and environmental values and needs, encompassed in the concept of sustainable development. This will require heritage institutions to come to terms with these conditions and begin to seek new solutions. Ultimately, if the heritage sector does not fully embrace sustainable development and harness the reciprocal benefits for heritage and society, it will find itself a victim of, rather than a catalyst for wider change.
>
> (UNESCO 2012)

The Ouro Preto Meeting recognized the need for a sustainable development policy in World Heritage and outlined its possible aim, scope and content, suggesting also a roadmap for its development, for consideration by the Committee. The latter reviewed the results of the Ouro Preto meeting at its 36th Session in St. Petersburg, 2012, and adopted Decision 36 COM 5C, requesting the World Heritage Centre, with the support of the Advisory Bodies, 'to convene a small expert working group to develop, within a year, a proposal for a policy on the integration of sustainable development into the processes of the *World Heritage Convention*' (WHC 2012).

The overall goal of the policy was to assist State Parties, practitioners, institutions, communities and networks, through appropriate guidance, to harness the potential of World Heritage properties, and heritage in general, to contribute to sustainable development and ensure that their conservation and management strategies are appropriately aligned with broader sustainable development objectives. In the process, of course, the primary objective of the World Heritage Convention, which is to protect the World Cultural and Natural Heritage, should not be compromised.

In requesting a policy on sustainable development, the Committee was acting in line with the decisions of the General Assembly of the State Parties to the Convention, which, at its 18th Session in Paris, 2011, had already adopted a 'Strategic Action Plan for the Implementation of the Convention, 2012–2022' (UNESCO 2015b), including various references to sustainable development. In its 'Vision for 2022', notably, the Strategic Action Plan called for the World Heritage Convention to 'contribute to the sustainable development of the world's communities and cultures', while Goal N.3 of the Plan required that 'heritage protection and conservation consider present and future environmental, societal and economic needs', which was to be achieved particularly through 'connecting conservation to communities'. It was expected that in drafting the policy, account would be taken of the outcomes of the numerous events (around 100) organized across all regions of the world in the framework of the fortieth anniversary of the Convention, whose official theme was 'World Heritage and Sustainable Development: the Role of Local Communities', as well as of the Rio + 20 Conference.[4]

Drafting the policy proposal

As a first step in implementing Decision 36 COM 5C, the World Heritage Centre drafted a working document to guide the work of the experts. This explained the background of how the Decision came to be and provided a proposal for a conceptual framework articulating the various dimensions of sustainable development against which the policy would be developed. It was based on this framework that the experts would be identified to join the group requested by the Committee. It was decided to draw from the document *Realizing the Future We Want for All* (United Nations System Task Team on the Post-2015 UN Development Agenda 2012), established by the UN Secretary General in 2011 to support UN system-wide preparations for the post-2015 UN development agenda, because its methodology represented the most recent comprehensive approach to sustainable development that existed at the time the policy was requested. The vision outlined in this document is shown in Figure 2.1. It included three 'overarching principles'; that is, human rights, equality and sustainability, and four 'core dimensions', namely inclusive social development, environmental sustainability, inclusive economic development and peace and security. This was also the approach taken by the Secretariat of the UNESCO 2003 *Convention on the Safeguarding of Intangible Cultural Heritage*, which was at the time engaged in a similar process to integrate sustainable development within its *Operational Directives* (UNESCO 2016c).[5]

Eight experts were thus selected to cover the four core dimensions, plus human rights, gender equality, resilience/disaster risk reduction (including climate change)

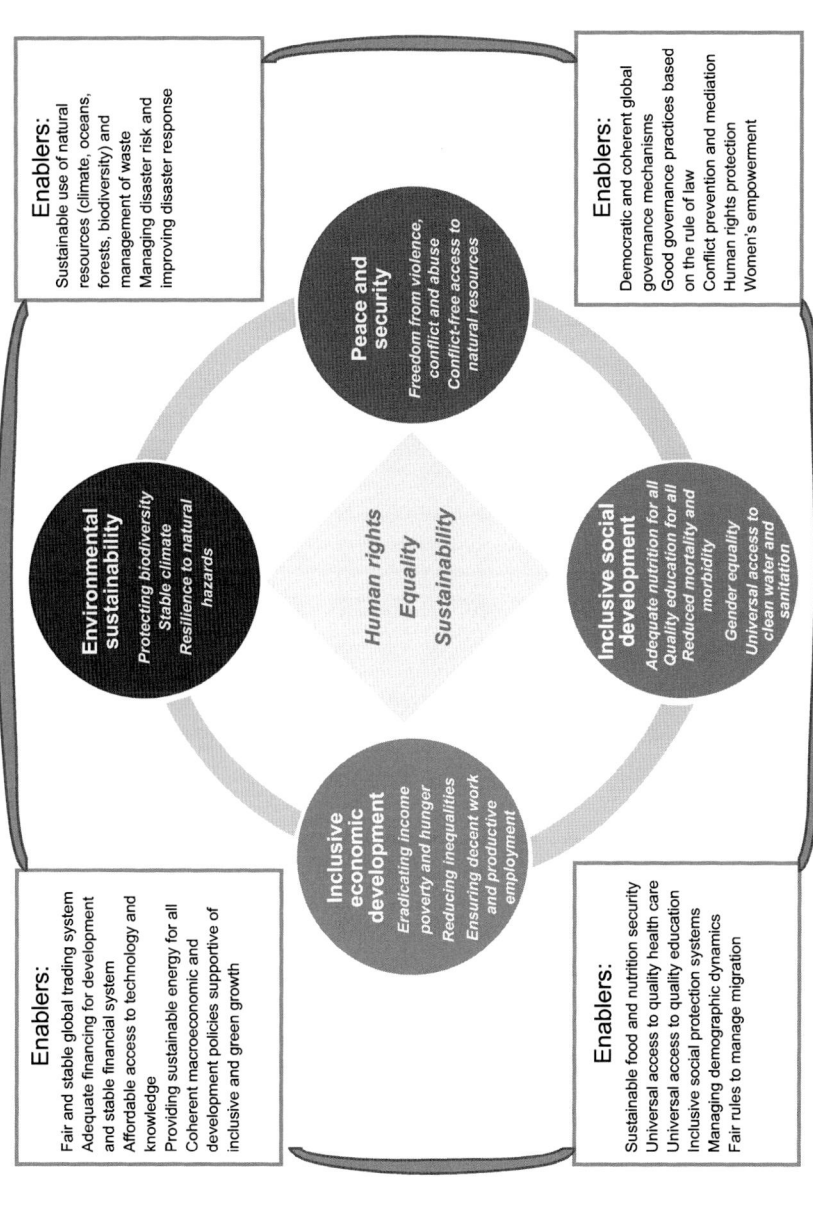

Figure 2.1 An integrated framework for realizing the 'future we want for all' in the post-2015 UN development agenda

Source: UN System Task Team on the Post-2015 UN Development Agenda 2012

and indigenous peoples/local communities. Such an approach was endorsed by the Committee at its 38th Session in Doha, 2014, by its decision 38 COM 5D (WHC 2014). The eight experts were asked to prepare an initial policy statement – each on his/her own topic – indicating which new principles should guide, in their view, the World Heritage community in relation to the relevant dimension of sustainable development and including definitions of key terminology. The process moved forward rather slowly, due to lack of funding, and it was only in October 2014, at the invitation of the German authorities and the Brandenburg University of Technology Cottbus-Senftenberg, that the group of experts could meet face to face, in Cottbus, together with representatives of the World Heritage Centre and the three Advisory Bodies.

Following the Cottbus Workshop, the group continued its work revising the policy statements and met a second time in Ninh Binh, Viet Nam, from 22 to 24 January 2015, with financial support from the Vietnamese government. This second meeting included the participation of World Heritage site managers from different regions and several Vietnamese officials, 'which enabled constructive criticism from those who had experience implementing the Convention on the ground' (UNESCO 2015c). Following the Ninh Binh meeting, it was agreed that the policy would be structured around the four core dimensions of sustainable development, as defined in the above-mentioned report *Realizing The Future We Want for All*, under which other related themes were subsumed (e.g. gender equality and human rights were now covered under 'Inclusive social development', while strengthening resilience to natural hazards and climate change was covered within 'environmental sustainability'). For each aspect, short but compelling policy statements were drafted, seeking to provide clear guidance on what State Parties and other actors within the Convention should do.

It was also decided to develop a series of general principles not related to a specific dimension of sustainable development. These included the three overarching principles of human rights, equality and sustainability, but they also addressed transversal considerations such as the link between biological diversity and local cultures; the interdependent and mutually reinforcing nature of all dimensions of sustainable development; the need to integrate conservation and management approaches for World Heritage properties within their larger regional planning frameworks; and, finally, the critical roles of capacity-building and education to enable the implementation of the policy.

When the draft of the policy was discussed at the 39th Session of the Committee in Bonn, 28 June–8 July 2015, the reaction was generally favourable. Noting the very different context surrounding World Heritage properties across the world, including in socio-economic terms, some Committee members stressed the importance of ensuring that the policy would envisage a certain degree of flexibility to reflect local conditions. ICCROM, on behalf of the three Advisory Bodies, welcomed the draft policy, noting as well how this was giving substance to the principles expressed in the fifth 'C' for communities, the strategic objective adopted by the Committee in 2007. Observers and representatives of non-governmental organizations also took the floor to express their overall support for the policy.

Considering the importance and complexity of the issues at stake, the Committee nevertheless requested that State Parties be given an opportunity to express their comments on the text through a formal consultation process. The Committee also asked that a revised version of the policy be prepared by the World Heritage Centre, taking into account these comments, as well as the outcomes of ongoing discussions on the UN Post-2015 development agenda, taking place within the UN General Assembly. The latter was expected to adopt a set of new sustainable development goals for the period 2015–2030. The revised version of the policy was to be presented to the General Assembly of the State Parties to the Convention at its 20th Session in Paris, November 2015, for final adoption.

A formal consultation process was thus launched, in which 21 State Parties chose to participate. Their comments, together with those expressed at the 39th Session of the Committee in Bonn, were addressed through changes to the text of the draft policy.[6] In the meantime, a new set of 17 Sustainable Development Goals (SDGs) was agreed upon by the UN General Assembly in September 2015, as reflected in the declaration 'Transforming our world: the 2030 Agenda for Sustainable Development (United Nations 2015). The basic structure of the policy was not modified to mirror the 17 goals. However, clear linkages between the two frameworks were identified in its final version. For example, the 2030 UN Agenda for Sustainable Development identified 'planet, people, prosperity and peace', as areas of critical importance, which corresponded to the environmental, social and economic dimensions of the policy, together with peace and security. Eventually, the revised text of the policy was adopted on 6 November 2015 by the General Assembly of the State Parties to the World Heritage Convention at its 20th Session in Paris.

The relationship between sustainable development and World Heritage viewed through different lenses

The long process that led to the definition of the policy revealed how the various actors within the Convention, from State Parties to Advisory Bodies, individual experts and NGOs, held different views on the nature of the relationship between World Heritage, conservation and sustainable development, depending also on which dimension of sustainable development was being considered. These views were manifested at various stages of the process as the scope and contents of the policy were being progressively developed.

One point of view was the recognition that World Heritage was, in itself, a critical component of human wellbeing and sustainability. According to this perspective, by simply fulfilling its original mission, that is, by protecting the OUV attributes of listed property, the Convention was *ipso facto* contributing to sustainable development. This position came often from the natural heritage side, when it was argued that the safeguarding of hundreds of the world's most important natural protected areas was obviously a major contribution to environmental sustainability, and therefore to sustainable development. According to this position, sustainable development was a goal that had to be achieved at a scale often larger than that of the individual World Heritage properties. These, on the other hand, represented a select number of areas containing exceptional natural values, often threatened by development pressure such as extractive industries. It was therefore considered appropriate and even necessary – in conserving and managing natural World Heritage properties – to focus in particular on one dimension of sustainable development, notably by protecting biological diversity and ecosystem services and benefits, assuming that other dimensions could be pursued elsewhere.

A similar position was expressed also from the cultural side of the World Heritage spectrum. The underlying assumption was that, next to its environmental, social and economic legs, the international community should have recognized the cultural dimension of sustainable development, often referred to as its 'fourth pillar'. Those supporting this view considered that a policy on sustainable development, applied specifically within the context of the Convention, should have insisted primarily on the cultural (and natural) values of World Heritage, promoting these as essential parts of sustainable development and inter-related with social and economic elements. The policy, in a sense, was not so much seen as a means to mainstream a series of new concerns in World Heritage, beyond heritage protection, but rather as an opportunity to affirm heritage's own relevance to sustainable development.

In addition to a legitimate wish to see heritage recognized as a major component of sustainable development, an underlying concern was that, by integrating a wide variety of other objectives in the practice of the Convention and placing them on equal footing with heritage protection, its original aim would be compromised. Some feared that the inherently vague notion of sustainable development could have been used as a sort of 'Trojan horse' to undermine the very core of the Convention's mission. Seen from this viewpoint, the idea of an official go-ahead to, for example, 'inclusive economic development' to be handed down from the Committee, the most authoritative voice in heritage, could have seemed potentially threatening or undermining to protection efforts in cases of development conflict.

There were also concerns expressed about whether sustainable development could be covered within the mandate of the Convention and, accordingly, whether the Committee could be entrusted with a role in dealing with it. One Member State, indeed, wondered whether, from a strict legal point of view, it was possible to introduce within the Convention a new set of requirements that were not envisaged in the original text of 1972 ratified by over 190 State Parties. In its view, the negotiation among possible conflicting objectives (that is, heritage conservation vs. other sustainable development goals) should remain the responsibility of the individual States, based on existing international and national laws, and not the job of the Convention, which had no role in these matters.

These concerns were reflected in the final text of the policy in two ways. First, where reference is made to the fact that 'by identifying, protecting, conserving, presenting and transmitting to present and future generations irreplaceable cultural and natural heritage properties of Outstanding Universal Value (OUV), the World Heritage Convention, in itself, contributes significantly to sustainable development and the wellbeing of people' (UNESCO 2015a: Paragraph 1.3). Secondly, the policy clarifies, wherever necessary, that the OUV of the listed properties should never be compromised in the pursuit of sustainable development.

At the other end of the spectrum, many observers recognized that the Convention needed to align its practice with existing international humanitarian agreements and other multilateral environmental agreements (MEAs) and assume its share of social responsibility. Forty years after its adoption, it was not possible for the Convention to continue to focus exclusively on the protection of OUV considering that the number of listed properties was now over 1,000, including around 250 urban settlements. Integrating sustainable development, it was argued, required harnessing the missed opportunities for sustainable development from a conservation and management strategy that focused only on OUV. It also required addressing the conundrum of what happens when the OUV management is the cause of conflict within its surroundings. If the surrounding environment or community is endangered or damaged because of heritage protection, are we then not disavowing our most vital elements, humanity and nature working together as a whole, and thereby doing a disservice to the heritage, without which humanity and nature's successful interplay would be irretrievably lost? The escalation of larger global problems, such as climate change, meant that in determining how to link conservation and development, the hardest questions needed to be asked: If humanity and nature were to fail, what would be the value of heritage, at all? This rightly begged the question: When saving heritage, what exactly needed saving, why and who for? What do we do when heritage is saved at the expense of other elements of society and reasonable response to global challenges? The inclusion of sustainable development into World Heritage management policy was meant to address this contradiction, and enable better outcomes for both heritage and humanity, allowing both to be better equipped to strengthen one another. In this context, the over 1,000 World Heritage properties appeared to provide a unique opportunity to promote innovative models of sustainable development across the world.

The comments received from the State Parties and the debates within the Committee highlighted other differences in the way the policy was interpreted. In reviewing its provisions, for example, one State Party welcomed the spirit of the policy but expressed its concerns about the excessive constraints that could be imposed on the development of certain sites in the name of environmental sustainability. Another State Party noted how the high number of properties on the World Heritage List in Danger located in developing countries was a testimony to the need for economic development as a condition for the appropriate conservation of heritage. In its comments on the draft text of the policy, another State Party noted that different approaches should be applied in implementing the policy as between developed and developing countries, the latter still needing to achieve economic prosperity. In making these points, these State Parties appeared to understand the policy as an opportunity to enable what they felt was the necessary integration between conservation and economic development. Their view was that the prevention of their country's development, in the name of heritage conservation, would prevent their society from thriving and reaching the level of development that other countries already enjoyed. When the Convention was established, developed countries already had a head start; they had had decades or even centuries to build major infrastructure near their heritage, making the transition to living side-by-side with heritage a natural evolution. In most cases, this had already happened before the World Heritage Convention was even established. On the other hand, developing countries, by their very nature, did not have the same financial means, often leaving their heritage to be inscribed in a pristine, untouched condition. However, while their heritage may have been valuable to all of humanity, these countries were still working toward achieving higher living standards for their populations, which meant building new infrastructure, creating jobs and potentially encroaching on the country's heritage. For some stakeholders, at a certain point, quality of life for the country's inhabitants supersedes the intrinsic value of heritage. Asking developing countries to freeze in time, for the rest of the world's enjoyment, could be viewed as an infringement on their rights to attain an equal standard of living.

Conversely, other State Parties and some NGOs interpreted the policy as an opportunity to reiterate the need for adequate controls on development, for example, in relation to a call for a 'No-go' commitment by State Parties and leading industry stakeholders under which extractive activities would not be permitted within World Heritage properties.[7] Moving to another dimension of the policy, a State Party expressed concern about the notion of indigenous peoples, a notion that did not exist in its national legislation, which only referred to generic notion of 'citizens', all sharing equal recognition and rights. An NGO representing the interests of indigenous peoples, on the other hand, called for a strengthening of the provisions concerning the latter within the policy, which in its view should have been also made binding within the procedures of the Convention referring to wider global standards adopted.

In drafting the policy, all these conflicting views had to be acknowledged and an acceptable compromise found. The process stretched each stakeholder's bounds of comfort, pushing them to consider the scope and value of heritage from another standpoint, which at the same time revealed exactly why a more integrative view is needed. With the adoption of the policy by the General Assembly of the State Parties to the Convention, all parties are hereafter committed to working toward an agreed and common framework, one that hopefully will break the silos approach of the past.

Implementing the policy: current efforts and challenges ahead

World Heritage management is exemplary and has implications for managing other lesser-known properties worldwide. With that in mind, how will the policy now be implemented? The policy adopted by the General Assembly of the State Parties to the World Heritage Convention contains a series of principles and aspirational goals for all the relevant dimensions of sustainable development. The actual implementation of the policy on the ground, however, will require translating these principles into operational procedures and practical guidance. This will involve introducing a number of appropriate changes to the Operational Guidelines.

The General Assembly of the State Parties to the Convention, indeed, requested proposals for changes to the Operational Guidelines in its resolution 20 GA 13 (UNESCO 2015c) when adopting the policy. In addition, the General Assembly asked for proposals on indicators for measuring the progress of the policy's implementation, as well as for capacity-building initiatives, needed to enable implementation, including an indication of the related costs. The request was directed to the World Heritage Centre, in consultation with the Advisory Bodies, 'once a clear framework for the future *Policy Guidelines*, including its scope and structure, has been adopted by the General Assembly' (UNESCO 2015c).[8] In fact, at its 39th session in Bonn, 2015, the Committee had already revised the Operational Guidelines and included, *inter alia*, a reference to local communities and indigenous peoples in paragraphs 40 and 123 and in particular to their involvement in the conservation and management of a World Heritage property and in the nomination process.

While a comprehensive set of proposals has not yet been elaborated and formally presented to the Committee, the reflection has already started, for example, at a workshop held in Vilm, Germany, between 14 and 17 November 2016, entitled 'World Heritage and Sustainable Development – From Policy to Action'. The Workshop was organized by the German Federal Agency for Nature Conservation, together with the three Advisory Bodies to the World Heritage Convention in close collaboration with the UNESCO World Heritage Centre. The workshop noted the need to move forward with the implementation of the new policy based on the strong mandate provided by its adoption by the General Assembly of all State Parties to the Convention, without waiting for the statutory amendments to the Operational Guidelines. It identified the key processes of the Convention where the principles of the new policy could be integrated, from tentative listing and nominations to management, monitoring and reporting on properties, and made specific suggestions for the policy's implementation. At a more general level, the workshop emphasized opportunities for mainstreaming the policy within capacity-building strategies, partnerships and communication and, of course, in conservation and management planning and programs at national and site levels.

Even in the absence of an explicit policy, numerous efforts have been undertaken, and are still ongoing, to consider environmental, social and economic aspects in conservation plans and programs, including in a World Heritage context. Document WHC/16/40.COM/5C (UNESCO 2016a), submitted to the Committee at its 40th Session in Istanbul 2016 by the UNESCO Secretariat, provides information on a range of recent activities spearheaded by UNESCO that have relevance to the policy. What is missing in most of these initiatives, however, is a coherent and structured approach whereby all dimensions of sustainable development are, as stated in the policy, addressed and recognized as 'interdependent and mutually reinforcing, with none having predominance over another and each being equally necessary' and integrated equally for natural, cultural and mixed properties in all their diversity.

To achieve this, significant and long-term investments will also be required. The body of knowledge on the relationship between World Heritage and sustainable development will need to be considerably strengthened, including by identifying relevant case studies and drawing from them the relevant lessons. Guidance will also need to be developed, for both State Parties, at central and site levels, and for Advisory Bodies, to enable the appropriate integration of human rights, equality and sustainability concerns into World Heritage work. A set of indicators, moreover, will be required, to assess progress in implementing the policy, which would need to be incorporated within established monitoring and reporting mechanisms within the Convention, such as the Periodic Reporting process. The latter, in fact, is currently being revised in view of the launching of its third cycle and initial proposals for the integration of sustainable development concerns are already being developed for inclusion.

Not surprisingly, the main difficulties that lie ahead for achieving the full implementation of the policy stem from its ground-breaking character and ambition. By recognizing that heritage protection is only one element within the larger equation of human wellbeing, the policy has at the same time acknowledged the complex interrelations between conservation, on one hand, and all other dimensions of sustainable development, on the other, and requires that all these concerns are considered together.

In doing so, the policy poses a fundamental challenge to the field of conservation, as it inevitably blurs the boundaries between heritage and other societal concerns, thereby strengthening the relevance and legitimacy of many other stakeholders, disciplines and areas of expertise to be considered in decisions about heritage. The application of the policy into practice will have to acknowledge this and provide the necessary mechanisms for the integration of a diverse range of perspectives, and actors, into a single process at various levels, notably social, institutional, technical and financial. Only in this way will it be possible to find the appropriate and acceptable solutions to the above-mentioned equation.

Fundamentally, this new approach recognizes that the conservation and management of heritage is no longer just a technical question, regulated by a set of ethical principles and guidelines established by experts within a single discipline. It is instead part of the larger political debate on the appropriate use of public resources and the principles that should underpin the government of society, where a compromise needs to be found among different interests and visions of the world.

How these considerations may affect the institutional process regulating the Convention is, at present, still an open question. Going beyond the 'World Heritage box', and indeed beyond the narrow boundaries of the heritage field, is bound to create discomfort if not tensions among those who have presided over this area of work in past decades. New players will enter the arena, with different priorities, ranging from human rights, gender equality and poverty reduction to environmental sustainability, pushing for new rules of the game. Perhaps new types of expertise from the mainstream sustainable development sector will be required to advise the Committee, in addition to the three existing Advisory Bodies.

Essentially, the recognition of the inherently political nature of heritage management and protection, and of heritage's close relation with issues of equality, democracy and respect for human rights, may engender a completely new range of discussions in the implementation of the Convention. What was in the past conveniently considered an exclusively technical question, regulated by norms living in a world of their own, will in the future become an integral part of the broader debate about which values and principles should regulate our societies. State Parties, in other words, will be expected to demonstrate not only that the physical attributes of a World Heritage property are preserved but that human rights are respected, local communities are meaningfully involved in decisions, gender equality is pursued, and so on. If the Committee debates about the state of conservation of properties have sometimes been tense in the past, the introduction of the policy on sustainable development, with its new requirements touching on critical aspects of governance, is bound to expose differences in ideological and political visions of the world, with the potential for even deeper controversies. Conversely, decisions by the Committee that take into account the wider spectrum of sustainable development concerns would enjoy a broader social legitimacy.

In the longer term, the introduction of a sustainable development perspective into World Heritage – with its inherent people-centred approach – might also result in an evolution of the conceptual standpoints of the Convention. In the face of changing conditions, including climate change, and based on consideration of human rights, the question might arise, by way of example, about whether Statements of OUV of listed properties should be intended to continue 'forever', as is the case at present, or should be subject to periodical review through a broad consultative process.

Clearly, the policy will give a much more important role to civil society and its organizations, as also anticipated by the Committee in its Decision 40 COM 5C (paragraphs 8 and 9) (World Heritage Committee 2016). In this respect, the implementation of the policy on sustainable development could be instrumental in giving concrete application to another important policy document adopted by the Committee in recent years; that is, the World Heritage Capacity Building Strategy (UNESCO 2011) This Strategy recognized, for the first time, that in addition to practitioners and institutions, a third target audience needed to be addressed, that of communities and networks, which was an essential consideration with a view to ensuring 'a more dynamic relationship between heritage and its context and, in turn, greater reciprocal benefits by a more inclusive approach' (UNESCO 2011: 4). The table containing a list of priority actions in the Annex to the World Heritage Capacity Building Strategy, in fact, already provides several useful indications how the policy on sustainable development might be implemented.

In conclusion, the overall message of this policy is that it is time we learn to live with our heritage rather than protecting it as something *apart from* our living, breathing societies. By putting heritage within the sphere of the sustainable development agenda and aligning it with existing humanitarian and multilateral environmental agreements, this policy establishes an essential link between the heritage community and the rest of the world. To move forward with this policy is to acknowledge that to save heritage we must concern ourselves with issues 'beyond' heritage. Only then are we assured the best chance that our heritage will survive.

Notes

1 Disclaimer: The authors are responsible for the choice and the presentation of the facts contained in the article and for the opinions expressed therein, which are not necessarily those of UNESCO and do not commit the Organization.
2 The policy itself is accessible from UNESCO World Heritage Centre (2015). World Heritage and Sustainable Development at http://whc.unesco.org/en/sustainabledevelopment/
3 The Budapest Declaration on World Heritage states that the members of the Committee 'seek to ensure an appropriate and equitable balance between conservation, sustainability and development, so that World Heritage properties can be protected through appropriate activities contributing to the social and economic development and the quality of life of our communities'.
4 The World Heritage Centre prepared an analytical summary of the results of these events, which is accessible at: http://whc.unesco.org/en/sustainabledevelopment/.
5 The *Directives* were indeed modified, through the inclusion of a new section on sustainable development, by the General Assembly of the State Parties to the 2003 Convention at its sixth meeting (resolution 6.GA 7, accessible at: www.unesco.org/culture/ich/en/6.ga).
6 A compilation of all comments received by the State Parties, together with the answers provided by the Secretariat of the World Heritage Convention, is accessible at: http://whc.unesco.org/en/sessions/20ga/documents.
7 See footnote 18 on page 9 of the policy.
8 By '*Policy Guidelines*', the General Assembly referred to a compendium – whose scope and format is still to be defined – of all the policies agreed to by the Committee or the General Assembly itself, both in the past and in the future. The establishment of these *Policy Guidelines* was requested by the Committee, in its Decision 35 COM 12B (paragraph 11), adopted at its 35th Session (Paris, 2011), in which it decided 'to establish a four-year cycle for updating the *Operational Guidelines* and that the *Operational Guidelines* should be restricted to operational guidance, and that a new document, "*Policy Guidelines*", be developed as a means to capture the range of policies that the Committee and the General Assembly adopt'. At the time of writing of this paper (March 2017), these *Policy Guidelines* had not yet been developed.

References

UNESCO (2002). *The Budapest Declaration on World Heritage*. Available at: http://whc.unesco.org/en/decisions/1217/ (accessed 29 March 2017).
UNESCO (2010). Report of the World Heritage Committee Thirty-Fourth Session. *Item 5 of the Provisional Agenda: Reports of the World Heritage Centre and the Advisory*

Bodies: Decision 5D, World Heritage Convention and Sustainable Development. Available at: http://whc.unesco.org/archive/2010/whc10-34com-5De.pdf (accessed 29 March 2017).

UNESCO (2011). Report of the World Heritage Committee Thirty-Fifth Session. *Item 9b of the Provisional Agenda: Global Strategy for a Representative, Balanced and Credible World Heritage List, Presentation and Adoption of the World Heritage Strategy for Capacity Building*. WHC-11/35.COM/9B, 19–29 June 2011. Available at: http://whc.unesco.org/archive/2011/whc11-35com-9Be.pdf (accessed 29 March 2017).

UNESCO (2012). *Proceedings of the Consultative Expert Meeting on World Heritage and Sustainable Development* (Ouro Preto, Brazil), 5–8 February 2012. Available at: http://whc.unesco.org/uploads/events/documents/event-794-2.pdf (accessed 29 March 2017).

UNESCO (2015a). Item 13 of the Provisional Agenda: World Heritage and Sustainable Development. *World Heritage Committee: Twentieth Session of the General Assembly of the State Parties to the Convention Concerning the Protection of the World Cultural and Natural Heritage*. WHC-15/20.GA/13, Paris, 18–20 November 2015. Available at: http://unesdoc.unesco.org/images/0023/002355/235552E.pdf (accessed 29 March 2017).

UNESCO (2015b). UN General Assembly Resolution 20/12. *Future of the World Heritage Convention: Outcomes and Progress in the Implementation of the Strategic Action Plan*, 18–20 November 2015. Available at: http://whc.unesco.org/archive/2015/whc15-20ga-12-en.pdf (accessed 29 March 2017).

UNESCO (2015c). UN General Assembly Resolution 20/13. *World Heritage and Sustainable Development*, 18–20 November 2015. Available at: http://whc.unesco.org/en/decisions/6578/ (accessed 15 May 2017).

UNESCO (2016a). *Item 5 of the Provisional Agenda: Reports of the World Heritage Centre and the Advisory Bodies – World Heritage Committee – Fortieth Session*. WHC/16/40.COM/5C, 10–20 July 2016. Available at: http://whc.unesco.org/archive/2016/whc16-40com-5C-en.pdf (accessed 29 March 2017).

UNESCO (2016b). *Operational Guidelines for the Implementation of the World Heritage Convention*. Available at: http://whc.unesco.org/en/guidelines/ (accessed 29 March 2017).

UNESCO (2016c). *Sixth Session of the General Assembly of State Parties to the Convention for the Safeguarding of Intangible Cultural Heritage: Revision of the Operational Directives for the Implementation of the Convention*. ITH/15/6/GA/7, Paris, 29 April 2016. Available at: https://ich.unesco.org/en/6.ga (accessed 15 May 2017).

UNESCO World Heritage Centre (2015). *World Heritage and Sustainable Development*. Available at: http://whc.unesco.org/en/sustainabledevelopment/ (accessed 15 May 2017).

United Nations (2015). *UN General Assembly Resolution 70/1*. Transforming Our World: The 2030 Agenda for Sustainable Development. Available at: https://sustainabledevelopment.un.org/post2015/transformingourworld (accessed 29 March 2017).

United Nations System Task Team on the Post-2015 UN Development Agenda (2012). *Realizing the Future We Want for All: Report to the Secretary General*. Available at: www.un.org/millenniumgoals/pdf/Post_2015_UNTTreport.pdf (accessed 15 May 2017).

United Nations World Commission on Environment and Development (1987). *Our Common Future*. Oxford: Oxford University Press.

World Heritage Committee (WHC) (2007). *Evaluation of the Results of the Implementation of the Committee's Strategic Objectives* (Decision 31 COM 13A). Available at: http://whc.unesco.org/en/decisions/5196 (accessed 29 March 2017).

World Heritage Committee (WHC) (2010). *World Heritage and Sustainable w* (Decision 34 COM 5D). Available at: http://whc.unesco.org/en/decisions/4232 (accessed 29 March 2017).

World Heritage Committee (WHC) (2012). *World Heritage Convention and Sustainable Development* (Decision 36 COM 5C). Available at: http://whc.unesco.org/en/decisions/4610 (accessed 29 March 2017).

World Heritage Committee (WHC) (2014). *World Heritage and Sustainable Development* (Decision 38 COM 5D). Available at: http://whc.unesco.org/en/decisions/5799/ (accessed 29 March 2017).

World Heritage Committee (WHC) (2016). *World Heritage Convention and Sustainable Development* (Decision 40 COM 5C). Available at: http://whc.unesco.org/en/decisions/6776/ (accessed 29 March 2017).

Chapter 3

Historical, theoretical and international considerations on culture, heritage and (sustainable) development

Sophia Labadi

The UNESCO *Policy on the integration of a sustainable development perspective into the processes of the World Heritage Convention* (henceforth policy on World Heritage and Sustainable Development) represents a milestone in the implementation of this convention (UNESCO 2015). It provides a roadmap for a more effective engagement with sustainable development principles at World Heritage sites. However, this policy, its importance and relevance cannot be understood without considering the wider theories and frameworks on heritage and (sustainable) development. This chapter aims to chart these different theories and approaches related to culture, heritage and (sustainable) development, particularly those adopted at the level of the UN and UNESCO. The overall goal is to frame this newly adopted policy and this edited collection within a wider historical, theoretical and international framework.

The chapter begins by considering the concept of development at international and national levels, from the 1940s onwards. It focuses on understanding how development is seen as progress, as opposed to the concept of heritage, which is often understood in terms of the past and traditions. The shortcomings and failings of this understanding of development will be highlighted, as well as the emergence of a cultural turn in international development led by UNESCO. The chapter will then consider two recent trends: first, the increased consideration of heritage and culture as core elements of the concept of sustainable development, and, second, the persistent, yet paradoxical, marginalization of cultural heritage from reflections, theories and models of international aid and (sustainable) development.

Development versus heritage

From the 1940s to 1960s, development was considered almost solely in terms of progress and economic growth. Rostow's *The Stages of Economic Growth* (1960) stands as a classic illustration of this understanding of development. To be considered as developed, 'traditional societies' needed to go through stages of economic growth that would see them 'drive to maturity' and reach an 'age of high mass consumption' (Rostow 1960). Another approach, the structural change theory, aimed to change the economic structure of developing countries with measures to increase employment in modern and industrial sectors, rather than in the agricultural or subsistence sectors (Lewis 1954: 139–191; Ranis and Fei 1961: 533–565). These models are united in their perception of development as purely economic, based on outputs and measures of productivity, most notably measures of gross domestic product per person in the population ('GDP per capita') and related measures of employment, wages and levels of consumption (Labadi and Gould 2015: 199). These economic approaches also aim to impose Western models of development, as it was widely believed that this was the only model that worked. Western cultural values were considered key factors behind successful growth in capitalist economies, borrowing from and expanding on Max Weber's classical work on *The Protestant Ethic and the Spirit of Capitalism* (Weber 1930; see also Sen 1998: 40–41).

These approaches led to new geo-political realities and spatiotemporal dislocations, with on the one hand, the developed world of Western nations, considered to have fully entered modernity, and, on the other hand, developing countries, in their great majority former colonies, that had not yet encountered modernity and progress (Escobar 1995; Kothari 2011: 68). In this process, developed countries and international development institutions (e.g. the World Bank or the International Monetary Fund) created knowledge on developing countries through multiple technical studies and issues, or 'abnormalities', within developing economies (Escobar 1995: 88), such as poverty, hunger, small farmers or high levels of illiteracy. The knowledge generated through these studies provided Western countries and Western-based international development institutions with the power to define the populations of developing countries and the required courses of action to solve these identified issues. For some, these new 'realities' represented neo-colonialist endeavours, as they were a means of bringing people in developing regions under control (Escobar 1995; Ferguson 1994). Ferguson, for instance, explained how a 1975 World Bank Country report on Lesotho presented a new reality of underdevelopment, soil deterioration, food shortages, and subsistence economy. However, academic studies of Lesotho indicated a contradictory reality with a regionally integrated economy and a producer of cash crops for the South African market (Ferguson 1994: 27). These World Bank reports and the associated issues created a new reality to justify intervention from the World Bank, which happened to have the right expertise, types of interventions and solutions that Lesotho needed (Ibid. 70). In this process, the World Bank did not focus on the important issues of existing geo-political powers and the complex relationships between South Africa and Lesotho that would have led to relevant changes.

According to these frameworks, culture and heritage were often considered as the direct opposite of economic development. Culture, notably traditional culture, and heritage were considered to represent a backwards vision of the past (Basu and Modest 2015: 4–8). Worse, culture and heritage were even regarded as inhibitors of development in terms of progress and modernity (Abraham and Platteau 2004: 210–233; Labadi 2017a: 47–48). These focused criticisms on culture and heritage were means of obscuring unfair global structures of production and distribution, as well as the unfavourable terms of trade underdeveloped nations experienced in relation to developed countries (Prah 2011: 158). To reach development, local communities were encouraged to move beyond their culture and heritage, as they constituted 'cultural blockage', change their attitude and adopt 'modern' (in other words, occidental) cultural values. They were also encouraged to adopt Western approaches and values regarding heritage conservation (Jopela 2017; Ndoro and Wijesuriya 2015) These considerations, still valid today, have meant that many people from developing countries privilege occidental values and have no interest in their own culture which they consider as 'primitive' or 'backward' (Abraham 1978, quoted in Basu and Modest 2015: 16). This negative cultural identity, often driven by political or socio-economic motives, has had a major impact on creating stigma and self-depreciation. In turn, these have led to the negation of cultural, social and economic opportunities for minorities. Arizpe, for instance, documented how stigma attached to Indians in Mexico led mestizo families to monopolize jobs and business opportunities (1978; Arizpe 2004: 172). Similarly, the politically motivated destruction of some cultural heritage has been conducted in the name of development projects. These acts of destruction have aimed to prolong the cultural, social and economic domination, marginalization or exclusion of ethnic minorities, as was the case, for instance, with the destruction of some cultural heritage deemed of 'minor importance' during the construction of the Three Gorges Dam in China (Le Mentec 2006).

These acts of depreciation of culture and heritage for political, social or economic motives, or as a means of defining populations of developing countries, should not hide wider trends of destruction of cultural heritage to make way for development projects around the world. The ICOMOS *Heritage at Risk* series and the numerous state of conservation reports prepared for the World Heritage Committee provide many examples of monuments, groups of buildings and sites that have been at risk of destruction or have been destroyed in the name of development (see also Martínez Yáñez 2015: 175–195). These trends have many causes, including the belief that new buildings are cheaper to build than to restore, conserve and maintain old ones. In addition, heritage sites rarely bring sufficient economic benefits on their own, leading to the need to build commercial properties that may threaten these sites. Elsewhere, I have explained that this trend is still ongoing, with the example of the World Heritage site of Liverpool Maritime Mercantile City (inscribed on the World Heritage List in 2004 and on the World Heritage List in Danger since 2012) (Labadi 2016: 137–150). Still one of the most deprived territories in England, Liverpool will see a major redevelopment scheme of the historic docklands north of the city centre. This redevelopment project, called Liverpool Waters, will provide 1.7 million square metres of mixed use development floor space across 60 hectares. The scale and density of this proposed development has directly threatened the outstanding universal value of this World Heritage site. A core issue with this project is the lack of discussion between different stakeholders and the weak bargaining power of local authorities, effectively removing the forces that might have prevented this example of economic development happening at the expense of cultural heritage (ibid.; see also Gould and Pyburn 2017).

The cultural turn in development

These models of development as economic growth, modernization and progress have faced mounting criticism since at least the 1960s. The work of the Club of Rome is just one example of such a critical approach. It expressed concerns that overpopulation, exploitation of raw materials, industrial productions and mounting pollution would generate a collapse of the world ecosystems and economy and provided different scenarios for a sustainable future (Meadows et al. 1972). The *Convention Concerning the Protection of the World Cultural and Natural Heritage* (the World Heritage Convention or the Convention), adopted by UNESCO in November 1972 can be considered to reflect these concerns (Labadi 2017a: 45–60; Labadi in press). The World Heritage concept was indeed born out of the need to protect heritage of outstanding universal value threatened by, among other things, infrastructure and economic development projects. The first paragraph of the Preamble to the convention is quite clear when it stresses that:

> The cultural heritage and natural heritage are increasingly threatened with destruction not only by the traditional causes of decay, but also by changing social and economic conditions which aggravate the situation with even more formidable phenomena of damage and destruction.
>
> (UNESCO 1972)

This preamble clearly refers to the process of rapid industrialization and urbanization of the 1960s and 1970s that led to the destruction of the non-renewable resources embodied in heritage sites. Implicit reference is also made to the international campaign to salvage the two Abu Simbel Temples in Egypt dating from the reign of Pharaoh Ramesses II in the 13th century BCE. These temples were moved in 1968 onto an artificial hill to protect them from being submerged after the construction of the Aswan High Dam.

Concerns for the protection of non-renewable resources and the limits of growth gave rise to the concept of sustainable development, the theme of this book and the 2015 UNESCO policy on World Heritage and Sustainable Development. Sustainable development is usually defined, in the words of the World Commission on Environment and Development (the 'Brundtland Report'), as 'development that meets the needs of the present without compromising the ability of future generations to meet their own needs' (WCED 1987: Paragraph 27). Sustainable development is often associated with finding a balance between the three pillars of sustainable development – economic, social and environmental sustainability – that were adopted at the Earth Summit in Rio de Janeiro in 1992 (Spenceley 2008: 1; United Nations 1997). As reflected in the policy on World

Heritage and Sustainable Development, a fourth pillar, peace and security, was recently added to this traditional trio (UNCSD 2012: 24).

This concept of sustainable development has faced many criticisms. It is ambiguous and does not clearly explain how these four paradoxical pillars, which often correspond to different objectives and methods, can be holistically implemented. Indeed, how can economic growth go hand in hand with environmental protection and social inclusion and cohesion (Labadi 2013: 98–99)? For some, it is inconceivable to talk about the sustainable use of non-renewable resources, as exploitation of this finite stock will inexorably lead to its exhaustion (Turner 1988). Besides, intergenerational equity – the core principle of sustainable development according to the definition from the Brundtland Report – is also problematic (Meskell 2011: 27). In our unjust and unequal world, how can those who are already deprived of resources bequeath them to future generations? How can this principle of intergenerational equity work in a global context where instant profit is so valued to the detriment of long-term benefits? Finally, this definition does not take account of the concept of culture and the paradigmatic shift that has attempted to put it at the heart of sustainable development.

This paradigmatic shift started in the 1970s as a reaction to the models of development and growth presented in the first part of this chapter. This shift represented a new direction as people sought to place local cultures at the heart of development, and promote 'endogenous development' (Escobar 1995; Blake 2015: 155). This shift also revealed the arbitrary nature of the dual categories that structured the models of development presented in the previous section, including local/global, traditional/modern, developed/underdeveloped and scientific/unscientific. On the other hand, this shift insisted upon the fluid and interconnected nature of these categories. Examples abound of hybrid cultural processes on the grounds that are ways in which modernity is being reinterpreted and adapted at the local level. One example concerns environmental sustainability and local responses and adaptation to actual or potential impacts of changing climate conditions (Task Force on Climate Change, Vulnerable Communities and Adaptation 2003: 5). Traditional knowledge systems are increasingly recognized as powerful tools for monitoring climate change and for implementing successful adaptation strategies. Archaeological evidence from the Pacific Islands demonstrates, for instance, that local communities have adopted successful strategies for dealing with climate variability for over three millennia (Long and Smith 2010: 179–181).

This approach to development was reaffirmed and fine-tuned during the UN World Decade for Cultural Development (1988–1997). The ambitious aims of this decade were to find new models of development which would place a greater emphasis on the 'characteristics of the natural and cultural environment', as well as 'the needs, aspirations and the values of the populations concerned' (UNESCO 1987: 15). Cultural heritage was recognized as 'one of the major assets of a multidimensional type of development' (UNESCO 1990). These ideas were fully developed in *Our Creative Diversity* (1995), which was drafted by the World Commission on Culture and Development and represents a major output from this decade. A whole chapter of this report focuses on cultural heritage and, 20 years before the policy on World Heritage and Sustainable Development, developed a number of similar principles (World Commission on Culture and Development 1995: 175–204). This report details the importance of a bottom-up and participatory approach to the conservation, management and interpretation of cultural heritage, based on the values given to heritage by local communities. This publication also warns against the devastating effects of wide scale tourism development on local cultures. It encourages ethical tourism that meets the needs of local communities, and which is also devised by these communities on their own terms. This report also moves away from the perception that development equates to economic growth and progress. On the other hand, it adopts and promotes the notion of human development, relocating the human at the heart of development processes.

Taking this further, Sen has also defined human development as a set of capabilities that people can choose from to achieve what they want to be and do and to achieve a full and satisfying life. His focus is on the opportunities offered to people and on removing obstacles so that individuals have the freedom to live the life they have reason to value. He has identified culture as one of these sets of capabilities that can help individuals to achieve their wellbeing (Sen 1980, 1992; see also Labadi 2017b for an application of the capability approach to museums). For Sen, culture is core to wellbeing, as it improves people's lives through being a vehicle for expressions of feelings, desires, frustration and values. For this reason, enhancing cultural activities and the freedom and opportunities to take part in them can be seen as constitutive of development (Sen 2004: 39). Sen also explains the importance of cultural heritage, not only for economic growth, but also for providing physical evidence of the peaceful coexistence of different communities, which can be considered essential to enhancing peace. The World Heritage list is filled with such sites promoting this peaceful coexistence between different communities, including Butrint in Albania (originally inscribed on the list in 1992), which highlights a diversity of remains from Greece and Rome, as well as Christian and Islamic influences.

Two major additional events and publications at the end of the twentieth century further contributed to making the links between culture and development more explicit: the 1998 International Conference on Cultural Policies for Development organized by UNESCO and held in Stockholm and its associated report (UNESCO 1998) and the publications *Culture Counts. Towards New Strategies for Culture in Sustainable Development* (UNESCO and Government of Italy 1999). These events and documents introduced a number of key ideas that were more fully fleshed out in the 2015 policy on World Heritage and Sustainable Development. They highlight that culture should stand at the heart of the implementation of the economic and social pillars of sustainable development. The 1999 Culture Counts document, for instance, refers to the economic growth generated by tourism, but insists on the need for these revenues to be channelled back for site conservation and to strengthen local communities' capacities through employment, among other things. In addition, cultural heritage is presented as a form of social and human capital that promotes the cohesion and inclusion of local communities as a vector of identity. Educational projects at heritage sites are the best medium to strengthen the cohesion and inclusion of local communities. It has also been suggested that cultural impact assessment tools should be integrated in all development programs and projects to ensure full respect of local cultures and cultural heritage. Finally, the document *Culture Counts* identifies training in the field of culture as essential and as a key priority to ensure a more strategic and central relocation of heritage within development programs and projects.

At the turn of the millennium, an extensive trail of documents thus detailed the reasons why culture and heritage should stand at the heart of sustainable development. But how has the concept of sustainable development been integrated within the World Heritage convention system, and how has cultural heritage been integrated within the international development agenda in the 21st century?

Heritage and culture: core elements of sustainable development?

This concept of sustainable development became officially associated with the process of identifying, conserving and managing World Heritage properties for the first time in the Budapest Declaration of 2002, which expresses the need to:

> Ensure an appropriate and equitable balance between conservation, sustainability and development, so that World Heritage properties can be protected through appropriate activities contributing to the social and economic development and the quality of life of our communities.
>
> (UNESCO 2002: 4)

References to sustainable development within the official framework of the convention have increasingly taken centre stage, in particular with the World Heritage Paper 13, which insisted upon the importance of local communities involvement (de Merode, Smeets and Westrik 2013) or the 2005 revision of the Operational Guidelines (Paragraphs 6 and 119 make direct references to sustainable development). This trend continued in 2012 with the fortieth anniversary of the Convention, the celebratory theme of which focused on 'World Heritage and Sustainable Development: the Role of Local Communities' (Galla 2012). Despite these mentions, it has been documented that the implementation of this convention suffers from unsustainable development trends, including unsustainable economic development of World Heritage sites in the form of infrastructure or tourism development (Labadi 2013: 95–112). One example is the Mahabodhi Temple Complex at Bodh Gaya in India, inscribed on the World Heritage List in 2002 for its association with the life of Lord Buddha. The Gaya International Airport, which opened in 2002, has led to increased visitors from Bangkok, Sri Lanka, Nepal, Burma, and Bhutan (Geary 2008: 13; see also Labadi in Press). In 2013, the Airports Authority of India (AAI) made requests for the extension of this airport, further reflecting this boom in regional tourism (Winter 2010: 117–129). This increase has led to more tourist facilities. Yet, the Urban Development and Housing Department of the Government of Bihar has recognized that boarding and lodging facilities for tourists are 'largely unregulated' (Intercontinental Consultants and Technocrats Pvt. Ltd 2010: 8). Another issue concerns the marginalization of local communities in accessing the inscribed sites, and in taking part in their conservation, management and interpretation. Involving communities can be a difficult endeavour, as potential conflicts exist over who should identify and manage heritage (see Deacon et al. 2004: 42), who should represent the community and how local communities can make enlightened decisions concerning projects that might bring economic benefits in the forms of jobs on the one hand but destroy their heritage and social connections on the other. It might be argued that these trends have been the result of a lack of inclusion of clear guidelines on World Heritage and sustainable development in the working documents of the Convention. Hence, the importance of the 2015 policy.

The wider UN framework reflects this ambiguous attitude towards culture, heritage and (sustainable) development. There was no mention of culture or heritage in the Millennium Development Goals (MDGs, 2000–2015), which identified ambitious targets to eradicate extreme poverty, to enhance the capabilities of poor people through improved access to education, healthcare and political rights and to improve environmental sustainability. One explanation for this exclusion might be the consideration that culture and heritage constitute obstacles to development. This consideration echoes the theories opposing development and culture that flourished in the 1940s to 1960s, as presented at the beginning of this chapter. The misconception that culture and heritage hinder development seems to be so widespread that the 2004 UNDP's Human Development Report entitled *Cultural Liberty in Today's Diverse World* started by debunking five myths about how cultural diversity leads to social fragmentation, political conflict and weak economic development (UNDP 2004: 2). This report calls for a greater respect for the diversity of culture and heritage. It also makes clear that development takes many forms and does not necessarily need to be based on Western values, thus criticizing the ideas that Max Weber developed in *The Protestant Ethic and the Spirit of Capitalism* (Weber 1930) that are still heavily subscribed to. To illustrate this point, this UNDP document takes the example of Confucian values and their associated cultural manifestations and heritage, which did not prevent the impressive economic growth of Eastern Asian countries such as Japan or South Korea (UNDP 2004: 5).

A ground-breaking experimental investment of 95 million USD was made by the government of Spain in 2006 to support culture and development programs, under a scheme entitled the MDG-Fund Culture and Development Thematic window. The aim of this program was to accelerate progress towards the achievement of the MDGs through funding 18 culture and development projects on all the five continents, including in Bosnia and Herzegovina, Cambodia, Ethiopia and Uruguay. This program also aimed to demonstrate that culture is essential to the implementation of the MDGs. A number of World Heritage sites were the focus of these projects. The Island of Mozambique inscribed on the World Heritage List in 1991 was part of a wider 5 million USD project which aimed to *Strengthen Cultural and Creative Industries and Inclusive Policies in Mozambique*. This project, which ran from 2008 to 2013 aimed to contribute to MDG 1 through the creation of four new tourism tours on the island and the associated creation of job opportunities, contributing to poverty reduction. MDG 3 was also implemented by creating employment opportunities targeted at women, as well as the creation of women-run cultural businesses. This project also contributed to MDG1 and MDG3 through developing or enhancing community entrepreneurship, through training members of local communities (including women) in business development and in the provision of new cultural products. However, many projects funded by this thematic window at World Heritage sites fail to clarify whether targeted participants escaped poverty by earning a decent living through these new opportunities. In addition, these 18 programs remained scattered; no general guidelines were drawn on how to scale up these projects or to streamline culture into development projects and policies in a more systematic manner. In addition, only the government of Spain supported these efforts on culture and development and 'ambiguities remain regarding the actual level of commitment of (other) donors and beneficiary countries to this agenda' (De Beukelaer and Freitas 2015: 215).

Despite these limits, culture and heritage have increasingly been associated with sustainable development, as testified by the profusion of events and activities organized and publications and declaration released on this topic in the past ten years. Of particular relevance are the two resolutions adopted by the UN in 2010 and 2011 on culture and development (UN 2010, 2011). These resolutions invite governments and relevant stakeholders to include culture into all development policies, raise awareness of the importance of culture and cultural diversity for sustainable development as well as support and assist the development of cultural sectors through technical and vocational training. Other documents and events, including UNESCO's 2012 Thematic Think Piece on *Culture: a driver and an enabler of sustainable development* or the International Congress's *Culture: Key to Sustainable Development* (Hangzhou, China, May 2013) explain that culture in general and heritage in particular should be considered as transversal and cross-cutting themes which affect all dimensions of development and the MDG. Culture and heritage contribute to poverty eradication through tourism and income generation, strengthen food production through the adaptation of traditional land-management systems, contribute to education through local knowledge, as well as mitigate the effects of climate change through traditional environmental management practices (UNESCO 2012). In the same vein, a third UN resolution on culture and development was adopted in December 2013 that recognized the role of culture in implementing the three pillars of sustainable development and requested due consideration to culture and sustainable development in the preparation of the work for the post-2015 period (UN 2013). Other initiatives, including the '#culture2015goal campaign', call for a specific goal devoted to culture.

Despite all these efforts, events, publications and declarations, culture and heritage are not as present in the 2015 SDGs as one might have expected them to be, considering that no specific goal mentions culture or heritage directly. However, culture and heritage are mentioned in some of the 164 targets of the 17 overall goals. This represents an improved situation compared with the MDGs, which did not mention culture or heritage at all, and reflects the more inclusive nature of the SDGs. More specifically, World Heritage is mentioned as part of Goal 11 that aims to 'Make cities inclusive, safe, resilient and sustainable'. Target 11.4. aims to 'Strengthen efforts to protect and safeguard the world's cultural and natural heritage'. Tourism is mentioned at least twice, in very similar terms. First, Goal 8 aims to develop 'decent work and economic growth'. Target 8.9 aims, by 2030, to enable relevant stakeholders to 'devise and implement policies to promote sustainable tourism that creates jobs and promotes local culture and products'. A similar idea is presented in Goal 12, which aims to 'ensure sustainable consumption and production patterns'. Target 12.b. aims to 'develop and implement tools to monitor sustainable development impacts for sustainable tourism that creates jobs and promotes local culture and products'. Finally, Goal 4 aims to 'Ensure inclusive and quality education for all and promote lifelong learning'. Target 4.7 aims to promote 'a culture of peace and non-violence, global citizenship and appreciation of cultural diversity and of culture's contribution to sustainable development'.

These different targets do not reflect the rich contribution of culture and heritage to sustainable development, and a number of key ideas are not mentioned, including the importance of heritage for environmental sustainability, the potential of heritage to enhance quality of life and wellbeing of all stakeholders, the role of culture to ensure gender equality or the importance of heritage for peace and security. These shortcomings might still reflect the lack of guidelines on the degree to which culture and heritage contribute to these goals and the wider sustainable development framework (Basu and Modest 2015: 26). Considering these silences, the policy on World Heritage and Sustainable Development is a welcome initiative. It provides a much-needed roadmap on how to ensure that World Heritage fully contributes to sustainable development and the implementation of the SDGs.

Conclusion

This chapter has detailed the increasing references to culture and heritage as a transversal and cross-cutting theme that affects all dimensions of development. This trend started in the 1970s when people started to contest that development was uniquely defined by economic growth, progress and modernity and that one model of development could fit all situations. This cultural turn in development has accelerated in the past ten years, as UNESCO has pro-actively campaigned for culture and heritage to be considered as a driver and an enabler of sustainable development. However, the results of these efforts and campaigns cannot be deemed completely successful. It is true that some of the 164 targets of the 17 SDGs mention culture and heritage. This represents a welcome change, compared with the previous international framework of the MDGs, which failed to refer to culture or heritage. Yet, none of the 17 goals mention culture and heritage, and the targets do not refer to the rich contributions of culture and heritage to sustainable development.

One reason for these limited references in the SDGs might be the continued belief in models of (sustainable) development that exclude culture and heritage. These models associate development with economic growth, Western capitalism and notions of occidental modernity. Yet, putting culture and heritage at the heart of sustainable development requires a Copernican revolution. It requires the recognition that developed and developing countries, modern and traditional societies, backward and advanced countries are constructed notions that might not have a real underpinning, but have been constructed for social, political and economic motives. These omissions might also be due to the limited evidence that culture and heritage contribute to sustainable development and the lack of wide scale data. Under these circumstances, the policy on World Heritage and Sustainable Development might be a first step towards ensuring that heritage fully contributes to the implementation of the SDGs.

References

Abraham, A. and Platteau, J.-P. (2004). 'Participatory development: Where culture creeps in', in V. Rao and M. Walton (eds), *Culture and Public Action*. Stanford, CA: Stanford University Press.

Arizpe, L. (1978). *Migración, etnicismo y cambio económico*. Mexico: Colegio de México.

Arizpe, L. (2004). 'The intellectual history of culture and development institutions', in V. Rao and M. Walton (eds), *Culture and Public Action*. Stanford: Stanford University Press.

Basu, P. and Modest, W. (2015). 'Museums, heritage and international development: A critical conversation', in P. Basu and W. Modest (eds), *Museums, Heritage and International Development*. London: Routledge.

Blake, J. (2015). *International Cultural Heritage Law*. Oxford: Oxford University Press.

Deacon, H., Dondolo, L., Mrubata, M. and Prosalendis, S. (2004). *The Subtle Power of Intangible Heritage*. South Africa: HSRC Publishers.

De Beukelaer, C. and Freitas, R. (2015). 'Culture and sustainable development: Beyond the diversity of cultural expressions', in C. de Beukelaer, M. Pyykkönen and J. P. Singh (eds), *Globalization, Culture, and Development: The UNESCO Convention on Cultural Diversity*. London: Palgrave-Macmillan.

De Merode, E., Smeets, R. and Westrik, C. (eds) (2013). *Linking Universal and Local Values: Managing a Sustainable Future for World Heritage*. Paris: UNESCO.

Escobar, A. (1995). *Encountering Development: The Making and Unmaking of the Third World*. Princeton, NJ: Princeton University Press.

Ferguson, J. (1994). *The Anti-Politics Machine: 'Development', Depoliticization and Bureaucratic Power in Lesotho*. Minnnesota: University of Minnesota Press.

Galla, A. (ed) (2012). *World Heritage: Benefits Beyond Borders*. Cambridge: Cambridge University Press.

Geary, D. (2008). 'Destination enlightenment: Branding Buddhism and spiritual tourism in Bodhgaya, Bihar', *Anthropology Today*, 24, 11–14.

Gould, P. and Pyburn, A. (eds) (2017). *Collision or Collaboration: Archaeology Encounters Economic Development*. Cham: Springer.

Intercontinental Consultants and Technocrats Pvt. Ltd (2010). *City Development Plan (2010–30)*. Bodh Gaya: Urban Development and Housing Department Government of Bihar.

Jopela, A. (2017). *The Politics of Liberation Heritage in Postcolonial Southern Africa with Special Reference to Mozambique*. Unpublished PhD thesis, University of Witwatersrand.

Kothari, U. (2011). 'History, time and temporality in development discourse', in C. A. Bayly, V. Rao, S. Szreter and M. Woolcock (eds), *History, Historians and Development Policy: A Necessary Dialogue*. Manchester: Manchester University Press.

Labadi, S. (2013). *UNESCO, Cultural Heritage, and Outstanding Universal Value*. Plymouth, MA: AltaMira Press.

Labadi, S. (2016). 'Measuring the socio-economic impacts of heritage-led development: The cases of Liverpool (UK) and Lille (France)', in S. Labadi and W. Logan (eds), *Urban Heritage, Development and Sustainability*. London: Routledge.

Labadi, S. (2017a). 'UNESCO, heritage and sustainable development: International discourses and local impacts', in P. Gould and A. Pyburn (eds), *Promise and Peril: Archaeology Engaging with Economic Development*. New York: Springer.

Labadi, S. (2017b). *Museums, Immigrants, and Social Justice*. London: Routledge.

Labadi, S. (in press). 'Re-examining World Heritage and sustainable development', in V. Bharne and T. Sandmeier (eds), *Routledge Companion of Global Heritage Conservation*. London: Routledge.

Labadi, S. and Gould, P. (2015). 'Sustainable development: Heritage, community, economics', in L. Meskell (ed), *Global Heritage: A Reader*. Oxford: Wiley-Blackwell.

Le Mentec, K. (2006). The Three Gorges Dam Project: Religious Practices and Heritage Conservation. *China Perspectives*, 65 May–June 2006 (online). Available at: http://chinaperspectives.revues.org/626 (accessed 2 July 2017).

Lewis, W. A. (1954). 'Economic development with unlimited supplies of labour', *The Manchester School*, 22(2), 139–191.

Long, C. and Smith, A. (2010). 'Cultural heritage and the global environmental crisis', in S. Labadi and C. Long (eds), *Heritage and Globalization*. London: Routledge.

Martínez-Yáñez, C. (2016). 'Corporate visual impact on urban heritage: The corporate social responsibility framework', in S. Labadi and W. Logan (eds), *Urban Heritage, Development and Sustainability*. London: Routledge.

Meadows, D. H., Meadows, D. L., Randers, J. and Behrens III, W. (1972). *The Limits to Growth: A Report for the Club of Rome's Project on the Predicament of Mankind*. New York: Universe Books.

Meskell, L. (2011). *The Nature of Heritage: The New South Africa*. Oxford: Wiley-Blackwell.

Ndoro, W. and Wijesuriya, G. (2015). 'Heritage management and conservation: From colonization to globalization', in L. Meskell (ed), *Global Heritage: A Reader*. West Sussex: Wiley Blackwell, pp. 131–149.

Prah, K. K. (2011). 'Culture: The missing link in development planning in Africa', in L. Keita (ed), *Philosophy and African Development: Theory and Practice*. Dakar: Council for the Development of Social Science Research in Africa.

Ranis, G. and Fei, J. C. H. (1961). 'A theory of economic development', *The American Economic Review*, 51(4), 533–565.

Rostow, W. W. (1960). *The Stages of Economic Growth: A Non-Communist Manifesto*. Cambridge: Cambridge University Press.

Sen, A. (1980). 'Equality of what?', in S. McMurrin (ed), *The Tanner Lectures on Human Values*. Salt Lake City: University of Utah Press.

Sen, A. (1992). *Inequality Re-Examined*. Oxford: Clarendon Press.

Sen, A. (1998). 'Asian values and economic growth', *UNESCO World Culture Report*, 40–41.

Sen, A. (2004). 'How does culture matter?', in V. Rao and M. Walton (eds), *Culture and Public Action*. Stanford: Stanford University Press.

Spenceley, A. (2008). 'Introduction: Responsible tourism in Southern Africa', in A. Spenceley (ed), *Responsible Tourism: Critical Issues for Conservation and Development*. London: Earthscan.

Task Force on Climate Change, Vulnerable Communities and Adaptation (2003). *Livelihoods and Climate Change: Combining Disaster Risk Reduction, Natural Resource Management and Climate Change Adaptation in a New Approach to the Reduction of Vulnerability and Poverty*. Manitoba: IISD.

Turner, K. R. (1988). 'Sustainability, resource conservation and pollution control: An overview', in K. R. Turner (ed), *Sustainable Environmental Management*. London: Belhaven Press.

UNCSD (2012). *The Future We Want*. Rio de Janeiro: United Nations (online). Available at: www.uncsd2012.org/content/documents/727The%20Future%20We%20Want%2019%20June%201230pm.pdf (accessed 1 July 2017).

UNESCO (1972). *Convention Concerning the Protection of the World Cultural and Natural Heritage*. Paris: UNESCO.

UNESCO (1987). *A Practical Guide to the World Decade for Cultural Development 1988–97*. Paris: UNESCO.

UNESCO (1990). *The Third Medium Term Plan (1990–95) (25C/4)*. Paris: UNESCO.

UNESCO (1998). *Final Report: International Conference on Cultural Policies for Development*. Paris: UNESCO.

UNESCO (2002). *Decisions Adopted by the 26th Session of the World Heritage Committee*. WHC-02/CONF.202/25, 24–29 June 2002. Paris: UNESCO.

UNESCO (2012). *Culture: A Driver and an Enabler of Sustainable Development*. Thematic Think Piece (online). Available at: www.unesco.org/new/fileadmin/MULTIMEDIA/HQ/post2015/pdf/Think_Piece_Culture.pdf (accessed 2 July 2017).

UNESCO (2015). *Policy Document for the Integration of a Sustainable Development Perspective into the Processes of the World Heritage Convention* (online). Available at: http://whc.unesco.org/en/sustainabledevelopment/ (accessed 2 December 2017).

UNESCO and Government of Italy (1999). *Culture Counts: Towards New Strategies for Culture in Sustainable Development*. Paris: UNESCO.

United Nations (1997). *Agenda for Development*. New York: United Nations.

United Nations (2010). *Resolution 65/166: Culture and Development*. New York: United Nations.

United Nations (2011). *Resolution 66/208: Culture and Development*. New York: United Nations.

United Nations (2013). *Resolution 68/223: Culture and Sustainable Development*. New York: United Nations.

Weber, M. (1930). *The Protestant Ethic and the Spirit of Capitalism*. London: George Allen and Unwin Ltd.

Winter, T. (2010). 'Heritage tourism: Dawn of a new era?', in S. Labadi and C. Long (eds), *Heritage and Globalization*. New York: Routledge.

World Commission on Culture and Development (1995). *Our Creative Diversity*. Paris: UNESCO.

World Commission on Environment and Development (1987). *Our Common Future: From One Earth to One World: Report of the World Commission on Environment and Development*. New York: United Nations.

Part II

Policy dimensions and overarching principles

Chapter 4

Inclusive economic development in the urban heritage context

Christian Ost

With its post-2015 sustainable development agenda, the United Nations (UN 2015) adopted a set of goals to help define the future global development framework that will succeed the Millennium Development Goals (MDGs). Based on the UN Task Team Report *Realizing the Future We Want for All* (UN 2012), this new agenda addresses the issue of sustainable development as being dependent on four factors: environmental sustainability, inclusive social development, inclusive economic development and peace and security.

Inclusive economic development can be defined as follows: 'Sustainable development involves stable, equitable and inclusive economic growth, based on sustainable patterns of production and consumption' (UN 2012). In this regard, inclusive economic development is not in opposition to economic growth nor incompatible with a general increase in output that will provide more goods and services to the economy as a whole. Putting emphasis on inclusiveness and sustainability deals with benefits from growth, how they are distributed across the economy and how multiple stakeholders will get fair shares of the fruits of growth.

The aim of this chapter is to explain that when investing economic resources in cultural and natural heritage, it does not only provide expected economic benefits in terms of jobs and income, but it potentially also promotes social, equitable and inclusive benefits for all. In the field of heritage, inclusive economic development favours a people-centred economy, making economic growth and social equity compatible by relying on local use of resources and fair competition in a global market. This the emphasis that is put on inclusive economic development in UNESCO's 2015 *Policy for the integration of sustainable development into the processes of the World Heritage Convention* (hereafter the World Heritage and Sustainable Development policy) clearly underlines the major role of economic policies and the importance of addressing poverty alleviation, climate change issues and growing social inequalities. Furthermore, it sets this new agenda within the three overarching and cross-cutting principles of human rights, equality and long-term sustainability.

This chapter comprises four sections. The first section emphasizes historic parallels between economic changes and heritage conservation from a global perspective. The second section addresses some implications of this dynamic framework and describes the concept of economic inclusiveness, in particular in the urban heritage context. The next section analyses the content of the 2015 policy in terms of its integration of economic sustainability into the processes of the World Heritage Convention of 1972. Finally, the chapter makes recommendations for revising the Operational Guidelines, which is still to be undertaken.

Historic coincidence between economic growth and heritage conservation

UNESCO has devoted substantial efforts to turning cultural heritage conservation into a driver for promoting peace, intercultural cooperation and protection of local identity. As successful as this project has been (1,073 World Heritage monuments and sites listed in 167 countries), heritage conservation still faces many challenges, the roots of which often come from the social and economic environments.

In Europe, the protection of cultural heritage that was initiated formally after World War II for embracing values of peace and identity has been developed within a long period of reconstruction and economic growth, accompanied by expanding international trade and cooperation. When the World Heritage Convention was adopted in 1972 (UNESCO 1972), it was in effect an achievement of almost 30 years of reflection, debate and discussion on the need to preserve a common world heritage. It is noteworthy that the debate leading up to the adoption of the 1972 Convention came in a time of world economic transition, characterized by discussions about the implications of excessive growth in the Western world and the rise of a global environmental agenda (Meadows et al 1972). Later, heritage conservation would indeed follow the economic trend of globalization, by extending outside of Europe, following a shift of economic gravity to the East, with implications on the definition of heritage itself that integrated cultural diversity and intangible significance.

Another major shift came from the growing world population, migrations, rural exodus, and urbanization to a level unprecedented in history. Conservation of cultural and natural heritage increasingly faced more complex issues than those to which conservation specialists were accustomed thus far. This also led to heritage conservation embracing a broader set of principles and practices in order to engage with more systemic and holistic approaches. In the context of urban heritage conservation, for example, this has involved looking at broader urban ensembles, heritage cities and historic urban landscapes to address the comprehensive significance of places (*genius loci*) entailing architectural and historic values, but also economic and social values.

In 2012, UNESCO celebrated the fortieth anniversary of the adoption of the World Heritage Convention amid new contemporary challenges, among them crucial economic issues such as mass tourism and new urban development projects. The forces of change in urban conservation are prompting UNESCO to explore innovative tools to help site managers, urban planners and conservation specialists respond to these worldwide challenges. In their Strategic Plan 2012–2022, the World Heritage Committee and the General Assembly of the State Parties to the 1972 Convention implicitly acknowledged that concrete sustainable development gains could derive from the implementation of the Convention (UNESCO 2012a);

in other words, implying that World Heritage should clearly consider the social, economic and environmental needs.

Two succeeding expert meetings held in Paraty (UNESCO 2010) and Ouro Preto (UNESCO 2012b) underlined the need for heritage conservation to take into consideration the surrounding economic conditions in order to avoid the risk that cultural heritage would 'find itself a victim of, rather than a catalyst for wider change'. That was a major breakthrough in heritage economics, suggesting a shift from the established view that conservation may generate some marginal economic benefits to the acknowledgment that cultural and natural heritage definitely contribute to economic sustainability (Europa Nostra 2015). Not only does culture matter for itself, but it was now increasingly accepted that culture matters for economic growth. This new perspective was eventually encapsulated in principles of sustainable development with the four-pillar paradigm of cultural, social, economic and environmental (UNESCO 2013) and the adoption of the World Heritage and Sustainable Development policy (UNESCO 2015).

Bringing together conservation and economics has been an objective for scholars and practitioners for a long time. Professor William Hendon, founder of the *Journal of Cultural Economics*, organized the first international conference on cultural economics at Edinburgh in 1979. The path of cultural economics eventually led to the integration of economic principles and recommendations in official UNESCO and ICOMOS documents. The scientific contribution to this quest has been greatly facilitated by the analysis of natural resources by environmental economists during the 1970s and the subsequent integration of these early findings into mainstream economics (Arrow and Fisher 1974). The branch of cultural economics itself was also nurtured by the wave of consumer research applying basic microeconomic principles to the analysis of cultural consumer's behaviour (Baumol and Bowen 1966).

The role of public governance has changed profoundly during the last decades because of the need to compensate crisis-induced economic and social costs and rising public debt – a concern still relevant today. Policy documents on conservation put emphasis on sound governance and effective management of heritage properties, which again reflects the principles of efficiency, transparency and accountability that management theory has put forward in recent years.

The dynamics of the current global economic system, which is characterized by fast changes across places and time, present new challenges. However, while mobility and exchange of resources and goods are clearly prioritized today, most cultural and natural heritage properties are immoveable, although their use may change particularly as the result of the massive movements generated by cultural tourism. Another feature of how current dynamics of the economic system can be challenging for heritage is the decreasing lifetime of goods (called economic obsolescence), whereas cultural and natural heritage, as well as conservation, are fundamentally embedded in long-term considerations.

Although short-term objectives can be managed satisfactorily within long-term sustainable goals, the integration of economics into the processes of the World Heritage Convention has to overcome obstacles generated by the misunderstanding of common economic principles. For example, the shortening these days of the repayment period for financial loans makes it difficult to fund conservation in the long term. In promoting frequent and short-term adaptive re-use of heritage resources for the community's needs, heritage economics may eventually match short-term conditions with long-term conservation goals. Similarly, in promoting local decision-making and community approach, heritage economics can match local cultural awareness with Outstanding Universal Value (OUV). Current models of inclusiveness emphasize resources allocation throughout circular economic schemes – that is, product lifecycles with greater recycling and re-use – in order to bring benefits for both the environment and the economy (Webster 2015).

Economic inclusiveness in the urban context

World Heritage properties may contribute to the achievement of sustainable objectives because of the values that they pass on and because these values may help to reconcile cultural identification with better ways of living and working. Given the four-pillar paradigm of sustainable development, economic inclusiveness would aim to make economic values compatible with cultural values, in such a way that economic efficiency (best allocation of cultural and natural resources) is linked with social inclusiveness and protection of the OUV of cultural and natural heritage. Such economic conditions need to be tailor-made to the characteristics of cultural and natural heritage and wider social conditions and will differ from common rules of economic efficiency.

Economic inclusiveness can, amongst other things, be addressed by reviewing the concept of opportunity cost; e.g. the value of the best alternative forgone to preserve heritage, or the benefits from alternative use of ground or built properties. The higher the opportunity cost, the more difficult it will be to conserve heritage from an economic perspective. When facing a modern urban development project, for instance, the economic inclusiveness approach would challenge the way the opportunity cost is assessed by developers. In fact, the opportunity cost of conservation should be reduced by both the extra environmental costs of new buildings and the non-values generated by heritage conservation.

The question of economic inclusiveness is really at stake in urban areas, where the opportunity cost raises questions of conflicting interests, multiple stakeholders, gentrification and new development projects. All of those issues rely on the alternative use of space potentially threatening heritage and on the expected economic value generated by different (sometimes opposite) uses of built heritage. This makes the urban heritage context particularly interesting to explore the question of inclusiveness.

Conditions for economic inclusiveness in the urban heritage context

Among the different charters, declarations and memoranda produced by UNESCO over the last 40 years, there is some consensus on the complexity of historic city planning and management. Initial considerations were addressed for the safe-guarding and contemporary role of historic areas in the Nairobi Recommenda-tion, highlighting the environment as directly linked to historic areas 'in space, or social, economic or cultural ties' (UNESCO 1976). Of particular value are the ICOMOS Charter for the Conservation of Historic Towns and Urban Areas 1987 ('Washington Charter') and the UNESCO Declaration on the Conservation of Historic Urban Landscapes 2005 ('Vienna Memorandum'). The Washington Charter indicates that 'in order to be most effective, the conservation of historic towns and other historic urban areas should be an integral part of coherent poli-cies of economic and social development and of urban and regional planning at every level' and that 'the conservation plan should aim at ensuring a harmonious relationship between the historic urban areas and the town as a whole' (ICOMOS 1987). The Vienna Memorandum indicates how economic information can help the planning and management process, underlying that 'investigating the long-term effects and sustainability of the planned interventions is an integral part of the planning process and aims at protecting the historic fabric, building stock and context' and that 'economic aspects of urban development should be bound to the goals of long-term heritage preservation' (UNESCO 2005).

Clearly, urban conditions for economic inclusiveness make sense only in holis-tic and systemic perspective. This requires a macro-perspective, which takes into consideration an entire area with its multiple stakeholders, an approach particu-larly relevant for the historic urban landscape approach (Bandarin and van Oers 2012, 2014).

The concept of cultural capital

The macro-perspective suggests an all-embracing urban historic aggregate of cultural assets, which can be understood through the concept of cultural capi-tal. Originally inspired by the environmental definition of natural capital devel-oped in the 1990s (El Sarafy 1991), this concept was first developed by cultural economist David Throsby (1999, 2002). It has been extensively applied to urban issues, where cultural capital runs parallel to other forms of capital such as physi-cal (infrastructure), human, intellectual and social capital.

World Heritage properties inscribed under cultural criteria may be considered as a form of cultural capital. They need resources to be built in the first place, they require adequate investment to prevent capital deterioration and, importantly, they provide for other goods and services over time. Many forms of cultural capital make up the multi-faceted complex urban realm of World Heritage properties, from immovable cultural heritage to collections of museums, art galleries, librar-ies, archives as well as intangible cultural heritage (oral traditions, performing arts, festivals, rituals etc.). Urban cultural capital is made up of assets that may potentially generate economic streams of services over time. They may become products for consumption by residents or visitors to the city and thus further con-tribute to the production of goods and services.

In the context of the historic urban landscape, the concept of cultural capital aims to describe how tangible and intangible heritage thus turn into assets that yield a flow of economic goods and services over time. Typically, World Heritage properties are surrounded by various built, moveable and intangible assets, many of which 'contribute to the cultural capital of the place. These assets are bonded together within spatial assets (public spaces, parks, urban furniture, river fronts) that may possess historic and cultural significance, or simply contribute to a sense of place and identity' (Marcus 2010).

The definition of urban cultural assets also addresses human, social and environmental values. These furthermore relate to questions of cultural identity, sense of place and social cohesion, raising challenging dynamics such as gentrification and environmental issues like the mobility of people and goods, and provision of waste disposal and utilities. Such social and environmental outcomes are key issues to consider in addressing urban sustainability and inclusiveness. Inclusive economics may thus identify types of production and consumption of goods and services and how categories of income and jobs aim at improving wellbeing in a sustainable and equitable way. This equally concerns a wide range of uses of heritage buildings such as the nature of cultural events, improvement of public spaces, tourism management, arts and crafts activities, attracting new businesses.

This raises the question of activation that is how urban cultural assets are turned into economic resources in order to generate economic values. When applied to different kinds of assets, activation embraces different meanings and possible consequences. World Heritage properties are activated when they provide real estate values, become a source of cultural tourism or other otherwise provide services. Moveable assets around World Heritage properties are typically activated in designated museums or art galleries. Intangible assets are activated when practiced, promoted or made accessible to the public. Spatial assets, in turn, are activated to fit transportation, utilities or specific events. But activation is just a prerequisite to economic inclusiveness, the latter being achieved when private or public activation of heritage properties gives rise to the consideration of wider sustainable values, with equitable and shared costs and benefits.

Urban conservation in World Heritage cities can work out better sustainable activation by, for example, finding the right adaptive re-use for heritage buildings, managing cultural sites and monuments in a sustainable way (preventing mass tourism), promoting conservation works with local skills, jobs, resources, creating incentives aimed for attracting more residents, businesses, artists and entrepreneurs and preventing gentrification and urban exodus. Other factors to be considered include the state of conservation of heritage properties, the local community awareness of and rights of access to heritage, the community participation in the process of conservation, the legal framework and the type of governance, the spatial integration of cultural assets across an area, and the quality of public spatial assets (Gehl and Gemzøe 2004).

Economic inclusiveness, World Heritage and sustainable development

The policy document adopted by the General Assembly of the State Parties to the Convention at its 20th Session in November 2015 (Resolution 20 GA 13, Paris, 2015) includes inclusive economic development as one of its main sections. The economic perspective is discussed along three axes, each of them entailing several statements.

Ensuring growth, employment, income and livelihoods

Heritage conservation may entail income, jobs, growth, revenues and ultimately even economic benefits for the whole community. The first principle aims to ensure growth, employment, income and livelihoods from heritage conservation. As such, emphasis is put on the fact that economic values are not just about quantity (number of jobs, thousands of USD, number of visitors, property prices), but also qualitative factors such as satisfaction ('utility' as economists designate it), wellbeing, skills or welfare.

Heritage economics consider economic values together with cultural values. 'Economic behaviour cannot be beyond, or separate from culture, which by definition is *"ways of living together"* or attitudes and behaviours passed on' (Mason 2002: 10). Economic values can be considered in terms of stock value or flow value. A typical stock value measurement for a heritage building is given by its property price, but most heritage monuments and sites may be understood in terms of their flow estimate, i.e. the value of all benefits they generate over time for various stakeholders. An important feature for cultural heritage is that it contributes to both private (individual) and public (collective) values.

A World Heritage property may be considered as an economic public good notwithstanding the nature of its owner. 'There are two things in a building: its use and beauty. Its use belongs to the owner, its beauty to all, to you, to me, to us all', as Victor Hugo stated in his 1825 *Note on destruction of monuments in France*. Most World Heritage properties are economic public goods, being both non-excludable (individuals cannot be effectively excluded from use) and non-rival (use by one individual does not reduce availability to others). Enhancing heritage properties as an economic public good may increase through public events such as an open monument day, festivals featuring intangible assets and available to all. In this regard, policies that encourage and regulate public access to World Heritage may strengthen the cultural identity of communities, while extending the scope of potential economic benefits. Adopting a broad economic perspective for the management and conservation of World Heritage requires a balance between efficient market mechanisms and inclusive public policies. It is acknowledged that many outcomes from heritage management and conservation go beyond the market as they provide impacts on stakeholders (Throsby 2010).

In brief, sustainability may possibly cover all categories of economic values including individual values from market transactions of cultural heritage taken as a private good (these are mostly termed as use values) as well as collective values, derived from the heritage taken as a public good (these are mostly termed as non-values). Sustainable development is predicated on the efficient balance between market mechanisms and public interventions, not least in terms of addressing externalities, which are impacts on third parties (sometimes termed indirect or induced impacts) that may result from market failures and be corrected by regulations (Klamer and Zuidhof 1998).

In a global world where market dominance often generates conflicts with heritage conservation, the need for adjusting appropriate policy interventions on market processes are key factors to ensure sustainable growth that benefits all stakeholders in and around Word Heritage properties. Such policy interventions need to go along with innovative private-public partnerships, economic incentives, equitable benefit-sharing and sectoral cooperation.

Heritage economics literature thus offers both documentation and methodologies on how to conduct values assessment for cultural built heritage and how to integrate economic fiscal incentives in heritage conservation (for example, Pickard 2009). The implementation of conservation projects, for example, may address economic outcomes in terms of income and jobs. Conservation and restoration works are known for their labour-intensive character, providing also job opportunities with high level of artistic and technical skills. It is also documented how conservation works may bring flows of fiscal revenues to local and national authorities or long-term indirect outcomes in future local budgets, health improvement, crime reduction and better social cohesion, all of which may ultimately result in economic public benefits, and better liveability. The sustainability of these outcomes depends on whether and how there is decent income, employment and livelihoods for local communities, including marginalized populations.

Promoting economic investment and quality tourism

As indicated above, the integration of sustainable development into the processes of World Heritage conservation is an issue that evolves over time. In particular, it concerns the ability of conservation to address the challenges of changes, for example, in finding out the best adaptive re-use for a heritage building. Sound and sustainable economic investments and planning is required to maintain the cultural capital, while fully respecting the cultural values of the built heritage. When World Heritage properties are taken into consideration, economic investments are often mainly tourism-oriented, as the objectives are either to increase the number of visitors and the quality of their visit or to improve site management, tourism facilities and surrounding infrastructures.

The aim of heritage protection, in turn, is to preserve cultural values that are significant to and, secondly, exert an attraction effect on communities, small and large, diverse and sometimes very remote. The attraction is itself a basis for substantial economic benefits, which unfortunately are sometimes accompanied by costs or negative externalities. This is the challenge for sustainable tourism: to manage tourism growth in and around World Heritage properties in terms of maximizing the positives and minimizing the negatives (Pedersen 2002).

It is acknowledged today that tourism has a steady growth and has become one of the world's major service industries. While many actors remain convinced that cultural tourism may constitute an economic panacea through direct, indirect and induced effects brought along by visitors in the surrounding of World Heritage properties, there is also a growing concern for tourism sustainability. In this regard, the positive trend of mass tourism around the world has a down-side: the growing economic risk for World Heritage properties that are impacted by sometimes irreversible damages of unbridled growth in cultural tourism.

Inclusive economic development deals with this concern of mass tourism, encouraging sustainable tourism that entails respect for local communities, accurate interpretation of heritage and significant visitor experience (Fladmark 1994). It also encourages public policies and community-based initiatives to ensure benefit sharing in and around World Heritage properties. As in most sustainability processes, however, achieving sustainable tourism relies on some kind of economic market regulation. Mass tourism should be managed with the help of, among other things, a mix of interventions on quantity limitation (quotas, modulation of visitors, booking required for tour groups) and price control (admission fees, subsidies, social rebate).

But the central factor in tourism sustainability is to keep a strong local connection and participation because 'local people must benefit economically and see a clear link between the benefits and the need to protect the resource' (UNESCO 2010). Ideally, economic outcomes like tourism income and revenues should stay in local areas and be distributed among local stakeholders. Investments should make use of economic resources, jobs and craft skills from local communities. When the participation of local people in economic investment increases, benefits translate into greater awareness of cultural identity and bigger concern for protection by the community. Finally, part of local revenues from cultural tourism has to be reinvested in conservation and other heritage-related activities.

There is not inclusive economic development and heritage conservation if a bottom-up process of community participation has not been established. Sustainable investments in cultural tourism start with conservation, then extend to tourism-related infrastructures and then to non-tourism activities through induced benefits in terms of visibility, attractiveness or new opportunities for investors. Economic diversification is a key factor in inclusive economic development. World Heritage properties will benefit from visibility far away, across the world. The prestige consumption and investment that comes with universal recognition may generate opportunities as well as threats for businesses in various fields of economic activities. When properly managed, alternative sources of growth and economic diversification of places strengthen social and economic resilience in a way that also helps protect World Heritage properties.

Strengthening capacity-building, innovation and local entrepreneurship

The potential of cultural heritage places for adaptive re-use is an opportunity for many communities around the world. Investing in heritage – prevention, maintenance, repair, rehabilitation – is a continuing process that is dedicated to long-term growth and development. Just as economic investments are driven by technological innovations and market opportunities, conservation similarly benefits from new techniques and new innovative processes that may make heritage buildings properly fitted to contemporary activities. In so doing, conservation also contributes importantly to the dissemination of skills, knowledge and innovations. Capacity-building is essential for economic inclusiveness as it translates state-of-the-art world experience into local practicalities, processes and courses of action.

In economic development theory, it has been demonstrated that technological innovations can be considered as one of the critical factors for economic changes. Among others, Joseph Schumpeter described how innovations emerge in clusters and how managerial entrepreneurs contribute to interpret them into product, market and organizational changes and to disseminate such drivers for creativity throughout the whole economy (Schumpeter 1942). Stimulating creativity is also achieved by raising awareness of the cultural heritage and by conducting policies that encourage creative entrepreneurs and research centres to brand places and World Heritage properties. Tangible and intangible cultural heritage are not just drivers of innovation and creativity in the field of culture; they are also prevailing drivers of many social and economic initiatives and strong catalysts for innovative financing, business and governance models. For example, in relation to the intangible skills and knowledge involved in arts and crafts techniques, local expertise is encouraged through micro-financing and basic training to foster local economic development in a sustainable perspective.

Although culture may sometimes be considered subsidiary competence of many international or economic development projects, it is clearly at the heart of innovation goals and the development of new economic and social paradigms (Bruell 2013). In terms of the redevelopment and revitalizing of former industrial cities and sites all across the world, the cultural innovation and creativity that are applied to World Heritage properties become successful factors in attracting business opportunities, qualified jobs and economic growth. Unlike old industrial revolutions, the current wave of digital innovation and creativity is a worldwide opportunity that benefits equally to all parts of the world, since World Heritage properties are per se global economic resources.

Entrepreneurship, as applied to conservation, may contribute to the integration of sustainable development into the management processes of World Heritage properties by enabling the use of the sites as local resources to the satisfaction of local stakeholder' needs. As indicated before, the concept of a circular economy is totally compatible with sustainability and inclusiveness. Implementation of conservation projects, for example, may entail local economic outcomes in terms of income and jobs. Conservation and restoration works are known for their labour-intensive character that provides job opportunities with high levels of artistic and technical skill. Conservation policies based on capacity-building and coupled with a community approach may provide local training, on-the-job learning and, ultimately, reduction of rural exodus. In addition, local conservation works may bring flows of fiscal revenues to the local budget.

Cultural heritage tourism is often considered as the provider of major economic output. While direct outcomes from visits to monument and cultural sites can be caught as local benefits, indirect and off-site tourism expenditures can be more volatile and even withdrawn from local facilities (hotels, guest houses, bed-and-breakfasts, souvenir shops). The provision of cultural goods and services, which includes the production of traditional works of art or craft and other intangible assets, should therefore go hand in hand with local skills or talent development. For example, street vendors, food stalls and street artists may contribute to economic inclusiveness of World Heritage cities (Pillai 2014).

Real estate activities around World Heritage properties are commonly based on the perception that the properties present a risk of gentrification. To prevent this, local authorities must integrate housing policies into urban conservation to regulate urban changes and to monitor market prices through the use of appropriate indicators. Public heritage buildings seldom appear on the real estate market but still provide a local outcome in terms of uses, services and fiscal revenues (UNESCO 2016).

Local business outcomes go well beyond the scope of cultural tourism (Ahlfeldt, Holman and Wendland 2012). When properly managed, World Heritage properties attract new businesses and provide better quality of life on the working place (Haspel 2002). The prestige that comes along with universal recognition of heritage is therefore a huge (sometimes underutilized) potential for local investors. Public and semi-public authorities, on the local, regional and national levels and acting as representatives of larger communities, benefit from local short-term outcomes such as increased taxes and revenues, but often also reap long-term benefits such as health improvement, crime reduction, better social cohesion and improved transportation.

From conclusions to operational guidelines

This chapter has aimed at analysing how heritage economics can help to address some of the sustainability challenges faced by UNESCO and State Parties in relation to World Heritage site management. Historical evidence has been presented to suggest that heritage conservation and heritage economics are bound together and that still today, economic inclusiveness is a critical component to address sustainability. In particular, the discussion of urban context clearly shows how inclusive economic development and heritage conservation need to go hand in hand and how cultural heritage can be properly managed to contribute to economic sustainability goals while fully respecting cultural goals and the OUV of World Heritage properties. Analysis of the policy that was adopted in 2015 by the General Assembly of the State Parties to the 1972 Convention plainly envisages that economic change may result from appropriate heritage conservation processes and that such change is not restricted to tourism. The historic urban landscape recommendation exhorts decision makers to, among other steps, 'undertake a full assessment of the city's natural, cultural, and human resources' and 'to assess the vulnerability of urban heritage to socio-economic pressures'. The full assessment of resources is also an obvious prerequisite in testing economic inclusiveness (van Oers 2007).

As indicated in this chapter, sustainable outcomes will depend on the nature of cultural heritage activation. More consideration is needed for how World Heritage properties become cultural capital that is allocated for economic uses. World Heritage properties can be activated for the best (in the sense of providing affordable housing for inhabitants) or for the worst (such as triggering mass tourism that puts properties at risk). Hence, the integration of sustainable economics into the processes of conservation requires consideration of the potential uses of cultural properties against their actual uses and potential impacts. Such evaluation of 'before activation' versus 'after activation' indicates how to match cultural heritage with economic sustainability.

When UNESCO inscribes a place on the World Heritage list, the decision is founded on the recognition of the property's OUV and other factors. Despite the fact that there is no specific criterion in the World Heritage Convention related to economic values, the Operational Guidelines could recommend that the nominating State Parties test the capacity of a property to generate economic values over time – thereby providing the revenues to fund the maintenance, restoration and rehabilitation of the property – as well as the inclusiveness of such values in contributing to sustainable development. The inclusion of heritage economics in the management planning process could prevent unsustainable issues and impacts that may threaten the World Heritage property. The success of implementing UNESCO's policy for sustainable development will also be facilitated – or hampered – by the ability of public governance to cope with new innovative private and public partnerships and with a community-approach that embeds multiple types of stakeholders and non-governmental organizations (Macdonald and Cheong 2015).

The integration of a sustainable development perspective into all the processes of the World Heritage Convention will help to achieve both the identification of cultural capital that is at risk or resilient to economic changes and the formulation of urban policies that seize opportunities or overcome threats to cultural capital coming from mass tourism or new development projects. Monitoring and reporting about World Heritage properties could also include economic indicators for testing sustainability. Monitoring tourism, for example, is a commonly recognized requirement for site managers in their task of dealing limited carrying-capacity issues. Eventually, a risk assessment process that is applied to the World Heritage properties would include the identification of economic opportunities and threats faced by the natural and cultural heritage, considered as inclusive cultural capital.

References

Ahlfeldt, G., Holman, N. and Wendland, N. (2012). *An Assessment of the Effects of Conservation Areas on Values: Final Report*. London: London School of Economics and Political Science.

Arrow, K. J. and Fisher, A. C. T. (1974). 'Environmental preservation, uncertainty, and irreversibility', *Quarterly Journal of Economics*, 88(2), 312–319.

Bandarin, F. and van Oers, R. (2012). *The Historic Urban Landscape: Managing Heritage in an Urban Century*. London: Wiley-Blackwell.

Bandarin, F. and van Oers, R. (2014). *Reconnecting the City: The Historic Urban Landscape Approach and the Future of Urban Heritage*. London: Wiley-Blackwell.

Baumol, W. and Bowen, W. (1966). *Performing Arts, the Economic Dilemma: A Study of Problems Common to Theater, Opera, Music, and Dance*. New York: Twentieth Century Fund.

Bruell, C. (2013). *Creative Europe 2014–2020, a New Programme, a New Policy as well?* Stuttgart: Ifa-Edition Culture and Foreign Policy (online). Available at: www.ifa.de/fileadmin/pdf/edition/creative-europe_bruell.pdf (accessed 13 April 2017).

El Sarafy, S. (1991). 'The environment as capital', in R. Castanza (ed), *Ecological Economics: The Science and Management of Sustainability*. New York: Columbia University Press.

Europa Nostra (2015). *Cultural Heritage Counts for Europe, Report by the European Commission*. Krakow: International Cultural Centre on behalf of the CHCfE Consortium (online). Available at: http://blogs.encatc.org/culturalheritagecountsforeurope/outcomes/ (accessed 13 April 2017).

Fladmark, J. M. (1994). *Cultural Tourism*. London: Donhead.

Gehl, J. and Gemzøe, L. (2004). *Public Spaces, Public Life*. Copenhagen: Danish Architectural Press.

Haspel, J. (2011). *Built Heritage as a Positive Location Factor, Economic Potentials of Heritage Properties*. Scientific Presentation at the ICOMOS General Assembly in Paris (online). Available at: http://openarchive.icomos.org/1304/1/IV-3-Article3_Haspel.pdf (accessed 8 June 2017).

Hugo, V. (1825). *Note sur la Destruction des Monuments en France* (online). Available at: www.revuedesdeuxmondes.fr/guerre-aux-demolisseurs/ (accessed 6 August 2017). Translation by the author.

ICOMOS (1987). *Charter for the Conservation of Historic Towns and Urban Areas (Washington Charter)*. Washington, DC: ICOMOS General Assembly. (online). Available at: www.icomos.org/charters/towns_e.pdf (accessed 8 June 2017).

Klamer, A. and Zuidhof, P.-W. (1998). 'The v of cultural heritage: Merging economic and cultural appraisals', in Getty Conservation Institute (ed), *Economics and Heritage Conservation* (online). Available at: www.getty.edu/conservation/publications_resources/pdf_publications/pdf/econrpt.pdf (accessed 4 July 2017).

Macdonald, S. and Cheong, C. (2015). *The Role of Public-Private Partnerships and the Third Sector in Conserving Heritage Buildings, Sites and Historic Urban Areas*. Los Angeles: The Getty Conservation Institute.

Marcus, L. (2010). *Spatial Capital and How to Measure It: An Outline of an Analytical Theory of Urban Form*. Research paper. Stockholm: The KTH School of Architecture (online). Available at: www.diva-portal.org/smash/get/diva2:469880/FULLTEXT01.pdf (accessed 8 June 2017).

Mason, R. (2002). 'Assessing values in conservation planning: Methodological issues and choices', in M. de la Torre (ed), *Assessing the Value of Cultural Heritage*. Los Angeles: The Getty Conservation Institute.

Meadows, D. H., Meadows, D. L., Randers, J. and Behrens III, W. W. (1972). *The Limits to Growth: A Report for the Club of Rome's Project on the Predicament of Mankind*. Washington, DC: Potomac Associates.

Pedersen, A. (2002). *Managing Tourism at World Heritage Sites: A Practical Manual for World Heritage Sites Managers*. Paris: UNESCO.

Pickard, R. (2009). *Funding the Architectural Heritage: A Guide to Policies and Examples*. Strasbourg: Council of Europe Publishing (online). Available at: https://books.google.com. au/books?hl=en&lr=&id=Uaw3B4Id-8cC&oi=fnd&pg=PA1951&dq=Pickard,+R.+ (2009).+Conservation+in+the+Built+Environment,+Policy+Law+and+Practice&o ts=yxwbnnb1FW&sig=Iik9vDlVvwhFg7jrQeji3Yl2Zi4#v=onepage&q&f=false (accessed 25 September 2017).

Pillai, J. (2014). *Cultural Mapping: A Guide to Understanding Place, Community and Continuity*. Petaling Jaya, Malaysia: State Institute of Rural Development (SIRD).

Schumpeter, J. (1942). *Capitalism, Socialism, Democracy*. New York: Harper and Brothers.

Throsby, D. (1999). 'Cultural capital', *Journal of Cultural Economics*, 23(1–2), 3–12.

Throsby, D. (2002). 'Cultural capital and sustainability concepts in the economics of cultural heritage', in M. de la Torre (ed), *Assessing the Value of Cultural Heritage*. Los Angeles: The Getty Conservation Institute.

Throsby, D. (2010). *The Economics of Cultural Policy*. Cambridge: Cambridge University Press.

UNESCO (1972). *Convention on the Protection of World Cultural and Natural Heritage* (online). Available at: http://whc.unesco.org/uploads/activities/documents/activity-562-4. pdf (accessed 8 June 2017).

UNESCO (1976). *Recommendation Concerning the Safeguarding and Contemporary Role of Historic Areas* (online). Available at: www.icomos.org/publications/93towns7o.pdf (accessed 8 June 2017).

UNESCO (2005). *World Heritage and Contemporary Architecture: Managing the Historic Urban Landscape* (Vienna Memorandum) (online). Available at: http://whc.unesco.org/ archive/2005/whc05-15ga-inf7e.pdf (accessed 8 June 2017).

UNESCO (2010). *Paraty Meeting Outcome and Action Plan: Decision 34 COM 5D* (online). Available at: http://whc.unesco.org/archive/2010/whc10-34com_5De.pdf (accessed 20 April 2017).

UNESCO (2012a). *Resolutions adopted by the General Assembly of State Parties to the World Heritage Convention at its 18th Session* (online). Available at: http://whc.unesco. org/archive/2012/whc11-18ga-11-en.pdf (accessed 20 April 2017).

UNESCO (2012b). *Proceedings of the Consultative Expert Meeting on World Heritage and Sustainable Development* (Ouro Preto, Brazil), 5–8 February.

UNESCO (2013). *Hangzhou Declaration: Placing Culture at the Heart of Sustainable Development Policies* (online). Available at: http://unesdoc.unesco.org/images/0022/002212/ 221238m.pdf (accessed 20 April 2017).

UNESCO (2015). *Policy Document for the Integration of a Sustainable Development Perspective into the Processes of the World Heritage Convention* (online). Available at: http://whc.unesco.org/en/sustainabledevelopment/ (accessed 2 December 2017).

UNESCO (2016). *Culture Urban Future: Global Report on Culture for Sustainable Urban Development: Summary* (online). Available at: http://unesdoc.unesco.org/images/0024/002 462/246291E.pdf (accessed 8 June 2017).

United Nations (UN) (2012). *Realizing the Future We Want for All*. New York: Report to the Secretary General, UN System Task Team on the Post-2015 UN Development Agenda (online). Available at: www.un.org/millenniumgoals/pdf/Post_2015_UNTTreport.pdf (accessed 8 June 2017).

United Nations (UN) (2015). *Transforming Our World: The 2030 Agenda for Sustainable Development*. New York: Resolution adopted by the General Assembly, A/RES/70/1 (online). Available at: http://ggim.un.org/docs/meetings/GGIM6/TRANSFORMING%20 OUR%20WORLD.pdf (accessed 8 June 2017).

van Oers, R. (2007). 'Towards new international guidelines for the conservation of Historic Urban Landscapes', *City & Time*, 3(3), 34–51 (online). Available at: www.ceci-br.org/ novo/revista/docs2008/CT-2008-113.pdf (accessed 8 June 2017).

Webster, K. (2015). *The Circular Economy: A Wealth of Flows*. Chicago: Ellen Macarthur Foundation.

Chapter 5

Inclusive social development and World Heritage in urban areas[1]

Jyoti Hosagrahar

The General Assembly of the State Parties to the World Heritage Convention adopted in 2015 the *Policy for the Integration of a Sustainable Development perspective into the processes of the World Heritage Convention* (World Heritage and Sustainable Development policy) (UNESCO 2015). This document identifies inclusive social development as one of the three key dimensions of sustainable development that may bring benefits to the World Heritage properties and cultural heritage in general if integrated into their conservation and management systems.

Social inclusion, as conceived by the World Bank (2013: 3–4), is about improving the processes and terms by which people participate in society. They refer to the processes of improving the ability, opportunity and dignity of people disadvantaged on the basis of their identity to take part in society. According to the UNDESA's *2016 Report on the World Social Situation*, social inclusion is the process of improving the terms of participation for people through enhancing opportunities, access to resources, voice and respect for human rights (UNDESA 2016). The World Heritage and Sustainable Development policy places emphasis on the reduction of inequalities including its structural causes such as discrimination and exclusion as essential to achieve inclusive sustainable development. Going beyond reduction of poverty alone, it recognizes and addresses other kinds of deprivation, disadvantaged positions and lack of opportunity with the aim of fostering shared prosperity. People may be excluded from a range of development processes, opportunities and benefits due to their gender, race, ethnicity, migrant or refugee status, religion, disability, sexual orientation or other markers that confer them with subordinate positions in society. Social Inclusion values and indeed prioritizes human wellbeing over economic growth and is an objective of sustainable development.

This chapter focuses on social inclusion, particularly in urban areas, and examines the relationship of inequality and poverty as a broad deprivation and lack of opportunity in and around urban heritage areas, especially insofar as the management of the heritage is concerned. It argues for inclusive social development that can help to improve the abilities, opportunities and dignity of the communities in which the properties are embedded. The key objective of addressing Social Inclusion as a Sustainable Development principle with regard to the World Heritage

Convention (UNESCO 1972) is to promote those practices of conservation and management in and around urban heritage properties that can reduce inequalities and help to improve the abilities, opportunities and dignity of the communities in which they are embedded. A fundamental question underlies this objective: How can a more expanded understanding of heritage be integrated into a vision for a more inclusive and sustainable future?

The chapter has four sections. First, it outlines the contemporary urban context where socially inclusive development is sorely needed. It then goes on to elaborate the connections between poverty and social inclusion and shows the significance of socially inclusive development to the better management of heritage properties. The third section discusses some key assumptions made in this endeavour, some common misconceptions and new re-conceptions as well as some missed and newly opening up opportunities. The final section proposes key principles that should be taken into account when socially inclusive development is integrated into the processes of the World Heritage Convention as required by UNESCO's World Heritage and Sustainability policy. Brief case studies are introduced to illustrate main points in the argument.

While social inclusion is closely associated with issues around economic dimensions of inclusion, human rights, indigenous peoples and gender equality, these matters are not dealt with in detail in this chapter, since they are addressed specifically elsewhere in the volume. Also, while acknowledging the significance of natural heritage to sustainable development, the chapter focuses on cultural heritage, particularly in urban contexts. The difficulty of separating natural and cultural values is recognized, as too is the indivisibility of natural and cultural in the eyes of many peoples, especially indigenous, around the world. Nevertheless, given the large, and increasing, number of cultural heritage properties in urban areas facing intense pressures, this paper focuses on them with the hope that insights from this chapter can be useful also to other types of heritage.

Urbanization, cultural heritage and social inclusion

Heritage is that which is handed down from the past and valued today. Particular to a time and place, heritage expresses the cumulative knowledge and experience of generations, affirming and enriching cultural identities. The UNESCO heritage conventions, seen together, conceive of cultural heritage as both tangible heritage to be conserved in its authenticity (historic monuments, museum collections, archaeological sites and art and architecture) and intangible cultural heritage (local knowledge and practices, music, dance, theatre and crafts) that is to be safeguarded and transmitted from generation to generation. More broadly, heritage includes cultural relationships and practices with respect to the natural environment, including land management and water systems particular to a place and time. These, too, comprise both material things (such as inherited landmarks, hierarchy of open spaces and street patterns) and immaterial knowledge and practices (such as processions, water management and vernacular building). Cultural heritage also includes conservation of the material forms, safeguarding of living heritage transmitted across generations and the promotion of the creative practices that make places meaningful to local communities.

In all of these different forms of heritage, conservation practices and heritage management can enhance the engagement of local communities and their social inclusion or serve as a divisive and exclusionary force – sometimes perpetuating inherited practices of discrimination. Heritage conservation is not about a simple and uncontested temporal sequence from the old to the new. How, for example, do we go about conserving the forms, spaces and meanings that communities choose to remember collectively and that help satisfy the needs and aspirations of current and future generations? In recent years, scholars and experts in Europe, North America and Australia have been attentive to evaluating the economic value of heritage, especially through tourism and increased investments (Licciardi and Amirtahmasebi 2012; Hosagrahar 2015). While some detailed studies have been conducted in Europe on the economic impacts of heritage designation, for instance *Cultural Heritage Counts for Europe* (EU 2015), such impact studies are largely lacking in other parts of the world. Systematic and robust social impact assessments of heritage inscription and tourism have yet to be undertaken globally.

Urbanization in many emerging and developing economies has been rapid, incessant and often uncontrolled. The rampant growth of cities has resulted in deteriorating urban environments, inadequate water supply and sanitation and a vast increase in the numbers of urban poor and their varied experiences of deprivation whether they live in slums without access to many of the social amenities and infrastructure or in a decrepit historic urban core that may be overcrowded or abandoned. Such modes of urbanization have also been destructive of local ecologies, natural resources, including land and water bodies, and cultural resources, including built heritage, intangible heritage and creative industries.

Pressures for economic development and for prioritizing engagement with the global economy have accompanied rapid urbanization. In many societies, pressures for economic development have driven modernization efforts. The pressures of rapid urban growth have also made cities places of great inequality. In addition to debilitating social inequalities that define the identities of rural, ethnic and transnational migrants, inadequate infrastructure and lack of employment options have created inequalities in access to minimal housing, water, power, sanitation, schooling, health and employment opportunities.

Many people have migrated from rural areas to cities or across borders to other countries, pushed out of their homes by famine, drought and natural disasters, wars and persistent conflicts. Seeking survival or unable to continue in their ancestral villages or on their ancestral land, they have moved to urban areas in search of employment and education for their children. Despite the seemingly significant steps in the economic growth of many countries, the challenge of making cities inclusive remains. Faced with competing demands, many governments have pitted development against the management of cultural resources in the allocation of scarce funding. Hence, the conservation and management of cultural heritage has often received negligible funding in comparison to, for instance, infrastructure development for urban areas. In other instances, the management of cultural heritage has privileged some groups of people to the exclusion of others such as tourists over local communities or dominant ethnic or religious groups over others.

Received views of cultural heritage as monuments of artistic work expect only for investments into their material protection, with no relationship to sustainable development. Contrary to such a view, understanding the ways that local communities engage with heritage properties and elements and recognizing their role in conservation and management can help to reinforce the relationship between heritage local communities to the benefit of both heritage conservation and social inclusion (Hosagrahar 2017). Heritage has the potential to contribute to poverty alleviation and enhance sustainable livelihoods of local communities including those of marginalized populations. Some recent scholarship has begun to identify how cultural heritage can contribute to social inclusion (see, for instance, Erica Avrami 2016). Others, as in some of examples below, argue that improving the conditions of the local communities contributes to better management of the heritage properties.

Poverty and social inclusion

Recent scholarship has pointed out the complex ways in which poverty is experienced that make it a multi-dimensional concept (Hosagrahar 2013). Deprivation and exclusion exist not only for those whose incomes qualify as below the poverty line in that country; it also exists for others who may not be strictly below the statistical poverty line but who experience lack in a variety of dimensions including limited access to education, training, and employment, adequate housing, food, nutrition and healthcare and a living environment devoid of social conflicts (Roy 2003).

Many of the poor in South and Southeast Asia have low skills and education and work in insecure jobs as daily wage labour in agriculture, construction, or for contractors on a piece-work basis. The absence of an adequate, steady and reliable source of income is a major source of deprivation. Illiteracy, as well as limited access to mobility and transport, further reduces such people's opportunities to find suitable employment. Those in small towns and rural areas are often unable to find alternative employment opportunities.

Most urban poor live in sub-standard housing conditions without tenure rights, water, power, sewerage, drainage, transport, communications and infrastructure either because their houses are slums or because they live in deteriorating historic urban cores. Overcrowding in historic cities with complicated ownership and tenancy rights often masks the inadequacies and insecurities. Very often, squatter housing is constructed using materials that are cheap and lightweight, making it quick to assemble and disassemble, and is in locations vulnerable to natural hazards and risks, such as areas prone to earthquakes, floods and landslides. Historic urban centres, by contrast, may be built of permanent materials with ornate structures even if they are run down and sometimes in dangerous conditions. The social, demographic, political and economic changes have resulted in many historic cities, such as Cairo, Fez and Tunis, becoming overcrowded and their populations impoverished. Other urban areas, such as many *centros históricos* in Latin American countries, are being abandoned by businesses and homeowners (Rojas 1999; Scarpacci 2005). The invisibility of poor housing in small towns and historic centres allows unsafe and unhealthy conditions to persist (see, for example, State of Conservation reports for Fez, Morocco).

In urban areas, dependence on income to buy food rather than growing, breeding or collecting it forces many of the urban poor to battle against food insecurity and poor nutrition. Inadequate sanitation and an inadequate supply of clean water put them at risk of diseases and epidemics (Hosagrahar and Hayashi 2013). In rural areas and small towns, those in traditional built environments may have better access to food that they are able to grow themselves, along with the food that comes from the animals they maintain or from collecting food from forests in the vicinity. However, those without access to these resources face hunger even in rural areas.

Crippling social problems such as crime and violence are greatly exacerbated in overcrowded and poorly serviced historic urban environments, where negotiations over scarce resources can easily lead to conflicts. Systemic biases and exclusionary practices may exclude certain groups from the benefits of development in other places. The poor are most often located in these least desirable parts of cities or on those designated not for habitation. The poorest and the social outcasts such as new immigrants, ex-convicts, prostitutes and drug addicts form invisible ghettos in overcrowded or abandoned historic urban centres. Outside of the historic centres, locations such as seismic fault-lines, low-lying and marshy lands, the annual flood plains of rivers, and unstable hillocks leave the poor vulnerable to natural disasters. Furthermore, their houses, made of cheap and temporary materials, are easily destroyed and damaged. Floods, landslides, and earthquakes have often caused major destruction to the poor, who do not have the resilience to recover easily from disasters.

Access to and use of heritage places

The right of access to and use of heritage properties are not even across the social spectrum and change over time. Historical, political and demographic changes over time have meant that the communities that use and give meaning to heritage properties today are sometimes different from those that originally established the property. With multiple layers of history and historical meaning laid over the property, in some instances different communities of people have competing interpretations of and associations with the same heritage property. Often the interpretation, meanings and access of the dominant group in a society is privileged over others. In recent years, with galloping tourism, policies and management of heritage properties too often give primacy to tourists and the interests of the tourism industry over those of local communities.

Some sites have historically not permitted women to access some heritage properties, such as the Greek Orthodox spiritual centre at Mount Athos or the male sacred spaces on Olkhon Island in Japan, for example; others dictate segregation and differential use. Such exclusion of or differential access and use by women needs to be considered carefully in each instance. In general, continuing such practices of limited access perpetuates gender discrimination and needs to be modified from a human-rights based perspective (see chapters by Labadi and Larsen, this volume). However, in those instances where such gender specificity is an essential aspect of the meaning and identity of the place for the community in which the heritage property is embedded, it may be argued that the limited access should be retained as an associated practice of access and use.

Intangible cultural heritage and traditional practices

While scholars and preservation professionals often put a great deal of emphasis on the artistic value, material authenticity and symbolism of the built form, its morphology and iconography, the meaning of a heritage property inheres in many instances in the rituals, practices and associated knowledge of the communities that identify with the property or to whom the property belongs. Sometimes these practices belong to a community different from the dominant one that originally sponsored the heritage property or they may have meanings and practices that differ from narratives of practice of the dominant groups. In the management of the property, zealous conservationists sometimes privilege protection of the physical structure as an artefact excluding, even if unwittingly, through their policies, the traditional practices and rituals and the transmission of intangible heritage and associated knowledge. Inclusive practices of heritage conservation would be careful to include in the interpretation of heritage properties, their use and management, local communities, their intangible cultural heritage and local practices and associated knowledge treated as an integral aspect of the properties that are transmitted across generations.

Sustainable tourism and local communities

The management of many heritage places has been driven by the possibilities of global tourism. Numerous programs of the local, provincial and national governments, along with investors and hoteliers, have rushed to capitalize on burgeoning global tourism. That excessive tourism and large numbers of visitors pose a threat to heritage properties is has been recognized in recent years with efforts of some local and national authorities to manage visitor flows. More insidious and invisible has been the impact of poorly managed tourism policies on local communities, their intangible cultural heritage and social inequalities (see Alsayyad 2000). Increasing commercialization and commodification of heritage, both tangible and intangible, further exacerbates and perpetuates social inequities between those for whom the property and associated intangible cultural heritage elements mean something and those who view it as an aesthetic experience and heritage entertainment.

Case study: India

In some parts of India, for instance, forts and palaces have been retrofitted to function as hotels. Turbaned waiters and sumptuous decoration offer ordinary visitors the opportunity to live out for a day fantasies of opulence of the fabled Indian maharajas. Colourful fairs, house-boats, hand-crafted memorabilia, temple processions and camel rides are made available to eager tourists in search of 'real' (if imagined) exotic places. Colonial estates and bungalows have become upscale resorts. They too stand for luxury, spaciousness and the airy life of an erstwhile landed gentry (Hosagrahar 2017). Another kind of heritage-themed accommodation with an entertainment add-on that has enjoyed a growing popularity in recent years is 'heritage' hotels. Luxury hotels vie with each other to promise distinctive and memorable experiences and conjure tantalizing visions of the pleasure and decadence of a mythical orient as for instance in the heritage hotel in Manesar, Haryana. With enthusiasm, officials and entrepreneurs embrace exoticism and connive in their construction.

In Gurgaon for instance, there is an air-conditioned indoor market called *Culture Gully*. A *gully* in a typical north Indian historic town is a narrow, winding, street with houses on both sides (Hosagrahar 2017). Culture Gully is a lavishly designed market places for artisanal goods and handicrafts from all over India, along with heritage themed restaurants serving regional cuisine. Crafts, street performers and regional cuisines epitomize the theatrical packaging and presentation of heritage as an exotic commodity that corporate capital makes available in plush surroundings. Traditional street performers and folk artists lend colour and festivity to the whole streetscape making it reminiscent of a village fair – albeit dust-free – thereby offering an experience that has never been experienced in the subcontinent before. Meanwhile, the artisans and village communities are not able to participate in the social, economic and political decision-making around such staged theatrical displays that exacerbates the divisions between the modern global shopper and consumer of heritage entertainment and the traditional cultural producers frozen in time.

Challenges to integrating social inclusion in heritage management

Institutional forms and biases are a significant impediment to integrating policies on social inclusion in heritage conservation and management. Most agencies and institutions with a mandate for conservation and heritage management are expected to protect only the heritage; they do not have a mandate for addressing the needs of local communities or even to engage them in decision making. The inputs of international experts who focus on physical conservation of structures and the authenticity of its form often further alienate local communities. The very communities that may have managed the heritage structures in their midst for generations, officials suddenly begin to regard as a threat.

While some conservation theories and experts privilege visual composition and reconstruction, others regard that authenticity is in protecting the material form of the properties exactly as they were found. Such approaches to heritage as objects, oppose any development, even sustainable development of local communities, as antithetical and detrimental to heritage conservation. Other prevalent perspectives see the needs of local communities as secondary to the work of material conservation. They make no room for the changing socio-economic needs and aspirations of the local communities where the heritage properties belong.

A number of assumptions, misconceptions and missed opportunities in heritage management policies and practice also present challenges to social inclusion. Many conservation theories and approaches have privileged elitist conceptions of heritage as a glorification of artistic refinement and conservation as the as the preservation of the physical edifice and its artistic attributes. While such an approach may be appropriate for some types of heritage, for a vast majority, they result in the exclusion of engagement of ordinary people and the lived life of the heritage. Furthermore, such approaches find themselves in opposition to any type of change and development to address the needs of those who inhabit in and around the heritage and care for it. Socially 'blind' approaches to conservation in fact often reify existing social differences or exacerbate them under the guise of scientific neutrality.

Case study: Djenné, Mali

The old town of Djenné in central Mali, the oldest known city in sub-Saharan Africa, was recognized as globally significant urban heritage with its addition to the UNESCO World Heritage List in 1988 under criteria (iii) and (iv) (UNESCO 2017b). The Great Mosque of Djenné is an adobe building in the centre of the city with adobe houses around it forming the urban fabric. In the years following its inscription, while conservation experts from around the world marvelled at the adobe construction and focused on protecting the authenticity of both the built fabric and the Great Mosque, the primary concern of the local community in Djenné was related to socio-economic development, including improvement in roads, infrastructure and housing on the one hand, and opportunities for better education and employment on the other.

The socio-economic agenda received little support from the international community, however, and much of the external support for intervention focused on conservation of the adobe construction and the authenticity of the physical fabric. The growing threat of violent extremist groups became an increasing source of instability and raised concerns about the potential damage to the buildings and these factors eventually led to Djenné being inscribed on the list of World Heritage in Danger in 2016. Thus again, a wide range of scholars and experts from conservation to development and anthropology saw the approach to heritage management as one focused exclusively on conservation of the physical fabric as prioritized by external experts and they assumed this to be detrimental to the local communities. Indeed, the subsequent rise of radical groups and their violent attacks and extensive destruction of heritage in Timbuktu has greatly destabilized the local communities in Mali during the last few years.

Case study: Salvador da Bahia, Brazil

The historic city centre of Salvador da Bahia was founded in the middle of the 16th century and became the first capital of Portuguese America – and also the first slave market for slaves arriving to the new world to work on sugar plantations. It was inscribed on the World Heritage List in 1985 under criteria (iv) and (vi). As noted in the description of the site on the World Heritage Centre's website,

> This densely built colonial city *par excellence* of the Brazilian northeast is distinguished by its religious, civil and military colonial architecture dating from the 17th to the 19th centuries. Salvador de Bahia is also notable as one of the major points of convergence of European, African and American Indian cultures of the 16th to 18th centuries…. Echoes of this multicultural past survive to the present day in the historic centre's rich tangible and intangible heritage.
>
> (UNESCO 2017a)

Today, Salvador is the country's third largest city, with all the problems of infrastructure and inequalities in a burgeoning metropolitan area. However, the conservation approaches and initiatives undertaken following its designation, especially in the Pelourinho district of the historic centre, reassigning functions and relocating inhabitants, exacerbated the alienation and flight of the low-income local communities where conservation officials and businesses saw them as a threat to the heritage value of the historic urban area.

Isolated by new transportation highways, and public works, the historic centre had been decline since the 19th century. In the 1970s, the development of a new administrative and financial city centre on the outskirts of the historic city further reinforced the processes of degradation. When the city was inscribed in 1985, Pelourinho was home to prostitutes, drug traffickers and other marginal groups not welcome in the financial centres and planned urban areas.

> (Nobre 2002)

In 1991, the state decided to undertake regeneration of the historic area focusing on rehabilitation and restoration to tap into the economic potential of tourism. They carried out a number of public works to improve energy provision, telecommunications, sanitation, water supply and fire-fighting. Initially, emphasis was placed on refurbishing monuments and public buildings as well as the facades and eventually, several houses were also restored. Building uses related to tourism and entertainment were prioritized. By 2000, the state had purchased and owned more than fifty percent of the properties, having compensated the low-income populations to relocate and leave the neighbourhood. As hotels and guest houses proliferated, more and more residents left the historic centre and settled in neighbourhoods in surrounding areas. Some districts lost nearly 67 per cent of their population.

(Nobr+e 2002)

Such gentrification vastly diminished the densities and vitality of the city. Scholars and experts from those advocating human rights and cultural rights to conservation specialists saw the policies aimed at deliberate gentrification as detrimental and problematic. Much of the poor population was displaced to worse living conditions. Subsequent state efforts to redress the growing imbalance was aimed at retaining and rehabilitating the low-income population, using creativity and the intangible cultural heritage of the local people as a means to integrate them into the urban regeneration efforts.

Responses and opportunities to integrate social inclusion

UNESCO's ongoing advocacy for integrating culture and development is most significant in this regard including the most recent initiative on integrating culture into the UN Sustainable Development Agenda.[2] The Recommendation on Historic Urban Landscape (UNESCO 2011) broadens the notion of heritage conservation to include urban development in historical contexts. Going far beyond the idea of material conservation of built forms, the HUL approach is about managing urban change and integrating contemporary needs and services while conserving the forms, meanings and associated elements with cultural heritage (Bandarin and van Oers 2012). It integrates the goals of conservation of urban heritage with the goals of social and economic development and sustainable development of the urban areas in general. The work of the Aga Khan Trust has been pioneering in this regard in integrating heritage conservation with sustainable development for local communities, reviving and safeguarding local building crafts and other intangible cultural practices and management of water and other natural resources.

Many scholars have called for a more critical approach to heritage management so that structural inequities are exposed, analysed and the processes include the participation of all relevant stakeholders. Tim Winter (2013: 533), who helped establish the Association of Critical Heritage Studies, has argued for instance, for the importance of heritage management 'addressing the *critical* issues that face the world today, the larger issues that bear upon and extend outwards from heritage'. This fits well with the ambition of this 'Key Issues in Cultural Heritage' series, whose co-editors see heritage conservation as a form of cultural politics that 'can be used in positive ways to give a sense of community disparate groups and individuals or to create jobs on the basis of cultural tourism' but that can also be used to 'reshape public attitudes in line with undemocratic agendas or even to rally people against their neighbours' (Logan and Smith, Series Editors' Foreword, this volume).

Postcolonial perspectives in architecture and urbanism offer ways of thinking about built form and space as cultural landscapes that are at once globally interconnected and precisely situated in space and time. With intellectual roots in the struggles against Western European colonization of Asia and Africa in the nineteenth and early twentieth centuries, much of the scholarship has focused on the Global South that has been disdained or marginalized in received literature (Hosagrahar 2011). Postcolonial thought questions the dominance of universalizing paradigms and simplistic categorizations in conventional scholarship in architecture and urbanism focused on Western Europe and North America. Dichotomies such as those between West and non-West, traditional and modern, have persisted as rigid oppositions that deny both the interdependence and the inequalities in the relationship. Postcolonial perspectives challenge the notion of a universal modernism that privileges those in positions of power and authority, legitimating their right to define fundamental values, policies, operations and identities. They acknowledge, instead, the multiple dimensions of subordinate experiences. In so doing, postcolonial perspectives particularize universal narratives and globalize narrowly parochial ones (Hosagrahar 2011).

Case study: Sustainable Urbanism International

Sustainable Urbanism International (SUI), an Indian NGO, has focused on exploring the intersections of nature, community and the built environment to promote sustainable development. An integrated view of sustainability has highlighted the ways that local knowledges, building practices and hydrological systems have been integral to a cultural landscape. From collaborative inventorying of tangible and intangible heritage, to reviving and conserving historic lakes and stepped well, developing heritage-focused masterplans for the historic towns based on built forms and standards derived from historic neighbourhoods, reviving and adapting traditional technologies of earth construction for new structures, and strategies for generating livelihoods rooted in local culture and creative practices, SUI's approach has been to integrate heritage conservation with sustainable development including processes of design, participatory planning, and natural resource management.

(Hosagrahar 2011: 83)

Most recently, UNESCO has contributed significantly with Culture to the New Urban Agenda, adopted by all countries at the UN Habitat III meeting held in

Quito, Ecuador, in October 2016. The New Urban Agenda provides a 20-year roadmap to guide sustainable urban development across the globe (Hosagrahar 2017). At the same meeting, UNESCO launched its global report *Culture: Urban Future* report that presents a global overview of urban heritage safeguarding, conservation and management as well as the promotion of cultural and creative industries (UNESCO 2016). It is intended as a policy framework document to support governments in the implementation of the Agenda. The UNESCO World Heritage and Sustainable Development policy goes further by seeing inclusive social development as one of the key dimensions of sustainable development to which the World Heritage and other heritage programs must contribute.

Case study: Nablus, Palestine

The historic centre of Nablus (Palestine) continues to thrive despite growing challenges to its setting and identity. Since the 1990s, the city has faced increased development pressure from the expansion of adjacent urban blocks, calling for the adoption of a culture-driven urban development policy that supports safeguarding the city's distinctive cultural attributes. The cultural conservation, management and promotion policy in Nablus has focused on the adaptive reuse of abandoned and damaged buildings to benefit the local community. The renowned ancient caravanserai of Khan Al-Wakala was rehabilitated to become a mixed-used space offering a public arena for events, accommodation and cultural activities. In the rehabilitated family houses of Abdel Hadi, Hashim and Al-Amad, local institutions have offered educational services for youth and children, such as a kindergarten, and music and language classes. In addition, through a comprehensive conservation, management and research project, the abandoned Shikmu (Tell Balata) site, the earliest settlement in the Nablus area, was transformed into an archaeological park with an interpretation and visitor's centre. The project has enabled the local community to reconnect with the site and strengthen the local economy. The cultural assets of Nablus have been a strong driver for the city's sustainable development, and such interventions have empowered local communities, individuals and groups to interact and better understand the significant role of culture in their lives.

(UNESCO 2012, 2016: 137; 2017c)

Enhancing social inclusion with cultural heritage

As indicated by the brief cases studies, improving social inclusion requires appropriate policies and initiatives at the global, national, urban and site management levels. Greater opportunities must be found for achieving goals of equity and social justice by emphasizing local communities and the diversity of stakeholders, localities, contexts and historical continuities as well as policies and approaches that promote social inclusion promises. In this way, cultural heritage conservation and management has the potential to offer opportunities for a plural, more diverse and more contextually responsive urban environments. Outlined below are some principles that could help to guide conservation interventions and policies towards these ends. These principles are based on and further expand on the World Heritage and Sustainable Development Policy.

1 *Conservation and management of heritage properties must promote cultural diversity, inclusion and equity*

The conservation and management of heritage must aim to promote cultural diversity, inclusion and equity through policies and interventions that include all stakeholders, especially the local communities. This must ensure that the local communities' abilities, dignity and opportunities are improved as a result, their exclusion and economic inequalities reduced and their values and local knowledge of the heritage property respected.

a *Principle of building local capabilities with and through heritage conservation and management:*

> Amartya Sen's important work on underdevelopment and inequalities has emphasized local causes and inherent patterns as the backdrop to development efforts (Sen 1999, 2004). Arjun Appadurai has asserted the importance of expanding the opportunities of the poor to exercise their choices, to have their voices heard and to build the capacities to which they aspire (Appadurai 1990, 2003, 2013). People turn to culture as a means of self-definition and mobilization, while asserting that their cultural values are often the sole assets to which they have a claim. As an extension of Sen's idea of 'substantial freedom' (Sen 1999, 2004) and Martha Nussbaum's conception of 'central capabilities' (Nussbaum 2011), such approaches aim for individuals, households, communities, institutions and governments to achieve culturally informed sustainable human development by building on existing local assets and overcoming obstacles and limitations to their capabilities. For the marginalized, conservation policies and interventions that build on existing local assets enable communities and institutions to engage with development processes in order to engage in heritage on more equitable terms.

b *Principle of enhancing social cohesion:*

> Many heritage properties also include significant public spaces. Public spaces provide a unique opportunity to enhance social cohesion through encouraging use and access of a diversity of local communities. Serendipitous interactions of diverse communities in public space contribute to building intercultural understanding and trust. Social cohesion creates conditions for development

interventions, while cultural approaches promote inclusiveness, equity and diversity by recognizing and protecting cultural assets as valuable resources.

(see Hosagrahar et al. 2016)

c   *Principle of integrating safeguarding of intangible cultural heritage with conservation of built and natural heritage:*

From the extraction of natural building materials and building techniques and practices to ritual activities, meanings and knowledge associated with particular properties, local knowledge and intangible cultural heritage are an integral aspect of heritage properties. For the properties to remain meaningful and for better conservation, the intangible cultural heritage must be safeguarded and transmitted from generation to generation. However, intangible cultural heritage is not fixed in time. It evolves and changes with each generation. When such knowledge and practices are included, they are sometimes reduced to staged exhibitions rather than remaining as an integral aspect of the local community's identity and meaning. Some experts view evolving intangible cultural heritage as a loss of 'authenticity', even though this concept was rejected as inapplicable to intangible heritage by those formulating the UNESCO Intangible Heritage Convention (UNESCO 2003; see Logan 2017: 29). Many efforts to 'fix' it merely retain the aesthetic elements (such as colourful festivals) to the detriment of local knowledge and related practices. Strategies for better integrating intangible cultural heritage with the built are a key to social inclusion of the local communities.

2   *Conservation and management of heritage properties must promote inclusive governance and respect local communities*

Respect for human dignity creating enabling environments at community and societal levels are integral to human development. A vibrant and meaningful cultural life is an important dimension of human wellbeing and an end goal of development. Promoting respect for local communities demands a commitment to integrate and implement the full range of international standards on human-rights.

a   *Principle of participation in decision-making and management of heritage:*

Participation of local communities and stakeholders in the management of the heritage properties and decision-making related to its use and meaning as well as its conservation is a critical aspect of the governance of cultural heritage. Inclusive participatory management of heritage sites would be advantageous both for improved conservation of properties that have often been managed by the local communities for generations and for poverty alleviation as well as more effective development efforts. In contrast to previous efforts at top-down development programs and policies that international agencies and national governments have devised and implemented, cultural considerations engage not only with the outcomes but also with the processes through which poverty alleviation and sustainable development are addressed.

b   *Principle of inclusive development of local communities contributing to sustainable conservation of cultural heritage:*

Sustainable transformative change comes only when people are recognized as having the agency to act and direct their own destinies, thus ensuring that sustainable development efforts operate within the given cultural framework of society. Valuing cultural sensibilities and shaping locally appropriate development projects and interventions would enable the empowerment of those who are intended to benefit most from development efforts: the poor, the marginalized and the disadvantaged. Scholars like John Friedmann and Marshall Sahlins have proposed alternative approaches to development that restore the agency for change to those whom development efforts are most intended to impact, such as the poor (Friedmann 1992, 2011; Sahlins 2014). From such a perspective, giving members of the community an active role in directing their own destinies is crucial to sustainable and long-term conservation and management of heritage. The application of universal recipes for development can assume that local people are passive consumers with no role in managing their own resources. Culturally informed approaches recognize the role and agency of the poor, as well as the direct and indirect impacts on them of conservation policies and interventions, whether these are targeted to benefit them or to exclude them from considerations of their benefit.

c   *Principle of cultural access and participation:*

Access to cultural heritage properties, as well as cultural infrastructure and practices related to them are keys to ensuring that a diversity of meanings and uses are included in the management of the heritage property rather than emphasizing only a single, dominant one. All stakeholders, including local communities, are enabled and empowered to identify with the heritage properties in their own ways. When certain practices or uses seem to be detrimental to the conservation of the heritage values of the properties, a management decision to bar them impacts on the significance of the heritage property for some local communities who may easily remain excluded, sometimes exacerbating existing social differences. Cultural access and participation is also at the heart of gender equality and women's empowerment. The roles, responsibilities, access to resources and opportunities for women and men to participate in or benefit from mainstream development efforts and heritage vary greatly across place and cultural groups. In particular, women in many societies are often the producers, transmitters and caretakers of heritage, local knowledge and creative expressions. The human rights of women are also a cultural issue, as they can pit universal values and ethics against local particularities. This has been further discussed in this volume in the chapters on human rights and gender equality.

3   *Conservation and management of heritage properties must enhance the quality of life and wellbeing of all local-communities in and around heritage properties:*

When the quality of life and wellbeing of local communities are enhanced, their ability to participate in and contribute to the conservation and management of the heritage property is improved. The wellbeing of local communities is also directly linked with the transmission of intangible cultural heritage and local knowledge associated with the property.

a   *Principle of integrating communities' customary use of heritage property into its conservation and management:*

As many of the communities have been customarily using the heritage properties to provide their food, clean water, medicinal plants or sources of livelihood, conservation policies and management would need to find a way to integrate these uses in an equitable way.

b   *Principle of improving the basic infrastructure and services for communities in and around heritage properties:*

Providing basic infrastructure and services for communities in and around the heritage properties is essential to including them in the benefits of conservation efforts. Experience has shown that investing exclusively on the material conservation of heritage properties or removing local people from it exacerbate social exclusion and have had detrimental impacts on conservation. Promoting enhanced sanitation and environmental health would also be a way of managing the heritage property in a way that benefits all.

Conclusion

In order to implement the foregoing principles and promote social inclusion for sustainable development in and around heritage properties, global and local partnerships are necessary. Funding and technical support from international agencies as well as local, regional and national sources is essential. The principle of partnership here is key rather than top-down efforts with external experts. Following these key principles would also help counter the dominance of development efforts that target tourist preferences to the detriment of local communities, or the 'staging' of heritage properties. Keeping the focus of heritage conservation and management efforts on promoting cultural diversity, equity, inclusive governance and respect for all would be important steps towards localizing a global convention towards sustainable development in a local context.

Notes

1 Disclaimer: The opinions and positions expressed in the chapter are those of the author and not necessarily those of UNESCO.
2 UNESCO has been advocating an integrated view of culture and development since the mid-eighties. See timeline in UNESCO brochure, *Culture for the SDGs* (2018 forthcoming).

References

Alsayyad, N. (2000). *Consuming Tradition, Manufacturing Heritage: Global Norms and Urban Forms in the Age of Tourism*. London and New York: Routledge.

Appadurai, A. (1990). 'Disjuncture and difference in the global cultural economy', *Public Culture*, 2(2), 1–24.

Appadurai, A. (2003). 'Diversity and sustainable development', in UNESCO-UNEP (ed), *Cultural Diversity and Biodiversity for Sustainable Development*. Nairobi: UNEP (online). Available at: http://unesdoc.unesco.org/images/0013/001322/132262e.pdf (accessed 16 November 2017).

Appadurai, A. (2013). *The Future as Cultural Fact: Essays on the Global Condition*. New York: Verso.

Avrami, E. (2016). 'Making historic preservation sustainable', *Journal of the American Planning Association*, 82(2), 104–112.

Bandarin, F. and van Oers, R. (2012). *The Historic Urban Landscape: Managing Heritage in an Urban Century*. New York: Wiley.

European Union (2015). *Cultural Heritage Counts for Europe*. Final Report (online). Available at: www.encatc.org/culturalheritagecountsforeurope/outcomes/ (accessed 4 December 2017).

Friedmann, J. (1992). *Empowerment: The Politics of Alternative Development*. Chichester, UK: Wiley-Blackwell.

Friedmann, J. (2011). *Insurgencies: Essays in Planning Theory*. London and New York: Routledge.

Hosagrahar, J. (2011). 'Interrogating difference: Postcolonial perspectives in architecture and urbanism', in C. Crysler, S. Cairns and H. Heynen (eds), *A Handbook of Architectural Theory*. New York: Sage.

Hosagrahar, J. (2013). *Culture's Contribution to Achieving Sustainable Cities*. Background Note 3A-C for Culture: Key to Sustainable Development, Hangzhou International Congress, Hangzhou, China (online). Available at: www.unesco.org/new/fileadmin/MULTIMEDIA/HQ/CLT/images/SustainableCitiesFinalENG.pdf (accessed 15 November 2017).

Hosagrahar, J. (2015). 'Urban heritage and sustainable development: Challenges and opportunities in South Asia', in M.-T. Albert, R. Bernecker and B. Rudolff (eds), *Sustainability in Heritage-Related Disciplines*. Cottbus, Germany: Brandenburg Technical University and de Gruyter.

Hosagrahar, J. (2017). 'Culture: At the heart of the SDGs', *The UNESCO Courier*, April–June (online). Available at: http://en.unesco.org/courier/2017-april-june/culture-heart-sdgs (accessed 17 October 2017).

Hosagrahar, J. (2017). 'A history of heritage conservation in city planning', in C. Hein (ed), *Planning History Handbook*. New York, London: Routledge.

Hosagrahar, J., Fusco Girard, L., Soule, J. and Potts, A. (2016). *Concept Note: Cultural Heritage, the UN Sustainable Development Goals*. US ICOMOS (online). Available at: www.usicomos.org/wp-content/uploads/2016/05/Final-Concept-Note.pdf

Hosagrahar, J. and Hayashi, N. (2013). *Culture, Poverty and Wellbeing*. Background Note 2A for Culture: Key to Sustainable Development, Hangzhou International Congress, Hangzhou, China (online). Available at: www.unesco.org/new/fileadmin/MULTIMEDIA/HQ/CLT/images/CulturePovertyWellbeingENG.pdf (accessed 15 November 2017).

Licciardi, G. and Amirtahmasebi, R. (2012). *The Economics of Uniqueness: Investing in Historic City Cores and Cultural Heritage Assets for Sustainable Development (Urban Development)*. Washington, DC: World Bank.

Logan, W. (2017). 'UNESCO heritage-speak: Words, syntax and rhetoric', in C. Antons and W. Logan (eds), *Intellectual Property, Cultural Property and Intangible Cultural Heritage*. London: Routledge.

Nobre, E. A. C. (2002). 'Urban regeneration experiences in Brazil: Historical preservation, tourism development and gentrification in Salvador da Bahia', *Urban Design International*, 7, 109–124 (online). Available at: www.napplac.fau.usp.br/trabalhos/enobre/enobre_art12.pdf (accessed 16 October 2017).

Nussbaum, M. C. (2011). *Creating Capabilities: The Human Development Approach*. Cambridge, MA: Belknap Press (online). Available at: https://www3.nd.edu/~ndlaw/prog-human-rights/london-symposium/CreatingCapabilities.pdf (accessed 16 October 2017).

Rojas, E. (1999). *Old Cities, New Assets: Preserving Latin America's Urban Heritage*. Washington, DC: Inter-American Development Bank/Johns Hopkins University Press.

Roy, A. (2003). *City Requiem, Calcutta: Gender and the Politics of Poverty*. Minneapolis: University of Minnesota Press.

Sahlins, M. (2014). *Stone Age Economics*. 2nd revised ed. London: Routledge.

Scarpacci, J. L. (2005). *Plazas and Barrios: Heritage Tourism and Globalization in Latin American Centro Histórico*. Tuscon: University of Arizona Press.

Sen, A. (1999). *Development as Freedom*. New York: Oxford University Press.

Sen, A. (2004). 'How does culture matter?', in V. Rao and M. Walton (eds), *Culture and Public Action*. Palo Alto, CA: Stanford University Press.

UNESCO (1972). *Convention concerning the Protection of the World Cultural and Natural Heritage* (online). Available at: http://whc.unesco.org/en/conventiontext/ (accessed 15 October 2017).

UNESCO (2003). *Convention for the Safeguarding of the Intangible Cultural Heritage* (online). Available at: https://ich.unesco.org/en/convention (accessed 15 October 2017).

UNESCO (2011). *Recommendation on the Historic Urban Landscape* (online). Available at: http://portal.unesco.org/en/ev.php-URL_ID=48857&URL_DO=DO_TOPIC&URL_SECTION=201.html (accessed 17 October 2017).

UNESCO (2012). *EU and UNESCO Restore Nablus' Landmark Khan Al Wakalah to Its Former Glory* (online). Available at: www.unesco.org/new/en/media-services/single-view/news/eu_and_unesco_restore_nablus_landmark_khan_al_wakalah_to_i/(accessed 18 October 2017).

UNESCO (2015). *Policy Document for the Integration of a Sustainable Development Perspective into the Processes of the World Heritage Convention* (online). Available at: http://whc.unesco.org/en/sustainabledevelopment/ (accessed 29 August 2017).

UNESCO (2016). *Culture: Urban Future*. Paris: UNESCO (online). Available at: http://unesdoc.unesco.org/images/0024/002462/246291E.pdf (accessed 18 October 2017).

UNESCO (2017a). *Historic Centre of Salvador de Bahia* (online). Available at: http://whc.unesco.org/en/list/309 (online). Available at: http://whc.unesco.org/en/list/309 (accessed 17 September 2017).

UNESCO (2017b). *Old Towns of Djenné* (online). Available at: http://whc.unesco.org/en/list/116 (accessed 17 September 2017).

UNESCO (2017c). *The Old Town of Nablus and its Environs* (online). Available at: http://whc.unesco.org/en/tentativelists/5714/ (accessed 18 October 2017).

UNESCO (2018 Forthcoming). Culture for the Sustainable Development Goals: Implementing the 2030 Agenda with Culture. Paris: UNESCO.

United Nations (UN) (2015). *Sustainable Development Goals* (online). Available at: www.un.org/sustainabledevelopment/sustainable-development-goals/ (accessed 15 October 2017).

United Nations Department of Economic and Social Affairs (UNDESA) (2016). *Report on World Social Situation* (online). Available at: www.un.org/development/desa/dspd/report-on-the-world-social-situation-rwss-social-policy-and-development-division/rwss2016.html (accessed 16 November 2017).

Winter, T. (2013). 'Clarifying the critical in critical heritage studies', *International Journal of Heritage Studies*, 19(6), 532–545.

World Bank (2013). *Inclusion Matters: The Foundation for Shared Prosperity*. Washington, DC: World Bank.

Chapter 6

World Heritage and gender equality

Sophia Labadi

Achieving gender equality is integral to sustainable development. How can such a virtuous concept as sustainable development be achieved if women – 'half the sky', as the ancient Chinese proverb poetically call them – are marginalized, suffer from discrimination and inequalities and have their needs discredited? Gender equality is a top priority of the UN and its specialized agencies. This commitment, among other things, led to the creation of the United Nations Entity for Gender Equality and the Empowerment of Women initiative (better known as UN Women) in July 2010. Gender equality has also been a global priority at UNESCO (one of the only two, with Priority Africa) for almost a decade. In addition, achieving gender equality and the empowerment of all women and girls is a full Sustainable Development Goal (and was also a full Millennium Development Goal).

What were these programs, and what was their impact at the UN and UNESCO? What were the different theories that guided these programs? How has gender equality been addressed within the policy discourse and implementation of the World Heritage Convention? What are the key recommendations of the section on 'achieving gender equality' in the UNESCO 'Policy for the integration of a Sustainable Development Perspective into the processes of the World Heritage Convention'? Why were these recommendations proposed?

To address these questions, this chapter first provides a critical analysis of the different efforts by the UN and UNESCO to achieve gender equality and the empowerment of women, whilst also explaining the different theoretical frameworks which have guided these efforts. It then analyses how gender equality and the empowerment of women have been interpreted and implemented within the World Heritage framework, highlighting key issues and shortcomings. Having demonstrated the fundamental importance of the section on 'achieving gender equality' as part of the policy on World Heritage and sustainable development, a last section details its key features and how the author of this article took into careful consideration the existing issues with gender and World Heritage in the drafting process of the policy.

Gender equality at the UN and UNESCO – the wider framework

Gender equality and the empowerment of women have occupied a major position within the United Nations, as demonstrated by the impressive and diverse list of activities and events organized over more than 30 years. This includes the adoption of 1975 as the International Women's Year and 8th March as the International Women's day, which, every year, celebrates the social, economic, cultural and political achievements of women and the advances in respect of their rights as well as calling for action on empowering women and achieving gender parity. Another key event was the UN decade for women (1976–1985), a key result of which was the adoption in 1979 of the *Convention on the Elimination of All Forms of Discrimination against Women* by the UN General Assembly. This convention has so far been ratified by 189 Member States. It outlines women's social, cultural, political and economic rights, what constitutes discrimination or prejudice against women as well as measures for national actions to end these discriminations or prejudices in order to realize equality between women and men. In addition, four UN World conferences on women (organized in Mexico City in 1975, Copenhagen in 1980, Nairobi in 1985 and Beijing in 1995) have aimed at locating the issues facing women at the centre of the global arena and agenda, as well as to set common objectives and plans of action (Chen 1995: 477–478). The 1995 Beijing Declaration and the Platform for Action, in particular, recognized the crucial link between poverty eradication and gender equality. The continued and renewed importance that the UN gave to gender equality and the empowerment of women led to the creation of a single entity solely responsible for these themes, that is, the United Nations Entity for Gender Equality and the Empowerment of Women (better known as UN Women) in July 2010. This organization aims to coordinate the UN system's work on gender equality and the empowerment of women, to help intergovernmental bodies in the formulation of policies, standards and norms, as well as monitoring the implementation of these initiatives and related activities. It also aims to help Member States to implement these policies, standards, norms and activities.

Different philosophical and conceptual approaches have framed and guided all these different initiatives and events. This includes the 'Women in Development' approach, formulated in the early 1970s (Tinker 1990: 30). For proponents of this approach, women had been marginalized up until then or excluded from every aspect of development. They were particularly marginalized or excluded from key administrative and political roles related to the planning, development and implementation of development projects at international, national and local levels (Boserup 1970; Benaría and Sen 1982: 161; Rogers 1980). As a consequence, women had not benefited from development projects, which primarily adressed men's concerns, and benefited men first and foremost. According to this approach, greater inclusion of women in development projects, mainly in high-level roles, would help solve these issues of marginalization and exclusion.

However, another view, the 'Women and Development approach', inspired by Marxism and dependency theory, argues that women have in fact always been involved in development processes and projects. Yet, they have been heavily exploited in their majority and far more than men, particularly in developing countries. Examples abound, for instance, women artisans are often underpaid and work in an unregulated labor force, making souvenirs for tourists or crafts to be exported to North America, Europe or the Asian markets. Another example of this exploitation are the women that work in manufacturing, particularly in the clothing and textile sectors, who provide cheap and flexible labour and have only very few rights (Mies 1982; Lim 1983). This approach calls for women-only development projects which will remove them from capitalist, imperialist and patriarchal exploitation (ibid.: 80).

This 'Women and Development' approach has a number of shortcomings. Women are considered as a homogeneous and coherent group; in other words, they are essentialized. Another related issue is that men are always seen to be privileged and dominant. This has led to the stereotyping of both women and men. For instance, women from the Middle East are often portrayed as overtly submissive, whilst the reality is far more complex.

The 'Gender and Development' approach which has become dominant within the UN system developed out of the shortcomings of the 'Women in Development' and the 'Women and Development' approaches (Oakley 1972; Moser 1993). This 'Gender and Development' approach focuses on the interconnected social relations between women and men and the need to challenge gender roles. This approach moves away from considering gender issues uniquely through female lens (Ostergaard 1992: 6). Not only has this approach helped to consider the variability of gender relations in time and space (Schech and Haggis 2000: 96), but it has also helped to deconstruct some of the long-held stereotypes about women. The 'nimble fingers' of women, for instance, which has led to their massive employment in manufacturing jobs, has been explained as being learnt skills, rather than a natural characteristic (Elson and Pearson 1988: 21). One of the recent initiatives reflecting this approach is the 'HeForShe' campaign initiated by the UN Women in 2014. It was made visible, in part, thanks to the different actions taken by the actor Emma Watson, also UN Women Goodwill Ambassador, notably her 2014 speech and the 2015 live Facebook conversation, widely circulated online.[1] This initiative considers boys and men as central to addressing some of the social, economic, political and cultural issues leading to the marginalization and inequalities faced by girls and women. This popular campaign highlights that the issues and inequalities faced by women should not be constricted to, or only resolved by women. On the contrary, this initiative has approached the topic as a human rights issue that concerns everybody and deserves a collective solution.

Despite the different and diverse programs and activities developed and implemented by the UN, guided by these theoretical approaches, major problems still affect gender equality and women's empowerment, leading Koehler to sum up the current situation in these terms: 'Not a single country has achieved the gender equality goals agreed in 1995' (2015: 746). The long lists of targets associated with the UN Sustainable Development Goal 5 (henceforth SDG, adopted in September 2015) and its targets provide more specific indications of these problems. This goal aims to 'achieve gender equality and empower all girls and women'. The different associated targets include: the need to end 'all forms of discrimination and all forms of violence against women', to eliminate 'all harmful practices', to '[e]nsure women's full and effective participation and equal opportunities for leadership at all levels of decision-making' and to 'undertake reforms to give women equal rights to economic resources, as well as access to ownership and control over land and other forms of property, financial services, inheritance and natural resources, in accordance with national laws' (United Nations 2015). This list demonstrates that the previous Millennium Development Goal 3, which aimed to promote gender equality and empower women through eliminating gender disparity in primary and secondary education, might not have been as encompassing or successful as originally believed (Fehling, Nelson and Venkatapuram 2013: 1109–1122; Subrahmanian 2005).

UNESCO, as a specialized agency of the UN has had a parallel concern for gender equality and the empowerment of women. Since 2008, gender equality has been one of the Organization's two overarching global priorities, along with Priority Africa (Forss 2013: 1). This means that all sectors of UNESCO should initiate, develop and implement gender-specific activities and programs, interventions, partnerships and networks. To guide the actions of UNESO, two Gender Equality Action Plans have been adopted, the first one ran from 2008 to 2013 and the second one is running from 2014 to 2021. In addition, UNESCO has had a special unit dedicated to the promotion of the status of women and gender equality for almost 20 years (Forss 2013: 10). Maybe one of the most visible and well-known initiatives and partnerships is the L'Oréal-UNESCO 'For Women in Science' program which aims to recognize, promote and enhance the role of women in science though an award. Since 1998, the L'Oréal-UNESCO award has recognized more than 97 laureates from 30 countries. Every year, the laureates are the subjects of a highly visible promotion campaign with panels in airports and public transports. Another action has taken the shape of a training program on gender equality, supposedly mandatory for all UNESCO staff since 2005 (Forss 2013: iii). This program aims to make staff aware of the key concepts, goals and issues related to gender equality as well as introducing ways in which to implement them in their daily work. However, there have been no incentives or accountability mechanisms put in place to encourage staff to undertake this training program (ibid. iv). In addition, the program does not contain practical tasks related to developing gender specific activities, making it difficult to include this training in daily work and translate it into practice (ibid. 12). UNESCO's approach to gender equality and the empowerment of women has also been based on a strong commitment to cultural diversity and the enjoyment of culture as a driver and enabler of people-centered development, as detailed in the UNESCO Report on Gender Equality, Heritage and Creativity (UNESCO 2014a). But how has this concern for gender equality been applied to World Heritage?

Gender equality and World Heritage – taking stock

Gender equality seems to be a key idea and concern driving the implementation of the World Heritage Convention, particularly with the increased consideration given to local community involvement and to a human-rights approach to heritage conservation. As clarified by Farida Shaheed, the former Special Rapporteur in the field of cultural rights: 'The realization of equal cultural rights demands that women and girls are able to access, participate in, and contribute to all aspects of cultural life on a basis of equality with men and boys' (Shaheed 2014). In other words, a human-rights based approach to World Heritage cannot be possible without gender equality. This represents an evolution in the understanding and implementation of the World Heritage Convention, which, at the time of its adoption in 1972, did not make any reference to gender equality or the roles of women and men, as well as their empowerment through World Heritage (Rössler 2014: 61). Gender equality concerns all aspects of the convention, as gender relations are infused throughout the implementation of this legal instrument, from the identification of heritage, to its conservation and management and its interpretation. In addition, gender equality stands at the heart of integrating a sustainable development perspective within the processes of the World Heritage Convention. Indeed, no development can be sustainable, just and equitable without removing the inequalities facing half of the population.

Activities aimed at achieving gender equality and the empowerment of women within the implementation of the convention have been regularly reported on by the UNESCO Director General at the General Conferences (see, for instance, UNESCO 2013b, 2015a). These reports reveal that gender equality has been understood primarily as ensuring the parity in the participation of women and men in projects, activities and capacity-building workshops. This concern for parity has characterized all programs, including the World Heritage Education program and its youth fora and capacity building activities. In addition, specific activities at an individual property level have aimed to benefit women socially and economically, as is the case, for instance, in the project, 'Social inclusion of women and young people through earthen architecture driven traditional handwork techniques' implemented in the City of Cuenca, Peru (UNESCO 2015; see also Galla 2012 for more examples). Besides, it is worth mentioning the appointment, for the first time, of a woman, Dr Mechtild Rössler, as Director of the World Heritage Centre (as well as Director of the Heritage Division) in 2015. This is very important, considering that the latest version of the UNESCO Priority Gender Equality Action Plan notes the ' "glass ceiling" for women to reach senior management positions or to participate in decision-making processes' (UNESCO 2014b: 37). Finally, concerns for gender equality within the implementation of the convention have led to an entire issue of the World Heritage Review dedicated to this theme (UNESCO 2016).

However, important shortcomings can be identified in the current approach to gender equality as part of the implementation of the World Heritage Convention. First, the World Heritage Committee has not adopted a general gender policy, but has only occasionally referred to gender equality in its decisions (UNESCO 2013a). This absence makes the section on gender a vital part of the 'Policy for the integration of a sustainable development perspective into the processes of the World Heritage Convention' presented below. In addition, as I have just explained, too often, implementation of the gender priority within the framework of the convention has been equated with a balanced participation of women and men (or girls and boys) in different activities, projects or capacity-building workshops. This is clearly reflected in the performance indicators and benchmarks identified to monitor the implementation of the global priority on gender equality within the framework of the convention, as presented in the UNESCO Program and budget document (also known as 'the C/5'). The UNESCO Program and budget document for 2014–2017, for instance, identifies as the 'number of World Heritage properties where the balanced contribution of women and men to conservation is demonstrated' one of the performance indicators (UNESCO 2014: 163). However, this balanced participation does not necessarily lead to gender equality or the empowerment of women. It reflects more the 'women in development' theory presented previously. Indeed, these activities, indicators and benchmarks denote more a concern for the inclusion of women in training sessions and available opportunities than for the nature of this participation. It is unclear whether and how such participation changes the gender and power relations or the social construction of gender at World Heritage properties (see also Mosse 2005: 150).

Another issue concerns references to women in nomination dossiers, these being considered as key documents for the long-term interpretation, management and conservation of heritage properties. It could have been expected, naively, that these documents would have put women, gender equality and the empowerment of women at their heart to respect UNESCO's vision, approaches and priorities. However, in-depth analyses of a selection of 114 nomination dossiers revealed a clear marginalization of the references to women or gender relations (Labadi 2013: 77–93, 2007: 161–164). References to women amount to only a few sentences of some nomination dossiers, with some exceptions such as the Flemish Béguinages in Belgium, inscribed not only for their urban and architectural characteristics, but also for the cultural tradition of independent religious women in north-western Europe (Government of Belgium 1997). These few references strongly position women at the margin of the text, history and heritage, and make them invisible, secondary and forgettable. This marginalization stands in stark contrast to the long descriptions of famous men related to nominated properties. In a number of cases, famous men are used to define the outstanding universal value of the nominated property. This is not the case for most women in the sample analysed. Worse, some references tend to be a vehicle for stereotypical personal characteristics of women, describing them as sentimental, hysterical, prone to making decisions based on emotion and incapable of rational action. It could have been thought that this focus on the 'great men of history' could have changed in recent years, especially after UNESCO defined gender equality as one of its two global priorities. Yet, on the contrary, the focus on the great men of history has increased in the recent nomination dossiers. There are now entire dossiers focusing on great men and their deeds, as is the case with the serial nomination of 'The Architectural Work of Le Corbusier' (France, Argentina, Belgium, Germany, India, Japan and Switzerland), inscribed on the World Heritage List in 2016. This marginalization, or even invisibility has also been identified in States of Conservation Reports for natural heritage sites. Out of the 1,290 SOC reports assessed by IUCN, only nine referred to women or issues of gender equality and women's participation at these natural heritage sites (Bastian, Gilligan and Clabots 2016).

These results confirm previous publications on the matter which have also documented heritage and history as being predominantly male-centred (Smith 2008; Lowenthal 1998). This invisibility of women is more related to the fact that women's stories and actions are not as well promoted as men's deeds, rather than women being passive or only working in private spheres (see also Rössler, Cameron and Selfslagh 2016: 6). This invisibility thus reflects power relations at heritage properties, as well as who has the authority to decide what constitutes the significance of World Heritage (or heritage in general). Obscuring women in nomination dossiers is problematic as it reproduces gender inequalities. Indeed, best practice encourages the identification of all the values that make the property significant to ensure they guide the long-term management of the property. If the histories of women are not brought forward, then some important social, historical or cultural events related to them might not be recorded, and a holistic management of the property will never be implemented. Besides, to allow women to be empowered – that is, to take control of their lives through building self-confidence and self-reliance – women need to have their history and heritage recognized, valued and promoted. Indeed, such recognition would reveal that there exist many women who have done great deeds, just like their male counterparts in shaping World Heritage. Without this recognition, contemporary women will continue to be marginalized and stereotyped and to be considered as inferior to men. Above all, seriously taking account of gender relations at the property level would make it necessary to look 'at women's experiences vis-à-vis men and vice versa (as well as to other genders beyond the male-female binary) and the power negotiations involved in that' (Blake 2014: 50). This will never be possible if only men and their perspectives are considered and valued.

This invisibility of women was reflected, until recently, in the choice of experts from ICOMOS undertaking evaluation missions to evaluate the authenticity, integrity, protection, conservation and management of nominated properties. From 2006 to 2008, 70 per cent of ICOMOS experts were men (Tabet 2010: 25). This imbalance was repeated in the breakdown of World Heritage panel members from ICOMOS whose role was to adopt recommendations on nominated properties, with 77 per cent of men compared with 23 per cent of women, again from 2006 to 2008 (ibid: 29). This gender imbalance was also found, but exacerbated, in the IUCN evaluators who used to carry out site visits, with 33 male evaluators out of a total of 34 in the period 2001–2004 (Cameron 2005: 8). In response to these findings, both ICOMOS and IUCN have stated that they have taken steps to ensure a greater gender balance in the experts undertaking evaluation missions (Rössler, Cameron and Selfslagh 2016: 9), although no figures seem yet to have been published.

Moving forward: achieving gender equality at World Heritage properties

Such shortcomings just detailed made it necessary to include a section on 'Achieving gender equality', as part of the dimension on 'Inclusive Social Development', within the 'Policy for the integration of a sustainable development perspective into the processes of the World Heritage Convention'. To ensure policy coherence within the UN sustainable development agenda, this section on achieving gender equality reflects the SDG 5 and some of its key targets. The Priority Gender Equality Action Plan (2014–2021) was also used as a guide to draft the section, and I sought to respect its vision, principles, definitions and objectives. Besides this section on 'Achieving gender equality' fully reflects and respects the principles, ideas and recommendations proposed in the UNESCO report on Gender Equality, Heritage and Creativity (UNESCO 2014a: 135). Guidance was also provided by UNESCO Gender Equality division, and the IUCN Global Gender Office and their comments on earlier versions of the draft policy were also fully integrated. Finally, the section took into account the shortcomings I had identified of previous approaches to gender equality and the empowerment of women within the implementation of the World Heritage Convention.

This section of the policy aims to mainstream a gender perspective; that is, to make women's, as well as men's, concerns, experiences, knowledge and expertise integral dimensions of the design, implementation, monitoring and evaluation of policies and programs related to the World Heritage Convention (UNESCO 2014b: 15). This will pave the way to gender equality, that is, for 'women and men to enjoy the same status and have equal opportunity to realize their full human rights and potential to contribute to national, political, economic, social and cultural development' (UNESCO 2014b: 60). This will also help to ensure that women and men benefit equally from the implementation of the convention, and so that inequality is not perpetuated or exacerbated. To rectify this imbalance, the section adheres to, and integrates, the three interrelated components of the right to take part in cultural life as: (a) participation in; (b) access to; and (c) contribution to cultural life (Shaheed 2014). The section on gender equality also aims to empower women, that is, to ensure that they have control over their lives, gain skills, build self-confidence and develop self-reliance (ibid.). Finally, the section aims to facilitate the adoption by States Parties of 'gender-sensitive, gender-responsive and gender-transformative policies[2] and practices in the field of heritage', in line with the principles from the action plan (UNESCO 2014b: 38).

The definitions proposed were based on the UNESCO Priority Gender Equality Action plan, even though the definition of gender as the 'social meaning given to being a woman or a man' (UNESCO 2014b: 60) was criticized during the Cottbus and Ninh Binh meetings discussing the policy on World Heritage and sustainability. Indeed, for some experts, this definition was too simplistic: it did not go beyond the male/female binary and did not take account of the complexity and diversity of genders, including a-gender, gender-fluid or third gender. By adopting this definition from UNESCO, this section thus excludes some genders currently practiced and recognized.

More specifically, the section of the policy calls on States Parties, first, to 'ensure respect for gender equality throughout the full cycle of World Heritage processes, particularly in the preparation and content of nomination dossiers' (UNESCO 2015b). This focus on nomination dossiers aims to ensure that the interests, needs and priorities of both women and men are considered right from the earliest stages of the World Heritage process. In addition, such a focus could help to address some of the issues discussed earlier, in particular the invisibility of women and their views, values and history in nomination dossiers. Such representation should help to fight against negative stereotyping, and forms of discriminations against women as well as change power relations at site levels, in line with the first target of SDG 5. To achieve such a recommendation, more inclusive teams should be formed to prepare nomination dossiers and management plans, greater account should be paid to hidden, but nonetheless significant, histories at the site level and greater use should be made of international networks that have filled the gender gap. In addition, the format for the nomination of properties for inscription on the World Heritage List should be revised to ensure that the description of the property, its history and development and explanation of its outstanding universal value fully reflect the local cultural diversity and the key values they associate with the property. This will ensure a holistic and comprehensive approach to the protection of the outstanding universal value of the property, as well as its management and conservation.

Second, the policy urges State Parties to '[e]nsure social and economic opportunities for both women and men in and around World Heritage properties' (UNESCO 2015b). This recommendation was brought up during the discussions on the draft policy. It was recognized that providing equal social and economic opportunities to women and men is still rare, despite some notable projects such as those mentioned earlier. For this reason, women remain disproportionately affected by poverty, exploitation or marginalization. Hence, there was a need to request clearly that equal social and economic opportunities are provided for in and around World Heritage properties and not necessarily or solely in tourism. Implementing this recommendation would lead to income generation for women, poverty reduction and the empowerment of women. This second recommendation reflects one of the targets of the UN SDG 5, which aims to 'give women equal rights to economic resources, as well as access to ownership and control over land and other forms of property, financial services, inheritance and natural resources, in accordance with national laws'. A first step to implement this recommendation would be to gather best practices, as published, for instance, by IUCN (see, for instance, Koirala, Gurung and Sharma 2004) or by UN Women, to determine how these could be applied in and around World Heritage properties.

The third recommendation urges State Parties to '[e]nsure equal and respectful consultation, full and effective participation and equal opportunities for leadership and representation of both women and men within activities for the conservation and management of World Heritage properties' (UNESCO 2015b). This was carefully drafted to reflect UN SDG 5.5, which aims to ensure 'women's full and effective participation and equal opportunities for leadership at all levels of decision-making'. This element is not only about the mere participation of women but also about their opportunity to influence decision-making processes and to challenge and change power relations at national and local levels on using heritage for sustainable development. One way to implement this recommendation would be to revise the format for the nomination of properties for inscription on the World Heritage List and request explanations of the different consultations undertaken. It would then be important to analyse the different ways in which equal and respectful consultation and full and effective participation were undertaken and how they would be ensured throughout the full cycle of World Heritage processes and the long-term management of the property.

The last recommendation addresses issues concerning women's access to World Heritage properties. It reflects discussions held during the drafting of this policy concerning World Heritage properties whose access is forbidden to women. The exploratory discussion focused on one property in particular: Mount Athos in Greece. Inscribed in 1988, it is a holy mountain with around twenty monasteries inhabited by some 1,400 monks (Rössler 2014: 83). One of the fundamental practices of monastic life is the 'avaton', with one of its rules which forbids women and children from entering or staying on Mount Athos (Papayannis 2016: 16–17). However, as explained by Farida Shaheed and as already quoted: 'The realization of equal cultural rights demands that women and girls are able to access, participate in, and contribute to all aspects of cultural life on a basis of equality with men and boys' (2014). In order to do so, women should have the right to determine on an equal basis with men whether they want to access heritage properties, and which values or traditions should be kept or discarded. To respect and realize fully cultural rights at World Heritage properties, the last recommendation of the policy thus requires State Parties, when or where relevant,

> to ensure that gender-rooted traditional practices within World Heritage properties, for example in relation to access or participation in management mechanisms, have received the full consent of all groups within the local communities through transparent consultation processes that fully respects gender equality.
>
> (UNESCO 2015b)

The integration of this gender lens and wider sustainable development perspective into the processes of the World Heritage Convention will require the building of necessary capacities among practitioners, institutions, concerned communities and networks across a wide interdisciplinary and inter-sectorial spectrum, as highlighted in paragraph 11 of the policy (UNESCO 2015b). In addition, new research should aim at collecting best practices in implementing the different recommendations as well as in establishing gender-sensitive, gender-responsible and gender-transformative policies and practices. These best practices should be widely disseminated. Finally, gender-specific data and statistics should be regularly collected to monitor and measure progress, and inform future strategy. To assess the effectiveness of these initiatives, the Gender Equality Marker at UNESCO should be used. This tool aims to measure the extent to which initiatives or projects contribute to the promotion and realization of gender equality. It follows a simple four-point scale from 'gender unaware' to 'gender transformative'. A gender transformative activity, policy or program will provide, for instance, gender-related expertise, gender-related performance indicator(s) and corresponding target(s) or gender-related expected results. Using this tool will help to track progress and help to revise activity, policy and programs that do not show awareness of gender equality principles or will not lead to it. To ensure some accountability, a World Heritage gender focal point should be tasked to report back regularly to the Committee on progress on achieving gender equality.

Conclusion

This chapter has explained that both the UN and UNESCO, as one of the UN's specialized agencies, have made gender equality a key priority. Yet, many issues are still preventing the full achievement of gender equality and the empowerment of women, as illustrated by the long list of targets associated with the Sustainable Development Goal 5.

Within the framework of the World Heritage Convention, an increasing number of activities promoting gender equality have been implemented, with the importance given to local communities and the development of a human-rights approach to heritage conservation. However, these activities present a number of shortcomings, including a general focus on parity between women and men, rather than specifically on changing power relations and gender inequalities at World Heritage properties. In addition, key documents related to the implementation of the convention, particularly nomination dossiers, do not reflect principles or specific concerns of gender equality or the empowerment of women. No effort has been made to encourage States Parties to nominate sites associated with women or to include references to them in nomination dossiers. Thus, nomination dossiers have predominantly been male-centred, as reflected, for instance, with the recent inscription of the architectural work of Le Corbusier on the World Heritage List in 2016. This invisibility of women was reflected, until recently, in the choice of experts from the Advisory Bodies evaluating nomination dossiers. Above all, the Committee has never adopted a general gender policy.

These shortcomings have made the section on 'Achieving gender equality' a fundamental part of the 'Policy for the integration of a sustainable development perspective into the processes of the World Heritage Convention'. The section respects the UNESCO Priority Gender Action Plan and reflects some of the targets of the SDG 5. Suggestions for the implementation of this section include the need to revise the format of nomination dossier, to respect and reflect better cultural diversity in the different World Heritage processes or to gather best practices on providing equal social and economic opportunities to women and men and apply them at World Heritage properties. These changes, if implemented, would go a long way towards ensuring that gender equality and the empowerment of women become a reality at World Heritage.

Notes

1 Emma Watson's 2014 speech is available at: www.youtube.com/watch?v=gkjW9PZBRfk. Her 2015 live Facebook conversation is available at: www.facebook.com/emmawatson/posts/1032692416749648.
2 Gender sensitive, according to UNESCO, means 'acknowledging differences and inequalities between women and men as requiring attention'. Gender responsive includes the definition of gender sensitive but also articulates 'policies and initiatives which address the different needs, aspirations, capacities and contributions of women and men'. A gender transformative approach challenges 'existing and biased/discriminatory policies, practices, programs and affect change for the betterment of life for all'.

References

Bastian, L., Gilligan, M. and Clabots, B. (2016). *Gender and Protected Areas: Exploring National Reporting to the Ramsar Convention and the World Heritage Convention.* Washington: IUCN.

Benería, L. and Sen, G. (1982). 'Class and gender inequalities and women's role in economic development-theoretical and practical implications', *Feminist Studies*, 8(1), 157–176.

Blake, J. (2014). 'Gender and intangible heritage', in UNESCO (ed), *Gender Equality, Heritage and Creativity*. Paris: UNESCO, pp. 48–79.

Boserup, E. (1970). *Women's Role in Economic Development*. London: George Allen and Unwin.

Cameron, C. (2005). *Evaluation of IUCN's Work in World Heritage Nominations*. Gland: IUCN.

Chen, M. (1995). 'Engendering world conferences: The international women's movement and the United Nations', *Third World Quarterly*, 16(3), 477–494.

Elson, D. and Pearson, R. (1988). 'The subordination of women and the internationalization of factory production', in K. Young et al. (eds), *Of Marriage and the Market: Women's Subordination Internationally and Its Lessons*. London: Routledge, pp. 18–40.

Fehling, M., Nelson, B. D. and Venkatapuram, S. (2013). 'Limitations of the millennium development goals: A literature review', *Global Public Health*, 8(10), 1109–1122.

Forss, K. (2013). *Review of UNESO's Priority Gender Equality*. Paris: UNESCO.

Galla, A. (2012). *World Heritage: Benefits beyond Borders*. Cambridge: Cambridge University Press.

Government of Belgium. (1997). *Nomination of the Flemish Béguinages for Inclusion on the World Heritage List*.

Koehler, G. (2015). 'Seven decades of "development" and now what?', *Journal of International Development*, 27(6), 733–751.

Koirala, I., Gurung, R. and Sharma, D. (2004). *Monitoring Gender, Poverty and Social Equity in Natural Resource Management: Best Practice Resources and Annotated Bibliography*. IUCN Nepal Country Office.

Labadi, S. (2007). 'Representations of the nation and cultural diversity in discourses on World Heritage', *Journal of Social Archaeology*, 7(2), 310–330.

Labadi, S. (2013). *UNESCO, Cultural Heritage, and Outstanding Universal Value*. Plymouth, MA: AltaMira Press.

Lim, L. (1983). 'Capitalism, imperialism and patriarchy: The dilemma of Third World women workers in multinational factories', in J. Nash and M. P. Fernandez-Kelly (eds), *Women, Men and the International Division of Labour*. Albany: State University of New York Press, pp. 70–91.

Lowenthal, D. (1998). *The Heritage Crusade and the Spoils of History*. Cambridge: Cambridge University Press.

Mies, M. (1982). *The Lace Makers of Narsapur: Indian Housewives Produce for the World Market*. London: Zed Books.

Moser, C. (1993). *Gender Planning and Development: Theory, Practice and Training*. London: Routledge.

Mosse, D. (2005). *Cultivating Development: An Ethnography of Aid Policy and Practice*. London: Pluto Press.

Oakley, A. (1972). *Sex, Gender and Society*. London: Temple Smith.

Ostergaard, L. (1992). *Gender and Development: A Practical Guide*. London: Roy.

Papayannis, T. (2016). 'Mount athos-more than just a man's world', *World Heritage Review*, 78, 12–19.

Rogers, B. (1980). *The Domestication of Women: Discrimination in Developing Countries*. London: Tavistock.

Rössler, M. (2014). 'Gendered World Heritage? A review of the implementation of the UNESCO World Heritage Convention', in P. Keenan, K. Nowacka and L. Patchett (eds), *Gender Equality, Heritage and Creativity*. Paris: UNESCO, pp. 60–72.

Rössler, M., Cameron, C. and Selfslagh, B. (2016). 'World Heritage and gender', *World Heritage Review*, 78, 4–11.

Schech, S. and Haggis, J. (2000). *Culture and Development: A Critical Introduction*. Oxford: Blackwell Publishing.

Shaheed, F. (2014). 'Foreword', in UNESCO (ed), *Gender Equality, Heritage and Creativity*. Paris: UNESCO.

Smith, L. (2008). 'Heritage, gender and identity', in B. Graham and P. Howard (eds), *The Ashgate Research Companion to Heritage and Identity*. Aldershot: Ashgate, pp. 159–178.

Subrahmanian, R. (2005). 'Gender equality in education: Definitions and measurements', *International Journal of Educational Development*, 25, 395–407.

Tabet, J. (2010). *Review of ICOMOS Working Methods and Procedures for the Evaluation of Cultural and Mixed Properties*. Paris: ICOMOS.

Tinker, I. (1990). *Persistent Inequalities: Women and World Development*. Oxford: Oxford University Press.

UNESCO (2010). *Approved Program and Budget*. Paris: UNESCO.

UNESCO (2013a). *Item 13 of the Provisional Agenda: Draft Policy Guidelines: World Heritage Committee: 37th Session*. Paris: UNESCO.

UNESCO (2013b). *Report by the Director-General on UNESCO's Actions Promoting Women's Empowerment and Gender Equality-37th Session of the General Conference*. Paris: UNESCO.

UNESCO (2014a). *Gender Equality, Heritage and Creativity*. Paris: UNESCO.

UNESCO (2014b). *UNESCO Priority Gender Equality Action Plan–2014–2021*. Paris: UNESCO.

UNESCO (2015a). *Report by the Director-General on UNESCO's Actions Promoting Women's Empowerment and Gender Equality-38th Session of the General Conference*. Paris: UNESCO.

UNESCO (2015b). *Policy Document for the Integration of a Sustainable Development Perspective into the Processes of the World Heritage Convention* (online). Available at: http://whc.unesco.org/en/sustainabledevelopment/ (accessed 2 December 2017).

UNESCO (2016). *World Heritage and Gender Equality*. no. 78. Paris: UNESCO.

United Nations (2015). *Sustainable Development Goals*. Available at: www.un.org/sustainabledevelopment/ (accessed 7 March 2017).

The World Heritage and Sustainable Development Policy – a turning point for indigenous peoples?

Stefan Disko and Max Ooft

Throughout the history of the World Heritage Convention, indigenous peoples have frequently raised concerns regarding violations of their rights and a lack of regard for their cultural heritage, values and livelihoods in the implementation of the Convention. Following the adoption of the 2007 *United Nations Declaration on the Rights of Indigenous Peoples* (UNDRIP), these concerns have increasingly drawn the attention of international human rights bodies and mechanisms, several of which have urged UNESCO and the World Heritage Committee to take corrective action and ensure that the World Heritage Convention is implemented in accordance with the UNDRIP and that indigenous peoples are effectively involved in all relevant decision-making processes under the Convention. Considering the increasingly large number of World Heritage sites that are fully or partially located within the traditional territories of indigenous peoples, the importance and urgency of this matter is evident.

Initial steps in this regard were taken by the World Heritage Committee at its 2015 session in Bonn, when the Committee for the first time inserted references to indigenous peoples into the World Heritage Convention's Operational Guidelines (UNESCO 2016), including a provision encouraging States to obtain indigenous peoples' free, prior and informed consent when nominating sites to the World Heritage List. The session also saw the Committee's endorsement of a (draft) *Policy for the Integration of a Sustainable Development Perspective into the Processes of the World Heritage Convention*, subsequently adopted (in slightly revised form) by the General Assembly of State Parties in October 2015. The policy includes special sections on human rights and indigenous peoples, and represents the World Heritage Committee's most comprehensive and conclusive statement to date on the need to ensure respect for indigenous peoples and their rights in World Heritage processes. To be effective, however, the policy will need to be followed up with changes to the Operational Guidelines and other measures to translate its principles into actual operational procedures.

The present chapter discusses the significance of the World Heritage and Sustainable Development Policy in the context of indigenous peoples' struggle to ensure respect for their rights, cultures and values in the implementation of the World Heritage Convention. The first part provides a brief discussion on the relationship between sustainable development and indigenous peoples' rights, drawing on some of the key documents that define the concept of 'sustainable development' as understood by the United Nations. The respective documents make clear that respect for indigenous peoples' rights and positive measures to empower indigenous peoples are essential requirements for sustainable development. The second part of the chapter outlines some of the main concerns that indigenous peoples have raised in relation to the World Heritage Convention and presents some of the recommendations that human rights bodies have made on how the World Heritage Committee could address these concerns. The third part describes the steps taken so far to enhance respect for indigenous peoples and their rights in the implementation of the Convention. Finally, some thoughts are presented on potential follow-up actions that would help ensure that the World Heritage and Sustainable Development Policy is applied in practice and leads to positive change for indigenous peoples living in or around World Heritage sites.

Respect for indigenous peoples' rights as an essential requirement for sustainable development

From the UN reports and internationally agreed documents that define the concept of sustainable development as understood by the United Nations, it is very clear that respect for indigenous peoples' rights and the effective involvement of indigenous peoples in decision-making affecting them are considered as essential requirements for sustainable development.

The term 'sustainable development' was first popularized by the 1987 Brundtland Report, which also included what continues to be the most widely recognized definition of sustainable development: 'Sustainable development is development that meets the needs of the present without compromising the ability of future generations to meet their own needs' (United Nations 1987: 41). The report underlined that special attention and priority should be given to the needs of the world's poor and to empowering disadvantaged and vulnerable groups in order to enable them to fulfill their own aspirations. It contained a special chapter on the need to empower indigenous and tribal peoples, recognizing that

> few of them have shared in national economic and social development.... Many live in areas rich in valuable natural resources that planners and 'developers' want to exploit, and this exploitation disrupts the local environment so as to endanger traditional ways of life.... Social discrimination, cultural barriers, and the exclusion from national political processes make these groups vulnerable and subject to exploitation. Many groups have become dispossessed and marginalized, and their traditional practices disappear. They become victims of what could be described as cultural extinction.
>
> (United Nations 1987: 97–98)

The Brundtland Report highlighted the central importance of the 'recognition and protection of their traditional rights to land and the other resources that sustain their way of life', emphasizing that 'this recognition must also give local communities a decisive voice in the decisions about resource use in their area'. The report added that the protection of traditional rights should be 'accompanied by positive measures to enhance the well-being of the community in ways appropriate to the group's life-style' (United Nations 1987: 98).

A special chapter on 'Recognizing and Strengthening the Role of Indigenous People and their Communities' was also included in *Agenda 21*, adopted at the 1992 UN Conference on Environment and Development in Rio de Janeiro (United Nations 1992a: Chapter 26). Among other things, this chapter called on governments to 'provide support for the adoption by the General Assembly of a declaration on indigenous rights' and to consider ratification of the *Indigenous and Tribal Peoples Convention, 1989* (ILO Convention No. 169). The chapter also highlighted the need for governments and intergovernmental organizations to involve indigenous peoples in resource management, conservation strategies and development processes that may affect them, including the creation and management of protected areas. It called for the establishment of arrangements to strengthen the active participation of indigenous peoples in the formulation of policies and programs and their ability to initiate their own proposals. It also underlined the importance of recognizing and incorporating indigenous peoples' values, views, knowledge and practices in natural resource management and conservation policies and programs affecting them.

All these objectives are closely related to more general principles and objectives, whose essential importance for achieving sustainable development and ensuring that sustainable development benefits all has repeatedly been underlined by the UN Member States. These principles and objectives include, *inter alia*: respect for human rights; good governance; respect for cultural diversity; justice; equality and non-discrimination; democracy; public participation in decision-making and access to information (see, e.g., United Nations 1992b, 2002, 2012, 2015).

The outcome document of the 2012 UN Conference on Sustainable Development (Rio+20), *The future we want*, reiterated that sustainable development requires the meaningful involvement and active participation of indigenous peoples and 'stress[ed] the importance of the participation of indigenous peoples in the achievement of sustainable development'. Moreover, it 'recognize[d] the importance of the United Nations Declaration on the Rights of Indigenous Peoples in the context of global, regional, national and subnational implementation of sustainable development strategies' (United Nations 2012: paras. 43, 49).

This declaration, the UNDRIP, solemnly proclaimed by the UN General Assembly in 2007 after more than two decades of negotiations between representatives of indigenous peoples and States, reflects the existing international consensus regarding the rights of indigenous peoples in a way that is coherent with the provisions of other human rights instruments (Anaya 2011: para. 69). Based on a recognition of the 'urgent need to respect and promote the inherent rights of indigenous peoples ... especially their rights to their lands, territories and resources' (preamble), it affirms a wide range of individual and collective rights of indigenous peoples that constitute 'the minimum standards for the survival, dignity and well-being of the indigenous peoples of the world' (art. 43).

Central provisions of the UNDRIP affirm indigenous peoples' right to self-determination and to freely pursue their economic, social and cultural development (art. 3), their right to own, use, develop and control their lands, territories and resources (art. 26) and their right to participate in decision-making affecting them, through representatives chosen by themselves in accordance with their own procedures (art. 18). A related provision provides that States shall consult and cooperate in good faith with indigenous peoples 'in order to obtain their free and informed consent prior to the approval of any project affecting their lands or territories and other resources' (art. 32). The declaration's preamble expresses the conviction that 'control by indigenous peoples over developments affecting them and their lands, territories and resources will enable them to maintain and strengthen their institutions, cultures and traditions, and to promote their development in accordance with their aspirations and needs'.

Articles 41 and 42 of the UNDRIP establish a special obligation of UN agencies and intergovernmental organizations to promote respect for and act in accordance with the standards expressed in the Declaration and to establish ways and means of ensuring the participation of indigenous peoples on issues affecting them. UNESCO's former Director-General Koïchiro Matsuura welcomed the adoption of the UNDRIP as a 'milestone for indigenous peoples and all those who are committed to the protection and promotion of cultural diversity and intercultural dialogue' (Matsuura 2007). In 2013, the UNESCO General Conference adopted a new *Medium Term Strategy* (2014–2021) for the organization, according to which 'the Organization will implement the UNDRIP across all relevant programme areas' (UNESCO 2013b: para. 20).

Moreover, in October 2017 the Executive Board of UNESCO adopted a *UNESCO Policy on Engaging with Indigenous Peoples*, which repeats that, consistent with Article 41 of the UNDRIP, UNESCO, as a specialized agency of the UN, is committed to the full realization of the provisions of the Declaration (UNESCO 2017). The policy specifies that UNESCO's engagement with indigenous peoples is framed by the following provisions from the UNDRIP, which are of specific relevance to the Organization's mandated areas of work:

- Human rights and fundamental freedoms
- Equality and non-discrimination
- Self-determination, participation and free, prior and informed consent
- Cultural heritage, knowledge, traditional cultural expressions and languages
- Development with culture and identity
- Conservation and protection of environment
- Gender equality.

The policy provides in-depth guidelines on the application of the UNDRIP to the Organization's mandated areas, as well as mechanisms for mainstreaming the policy in its work.

Recurrent violations of indigenous peoples' rights in the implementation of the World Heritage Convention

There can be no doubt that the World Heritage Convention can play, and in some cases has played, a positive role for indigenous peoples by helping them protect their lands and territories, cultures and heritage from development pressures such as extractive industry activities or threats posed by major infrastructure projects. World Heritage sites can also create business and employment opportunities for indigenous peoples, for instance, in the tourism sector or directly in the management of sites. In some cases, World Heritage sites have been nominated at the initiative of indigenous peoples themselves, with a view to protecting ancestral lands or creating new livelihoods.[1] Further, the international attention and oversight that comes with World Heritage listing can potentially be used to encourage improved indigenous participation in decision-making processes, enhanced benefit-sharing or redress for past violations of indigenous peoples' rights. In evaluating World Heritage nominations and monitoring the state of conservation of listed sites, the World Heritage Committee and its advisory bodies IUCN and ICOMOS have increasingly called on State Parties in recent years to enhance the role of indigenous peoples in site management and consider their needs and interests.[2]

However, indigenous peoples have also repeatedly raised concerns regarding violations of their rights in the implementation of the Convention, not only at the national level in the nomination and management of specific World Heritage sites, but also at the global level in the practice of the World Heritage Committee, its advisory bodies and its secretariat (the UNESCO World Heritage Centre).[3] A recurrent, key problem is the frequent nomination and inscription of World Heritage sites in indigenous peoples' territories without the meaningful participation of the indigenous peoples concerned. As a consequence, but also due to the lack of directives and guidelines on these aspects, there is insufficient regard for indigenous peoples' land and resource rights, livelihoods, cultural heritage and values in the nomination documents and justifications for inscription adopted by the World Heritage Committee.

This problem is exacerbated not only by the lack of appropriate regulations to ensure the effective participation of indigenous peoples in decision-making processes under the World Heritage Convention, but also by the World Heritage Committee's problematic interpretation and application of the concepts of 'heritage' and 'outstanding universal value' (OUV) (see Disko 2017 for a discussion).[4] Based on the Convention's differentiation between cultural heritage and natural heritage, the Committee maintains a distinction between 'cultural' and 'natural' World Heritage sites that is highly problematic where indigenous peoples' territories and heritage are concerned. The vast majority of the indigenous sites on the World Heritage List are listed as natural sites, without any recognition of associated indigenous heritage values in the justification for inscription (Statement of OUV) and in disregard of the fact that '[f]or indigenous peoples, cultural and natural values are inseparably interwoven and should be managed and protected in a holistic manner' (EMRIP 2015: 20). References to 'man's interaction with his natural environment' and to 'exceptional combinations of natural and cultural elements' that were previously included in the inscription criteria for natural heritage sites were removed by the World Heritage Committee in 1992 (see Leitão and Badman 2015: 80), which has made it impossible to appropriately acknowledge indigenous peoples' relationship with their lands, territories and resources in the OUV of natural World Heritage sites.

Under the current regulations, indigenous cultural values, including interconnections between nature and culture, only become part of the justification for inscription when they are assessed to be of OUV in their own right, which is not a realistic possibility in the context of many sites. When they are not seen as 'exceptional' or 'unique' by government agencies, ICOMOS and/or the World Heritage Committee or not 'intact' or 'authentic' enough, indigenous cultural values are disregarded when the OUV of World Heritage sites is established. Consequentially, the values, interpretations and priorities of heritage experts, bureaucrats and diplomats assume greater importance than – and in many ways replace and undermine – the values attached to the sites by the traditional owners and custodians, who have inhabited, shaped and protected the respective areas for generations and whose lives and cultures are inseparably connected to them (Disko 2017: 73).

This lack of respect for indigenous peoples' own values attached to their lands and territories not only raises serious questions regarding the validity of the meanings attributed to the respective sites by UNESCO, but can also have significant adverse effects on indigenous peoples' livelihoods and living cultural heritage, as the justification for inscription may heavily affect future conservation strategies and management priorities. According to the Convention's Operational Guidelines, the Statement of OUV adopted at the time of inscription provides 'the basis for the future protection and management of the property', and States must ensure that human use within World Heritage sites 'does not impact adversely on the Outstanding Universal Value' (UNESCO 2016: paras. 155 and 119). If indigenous peoples' perspectives, cultural values and customary roles are not recognized and reflected when the OUV of a site is defined, this may significantly limit their future role in site management and decision-making and can also affect their substantive rights.

The marginalization of indigenous peoples in the management and governance of many 'natural' World Heritage sites is partly a result of this, although in most cases it is a continued legacy of the protected areas in question, which were often declared decades before they were included on the World Heritage List and often have a long history of injustices and human rights violations committed against indigenous peoples. In some World Heritage areas, indigenous peoples are essentially treated as threats to their own territories, and tight restrictions and prohibitions are imposed on indigenous land-use practices such as hunting, gathering, farming or animal husbandry, in violation of indigenous peoples' cultural and subsistence rights. These restrictions and prohibitions have had severe consequences for some indigenous peoples' food security, health and wellbeing and have sometimes come as a direct result of World Heritage status.[5] The World Heritage List also contains several protected areas from which indigenous peoples have been forcibly removed,[6] and, in some cases, this was even done with the intention of facilitating inscription on the World Heritage List as a 'natural site' (Titchen 2002). While the World Heritage Convention's Operational Guidelines recognize since 2005 that 'no area is totally pristine' and that '[h]uman activities, including those of traditional societies and local communities, often occur in natural areas … [and] may be consistent with the Outstanding Universal Value of the area where they are ecologically sustainable' (para. 90), there continues to be a 'misconception that World Heritage nomination requires community presence and rights to be extinguished for site recognition' as a natural World Heritage site (Larsen, Oviedo and Badman 2014: 78).

It is important to note that there are some World Heritage sites that are managed by indigenous peoples themselves or through co-management frameworks that provide for consensus decision-making between conservation agencies and indigenous peoples, and where indigenous peoples' rights are generally respected and fulfilled in conservation strategies.[7] However, these governance frameworks are the result of the domestic policies and laws of the respective State Parties or the political struggles of indigenous peoples, not the guidelines and requirements of the World Heritage Committee.

Recommendations of human rights bodies and mandate holders

Following the adoption of the UNDRIP in 2007, the many concerns voiced by indigenous peoples about violations of their rights in the context of the World Heritage Convention have increasingly drawn the attention of international human rights bodies and mechanisms, most notably the African Commission on Human and Peoples' Rights (ACHPR), the UN Permanent Forum on Indigenous Issues (UNPFII), the UN Expert Mechanism on the Rights of Indigenous Peoples (EMRIP) and the UN Special Rapporteur on the rights of indigenous peoples. The former Special Rapporteur James Anaya remarked in his 2012 report to the UN General Assembly:

> A recurring issue that has come to the attention of the Special Rapporteur relates to the impact on indigenous peoples of … World Heritage sites. […] Indigenous peoples have expressed concerns over their lack of participation in the nomination, declaration and management of World Heritage sites, as well as concerns about the negative impact these sites have had on their substantive rights, especially their rights to lands and resources.
>
> (Anaya 2012: para. 33)

The three above-mentioned UN mechanisms on indigenous rights, as well as the ACHPR, have therefore repeatedly urged the World Heritage Committee to review and revise the Convention's Operational Guidelines, with the effective participation of indigenous peoples, to ensure that the implementation of the Convention is consistent with the UNDRIP, that indigenous rights are respected in the management and governance of World Heritage sites and that no World Heritage sites are established in indigenous peoples' territories without their free, prior and informed consent.[8] They have also repeatedly called for the establishment of a mechanism through which indigenous peoples can effectively provide advice to the Committee. Similar recommendations were made by an international expert workshop on the World Heritage Convention and indigenous peoples held in 2012 in Copenhagen as part of the Convention's fortieth anniversary (Copenhagen Call to Action 2012) and the 2012 World Conservation Congress in Jeju (IUCN 2012).

Additionally, several of the mentioned bodies and mandate holders have emphasized the need for the World Heritage Committee to make efforts to ensure that harms and injustices suffered by indigenous peoples because of conservation activities are redressed in World Heritage sites. For instance, the World Conservation Congress has urged the Committee to work with State Parties to 'establish mechanisms to assess and redress the effects of historic and current injustices against indigenous peoples in existing World Heritage sites' (IUCN 2012), and the Special Rapporteur on the Rights of Indigenous Peoples has underlined the necessity of '[p]roviding redress for past injustices and violations of indigenous peoples' rights to which the establishment of World Heritage sites has contributed' (Anaya 2013).

EMRIP has also made some important observations regarding the World Heritage Committee's differentiation between 'cultural' and 'natural' heritage sites, and its implementation of the concept of 'outstanding universal value'. A 2015 study of EMRIP on the rights of indigenous peoples with respect to their cultural heritage underlines that:

> Heritage policies, programmes and activities affecting indigenous peoples should be based on full recognition of the inseparability of natural and cultural heritage, and the deep-seated interconnectedness of intangible cultural heritage and tangible cultural and natural heritage.
>
> (EMRIP 2015: 20)

In relation to the concept of OUV, the study notes:

> To be included on the World Heritage List, sites must be of 'outstanding universal value', a concept which can lead to management frameworks that prioritize the protection of those heritage aspects at the expense of the land rights of indigenous peoples. As a result, the protection of world heritage can undermine indigenous peoples' relationship with their traditional lands, territories and resources, as well as their livelihoods and cultural heritage, especially in sites where the natural values are deemed to be of outstanding universal value but the cultural values of indigenous peoples are not taken into account.
>
> (EMRIP 2015: 14–15)

EMRIP therefore issued the following advice to the World Heritage Committee:

> The World Heritage Committee should adopt changes to the criteria and regulations for the assessment of 'outstanding universal value' so as to ensure that the values assigned to World Heritage sites by indigenous peoples are fully and consistently recognized as part of their outstanding universal value.
>
> (EMRIP 2015: 23)

Similarly, the 2014 World Parks Congress recommended that:

> The World Heritage Convention should fully and consistently recognize Indigenous Peoples' cultural values as universal, and develop methods for recognition and support for the interconnectedness of natural, cultural, social, and spiritual significance of World Heritage sites, including natural and cultural sites and cultural landscapes.
>
> (IUCN 2014)

These recommendations are not meant to suggest that all heritage sites in indigenous peoples' territories should be considered as having OUV, nor do these recommendations challenge the idea of the World Heritage List as a select list and the prerogative of the World Heritage Committee to make the final judgment on whether a given site merits inscription or not. Rather, they imply concern over the fact that, under the current regulations, the Committee, States and the Advisory Bodies, in the process of declaring World Heritage sites, can (re)define, (re)interpret and (re)invent the significance of indigenous heritage sites without respecting the views of the indigenous peoples concerned and at the expense of their livelihoods and rights to protect, exercise and develop their cultural heritage and expressions (Disko 2017).

Corrective action by the World Heritage Committee

Already in July 2007, before the adoption of the UNDRIP, the World Heritage Committee passed a decision recognizing 'the critical importance of involving indigenous, traditional and local communities in the implementation of the Convention' and adopted a new strategic objective: 'To enhance the role of communities in the implementation of the World Heritage Convention' (Decision 31 COM 13A/13B). However, this did not lead to any changes to the Convention's Operational Guidelines, which continued to be entirely inadequate for ensuring the meaningful participation of indigenous peoples and respect for their rights in the implementation of the Convention, as they merely 'encouraged' State Parties to ensure the participation of 'a wide variety of stakeholders' in the identification, nomination and protection of World Heritage sites and did not contain any references to indigenous peoples (see UNESCO 2013c). Moreover, as evidenced by the repeated complaints received by the three UN mechanisms devoted to indigenous peoples' issues, the rights of indigenous peoples clearly continued to be ignored by the World Heritage Committee in key Convention processes, such as the inscription of sites on the World Heritage List.

In 2010 and 2011, the Permanent Forum on Indigenous Issues, which has a mandate to promote the UNDRIP within the UN system, sent representatives to the sessions of the World Heritage Committee in Brasilia and Paris. The purpose of this participation was to inform the Committee about the numerous concerns related to World Heritage sites that indigenous organizations had brought to the Permanent Forum's attention since its establishment in 2002, to transmit recommendations to the Committee on how to address these concerns and to initiate a dialogue with the Committee on how to implement the UNDRIP in the context of the World Heritage Convention (UNPFII 2010, 2011b). Prior to its 2011 session, the Committee also received a joint submission from a large number of indigenous organizations, deploring the continuous violations of indigenous peoples' right to free, prior and informed consent in the context of World Heritage nominations (IPO/NGO Joint Submission 2011).

These efforts led to the Committee's adoption, on the final day of its 2011 session in Paris, of two decisions that can be seen as an initial response by the Committee to the adoption of the UNDRIP and a first effort to incorporate the internationally recognized rights of indigenous peoples into the implementation of the World Heritage Convention. One of these, Decision 35 COM 12E, encouraged State Parties to '[i]nvolve Indigenous peoples and local communities in decision making, monitoring and evaluation of the state of conservation of the [World Heritage] properties' and to '[r]espect the rights of indigenous peoples when nominating, managing and reporting on World Heritage sites in indigenous peoples' territories'. The other decision, on the celebration of the Convention's 40th Anniversary in 2012, noted that considerations related to indigenous peoples 'should be included in the theme of the anniversary, "World Heritage and Sustainable Development: the Role of Local Communities"' (Decision 35 COM 12D). This decision provided the context for the international expert workshop on the World Heritage Convention and indigenous peoples that took place in September 2012 in Copenhagen as part of the fortieth anniversary. The workshop resulted in a 'Call to Action' addressing the urgent need to make the implementation of the World Heritage Convention consistent with the UNDRIP (Copenhagen Call to Action 2012), as well as a set of proposed amendments to the Operational Guidelines aimed at ensuring that indigenous peoples' free, prior and informed is obtained when parts of their lands or territories are identified, nominated or inscribed as World Heritage sites (ibid.: Annex).

The following year, at the Committee's session in Phnom Penh, the World Heritage Centre mentioned the workshop's Call to Action and proposed amendments in a working document prepared for the agenda item 'Revision of the Operational Guidelines', suggesting that the Committee consider any implications for future revisions of the Guidelines (UNESCO 2013a, 2013d). Following a brief debate about this in a working group during the Phnom Penh session, the Committee decided 'to re-examine the recommendations of this meeting [the Copenhagen workshop] following the results of the discussions to be held by the Executive Board on the [planned] UNESCO Policy on indigenous peoples' (Decision 37 COM 12.II).

Although UNESCO's Executive Board did not hold any discussions on this policy until 2017, the World Heritage Committee at its 2015 session in Bonn, acting on a proposal of the World Heritage Centre inspired by the results of the Copenhagen meeting (UNESCO 2015a: 7), for the first time added some references to indigenous peoples to the Operational Guidelines (while reiterating its decision to re-examine the recommendations of the Copenhagen meeting once the UNESCO Policy on indigenous peoples is adopted, see Decision 39 COM 11). The Guidelines now mention indigenous peoples among the list of potential 'partners' in the protection of World Heritage (para. 40) and encourage States to 'demonstrate, as appropriate, that the free, prior and informed consent of indigenous peoples has been obtained' when nominating sites for World Heritage listing (para. 123).

The adoption of this provision (para. 123) is a positive step towards enhancing respect for the participatory rights of indigenous peoples in the context of World Heritage nominations.[9] However, as the Permanent Forum on Indigenous Issues has criticized, the adopted provision is clearly insufficient, as involving affected indigenous peoples in the nomination process and obtaining their free, prior and informed consents is still not obligatory for State Parties, but merely recommended practice (UNPFII 2015). Moreover, the World Heritage Committee has rejected a proposal that all World Heritage nomination documents be made publicly accessible once UNESCO receives them (see IWGIA 2016: 521). Therefore, unless State Parties publish the nomination documents voluntarily, which they often do not do, they may not be accessible to affected communities until the site has already been inscribed on the World Heritage List. Indigenous peoples have repeatedly criticized this astonishing lack of transparency and access to information as incompatible with their right to participate in decision-making and the principle of free, prior and informed consent (see, e.g., IPO/NGO Joint Submission 2012; EMRIP 2015: para. 51).

The World Heritage Sustainable Development Policy

Another significant step towards enhancing the role of indigenous peoples in the implementation of the World Heritage Convention was taken in November 2015, when the General Assembly of State Parties adopted a comprehensive *Policy for the Integration of a Sustainable Development Perspective into the Processes of the World Heritage Convention* (UNESCO 2015b). Although the possibilities for indigenous peoples to participate in the drafting of the policy were very limited, the group of experts invited to develop the text included a former member of the UNPFII, Myrna Cunningham. The policy contains special sections on 'Respecting, protecting and promoting human rights' and 'Respecting, consulting and involving indigenous peoples and local communities', and emphasizes that '[r]ecognizing rights and fully involving indigenous peoples and local communities, in line with international standards is at the heart of sustainable development' (paras. 20–21). The UNDRIP is highlighted as an example for applicable international standards.

The policy affirms the need to 'view conservation objectives, including those promoted by the World Heritage Convention, within a broader range of economic, social and environmental values and needs encompassed in the sustainable development concept' and calls on State Parties to ensure that 'conservation and management strategies [for World Heritage sites] are aligned with broader sustainable development objectives' (paras. 2, 4). The policy makes it clear that, in order to be compatible with sustainable development objectives, conservation and management strategies must be based on respect for human rights (in particular environmental, social, economic and cultural rights) and should contribute to reducing inequalities, as well as its structural causes, including discrimination and exclusion. They should also contribute to fostering intergenerational equity and justice. The policy further underlines that State Parties should 'recognise the close links and interdependence of biological diversity and local cultures within the socio-ecological systems of many World Heritage properties' in applying a sustainable development perspective (paras. 6–8).

State Parties are therefore urged to adopt a rights-based approach and '[e]nsure that the full cycle of World Heritage processes from nomination to management is compatible with and supportive of human rights' (para. 20). They are also called upon to '[r]ecognise, respect, and include the values as well as cultural and environmental place-knowledge of local communities' in the conservation and management of World Heritage sites (para. 18). In regard to indigenous peoples specifically, the policy provides that State Parties should:

i   Develop relevant standards, guidance and operational mechanisms for indigenous peoples and local community involvement in World Heritage processes;
ii   Ensure adequate consultations, the free, prior and informed consent and equitable and effective participation of indigenous peoples where World Heritage nomination, management and policy measures affect their territories, lands, resources and ways of life;
iii Actively promote indigenous and local initiatives to develop equitable governance arrangements, collaborative management systems and, when appropriate, redress mechanisms;
iv   Support appropriate activities contributing to the building of a sense of shared responsibility for heritage among indigenous people and local communities, by recognizing both universal and local values within management systems for World Heritage properties.

(UNESCO 2015b: para. 22)

While the policy is aimed primarily at the State Parties, it does note that 'the implementation of its provisions will often require the contribution and support of the Secretariat, the Advisory Bodies and other relevant bodies' (para. 12). More-over, in adopting the policy, the General Assembly requested the Secretariat and the Advisory Bodies to develop proposals for changes to the Operational Guide-lines that would translate the principles of the policy into specific operational procedures, indicators for measuring the progress of the policy's implementation, and capacity-building initiatives needed to enable implementation (Decision 20 GA 13).

Conclusion and recommendations

With its emphasis on human rights and indigenous peoples, the World Heritage and Sustainable Development Policy undoubtedly represents a milestone – and hopefully a turning point – in the history of the World Heritage Convention. The adoption of the policy marks the first time that the World Heritage Com-mittee has called on State Parties to adopt a human-rights-based approach to the conservation and management of World Heritage sites, indeed, the first time that the Committee has mentioned human rights in one of its major decisions or policy documents at all.[10] The policy also represents the Committee's most comprehensive and conclusive statement to date on the need to ensure respect for indigenous peoples' rights in World Heritage sites and responds to some of the main concerns that indigenous peoples have voiced regarding the implemen-tation of the Convention. For indigenous peoples, the adoption of the policy is therefore clearly an important, positive step. If followed up by action, it can mark the beginning of a new era in the history and new strategic direction of the Convention, in which greater attention and respect is paid to the rights, values and interests of indigenous peoples and local communities living in or around World Heritage sites.

The Committee's lack of consideration of human rights to date is striking con-sidering that UNESCO's Constitution establishes the furthering of respect for human rights as one of the fundamental purposes of the organization (art. 1) and that UNESCO has a *Strategy on Human Rights*, adopted by the General Confer-ence in 2003, that is aimed at integrating a human rights-based approach into all of UNESCO's programs and activities (UNESCO 2003: paras. 10–15). In light of this, and given the many human rights concerns that continue to be voiced in relation to World Heritage sites, it is clear that in the area of human rights, much remains to be done before the World Heritage Convention can be seen as a 'global leader and standard-setter for best practice', as the State Parties to the Convention hope (UNESCO 2015b: para. 5).

The same can certainly be said in relation to indigenous peoples' rights specifi-cally, if one considers that other conservation organizations and intergovernmen-tal organizations have for years had policies aimed at implementing the UNDRIP within their programs and activities.[11] For instance, the IUCN World Conserva-tion Congress already resolved in 2008 'to apply the requirements of the UNDRIP to the whole of IUCN's Programme and operations', acknowledging that 'injus-tices to indigenous peoples have been and continue to be caused in the name of conservation of nature and natural resources' and recognizing that the UNDRIP is the 'accepted international mechanism for relieving the tremendous pressures and crises faced by indigenous peoples throughout the world as they endeavor to protect indigenous ecosystems, including biological, cultural, and linguistic diversity' (IUCN 2008a, 2008b). Moreover, in 2012, the World Conservation Congress passed a special resolution aimed at ensuring that the principles of the UNDRIP are respected in IUCN's work as an advisory body to the World Heritage Committee, acknowledging that 'indigenous peoples have suffered dispossession and alienation from their traditional lands and resources as a result of the establishment and management of protected areas, including many areas inscribed on the World Heritage List' (IUCN 2012).

Considering UNESCO's mission and its specific mandate within the UN system 'to ensure the preservation and promotion of the fruitful diversity of cultures',[12] it is clear that resolute action by UNESCO and the World Heritage Committee to ensure respect for the rights of indigenous peoples in the implementation of the World Heritage Convention has long been overdue. It is therefore all the more urgent and important for the Committee to elaborate and adopt the necessary changes to the Operational Guidelines to translate the principles of the World Heritage and Sustainable Development Policy into actual operational procedures, as the General Assembly of State Parties has requested it to do (Resolution 20 GA 13). The UNPFII has urged UNESCO to ensure the full and effective participation of indigenous peoples in this process (UNPFII 2015).

As the UNPFII also underlined, the effectiveness of the new World Heritage and Sustainable Development Policy 'will depend on the introduction of specific operational procedures that not only encourage but actually require State Parties to comply with international standards regarding the rights of indigenous peoples' (UNPFII 2015). Particularly, involving affected indigenous peoples in the preparation of nominations and obtaining their free, prior and informed consent before they are submitted must be mandatory requirements for States, not merely recommended practice; the same applies to the effective involvement of indigenous peoples in the conservation, management and monitoring of already listed sites, including all relevant activities of the Advisory Bodies.

Of fundamental importance for ensuring respect for indigenous peoples and their rights in World Heritage sites is also a renewed effort to overcome the divide between nature and culture under the World Heritage Convention, which is incompatible with indigenous peoples' holistic view of their heritage and leads to imbalanced management frameworks and approaches that are not appropriate for protecting indigenous heritage. Such an effort should not only include a reassessment of the World Heritage criteria, but also a reassessment of the way the concept of 'Outstanding Universal Value' is interpreted and applied. While 'recognizing both universal and local values within management systems for World Heritage properties', as the World Heritage and Sustainable Development Policy encourages State Parties to do (para. 22), is no doubt important, the recognition of local values does not replace the need for OUV to reflect indigenous peoples' own values and interpretations of World Heritage sites in their territories. For such reasons, the participants of the 2012 expert workshop in Copenhagen concluded that:

> comprehensive amendments to the Operational Guidelines are also necessary for enabling the World Heritage Convention to become an instrument that appropriately reflects and embraces the worldviews, values and heritage of Indigenous peoples, on an equal footing and with the same emphasis as it reflects and embraces the worldviews, values and heritage of the other peoples of the world. To achieve these ends, the Guidelines must be carefully reviewed, through an open and transparent process with the full and effective participation of Indigenous peoples.
>
> (Copenhagen Call to Action 2012: Annex)

For all these reasons, the World Heritage Committee and UNESCO should seriously consider the following recommendation of the Copenhagen expert workshop in their efforts to implement the World Heritage and Sustainable Development Policy:

> [The World Heritage Committee should] establish an open and transparent process to elaborate, with the direct, full and effective participation of Indigenous peoples, changes to the current procedures and operational guidelines and other appropriate measures to ensure that the implementation of the World Heritage Convention is consistent with the UNDRIP and a human rights-based approach.
>
> (Copenhagen Call to Action 2012)

The establishment, in dialogue with indigenous peoples, of such a process is also warranted in light of the recent adoption of the *UNESCO Policy on Engaging with Indigenous Peoples* by UNESCO's Executive Board (UNESCO 2017) and the World Heritage Committee's decision to re-examine the recommendations of the Copenhagen expert workshop following the adoption of this policy (Decision 37 COM 12.II). UNESCO and the World Heritage Committee can in this way act on their obligation to establish 'ways and means of ensuring participation of indigenous peoples on issues affecting them' (Art. 41, UNDRIP), as well as their conviction expressed in the World Heritage Sustainable Development Policy itself, that 'fully involving indigenous peoples and local communities, in line with international standards is at the heart of sustainable development' (UNESCO 2015b: para. 21).

Additionally, UNESCO should undertake a comprehensive review of World Heritage sites overlapping with indigenous peoples' territories to determine whether their governance arrangements and management frameworks are in line with international standards regarding indigenous rights in order to be able to consistently promote redress for past and present injustices and violations of indigenous rights. Proactively addressing the legacy of human rights violations against indigenous peoples in many World Heritage sites and reshaping the relation with and ensuring respect for indigenous peoples will be crucial for World Heritage to indeed become a 'global leader and standard-setter for best practice' in sustainable development.

Notes

1 A recent example is the nomination of Pimachiowin Aki (Canada), under consideration for inscription in 2018.
2 See Disko (2017: 42) for some examples.
3 For an overview of key concerns, see IWGIA and Forest Peoples Programme 2015.
4 Problems also frequently arise from the Committee's interpretation and application of the conditions of 'integrity' and 'authenticity', which can prevent an appropriate recognition and protection of indigenous peoples' cultural heritage and values. See IPO/NGO Joint Submission (2011: fn 13): 'We are concerned that the concepts of "outstanding universal value", "integrity" and "authenticity" are interpreted and applied in ways that are disrespectful of Indigenous peoples and their cultures, inconsiderate of their circumstances and needs, preclude cultural adaptations and changes, and serve to undermine their human rights'.
5 See, for instance, the case of the Ngorongoro Conservation Area, where a ban on subsistence cultivation imposed in 2009 resulted in a serious situation of hunger and malnutrition that affected most of the area's 70,000 residents and led to the deaths of several people. According to local indigenous organizations, the cultivation ban could be directly traced to the area's World Heritage status and the interventions of UNESCO and IUCN (PINGOs Forum et al. 2012).
6 Some examples are Bwindi Impenetrable National Park (Uganda), Kahuzi-Biega National Park (DR Congo), Thungyai – Huai Kha Khaeng Wildlife Sanctuaries (Thailand), Lake Bogoria National Reserve (Kenya) and Serengeti National Park (Tanzania).
7 Examples include Kakadu National Park (Australia), the Laponian Area (Sweden), SGang Gwaay (Canada) and Taos Pueblo (USA).
8 See, e.g., (UNPFII 2011a; ACHPR 2011; EMRIP 2012, 2015; Anaya 2013; Tauli-Corpuz 2016).
9 In 2016, the World Heritage Committee for the first time referred a nomination back to a State Party in order to allow it to 'resolve rights and livelihood concerns [of indigenous communities] and to achieve a consensus of support for the nomination … that is fully consistent with the principle of free, prior and informed consent' (Decision 40 COM 8.B11, Kaeng Krachan Forest Complex, Thailand). This decision was not least a result of the intervention of both the UN Committee on the Elimination of Racial Discrimination and the Office of the UN High Commissioner for Human Rights (IWGIA 2017: 623–624).
10 Apart from the reference to the rights of indigenous peoples in Decision 35 COM 12E (2011). Notably, human rights considerations are absent from both the *Strategic Action Plan for the Implementation of the World Heritage Convention 2012–2022* (Doc. WHC-11/18.GA/11) and the *Kyoto Vision* adopted at the closing event of the 40th Anniversary of the World Heritage Convention in 2012 (see http://whc.unesco.org/en/news/953).
11 E.g. the International Union for Conservation of Nature (IUCN), the International Fund for Agricultural Development (IFAD) or the Food and Agriculture Organization (FAO).
12 *UNESCO Universal Declaration on Cultural Diversity*, Preamble. According to article 4 of the declaration, 'The defence of cultural diversity … implies a commitment to human rights and fundamental freedoms, in particular the rights of … indigenous peoples'.

References

ACHPR (2011). *Resolution on the Protection of Indigenous Peoples' Rights in the Context of the World Heritage Convention* (African Commission on Human and Peoples' Rights Resolution 197).

Anaya, J. (2011). *Report of the UN Special Rapporteur on the Rights of Indigenous Peoples*. UN Doc. A/66/288.

Anaya, J. (2012). *Report of the UN Special Rapporteur on the Rights of Indigenous Peoples*. UN Doc. A/67/301.

Anaya, J. (2013). *Letter of the UN Special Rapporteur on the Rights of Indigenous Peoples to the World Heritage Centre*, 18 November 2013. Reproduced in UN Doc. A/HRC/25/74, p. 127.

Copenhagen Call to Action (2012). *World Heritage and Indigenous Peoples: A Call to Action*. Adopted by the International Expert Workshop on the World Heritage Convention and Indigenous Peoples, 20–21 September 2012, Copenhagen. Available at: http://whc.unesco.org/en/events/906 (accessed 5 October 2017).

Disko, S. (2017). 'Indigenous cultural heritage in the implementation of UNESCO's World Heritage Convention: Opportunities, obstacles and challenges', in A. Xanthaki et al. (eds), *Indigenous Cultural Heritage: Rights, Debates and Challenges*. Leiden: Brill, pp. 39–77.

EMRIP (2012). *Proposal 9: World Heritage Committee*. UN Doc. A/HRC/21/52, p. 7.

EMRIP (2015). *Promotion and Protection of the Rights of Indigenous Peoples with Respect to Their Cultural Heritage: Study by the Expert Mechanism on the Rights of Indigenous Peoples*. UN Doc. A/HRC/30/53.

IPO/NGO Joint Submission (2011). *Joint Statement on Continuous Violations of the Principle of Free, Prior and Informed Consent in the Context of UNESCO's World Heritage Convention*. Available at: www.forestpeoples.org/sites/fpp/files/publication/2012/04/joint-statement-indigenous-organizations-unesco-2.pdf (accessed 5 October 2017).

IPO/NGO Joint Submission (2012). *Joint Submission on the Lack of Implementation of the UNDRIP in the Context of UNESCO's World Heritage Convention*. Available at: www.forestpeoples.org/sites/fpp/files/publication/2012/05/joint-submission-unpfii.pdf (accessed 5 October 2017).

IUCN (2008a). *Implementing the U.N. Declaration on the Rights of Indigenous Peoples* (World Conservation Congress Resolution 4.052).

IUCN (2008b). *Indigenous Peoples, Protected Areas and Implementation of the Durban Accord* (World Conservation Congress Resolution 4.048).

IUCN (2012). *Implementation of the UNDRIP in the Context of the UNESCO World Heritage Convention* (World Conservation Congress Resolution 5.047).

IUCN (2014). *Promise of Sydney: Innovative Approaches for Change, World Heritage Theme*. Adopted at the World Parks Congress, 2014, Sydney. Available at: www.worldparkscongress.org/about/promise_of_sydney_innovative_approaches.html (accessed 5 October 2017).

IWGIA (2016). *The Indigenous World 2016*. Copenhagen: IWGIA.

IWGIA (2017). *The Indigenous World 2017*. Copenhagen: IWGIA.

IWGIA and Forest Peoples Programme (2015). *Promotion and Protection of the Rights of Indigenous Peoples with Respect to Their Cultural Heritage in the Context of the Implementation of UNESCO's World Heritage Convention* (Submission to EMRIP). Available at: www.ohchr.org/Documents/Issues/IPeoples/EMRIP/CulturalHeritage/IWGIA.pdf (accessed 5 October 2017).

Larsen, P. B., Oviedo, G. and Badman, T. (2014). 'World Heritage, indigenous peoples, communities and rights: An IUCN perspective', in S. Disko and H. Tugendhat (eds), *World Heritage Sites and Indigenous Peoples' Rights*. Copenhagen: IWGIA, pp. 65–82.

Leitão, L. and Badman, T. (2015). 'Opportunities for integration of cultural and natural heritage perspectives under the World Heritage Convention: Towards connected practice', in K. Taylor, A. St Clair and N. Mitchell (eds), *Conserving Cultural Landscapes: Challenges and New Directions*. New York: Routledge, pp. 75–92.

Matsuura, K. (2007). *Message from the Director-General of UNESCO on the Occasion of the Approval of the UNDRIP by the UN General Assembly*. Available at: http://portal.unesco.org/en/ev.php-URL_ID=39604&URL_DO=DO_TOPIC&URL_SECTION=201.html (accessed 5 October 2017).

PINGOs Forum (Pastoralists Indigenous NGOs Forum) et al. (2012). *Hunger in a World Heritage Site? Where Is the World?* Available at: www.iwgia.org/en/tanzania/1788-tanzania-hunger-in-a-world-heritage-site-where-is (accessed 5 October 2017).

Tauli-Corpuz, V. (2016). *Report of the Special Rapporteur of the Human Rights Council on the Rights of Indigenous Peoples*. UN Doc. A/71/229.

Titchen, S. (2002). *Indigenous Peoples and Cultural and Natural World Heritage Sites* (Conference Presentation). Available at: www.dialoguebetweennations.com/N2N/PFII/English/SarahTitchen.htm (accessed 5 October 2017).

UNESCO (2003). *Strategy on Human Rights*. Adopted by the General Conference of UNESCO on 16 October 2003 by 32 C/Resolution 27.

UNESCO (2013a). *Item 12 of the Provisional Agenda: Revision of the Operational Guidelines*. Doc. WHC-13/37.COM/12.

UNESCO (2013b). *Medium-Term Strategy 2014–2021*. Doc. 37 C/4.

UNESCO (2013c). *Operational Guidelines for the Implementation of the World Heritage Convention*. Doc. WHC.13/01.

UNESCO (2013d). *Report of the World Heritage Centre on Its Activities*. Doc. WHC-13/37.COM/5A.

UNESCO (2015a). *Item 11 of the Provisional Agenda: Revision of the Operational Guidelines*. Doc. WHC-15/39.COM/11.

UNESCO (2015b). *Policy Document for the Integration of a Sustainable Development Perspective into the Processes of the World Heritage Convention* (online). Available at: http://whc.unesco.org/en/sustainabledevelopment/ (accessed 2 December 2017).

UNESCO (2016). *Operational Guidelines for the Implementation of the World Heritage Convention*. Doc. WHC.16/01.

UNESCO (2017). *UNESCO Policy on Engaging with Indigenous Peoples*. Doc. 202 EX/9, Annex.

United Nations (1987). *Report of the World Commission on Environment and Development: Our Common Future*. Doc. A/42/427.

United Nations (1992a). *Agenda 21: A Programme for Action for Sustainable Development*. Adopted at the United Nations Conference on Environment and Development, 1992, Rio de Janeiro. Doc. A/CONF.151/26 (Vol. II), Annex.

United Nations (1992b). *Rio Declaration on Environment and Development*. Adopted at the UN Conference on Environment and Development, 1992, Rio de Janeiro. Doc. A/CONF.151/26 (Vol. I).

United Nations (2002). *Plan of Implementation of the World Summit on Sustainable Development* (Johannesburg, 2002). Doc. A/CONF.199/20, Annex.

United Nations (2012). *The Future We Want*. Outcome Document of the Rio+20 Conference on Sustainable Development, 2012, Rio de Janeiro. A/RES/66/288, Annex.

United Nations (2015). *Transforming Our World: The 2030 Agenda for Sustainable Development*. Doc. A/69/L.85, Annex.

UNPFII (2010). *Statement of the Permanent Forum on Indigenous Issues at the 34th Session of the World Heritage Committee*. Available at: http://xa.yimg.com/kq/groups/20674633/27593986/name/UNPFII+Statement+WHC+Final.docx (accessed 5 October 2017).

UNPFII (2011a). *Permanent Forum on Indigenous Issues: Report on the Tenth Session*. Doc. E/2011/43-E/C.19/2011/14.

UNPFII (2011b). *Statement of the Permanent Forum on Indigenous Issues at the 35th Session of the World Heritage Committee*. On file with the authors.

UNPFII (2015). *Statement of the Permanent Forum on Indigenous Issues at the 39th Session of the World Heritage Committee*. Available at: www.iwgia.org/images/newsarchivefiles/1234_Oliver_Loodes_Statement_on_Behalf_of_UNPFII_at_the_39th_session_of_orld_Heritage_Committee.docx (accessed 5 October 2017).

Chapter 8

Human rights, wrongs and sustainable development in World Heritage

Peter Bille Larsen

The new World Heritage and Sustainable Development policy puts an unprecedented explicit emphasis on mainstreaming human rights. In recent years, extensive critical literature and calls for redress have made the trouble in paradise abundantly clear in terms of rights violations, wrongs and discontent in some World Heritage sites. From the disregard of indigenous rights in natural heritage sites across several continents (Disko and Tugendhat 2014) to rights concerns raised in urban and archaeological settings, understanding is growing of human rights as a universal concern (Sinding-Larsen and Larsen 2017). Whereas rights issues in natural and cultural heritage may differ, there are also common experiences of displacement and dispossession. Rights to decent housing are often under threat by escalating price levels, gentrification or event resettlement in urban heritage areas, just as land and resources may become inaccessible due to enforced conservation measures and the fencing off of nature conservation areas.

Does the new policy offer the long-awaited reform and redress of this social deficit, or, conversely, the usual empty words that permeate heritage discourse, while hollowing out action opportunities for social empowerment and equity? The question is bewildering given the multiple agendas and policies as well as the many institutional layers between international mechanisms and reality on the ground. The answers, in turn, have important implications for State Party responses and civil society engagement.

As the author was closely involved in the initial stages of the drafting process of the policy, a critical perspective is now warranted to determine how and what such rights commitments actually transform practice. What arguments and evidence are there to consider whether the sustainable development policy merely cements a fundamentally peppered-up business as usual scenario with social equitable language or whether it in fact is leading to change? While the short history of subsequent World Heritage Committee meeting decisions since 2015 does not yet offer adequate time to judge progress, the initial celebratory honeymoon period is arguably over. There is today sufficient understanding prompting the need for urgent reform of World Heritage mechanisms. The first part of this chapter briefly introduces wording on human rights in the World Heritage and Sustainable Development policy and offers a reflexive analysis of the process leading to its adoption. The second part seeks to explore the relevance of critical stances potentially challenging the value and significance of this policy change. The final section reflects upon outstanding challenges and possible implications from a policy and practice perspective.

Key parameters of the new paradigm

At first sight, the new policy offers an unprecedented policy shift towards the mainstreaming of human rights principles and practice. State Parties are encouraged to uphold, respect and contribute to the implementation of the full range of international human rights standards and ensure that the full cycle of World Heritage processes from nomination to management is compatible with and supportive of human rights. The policy also encourages a rights-based approach, which promotes World Heritage properties as exemplary places for the application of the highest standards for the respect and realization of human rights. It equally speaks of standards and safeguards, guidance tools and operational mechanisms for assessment, nomination, management, evaluation and reporting processes compatible with an effective rights-based approach for both existing and potential new properties. Further language on indigenous and local community rights contribute to the comprehensive nature of the shift.

Much effort in wider sustainability conversations is about demonstrating the linkages between human rights and Sustainable Development Goals (SDGs) underlining shared grounds such as universal coverage and 'leaving no one behind'. Compared to the difficulties faced by human rights activists in wider sustainability politics, the specific World Heritage process eventually, it could be argued, has led to the formulation of major rights mainstreaming commitments. The World Heritage community has arguably shift from initial timid engagements with rights language (see discussion in Logan 2012) towards more explicit attention. In short, the language is much stronger and more explicit than the SDG goals with potentially massive implications for both new sites and legacy issues present in the existing 1,073 sites making up the World Heritage list. Despite imperfections and gaps in terms of rights language used (Morawa and Zalazar 2018), the policy commitments nonetheless represent a quantum shift for practice *if* implemented *à la lettre*. Furthermore, there is a shared emphasis on principles such as accountability, participation and non-discrimination, but equally so on the fundamental question of actual tools and mechanisms for implementation.

The question now is how to decrypt the actual significance of the new rights agenda recognizing how implementation is caught between normative muscle or the risks of down-sized normalization. On the one hand, it appears as an ambitious agenda for a challenged Convention with substantial legacy issues and, furthermore, at odds with growing trends of politicization (Meskell 2012). On the other hand, there is clearly a growing momentum to address the social deficit experienced in both natural and cultural sites across the globe. However, before discussing this in more detail, it is worthwhile to briefly describe the context for the articulation of rights in the sustainable development policy.

Recognizing diversity: a victory for weak expertise?

How did the policy, in the first place, result in such relatively strong wording on human rights mainstreaming? Where expertise in recent years has received a somewhat bad press as the incarnation of Western conservation hegemony (Smith 2006), this distinct process serves as a lesson on a different point, namely how expertise may also occupy a 'weak' positionality used to promote change and reform. In contrast with the view that expertise processes narrow down partici-pation to a few voices, it may, alternatively also be understood as an important interstitial space of resistance. The majority of 'experts' involved in the UNESCO policy process were not *per se* part of the system, but largely sought to chal-lenge trends of heritage being co-opted or side-lined by politics and short term profit-seeking. What is striking is thus not the grand ideals or the presence of a 'dominant' expert discourse, but rather the kinds of subtle and serendipitous techno-politics involved in crafting political alternatives to the deep challenges faced in the Convention.

At first sight, the process of developing the policy appeared much like many other expert-driven processes that have largely characterized UNESCO heritage deliberations since the early days. The drafting process was led by UNESCO civil servants, who identified experts responsible for contributing with draft language for a series of policy areas (see chapter by Boccardi and Scott, this volume). Yet beneath the apparent surface of strong expertise and bureaucratic power were equally signs of weakness in the bigger context. The policy work was under-taken on a voluntary basis. Lack of funding had long prevented the Secretariat from bringing people together. Background studies and much coordination were undertaken by interns and personally dedicated Secretariat staff. The expert con-sultation meetings relied on extra-budgetary means with additional funding from the Brandenburg Technical University at Cottbus, Germany, for an initial meeting and Vietnam as a State Party for the consultation meetings with practitioners in Ninh Binh.

The process was like so many other international processes framed as imple-menting a mandate established by a Committee decision. 'You are this group that the Committee has requested', as it was mentioned during the introductory state-ment of the first consultation (personal notes by the author).

While the authority of expert voice was confirmed, there were also concerns that strong rights language might be rejected given prior Committee responses to strengthen consultation mechanisms for indigenous peoples (Disko and Tugend-hat 2013). Yet, on the other hand, it was also noted how the Committee had agreed with proposed approaches to craft the policy, the methodology and human rights as one of the dedicated policy themes. Furthermore, the inclusion of rights language was carefully massaged to 'fit' by noting it as a fundamental and overarching principle suggested for Sustainable Development. By using language of harmonizing, updating and integrating decisions already adopted, a balancing act to maintain legitimacy took place. While such massaging is at times shunned by academics as political correctness, it is also part of pragmatic techno-politics in the international governance arena (Larsen 2013). As noted during initial discussions:

> World Heritage was built to conserve OUV, there were no references to human rights and gender. Yet, in the 21st century we are compelled to consider these issues in whatever we do. World Heritage is part of the United Nations. It is bound by definition to include these standards.
>
> (personal notes by the author)

In addition, interaction with a selected group of practitioners in Ninh Binh, Vietnam, allowed for testing ideas and language with site managers and heritage experts from Asia, Latin America and Africa. Consultations revealed divergent perspective on notions of rights, heritage and whether or not to conceptualize heritage as a resource, reflecting fundamental questions about the roles of the market, public authorities and society. Such questions revealed how rights concerns were, indeed, at the heart of responding to contemporary heritage dynamics.

Ultimately, a draft policy, revised after a round of State Party comments, was tabled with most of its initial rights language intact and adopted during the General Conference. Despite initial fears that State Parties would reject human rights language, there was an almost conspicuous absence of outright attempts to block it. Mali as a State Party had in its written comments prior to the meeting suggested to remove or minimize the use of the term indigenous peoples 'to avoid confusion'. France, in turn, had questioned the literal translation of community as '*communauté*', but also stressed how its constitutional principles of unity, indivisibility, equality and non-discrimination prevented it from recognizing the existence of peoples other than the nation. Nor was France in a position to recognize collective rights 'given that human rights are individual rights', as it was noted in a parenthesis (UNESCO 2015).

Notwithstanding such reservations, the relatively smooth adoption of the text was perceived as a small, but not insignificant, victory in the bigger minefield of World Heritage policy and practice. It was arguably more than simply 'the integration of a sustainable development perspective'. Active involvement of the Secretariat, Advisory Bodies and individual experts allowed for the pooling of multiple sustainability topics unlikely to be adopted on a stand-alone basis. As a bundle, however, a way was found into the incontestable terrain of sustainability. Yet, what informed and shaped the kinds of rights language listed in the policy?

What rights language? Filling the gap

Complementing more comprehensive analysis (Larsen 2017), the underlying premise informing the initial draft's language involved 'filling the gap' and harmonizing policy terminology. This 'theory of change' was largely based on the sheer absence of human rights language in the 1972 Convention. In addition to a decade-old call for the mainstreaming of human rights in the UN and UNESCO in particular (UNESCO 2003), prior to the World Heritage and Sustainable Development policy process, the 'Our Common Dignity' initiative coordinated by ICOMOS Norway had supported expert meetings and a first side-event on rights-based approaches at the World Heritage Committee in Doha (Ekern et al. 2012; Larsen, Oviedo and Sinding-Larsen 2014). Amund Sinding-Larsen, the coordinator of the Our Common Dignity Advisory Body initiative was subsequently invited to join the sustainable development policy process (whom I would later replace). This initiative sought 'to learn from practice' and had begun tabling proposals and new language on rights-based approaches. Such work was further fuelled by civil society critique of Advisory Bodies and UNESCO in their handling of several nomination cases overlapping with indigenous lands (Disko and Tugendhat 2014). Cases such as the rights of the Endorois in Lake Bogoria, Kenya, illustrated how indigenous rights, including international jurisprudence and reporting, could be easily ignored by World Heritage processes. Whereas the Kenya Lake System in the Great Rift Valley was inscribed in 2011, a 2009 decision by the African Commission on Human and Peoples' Rights to recognize rights of ownership, access and compensation arrangements remained unsettled, leading to both case-specific protests and broader calls for reform of the World Heritage system (Disko and Tugendhat 2014: 29).

In 2011, IUCN requested me to undertake a rapid view of the organization's nomination evaluation practice (Larsen 2012b), presumably due to previous work on protected areas, social safeguards and rights (Larsen 2006; Borrini-Feyerabend, Kothari and Oviedo 2004; Larsen and Springer 2008). This first review, which eventually led the IUCN to include a new section on community and rights in their evaluation format, was later complemented by discussions with the two other Advisory Bodies (Larsen 2012a) linking up with the Our Common Dignity initiative (Ekern et al. 2012; Sinding-Larsen and Larsen 2017). Conversations and interviews were undertaken with Advisory Body staff, but also individual experts and others working with the Advisory Bodies. These conversations made it clear that the World Heritage field, despite the statutory UNESCO commitments to human right was fraught with apprehension and trepidation. Yet, it was also clear that notions of human rights and dignity offered language to raise collective aspirations for social justice (Merry et al. 2010). This emerged both from initiatives like the Our Common Dignity initiative as well as rights claims and wake-up calls from indigenous representatives and support groups, such as the Indigenous Peoples of Africa Co-ordinating Committee, Forest Peoples Programme and the International Work Group for Indigenous Affairs. Equally important in creating momentum were a number of contentious nomination cases and international processes that raised concerns about indigenous rights being violated. In this sense, a form of convergence built legitimacy of rights concerned emerged through the activities of a relatively heterogeneous group of concerned officials, experts and activists engaging informally in the margins of the state-driven process of World Heritage to address the social deficit. While the space did not converge as such, both were contributing factors in terms of establishing the value conflict involved and the need for action. The very name 'Our Common Dignity' signalled commonality and the quest for a more just system in general, whereas many of the indigenous rights claims concerned specific grievances and a human rights agenda grounded in the affirmation of indigenous collective rights (Disko and Tugendhat 2013; Disko and Tugendhat 2014). It involved claims to indigenous rights such as the right to Free, Prior and Informed Consent, a right which was eventually adopted in the Operational Guidelines in 2015. From their perspective, rights were not merely a matter of values, but one of long overdue legal obligations and required changes in order to comply with international human rights standards.

The development of the World Heritage and Sustainable Development policy offered an important outlet and window of opportunity to table such proposals. It was also clear from the two consultation meetings that human rights required both specific attention, while being retained as a cross-cutting dimension of relevance to wider policy formulation in the fields of social and economic inclusion, gender and indigenous peoples. This dual thinking, despite suggestions to merge the two, was ultimately retained.

Progressive politics or pacification?

Do human rights principles offer potential for progressive politics of social justice, or are they rather at risk of instrumentalized pacification and subject to politics (Santos 2002)? Parts of the social sciences have grown increasingly sceptical about the emancipatory promises of human rights discourse. On the one hand, human rights are not immune to bureaucratization, or instrumentality, easily putting in jeopardy promises of social improvement. On the other hand, they can hardly be considered panacea to the panoply of social problems encountered in the heritage field (Logan 2007). This not only concerns the relative marginal role of cultural rights, but also concerns a wider range of ambiguities. Ranging from critical stances pointing to risks of fundamentalism (Hastrup 2003), feminist critique of narrow Western rights concepts (Merry 2006) or lack of trust in the UNESCO system (Horowitz 2016), anthropological critique has taken many paths since its initial calls for relativism (AAA 1947). Several criticisms have been waged about the relevance and utility of human rights language and approaches to resolve social justice concerns in the heritage field (Baird 2014; Meskell 2010). Baird, for example, speaks of the human rights approach as 'overreaching' and at risk of suffering from bureaucratic constraint, token participation and being out of touch with local concerns and values (2014: 148–149). Does the new policy language on human rights, indeed, merely rehash already established international language, while pre-empting social critique without any real teeth and consequences for practice? While there is a risk of local movements taking the social justice agenda within the World Heritage system for granted (Horowitz 2016), one should not lose sight of rights-based approaches as work in progress. Yet, it is also clear that there 'unfortunate tendency to shoehorn all important social goods into a human rights framework' (Donnelly 2005: 10). Human rights may appear as a false totality (Baxi 2012: 274), constituted in practice by a variety of normative texts. Nonetheless, not all social justice issues are resolved through human rights language, and further work is needed to harness pluralist approaches ("Caux Call for Action" 2016).

The issue I would argue here is not about whether or not human rights are relevant in the World Heritage field. While one may engage in a philosophical debate about whether human rights are a good approach to promote social justice, a more grounded route of investigation is also possible. Rights *are* present in today's world and thus whether *human* rights are addressed explicitly or are integral to World Heritage nomination processes and management practice is a real question. Furthermore, the adoption of human rights policy is not limited to the West, but arguably a highly globalized phenomenon. Human rights instruments are ratified and often grounded politically, even constitutionally, across the globe. While there are exceptions and reservations, this already justifies studying human rights implications as a matter of fact – even without explicit heritage attention. As Engle (2001: 559) argues: 'The question is not now, nor was it ever, whether to be for or against human rights. Rather, the debate has always been over the definition of those rights' (Engle 2001: 559). We might go even further here and argue that the debate is not merely about the definition of rights, but understanding their socially and politically grounded practice.

Asserting the relevance of human rights standards in the delineation of rights and responsibilities is thus at stake here alongside whether or not the implications are taken into account. If, indeed, human rights in heritage form part of the language and political repertoire for rethinking socially just and responsive heritage policy and practice, careful attention needs to be directed towards understanding the contested field of rights. An important question is thus whether a 'particular claim to justice actually contributes to the remaking of the world, or whether the rights-thinking implied actually distorts the nature of social and individual suffering' (Hastrup 2003: 310). This entails a confrontation between 'emergent cultures of rights and the entrenched culture of power' (Baxi 1995: 6). As Freeman has argued, institutionalization of human rights may not lead to better protection 'but to their protection in a form that is less threatening to the existing system of power' (Freeman 2002: 85). His point is exactly that institutionalization is a social process 'involving power, and that it should be analysed and not assumed to be beneficial' (ibid: 85). Critical social theory, it follows, offers potentially crucial insights (Cowan 2006). Anthropological engagement in terms of urgency, rescue and recuperation of heritage may be questioned in terms of essentialism (Berliner and Bortolotto 2013), just as defence of human rights can be challenged for its simplistic assumptions and even fundamentalism (Hastrup 2003). Neither argument, however, need provoke abstaining from engagement with heritage conservation nor agendas of social justice. Rather, they can deepen the nature of analysis.

Whereas critics may challenge the legalistic or narrow scope of rights, many indigenous rights claimants, on the contrary, champion the legal clarity of rights vs. vagueness of the stakeholder concept. It is also clear that many indigenous and local communities such as the Endorois in Kenya, Aboriginal peoples in Australia (Logan 2013) and the Karen in Thailand (Larsen and Buckley 2017) have used international human rights law to build legitimacy around claims in World Heritage processes. Such recasting of heritage effects through human rights law may be read as an 'act of instituting it and of demarcating right from wrong' (Hastrup 2003: 316). Human rights offer a unique basis of legitimation in the international arena (Habermas and Rehg 1998), particularly clear in global processes, a standard reference point – of highlighting social justice concerns as more than just a 'recommended' obligation. While rights language in such issues is used to catapult social justice issues into wider deliberations, the implications of this can – and needs to – be studied and problematized. What merits attention is thus *how* such issues are (un)identified, (un)addressed and (not) taken into account. The name of the game, in other words, is one of translation, vernacularization and concretization (Larsen 2018), not merely through promoting universalist practice, but granting universalist space for diversity.

Rights-based approaches may pass through renegotiations of focus as value systems, governance practices or bureaucratic mechanisms (Merry et al. 2010). The World Heritage and Sustainable Development policy includes a mix of this from referencing international human rights standards towards suggesting new safeguard approaches and operational mechanisms. The devil is, of course, in the detail in terms of how values are embedded or not between regulatory and emancipatory politics (Santos 2002). This raises specific questions about whether and how actual safeguards are put into practice or operational mechanisms modified. For hardened World Heritage practitioners, progress needs to be measured through concrete small steps, and the specific changes, not normative grand-standing. Systems are no more perfect then the practices that constitute their everyday social realities of heritage designation and management. Within competing rights regimes, state affirmation and legality in order to demonstrate effective protection of OUV far too easily trump the realization of human rights and social justice. Equally important are the risks of heritage being captured by massive development schemes with only scant attention to redistributive mechanisms and lost opportunities for local initiatives.

Up against such trends, the rights-based framework offers an alternative basis for the debate, planning and transformation of heritage management, as it also raises fundamental value debates about what matters in the first place. Parts of our work under the Our Common Dignity initiative have not only involved asserting complementary social values, but also stressing the multiple practical entry points for reforming the World Heritage system in terms of where and how rights are being considered (Sinding-Larsen and Larsen 2017). Key arguments, in this respect, have involved shifting from individual sites complaints towards addressing the functioning of the system as a whole.

Uncertainty

What we need to address as social scientists is not simply what ought to be in terms of more equitable heritage practice, but, as a first step, to shed light on how new rights language and social justice principles operate in practice (Cowan 2006). Are they real safeguards, voluntary measures or just aspirational statements without any teeth?

If the Sustainable Development policy aims to render human rights commitments explicit as a legal obligations, entitlements and responsibility rather than a remote possibility and voluntary initiative, our research equally demonstrates major discrepancies between these new aspirations and current practice (Larsen 2017; Sinding-Larsen and Larsen 2017). What constitutes human rights is not only perceived differently (Dembour 2010), rights clearly also appear and are addressed in different ways during the World Heritage Committee (Larsen and Buckley 2017). While some attempts are being made to raise the human rights flag in specific nominations and state of conservation reports (ibid), this is yet to be done systematically and many significant rights concerns remain ignored. Thus, 2015 evaluations, for example, led to Committee requests for rights action in the case of the Karen in the Kaeng Krachan Forest Complex nomination, whereas unresolved customary rights issues of ethnic minorities in Phong Nha Ke Bang remain unattended to (Larsen 2018). Uneven treatment of rights concerns is today common-place and demonstrates the social complexity involved.

Furthermore, efforts to provide people on the ground clear answers about everyday troubles – and opportunities – experienced in World Heritage are incipient and outdated compared to similar international processes. Perhaps the most striking feature of personal conversations held with indigenous and local community leaders making the effort to reach the World Heritage Committee meetings since 2013 have been the high degrees of uncertainty they expressed – uncertainty about whether they might risk relocation, uncertainty about whether their concerns about livelihoods and legacies of ignored cultural values would be heard, uncertainty about whether social promises made by State Parties would be kept. Yet, perhaps even more dramatic was the common uncertainty about social impacts in the first place.

Such uncertainties are not simply a sad coincidence or collateral damage in the name of World Heritage, but rather symptomatic of the lamentable state of World Heritage standards, in general, and the social sphere in specific. World Heritage standards do not currently offer adequate safeguards, but appear as negotiable markers in the landscape. Indeed, if anything, uncertainty characterizes how human rights issues are currently identified, claims perceived and responses crafted. Whether or not and how human rights are being addressed may vary from case to case and largely depends on attention from and capacity of civil society to trigger international attention (Larsen 2017). Rights dynamics in far too many cases, however, remain in a limbo more likely to be shaped by power and profit than by attention to people and poverty. Exceptions, fortunately, also demonstrate that socially responsible designation and remediation processes are possible. Cases of sustained Advisory Body and Committee dialogue with State Parties such as Kenya and Thailand have demonstrated the leverage of global mechanisms to draw attention to unresolved rights claims. In both cases, World Heritage processes have led to the renegotiation of management arrangements.

Building a rights-based World Heritage system is therefore not utopian, but a matter of political and institutional will and awareness. While there is growing understanding and goodwill, the institutional set-up urgently needs to bring in rights and social equity matters to the core of World Heritage practice. In this light, a major next step suggested by the Our Common Dignity process consists of recognizing human rights and social equity as part of the management pillar in the review of nominations and State of Conservation reporting (Sinding-Larsen and Larsen 2017). At the core of the quest is broadening the gaze from a narrow OUV-centred perspective towards one that takes the policy commitment to other social and environmental criteria seriously in the design and reform of World Heritage properties.

Will the 2017 Committee call for State Parties to mainstream 'sustainable development principles into their national processes' (Decision:41 COM 5C) lead to more systematic attention to rights concerns? While it does offer the hook on which to raise such concerns, more systematic engagement in reforming World Heritage processes throughout Operational Guidelines and the full cycle at the international level is needed to allow for more even national processes. There are now several follow-up measures in the pipeline by both the Secretariat and the Advisory Bodies such as training and awareness-raising, yet it remains to be seen to what extent efforts will be concentrated on picking low-hanging fruits such as documenting existing good practice or whether thorny concerns will also be taken on.

In a system characterized by uneven regulatory practice and a constant push to bypass standards, incremental small steps are more likely than systematic change. This raises the question whether efforts by indigenous peoples and local communities facing ongoing nomination processes or attempting to rework heritage legacies will be met with better conditions. For more ambitious social agendas to materialize, this will likely require clear-cut shifts in the Operational Guidelines supplemented by so-called upstream support. The latter term is used to describe early support efforts by the Secretariat and the Advisory Bodies to offer carrots for State Parties to improve practice rather than only present sticks *a posteriori*.

A basic condition for levelling the playing field will involve the recognition of human rights and social equity as governing principles of management is fleshed out in the Operational Guidelines. Considering that the Operational Guidelines *de facto* constitute policy in the World Heritage arena, more specific references to a human-rights-based approach are warranted. Secondly, it is critical to spell out the responsibility of State Parties to uphold their commitments to international human rights standards in key guidance Operational Guidelines concerned with nominations, performance indicators in management and State of Conservation reporting. In the meantime, much can of course be done by coalitions of community representatives, NGOs and experts to engage in transformative rights practice at different moments of the World Heritage cycle.

Concluding remarks

Is the new rights component merely a normalizing upgrade of policy aspirations to fit into the global international order and to sustain heritage business as usual, or can it genuinely contribute towards change and improvements for local inhabitants? Compared to other social justice agendas, the 'Our Common Dignity' initiative signalled not only a value debate, but also a pragmatic call for shifts in terms of nomination and management standards to deal with the legacy of wrongs.

The importance of lifting an issue like human rights out of obscurity through explicit wording is potentially substantial. It is today perfectly possible to imagine human rights concerns being addressed systematically in nomination, management, assessment and monitoring processes. It increasingly happens in some cases and there are no technical hindrances for a World Heritage system geared towards identifying unresolved rights grievances making use of convening power and the nomination momentum and financial backing to engage rights-holders in crafting socially responsive solutions. Furthermore, Advisory Bodies and other civil society organizations appear to be stepping up action to implement new rights commitments.

Yet, there is also a risk that human rights commitments are gladly forgotten when the going gets tough or reduced to procedural matters and boxes to ticked off. There is a genuine risk that the new policy merely serves to assert shared values, securing compliance at the level of expressed policy principles with little change in practice and action on the ground. Social standards can be undone, contained, or simply left in the archives of forgotten decisions for reasons all too evident. What are, for example, the chances that contentious historical legacies remain ignored if policy commitments are limited to aspirational statements? Hoping for immediate change to long-buried legacy matters may possibly remain wishful thinking.

What is clear is that a real rights filter to the design and management of World Heritage is yet to be applied systematically. As monitoring and accountability mechanisms remain in their infancy on other criteria than OUVs, the introduction of additional social and environmental performance standards is somewhat of a novelty. Yet, if World Heritage is recognized as a slow-moving train by sheer definition (covering the whole world and more than one thousand sites) then change cannot be expected overnight. Furthermore, while wheels of reform and incremental changes may be set in motion, the new sustainability principles are yet to offer navigable roadmaps for State Parties. Whereas the policy affirms international human rights standards, this is yet to be translated into a clear site of minimum standards for properties to enter the select club of World Heritage.

It is, however, not good enough to assume or hope for the positive spill-over effects to resolve human rights concerns and wider social justice issues. Real substantial and systemic change is required to translate policy into game-changing behaviour and actual change on the ground. While it is impossible to predict social change, human rights-based offer a basic framework for re-affirming both procedural principles as well as substantive matters to include in planning frameworks in far more explicit terms. Finally, we need to ask whether other and further social justice agendas are needed and required. The answer, found in the other chapters of this volume, is quite clearly affirmative. The need to rethink the redistribution of costs and benefits, address matters of poverty, social inclusion and gender inequalities, requires both human rights and alternative languages. Indeed, if we recognize that rights may be circumvented and constrain as much as empower, multiple repertoires of social justice are needed. Given the crippled and chronically underfinanced World Heritage system, societal engagement and legitimacy is today primordial. Rights-based approaches may very well form part of the bulwark needed to counter the current onslaught on World Heritage by extractive industries, commercial operations or blind nationalism.

References

AAA (1947). 'Statement on human rights', *American Anthropologist*, 49.

Baird, M. F. (2014). 'Heritage, human rights, and social justice', *Heritage & Society*, 7, 139–155.

Baxi, U. (1995). *Human Rights Education: The Promise of the Third Millenium*. New Delhi: Zakir Husain College.

Baxi, U. (2012). 'Changing paradigms of human rights', in J. Eckert, B. Donahoe, S. Christian et al. (eds), *Law against the State: Ethnographic Forays into Law's Transformations*. Cambridge: Cambridge University Press.

Berliner, D. and Bortolotto, C. (2013). 'Introduction. Le monde selon l'UNESCO', *Gradhiva*, 18, 4–21.

Borrini-Feyerabend, G., Kothari, A. and Oviedo, G. (2004). *Indigenous and Local Communities and Protected Areas: Towards Equity and Enhanced Conservation Guidance on Policy and Practice for Co-Managed Protected Areas and Community Conserved Areas*. Gland: World Commission on Protected Areas, IUCN.

Caux Call for Action (2016). *Caux Call for Action on Rights-Based Approaches in World Heritage*. Caux, Switzerland (January 19).

Cowan, J. K. (2006). 'Culture and rights after culture and rights', *American Anthropologist*, 108.

Dembour, M. B. (2010). 'What are human rights? Four schools of thought', *Human Rights Quarterly*, 32, 1–20.

Disko, S. and Tugendhat, H. (2013). *International Expert Workshop on the World Heritage Convention and Indigenous Peoples, 20–21 September 2012 – Copenhagen, Denmark*. Copenhagen: IWGIA.

Disko, S. and Tugendhat, H. (2014). *World Heritage Sites and Indigenous Peoples' Rights*. Copenhagen: IWGIA.

Donnelly, J. (2005). 'Human rights', in 23 wpn (ed). Available at: www.du.edu/gsis/hrhw/working/2005/23-donnelly-2005.pdf (accessed 1 March 2016).

Ekern, S., Logan, W., Sauge, B. and Sinding-Larsen, A. (2012). 'Human rights and world heritage: Preserving our common dignity through rights-based approaches', *International Journal of Heritage Studies*, 18(3), 213–225.

Engle, K. (2001). 'From skepticism to embrace: Human rights and the American Anthropological Association from 1947–1999', *Human Rights Quarterly*, 23, 536–559.

Freeman, M. (2002). *Human Rights: An Interdisciplinary Approach*. Cambridge: Polity.

Habermas, J. and Rehg, W. (1998). 'Remarks on legitimation through human rights', *Philosophy & Social Criticism*, 24, 157–171.

Hastrup, K. (2003). 'Violence, suffering and human rights: Anthropological reflection', *Anthropological Theory*, 3, 309–323.

Horowitz, L. (2016). 'Rhizomic resistance meets arborescent assemblage: UNESCO World Heritage and the disempowerment of indigenous activism in New Caledonia', *Annals of the American Association of Geographers*, 106, 167–185.

Larsen, P. B. (2006). *Reconciling Indigenous Peoples and Protected Areas: Rights, Governance and Equitable Cost and Benefit Sharing, Report Presented to the CBD COP 8*. The World Conservation Union, IUCN.

Larsen, P. B. (2012a). *Advisory Body Evaluations of World Heritage Nominations in Relation to Community and Rights Concerns, Independent Assessment, a Discussion Paper*. IUCN, ICOMOS Norway and ICCROM.

Larsen, P. B. (2012b). *IUCN, World Heritage and Evaluation Processes Related to Communities and Rights: An Independent Review*. Gland, Switzerland: IUCN World Heritage Programme.

Larsen, P. B. (2013). 'The politics of technicality: Guidance culture in environmental governance and the international sphere', in B. Müller (ed), *The Gloss of Harmony: The Politics of Policy Making in Multilateral Organisations*. London: Pluto Press.

Larsen, P. B. (2017). *World Heritage and Human Rights: Lessons from the Asia Pacific and the Global Arena*. London: Earthscan/Routledge.

Larsen, P. B. (2018). 'World heritage and ethnic minority rights in Phong Nha Ke Bang, Vietnam: Domesticating cosmopolitan assemblages', in P. B. Larsen (ed), *World Heritage and Human Rights: Lessons from the Asia Pacific and the Global Arena*. London: Earthscan/Routledge.

Larsen, P. B. and Buckley, K. (2017). 'The World Heritage Committee and human rights: Learning from event ethnography', in P. B. Larsen (ed), *World Heritage and Human Rights: Lessons from the Asia Pacific and the Global Arena*. London: Earthscan/Routledge.

Larsen, P. B., Oviedo, G. and Sinding-Larsen, A. (2014). *Building Capacity to Support Rights-Based Approaches in the World Heritage Convention: Learning from Practice*. IUCN, ICCROM and ICOMOS.

Larsen, P. B. and Springer, J. (2008). *Mainstreaming WWF Principles on Indigenous Peoples and Conservation in Project and Programme Management*. Gland, CH and Washington, DC, US: WWF.

Logan, W. (2007). 'Closing pandora's box: Human rights conundrums in cultural heritage protection', in H. Silverman and D. F. Ruggles (eds), *Cultural Heritage and Human Rights*. New York: Springer.

Logan, W. (2012). 'Cultural diversity, cultural heritage and human rights: Towards heritage management as human rights-based cultural practice', *International Journal of Heritage Studies*, 18(3), 231–244.

Logan, W. (2013). 'Australia, indigenous peoples and World Heritage from Kakadu to Cape York: State party behaviour under the World Heritage Convention', *Journal of Social Archaeology*, 13, 153–176.

Merry, S. E. (2006). 'Transnational human rights and local activism: Mapping the middle', *American Anthropologist*, 108, 38–51.

Merry, S. E., Levitt, P., Rosen, M. Ş. et al. (2010). 'Law from below: Women's human rights and social movements in New York City', *Law & Society Review*, 44, 101–128.

Meskell, L. (2010). 'Human rights and heritage ethics', *Anthropological Quarterly*, 83.

Meskell, L. (2012). 'The rush to inscribe: Reflections on the 35th session of the World Heritage Committee, UNESCO Paris, 2011', *Journal of Field Archaeology*, 37, 145–151.

Morawa, A. and Zalazar, G. (2018). 'The Interrelationship of the World Heritage Convention and International Human Rights Law: A Preliminary Assessment and Outlook', in P. B. Larsen (ed.), World Heritage and human rights: lessons from the Asia Pacific and the Global Arena. London: Earthscan/ Routledge.

Santos, B. D. S. (2002). 'Toward a multicultural conception of human rights', in B. Hernández-Truyol (ed), *Moral Imperialism: A Critical Anthology*. New York: New York University Press.

Sinding-Larsen, A. and Larsen, P. B. (2017). Our common dignity initiative: Rights-based approaches in World Heritage-Taking stock and looking forward (advisory body activities between 2011 and 2016): An advisory body report. IUCN, ICOMOS and ICCROM. Oslo: ICOMOS Norway.

Smith, L. (2006). *The Uses of Heritage*. London and New York: Routledge.

UNESCO (2003). *UNESCO Strategy on Human Rights*. Paris: UNESCO.

UNESCO (2015). *World Heritage and Sustainable Development: State Parties' Comments to the Draft Policy for the Integration of a Sustainable Development Perspective into the Processes of the World Heritage Convention (Provided by the Deadline of 31 August 2015), and Secretariat's Responses*. WHC-15/20.GA/13, Paris. Available at: http://whc.unesco.org/en/sessions/20GA/documents/.

Chapter 9

Heritage, Sustainable Development and the achievement of peace and security in our world

Ambitions and constraints

William Logan

It is self-evident that the possibilities for sustainable development and the sustainability of the world's cultural and natural heritage are undermined by war, civil conflict and other forms of violence including terrorist attacks on civilians. Since the World Heritage Convention is an integral part of UNESCOs' established mandate to build bridges towards peace and security, it follows that the World Heritage Committee and State Parties to the Convention should ensure that the processes established under the Convention are used to promote the achievement and maintenance of peace and security both between State Parties and within them. This chapter elaborates on these assertions, now embedded in UNESCO's new World Heritage and Sustainable Development policy (UNESCO 2015). It considers what this might mean for heritage practice within the World Heritage system, including nominations to the World Heritage List and World Heritage property management as well as because of the flow-down effect, in national and local heritage systems more generally. The chapter argues that while gaining acceptance of these assertions as policy principles in November 2015 was already a challenge, the follow-up task of operationalizing them as official guidelines will be even more difficult. Key issues that should be considered in revising the Operational Guidelines are raised and the question is asked about how meaningful the revisions can realistically be, given the range and strength of countervailing forces.

Impacts of conflict on sustainable development and heritage

Both the physical reality and the psychological fear of war, public disorder and violent crime have been scourges faced by humanity since time immemorial. Civilian populations need peace and security to maintain and build strong family and community relationships and care for their living environments. Commercial, industrial and infrastructure entrepreneurs want predictability before they invest in particular places and this cannot be guaranteed in the absence of peace and security. Although heritage was not yet paired with sustainable development, it was the destruction of historic cities during World War II and their insensitive reconstruction in post-war years that led to the Venice Charter (ICASHB 1964) and the establishment of International Council on Monuments and Sites (ICOMOS) in 1965.

The end of the Cold War in the 1990s suggested to scholars like political scientist Francis Fukuyama (1992) the emergence of a period in which United States hegemony might produce a peaceful capitalist-democratic world. It soon became apparent, however, that the collapse of the Soviet bloc unleashed a new set of conflicts – a spate of hot wars, both between and within states, that often focused on the cultural differences between neighbouring peoples. The conflicts in former Yugoslavia (Slovenia, Croatia, Bosnia, Kosovo etc.) and the southern republics of the ex-USSR (Georgia, Chechnya, East Prigorodny etc.) are examples. Deliberately targeting the cultural heritage of the enemy was rife, as in the bombing of the Old Bridge in Mostar and the Sarajevo Library in Bosnia-Herzegovina, aimed at undermining the morale of the opponents. In the Middle East such practice is the continuation of an age-old practice, going back to the destruction of the enemy's cities in ancient Mede, Persian, Greek and Roman times (De Cesari 2015). Sometimes it was accompanied by campaigns of ethnic cleansing: killing all the defeated enemy's men and boys or raping, carrying off and enslaving their women.

Conflict between religions

The Middle East and South Asia have been a major theatre for wars since the 1940s and increasingly since the 1990s, with dire results for heritage structures and artefacts as well as civilian populations ('collateral damage'). Some cases involve clashes between religions, as for instance with the destruction of Afghani Buddhist artefacts in the Kabul Museum by the Muslim Taliban, which provoked outrage from those who knew about it. This was followed by the blasting of the two standing Bamiyan Buddha statues in 2001, despite appeals from the UNESCO Director-General and other world political and religious leaders (Manhart 2016). It appears generally that the enormous tourism boost and global notoriety World Heritage inscription gives to places guarantees worldwide publicity for the perpetrators of any attack on those places, tourists and the communities living in and around them. It may be that association with UNESCO's World Heritage program heightened the risk of attack at Bamiyan.

The destruction in July 2012 of two fifteenth-century mausoleums of Sufi Muslim saints in the Timbuktu World Heritage site by Ansar Dine, a militant Islamist group linked to al-Qaeda, was another instance of inter-religious conflict. The group had captured most of the city in northern Mali in April 2012, prompting the World Heritage Committee in May to proclaim the site as World Heritage in Danger. Municipal officials in Mali considered the destruction to be a direct reaction to the UNESCO decision (Aljazeera 2012). Ansar Dine went on later in the year to destroy the remaining 16 mausoleums (BBC 2012), an attack that, according to Christian Manhart (2016: 288), was 'totally devoid of military or strategic necessity…. [The] only aim was to target the cultural and religious identity of the people, which is considered contrary to the Islamists' interpretation of the Koran'. The attack brought Timbuktu into the global media, however, and achieved the attention the group wanted for its ideological position. The destruction of Greco-Roman archaeological site of Palmyra, Syria, by the Islamic State (ISIS) during the years 2015–2017 is a similar case in point (Stanton 2015; Plets 2017).

Conflict within religions

The genesis of some recent Middle East conflicts is often see as lying in intra-Islamic rivalries that date from the death of the prophet Mohammad. As Vali Nasr (2016) explains, however, while Shiite and Sunni factions have frequently come to blows in the past, 'the violent paroxysm in today's Middle East is a modern phenomenon, a product of contemporary politics and priorities'. This complexity is seen in the Syrian civil war and in Yemen, where a proxy war is being waged between Wahhabi Saudi Arabia and Shiite Iran for regional dominance (Cote 2017; Meskell in press: ch. 8). Whatever the causes, destruction of cultural heritage has been enormous. The old cities of Damascus, Syria's capital, and Sana'a, Yemen's capital, which have been inscribed on the World Heritage List since 1979 and 1986 respectively, were given World Heritage in Danger status in 2013 and 2015. The aerial bombing of Sana'a in 2015 also damaged the old city of Saada and the archaeological site of the pre-Islamic walled city of Baraqish. The destruction provoked UNESCO's Director General, Irina Bokova, to condemn the attacks and to call, rather hopefully, on all parties to keep cultural heritage out of the conflict (NDTV 2015).

A decade earlier, the Shiite Al Askari Mosque in Samarra, Iraq, was bombed by Sunni forces in 2006, destroying its golden dome and eight of its ten minarets. The remaining minarets succumbed to another bombing the following year. Benjamin Isakhan (2016: 275) observes that not only was the heritage building itself destroyed, but, because the bombings can be perceived as attacks on the identity of the community that derives cultural or religious meaning from the building, the destruction can 'lead to a breakdown in social cohesion, as well as deadly counterattacks on the heritage sites and communities of the "other"'. Isakhan documents Iraq's devastating civilian casualties, horrific violence and unprecedented damage to some of the world's most sensitive heritage sites since the United States invasion in 2003. This includes the looting of the Iraq National Museum, which occurred immediately after the fall of Baghdad in April 2003, followed by irrevocable damage to Mesopotamian archaeological sites, an Abbasid-era palace and mosque, an Ottoman-era mosque and the Hashemite Parliament House.

Conflicts over ownership and benefits

Conflicts have broken out around World Heritage sites in other parts of the world and commonly revolve around the questions of who owns the heritage and who benefits from heritage conservation and associated tourism activities. Preah Vihear, a ninth-century temple complex dedicated to the Hindu god Shiva that was inscribed 2008, is a well-documented example (Hauser-Schäublin 2011; Logan 2012: 124; Meskell 2013). When the Cambodian nomination for World Heritage inscription of the temple was accepted in 2008, conflicting claims erupted into open hostilities, leaving 20 Cambodian and 16 Thai troops and several civilians dead (Wegener 2011: 27) and tens of thousands of other civilians displaced. In the case of the Tibetan Potala of Lhasa, which was inscribed on the World Heritage List in 1995, territorial expansion led to the migration of members of the dominant cultural group and the reduction of the traditional occupants to the position of an ethnic minority in what was formerly their own territory (Shepherd 2006; Menon 2013). The spread of Javanese through a *transmigrasi* (transmigration) process into outer Indonesian islands and New Guinea is similar (Rigg 1991). These cases raise human rights issues and may generate further conflict in future.

Customary land ownership systems being challenged in all continents, perhaps especially Africa, under threat here as in Africa. It should be noted that during the last decade a new set of conflicting ownership claims has arisen over intangible forms of cultural heritage, both between and within states (Antons and Logan 2017). In Southeast Asia, the commercial exploitation of traditional medicines has recently sparked diplomatic rows between Southeast Asian countries claiming ownership of such heritage (Antons 2009). Disputes between Malaysia and Indonesia erupted over 'ownership' of a traditional song that Malaysia had used in tourism advertisements (Asiagate 2007). These two states as well as Cambodia and Thailand have also claimed ownership of the style of hand movements used in traditional dances, again a form of intangible heritage that features in these countries' tourism (Denes 2017). The existence of many ethnic minorities straddling Asian state boundaries gives further rise to possible rival ownership claims as nationalism in the region grows.

Terrorist attacks

Although not new, a form of violence that has become more prevalent in recent years is terrorist attacks. These have impacted on both local workers and visitors at World Heritage and other tourism sites in the past and there is enormous risk of further atrocities. Not all such attacks are, strictly speaking, terrorist attacks if terrorism is defined as the unlawful use of violence and intimidation, especially against civilians but also to coerce governments or their agencies in the pursuit of political or social objectives. Some attacks are the work of individuals with a personal grievance against a government or agency. While the causation is different, the results can be identical – inflicting death and injury on civilians, damaging heritage structures and destroying the intangible heritage embodied in the dead. The immediate response is also the same, although for the longer term determining the underlying causes is important if societies are to understand and deal with these quite different threats to a society's peace and security.

Take the Peruvian example of the Historic Sanctuary of Machu Picchu, inscribed in 1983. In 1986, terrorists blew up the train that takes tourists from Cuzco to the town of Aguas Calientes, where thousands of tourists connect daily to reach the Incan ruins. Seven tourists were killed and 38 wounded (*The New York Times* 1986). The terrorists were probably from the Sendero Luminoso (Shining Path), a Maoist guerrilla group that had been fighting the government for six years. Tourism to Peru fell by almost 30 per cent during those years, although 1986 was the first time violence was directly targeted at tourists. There have been many, more murderous attacks on tourists in Egypt since the 1980s, culminating in the Luxor massacre of 58 foreign visitors and four Egyptians in 1997 when terrorists, probably linked to al-Qaeda, stormed the Temple of Hatchepsut in the Ancient Thebes and its Necropolis World Heritage property. In the following year tourists visiting Egypt fell by 12.8 per cent and tourism income by one-third (Meskell 2005: 137).

Twenty years later, tourists and other civilians are still being targeted elsewhere around the world, as in Barcelona in August 2017, when 16 pedestrians were killed and over 100 wounded by a car driven down Las Ramblas, a major tourism attraction just a stone's throw of the Palacio Güell, one of the components of the Gaudi World Heritage property inscribed in 1984. Demonstrating a global copycat effect, motor vehicles have also been used recently to kill and maim local and international visitors, residents and workers in Nice (July 2016), Berlin (December 2016), Columbus, USA (November 2016), and London (March and twice in June 2017), Melbourne (January 2017) and Stockholm (April 2017) (CNN 2017). The Australian attack, which killed six people, turned out to be the action of a mentally ill man with no links to terrorist networks, but all these attacks, no matter whether they are by terrorists or isolated individuals, show the urgent need for new management measures to make popular places safer. Physical barriers such as concrete walls and bollards seem to be a basic requirement. Tighter security checks will be needed on visitors entering heritage sites, World Heritage-listed or otherwise, although this is problematic when the site is a historic town centre or a cultural landscape.

UNESCO, peace and security

It is the concerted attempts to undermine the fabric of societies by destroying the physical symbols of their cultural identity that heritage organizations like UNESCO seek to neutralize, whether such attacks are in time of war, in the form of terrorist attacks or through other violent crime. UNESCO's founding Constitution, adopted in November 1945, makes clear this ambition, the text starting with the key sentence, '[t]hat since wars begin in the minds of men, it is in the minds of men that the defences of peace must be constructed'. These words have remained in the Constitution even though it has been amended many times. While responding to the World War II context, they reflect the hostility that we so commonly show when meeting peoples with cultural practices that are strange to us (Logan, Langfield and Nic Craith 2010: 6). As a result cultural diversity often becomes the cause of conflict – or at least the excuse for it. Numerous international normative statements insist, however, that humans have the right to maintain their diversity and cultural identity, both of which rest on their cultural heritage. What is needed according to the UNESCO Constitution is a process of intercultural dialogue and understanding that will make possible the achievement of greater tolerance and, ultimately, peace in this world.

Chief among the multilateral instruments and other mechanisms that UNESCO uses to channel the behaviour of Member States towards their own heritage and the heritage of others is the *Convention for the Protection of Cultural Property in the Event of Armed Conflict* (commonly known as the 1954 Hague Convention). Together with its two Protocols (1954 and 1999), the convention provides for the protection of both movable and immovable property during international and civil wars, including times of occupation. Its operation has not been, however, without problems (Techera 2007; Vdoljak 2016). State Parties to the Hague Convention are slack in attendance at committee meetings (Meskell in press: ch. 7). The United States of America did not become a State Party until 2009, and the United Kingdom has still to sign up. The self-declared and recently defeated ISIS was not internationally recognized and was therefore ineligible to become a State Party. The Convention follows the Red Cross model in specifying a symbol – in this case, a blue shield – to mark cultural property that should not be attacked. This appears to have reduced the destruction of monuments and sites in the 1991 and 2003 Iraq wars, although not the looting of museums (Techera 2007). By contrast, in the 1990s Balkan wars the blue shield mechanism seems merely to have advertised to belligerents on various sides the significant cultural symbols that should be targeted (Gerstenblith and Wilkie 2017: 4), which raises the question whether the mechanism should be used at all.

As Erika Techera (2007) observed, when cultural property is damaged or destroyed the effectiveness of the Hague Convention and other international instruments is often called into question. However, she argues that

> As can be illustrated by the loss of the Bamiyan Statues … [and] the attacks near the Monastery of Decani in Kosovo, [World Heritage-listed since 2004], there is little that the law can do to protect cultural property from deliberate and wilful destruction. Only a change in global attitudes and increased respect for our differing cultures can protect such items. Each and every country has a responsibility to publicly educate not only those involved in the military and defence forces but also its citizens, that cultural property should be protected for the future of all people.

It should be noted that international instruments such as the 2001 *Universal Declaration on Cultural Diversity* (2001) and the UNESCO *Declaration concerning the Intentional Destruction of Cultural Heritage* (2003) are not binding in the way conventions are and merely have moral authority. This means that UNESCO has to engage in a very considerable diplomatic and promotional effort to persuade the

Member States to behave in particular ways towards the heritage located within their territory, to accept the heritage of humanity notion and, if necessary, to put national interest aside in order to acknowledge the higher obligation to protect World Heritage or intangible elements on the Representative List (Logan 2017).

The conflicts discussed above show that UNESCO's efforts have so far been but a drop in the ocean, completely inadequate to the peace-building task before it. This is not to argue that UNESCO should stop striving to achieve its primary mission but that it should do more and do it better. Regrettably, the operation of its most popular convention – the 1972 World Heritage Convention – has not worked to maximize the mutual benefits that heritage protection and sustainable development could derive from the achievement and maintenance of peace and security. With nearly universal ratification of the World Heritage Convention by UNESCO Member States (193 State Parties out of 195 UNESCO Member States) and with 1,073 properties located in the territory of 167 State Parties, as well as known to and visited by countless people across the world, the system that has developed under the Convention could have, but so far has not held itself up as a model of how an organization works to bring heritage conservation to the service of both sustainable development and the attainment of peace and security.

Peace and security in the UNESCO World Heritage and Sustainable Development Policy

By bringing peace and security into 2015 World Heritage and Sustainable Development policy, the General Assembly of State Parties to the World Heritage Convention signalled that the World Heritage system is to be refocused in ways that will better help achieve UNESCO's constitutional ambition as well as the UN sustainable development goals. The positive impact that protecting and publicizing natural and cultural heritage might have on increasing understanding of other cultures has, of course, always underlain UNESCO's 'international campaigns for the safeguarding of the heritage of mankind [sic]' managed through UNESCO's Division of Cultural Heritage (DCH) and the inscription and monitoring of World Heritage by the World Heritage Committee and, after 1992, its secretariat, the World Heritage Centre. In the mid-1990s this link was made explicit by Federico Mayor (1995), then UNESCO Director-General, and other leading officers such as the DCH director, Mounir Bouchenaki, who described heritage at the 1997 ICCROM General Conference as offering the new way of conceptualizing culture as a 'culture of peace' (ICCROM 1997: 19).

Under the heading 'Fostering peace and security', the policy reminds State Parties that, as one of UNESCO's multinational normative instruments, the World Heritage Convention must play its part in working towards the organization's constitutional mission (UNESCO 2015: paragraph 28). The policy argues, therefore, that it is 'incumbent upon State Parties … to ensure that the implementation of the World Heritage Convention is used to promote the achievement and maintenance of peace and security between and within State Parties'. It asks State Parties to use their critically important role to ensure that the implementation of the World Heritage Convention, including the establishment of the World Heritage List and management of inscribed properties, is done in such a way that conflicts are prevented and cultural diversity is respected within and around World Heritage properties (paragraph 29).

Ensuring conflict prevention

The policy highlights four aspects of the State Parties' responsibilities in relation to fostering peace and security: ensuring conflict prevention (paragraph 30), protecting heritage during conflict (paragraph 31), promoting conflict resolution (paragraph 32) and contributing to post-conflict resolution (paragraph 33). What is new and probably most important of these is using the World Heritage system to ensure that conflict does not occur in the first place. To this end, five measures are recommended. First, scientific studies and research methodologies should be supported that are aimed at demonstrating the contribution that the conservation and management of World Heritage properties and their wider setting make to conflict prevention and resolution. This especially includes studies conducted by local communities that draw on their traditional ways of solving disputes. Second, an inclusive approach to identifying, conserving and managing World Heritage properties should be used. This will seek to promote consensus among stakeholders and celebrate cultural diversity as well as a better understanding of and respect for the heritage belonging to others, particularly neighbouring State Parties.

Third, State Parties should consider nominations to their Tentative Lists and to the World Heritage List that have potential to generate fruitful dialogue between State Parties and different cultural communities. Fourth, cross-culturally sensitive approaches should be adopted in the interpretation of World Heritage properties to visitors, local communities and other stakeholders. This, the policy notes, is particularly important when nominating or managing heritage places associated with conflicts. Fifth, where appropriate, consideration should be given to identifying, nominating and managing transboundary (aka transnational) heritage properties that have the potential to foster dialogue between neighbouring State Parties or non-contiguous State Parties sharing a common heritage.

Protecting heritage during conflict

During the period of armed conflict, the policy calls on State Parties to refrain from both using a World Heritage property and its immediate surroundings for purposes that are likely to expose them to damage and directing any act of hostility against them. They should ensure that their armed forces are understand and comply with provisions of the 1954 Hague Convention and its Protocols or, in cases where a State Party is not a signatory to Hague, to the principles of international customary law protecting cultural property in the event of armed conflict.

They should also ensure that the management and conservation of World Heritage properties are adequately covered in military planning and training programs.

Promoting conflict resolution

The policy points to the inherent potential of World Heritage properties and of their conservation to contribute to conflict resolution and the re-establishment of peace and security. Heritage conservation projects can act as mechanisms to re-establish cooperation between previously warring State Parties or communities within them and because of this they should be included, where appropriate, in conflict management and negotiations aimed at ending conflicts.

Contributing to post-conflict recovery

The policy envisages World Heritage properties and their wider settings making a significant contribution to the economic and social reconstruction of conflict-affected communities by rebuilding group identity, supporting jobs and generating income for the local economy. To enable this to happen, however, the policy calls for State Parties to use the inclusive approaches promoting engagement of multiple stakeholders that are required by other sections of the policy. State Parties need first of all to ensure, where appropriate, that the protection of World Heritage properties and their settings are included as a priority in UN and other regional peace-keeping and post-conflict initiatives and interventions. This must be followed up with the adoption of appropriate legal, technical, administrative and financial measures to support the recovery of World Heritage properties and their integration into public programs and policies. Not only the physical heritage features should be reinstated but intangible elements associated with the World Heritage properties that may have been negatively impacted by the conflict should be revitalized.

Operationalizing the 2015 policy

In approving the draft policy in November 2015 the General Assembly of State Parties to the World Heritage Convention requested the World Heritage Centre and Advisory Bodies to develop in consultation with State Parties and 'all relevant stakeholders' a set of proposals for the changes that would be necessary to translate the principles into specific operational procedures. Only when such proposals are also adopted by the World Heritage Committee and the General Assembly will it become clear what the policy really means for heritage practice at World Heritage sites and what flow-on effects will impact on national and local practice.

Nominations

There are many difficult questions to be considered in reformulating the *Operational Guidelines for the Implementation of the World Heritage Convention* to strengthen the World Heritage system's focus on fostering peace and security. With regard to nominations, for instance, should State Parties be encouraged to include on their Tentative Lists and then prioritize for nomination to the World Heritage List those sites focusing on dialogue creation or celebrating the achievement of peace, security and harmonious cultural diversity? Conversely, should the inclusion in tentative lists and the nomination of sites that would heighten tensions between states or within national communities be discouraged or even ruled out? Would a positive response to this question mean that in future inscriptions such as Japan's 'Sites of Japan's Meiji Industrial Revolution: Iron and Steel, Shipbuilding and Coal Mining' (inscribed 2015) no longer be possible? In this case South Korea, North Korea and China had objected strongly to the listing of the industrial ruins on Hashima Island, 15 km off the coast from Nagasaki, where their nationals were used as forced labour before and during World War II (Reiji 2015).

War-related sites usually present inscription difficulties given that there are winners and losers and, if the war is recent, tensions linger not far below the surface. The nomination of battlefields is usually less provocative if an interval of time has passed, as for example with Waterloo ('Waterloo Battlefield, the end of the Napoleonic era' was added to Belgium's Tentative List in 2008 but has not yet been nominated to the World Heritage List). It might have been thought that the battlefields of the American Civil War were sufficiently remote in time to have lost their power to generate conflict. The civil unrest that was ignited in Charlottesville, Virginia, in August 2017 by the demolition of a statue of a Confederate soldier puts paid to such confidence. What of the five Normandy beaches, the sites of the D-Day landings by American, British and Canadian troops in June 1944 that led to the retaking of Western Europe from Nazi Germany? These are clearly important heritage places for the Allied nations and probably also to Germany today. Keir Reeves et al. (2016: 3) maintain, however, that all twentieth-century war-related sites are not yet ready yet for major commemoration events. This may be over-pessimistic: it seems rather to depend on how many generations have passed, the extent to which personal memories of war have died out, how twentieth-century history is treated by scholars, teachers, the media and politicians, and whether there are reconciliatory measures in place.

There has certainly been a flurry of listing activity in Western Europe in the last few years, mostly related to the Western Front and no doubt connected with major World War 1 and II anniversaries. The Normandy landing beaches were added to France's Tentative List in 2014 and they remain there for the time being. Belgium and France have, however, submitted separate but coordinated World War I serial site nominations to their Tentative Lists in 2014 and to the World Heritage List in 2018 for a set of 105 World War I places – 25 in Belgium, 80 in France. Should these kinds of war-related nomination be discouraged or proscribed under the new policy? It is noteworthy that in the broad consultation with all State Parties as requested by the World Heritage Committee when it endorsed the draft policy in its Bonn session in mid-2015, it was only France that expressed concern about the wording in the draft advocating avoidance of war-related nominations. It commented that this was imposing 'rather a priori negatives on this type of heritage' – as indeed it was. As required by the Committee, the view of the State Party was taken into account, and the wording was softened in the final draft that went to the General Assembly.

The French and Belgian nomination documents, entitled the 'Funeral and Memorial Sites of the First World War (Western Front)', do not emphasize winners and losers but instead focus on the completely new, industrial and total form of war that was first seen in World War I and the new kind of esteem given to the dead (France 2015). Setting aside the question of whether this definition of the Outstanding Universal Value (OUV) is a response to the difficulty of fitting battlefields into the World Heritage criteria or an indirect celebration of victory, the nominations have identified a new way that societies dealt with their military dead, although not the civilian dead. In the liberal democracies that were then emerging in Western Europe, the rights of the individual were a core value, and those who died in the defence of the state were deemed to be entitled to individual honour. This acknowledgement by states on both sides of the conflict led to a completely new funeral and memorial approach with the equality of all in death being translated into the uniformity of graves, with no separation by military rank although with the individual's religious belief able to be shown on the headstones. This common approach led, after the war, to further cooperation and a sense of reconciliation, leading eventually to the signing of an agreement between France and Germany that granted permanent status to German war graves of both world wars located on French soil (France 2015: 57).

Site management

Generalizing from the Franco-Belgian example, should transboundary nominations be prioritized by the World Heritage Committee on the grounds that they encourage dialogue and cultural understanding between neighbouring states? Their 'symbolic value for peaceful cooperation between nations as well as practical benefit for coordinated or joint conservation management' has long been recognized, according to the World Commission on Protected Areas (Sandwith et al. 2001: 1). The World Heritage list already contains 37 transboundary inscriptions involving 67 State Parties, but the management experience these have had is not without problems and may give other State Parties hesitate. Such inscriptions are far more complex and challenging than single-site nominations, as Ona Vileikis (2016: 507–508) has explained in her case study of the Silk Roads: while they might, as highly recommended by the Operational Guidelines (UNESCO 2016: paragraph 135), have a single main management system, each component part requires a specific approach based on its own characteristics – different policies and management procedures and often different languages and present-day cultural values. Greater amounts of data need to be handled, and larger numbers of stakeholders will be involved. Vileikis concludes that, instead of strengthening peaceful cooperation, all these aspects can create a breeding ground for a variety of conflicts regarding site management.

The political context is always important: agreements about transboundary properties may be honoured where political parties in each state are stable, but what guarantees are possible when states face political turmoil? A thorough review of the existing transboundary inscriptions by the World Heritage Centre might help determine their efficacy in achieving dialogue. The Vietnamese and Palestinian case studies by Logan (2010) and Hammami (2016) raise the issue of what happens, too, when diasporic communities become involved, particularly when their view of what is nationally significant heritage differs from that held by the national government.

Reconciliation seems to be a key concept for the peace and security dimension of the World Heritage and Sustainable Development policy. Although not without semantic difficulties and sometimes dubious use by the political regimes in some post-trauma states (Logan and Reeves 2009), the concept can help both in determining which conflict-related sites are worthy of inscription and in the management of sites, including their interpretation to visitors. The concept is already integral to the OUV of several places already inscribed, such as Senegal's Gorée Island (inscribed 1978), Japan's Genbaku Dome (1996) and South Africa's Robben Island (1999). These places have, according to Christina Cameron (2010: 118), 'can contribute to sustaining memories and understanding the roots of conflict. Their positive capacity to foster a broad-based contemporary dialogue about human rights underscores their global importance'. The concept of reconciliation would allow more 'places of pain and shame' (Logan and Reeves 2009) to be inscribed, perhaps working with the International Coalition for Sites of Conscience to identify candidates. It has special relevance to sites related to recent wars, as Kobayashi and Ziino (2009) show in their study of the Japanese War Cemetery in the New South Wales town of Cowra.

Colonial places can also represent painful past events and current injustices, and their conservation and inscription can give rise to heightened tension (Batten 2009). The inscription, management and interpretation of such places need to have clear community engagement and support and not just be designed to perpetuate notions of colonist glory. Such places arguably need to be or have the potential to become sites of reconciliation. Perhaps the Operational Guidelines should be revised to require the management plans that are now an obligatory part of nomination dossiers to include, for conflict-related sites, an interpretation plan that is cross-culturally sensitive and focused on reconciliation. Structural issues might also be addressed as part of broader reconciliation plans.

How serious are we?

As I write (late 2017), the world is facing the threat of nuclear warfare in the Korean Peninsula, a worsening civil-cum-proxy war in Yemen and ethnic cleansing, if not genocide, in Myanmar. The first conflict, the greatest crisis in that part of the world in 60 years, threatens to engulf not only the two Koreas, but also Japan, China, American Guam and perhaps further afield. The war in Yemen started in 2014 and for a while it seemed some Yemeni thought it would be short-lived. The local community and the national heritage agency were planning in late 2015 to reconstruct some of the houses in the World Heritage-inscribed Old City of Sana'a that had been destroyed by the Saudi-led coalition air raids earlier in the year. They planned to use traditional techniques and base their work on existing documentation of the destroyed buildings. This seemed to show how heritage can be used to support community resilience (Giovanni Boccardi pers.comm. 2/10/2015). Such optimism now seems to have dissipated. The war is estimated to have already killed 8,600 citizens. One-third of the country around Sana'a is under siege, and an estimated 20 million people are deprived of humanitarian aid and suffering reputedly the world's largest food security emergency (BBC 2017).

Around a million Rohingya Muslims have been denied Myanmar citizenship, attacked and chased out of their home territory in Rakhine State, despite many families having lived there since well before the colonial British created Myanmar (then Burma) (Logan in press). The Rohingya disaster is already spreading tension throughout Muslim nations in Southeast Asia, potentially impacting on the World Heritage-listed Buddhist complex of Borobudur in Indonesia which has been selected as the site of a major anti-Myanmar demonstration (Reuters 2017). There have been reports that the actions of the Myanmar army and the inaction of Myanmar's de facto president, Aung San Suu Kyi, have already made Rakhine State a prey to penetration by ISIS and other terrorist groups (Latiff 2017).

Against events like these, what can be realistically expected of the peace and security component of UNESCO's World Heritage and Sustainable Development policy? The World Heritage Convention has no clause about conflict resolution, but it does allow for technical cooperation and the Operational Guidelines are relevant for World Heritage sites needing repair after physical damage. We must, however, never forget the people caught up in conflicts or accept loss of life as merely the collateral damage of war. Cultural heritage may concern sites and monuments but it is also, in its intangible forms, embodied in people. I recall the inspirational address by a leading Rwandan administrator at a Forum UNESCO conference in Valencia explaining how the cultural heritage of his people was lost with every death in that country's civil war in 1990–1993. By coincidence, his address was made on 11 September 2001, reminding us again of the need these days to include terrorist attacks in our conceptualization of peace and security.

Clearly, the World Heritage and Sustainable Development policy will not be able to achieve much, given the range and strength of countervailing forces. These include the entrenched character of hostilities between and within states, the powerful arms industries in and sheltered by many states and the ability of people living in comfortable conditions, mostly in developed states, to turn a blind eye to the conditions of poverty and conflict in which their fellow humans have to live.

Nevertheless, the UNESCO policy can make a useful contribution to improving peace and security. It is a reminder to State Parties to the World Heritage Convention that they – or most of them – have already signed up to a range of commitments under other international normative instruments, such as the *Universal Declaration of Human Rights* (UN 1948), the 1954 Hague Convention, the 1966 *the International Covenant on Civil and Political Rights* (UN 1966) and the *UN Declaration on the Rights of Indigenous Peoples* (UNPFII 2007). It also encourages support for and collaboration with other mechanisms and agencies seeking peace, security and social justice, such as the UNESCO committees responsible for the Intangible Cultural Heritage system, the International Committee of the Blue Shield and the International Criminal Court.

Approval of World Heritage and Sustainable Development policy in November 2015 was indeed an important step, therefore, even though it is still framed at the level of aims and principles. The over-riding challenge in the current operationalization stage will be to determine what guidelines might be both acceptable to the World Heritage Committee and the General Assembly of State Parties and effective in the field. The critical issue here is deciding how far restrictions should and can be taken. The Operational Guidelines are guidelines after all, and to change them into binding regulations may not be feasible. Attempts by the World Heritage Committee and its secretariat to restrict the State Parties actions have in the past been resisted and undermined, the Committee's decision at its Cairns meeting in 2000 to slow down the rate of nomination by State Parties already well represented on the World Heritage List being a case in point (UNESCO 2007: 41; Logan 2012: 126). Even so, if UNESCO, the World Heritage Committee and the General Assembly of State Parties to the World Heritage Convention were really serious about achieving their peace and security mission, they should not balk at making the necessary hard operational decisions.

Perhaps they should penalize those State Parties prosecuting wars or violence against civilians or refusing to uphold basic human rights. In Myanmar, for instance, should UNESCO have withdrawn the technical assistance it was providing for the development of a nomination dossier for Bagan once the UN had condemned the ethnic clearance taking place. Not to have done so invites accusations of complicity. Perhaps it should now refuse to process the Bagan nomination further until Myanmar reverses its policies and enables the Rohingya to return from refugee camps in Bangladesh. Would the State Parties in the World Heritage Committee and General Assembly refuse, however, to bar Myanmar from submitting nominations? Non-interference in the internal affairs of other states might be the ostensible reason for such a refusal, although perhaps this would hide an underlying fear that they, too, could be subjected to similar human rights-related scrutiny.

Returning to the Yemen example, should and would the State Parties censure the United Kingdom for selling weapons – illegally under the Geneva Convention – to Saudi Arabia for use on the Yemeni, including cluster bombs designed to inflict maximum civilian casualties (Mason and MacAskill 2016)?

Would they censure Australia for conducting training exercises with the Saudi navy, the agency responsible for blockading the import of humanitarian supplies of food and medicine into western Yemen, which is certainly a crime against humanity (McNeill 2017)? Would criticisms, should they be made, have the desired effect? How would the criticized State Parties react? Walk out, like the US – by far the largest supplier of arms to Saudi Arabia – and Israel?

In the end, then, the success or failure of the peace and security component of the World Heritage and Sustainable Development policy will depend on how serious UNESCO, the World Heritage Committee and General Assembly are about working towards the achievement of peace and security in our world. As heritage practitioners, members of ICOMOS and citizens of the State Parties, whether in policy-making situations, in academia or out in the field, we all have a role to play persuading UNESCO and its regional and country offices to take the matter with the utmost seriousness. Significant new contributions are coming from academics and practitioners. A number of international law scholars such as Alessandro Chechi (2014) and Ana Vdoljak (2016) are exploring how the current World Heritage system might be improved. Marina Lostal Becceril (2017) has reacted to the lack of integration between the World Heritage Convention and the other UNESCO instruments and programs and proposes a specific protection regime for cultural and natural World Heritage sites.

What should UNESCO's managers do under these circumstances? UNESCO is an intergovernmental organization made up of State Parties that jealously guard their independence and right to put national interests first (Logan 2012). Of course, UNESCO should continue to toe the fine line, relying on rhetoric to coax State Parties into adhering to the World Heritage and Sustainable Development policy in all its dimensions. It might also be the right moment to push the pursuit of peace and security well beyond the technical and administrative to consider, as Lynn Meskell (in press: ch. 8) argues, the deeper issue of the 'stark inequities that still exist between different nations' and to reflect on the 'ways in which World Heritage has been instrumentalized by various international actors, whether Ansar Dine, ISIS or UNESCO, to promote their particular, divergent worldviews'. This might be the best way in the long term to gain full benefit from the potential for heritage to contribute to peace and security. In the short term, the Operational Guidelines will be revised – a daunting task if the philosophical, political and practice considerations surveyed in this chapter are taken into account. It is only when the proposed revisions are approved by the State Parties in the World Heritage Committee and General Assembly that will we see how much the World Heritage system can be changed at the current time to accommodate UNESCO's World Heritage and Sustainable Development policy, in particular the fostering of peace and security. Only then will we see what the policy might mean for heritage practice at World Heritage sites, what flow-on effects might impact on national and local practice and what contribution World Heritage might make to the more sustainable development of our world.

References

Aljazeera (2012). Ansar Dine Fighters Destroy Timbuktu Shrines. *Africa News*, 1 July (online). Available at: www.aljazeera.com/news/africa/2012/06/2012630101748795606. html (accessed 25 August 2017).

Antons, C. (2009). 'Traditional knowledge in Asia: Global agendas and local subjects', in R. Peerenboom (ed), *Regulation in Asia: Pushing Back on Globalization*. London: Routledge.

Antons, C. and Logan, W. (eds) (2017). *Intellectual Property, Cultural Property and Intangible Cultural Heritage*. London: Routledge.

Asiagate (2007). Malaysia Urges Indonesia to Drop Suit Over Folk Song, 5 October (online). Available at: http://goldsea.com/Asiagate/710/05song.html (accessed 7 December 2017).

Batten, B. (2009). 'The Myall Creek Memorial: History, identity and reconciliation', in W. Logan and K. Reeves (eds), *Places of Pain and Shame: Dealing with 'Difficult Heritage'*. London: Routledge.

BBC (2012). Timbuktu Mausoleums 'Destroyed'. *Africa News*, 23 December (online). Available at: www.bbc.com/news/world-africa-20833010 (accessed 25 August 2017).

BBC (2017). Yemen Crisis: Who Is Fighting Whom? *World News*, 2 December (online). Available at: www.bbc.com/news/world-middle-east-29319423 (accessed 7 December 2017).

Cameron, C. (2010). 'World Heritage sites of conscience and memory', in D. Offenhäuser, W. Zimmerli and M.-T. Albert (eds), *World Heritage and Cultural Diversity*. Cottbus: German UNESCO Commission.

Chechi, A. (2014). *The Settlement of International Cultural Heritage Disputes*. Oxford: Oxford University Press.

CNN (2017). 'Terrorist attacks by vehicle fast facts', *CNN International Edition*, 6 November (online). Available at: http://edition.cnn.com/2017/05/03/world/terrorist-attacks-by-vehicle-fast-facts/index.html (accessed 7 December 2017).

Cote, R. (2017). Iran and Saudi Arabia's Proxy War in Yemen. *Center for International Maritime Security*, 20 April (online). Available at: http://cimsec.org/iran-saudi-arabias-proxy-war-yemen/32230 (accessed 11 September 2017).

De Cesari, C. (2015). 'Postcolonial ruins: Archaeologies of political violence and IS', *Anthropology Today*, 31(6), 22–26.

Denes, A. (2017). 'Culture by decree: Thailand's intangible cultural heritage bill and the regulation of thai-ness', in C. Antons and W. Logan (eds), *Intellectual Property, Cultural Property and Intangible Cultural Heritage*. London: Routledge.

France (2015). *Sites funéraires et mémoriels de la Première Guerre mondiale (front de l'Ouest). Proposition d'inscription franco-belge sur la Liste du patrimoine mondial de l'UNESCO. Candidature sérielle et transnationale* [Funeral and Memorial Sites of the First World War (Western Front). Franco-Belgian Nomination for Inscription on UNESCO's World Heritage List. Serial and transnational application] (online). Available at: http://verdun-meuse.fr/images/pages/Dossierfinalseptembre11.pdf (accessed 28 August 2017).

Fukuyama, F. (1992). *The End of History and the Last Man*. New York: Free Press.

Gerstenblith, P. and Wilkie, N. C. (2017). *The U.S. Committee of the Blue Shield and the Blue Shield Movement* (online). Available at: www.culturalheritagelaw.org/resources/Pictures/NATO%20Legal%20Gazette_Patty%20Gerstenblith%20and%20Nancy%20C.%20Wilkie.pdf (accessed 28 August 2017).

Hammami, F. (2016). 'Issues of mutuality and sharing in the transnational spaces of heritage: Contesting diaspora and homeland experiences in Palestine', *International Journal of Heritage Studies*, 22(6), 446–465.

Hauser-Schäublin, B. (2011). 'Preah Vihear: From object of colonial desire to a contested World Heritage site', in B. Hauser-Schäublin (ed), *World Heritage Angkor and Beyond: Circumstances and Implications of UNESCO Listings in Cambodia*. Göttingen: Universitätsverlag Göttingen.

ICCROM (1997). *General Assembly Minutes, 20th Session*, 10–12 December.

International Congress of Architects and Specialists of Historic Buildings (ICASHB) (1964). *International Charter for the Conservation and Restoration of Monuments and Sites* (Venice Charter) (online). Available at: www.icomos.org/charters/venice_e.pdf (accessed 28 August 2017).

Isakhan, B. (2016). 'Heritage under Fire: Lessons from Iraq for cultural property protection', in W. Logan, M. Nic Craith and U. Kockel (eds), *A Companion to Heritage Studies*. Chichester, UK: Wiley Blackwell.

Kobayashi, A. and Ziino, B. (2009). 'Cowra JapaneseWar Cemetery', in W. Logan and K. Reeves (eds), *Places of Pain and Shame: Dealing with 'Difficult Heritage'*. London: Routledge.

Latiff, R. (2017). Myanmar Faces Danger from Islamic State Militants, Malaysian Police Say. *Reuters World News*, 4 January (online). Available at: www.reuters.com/article/us-malaysia-security-rohingya/myanmar-faces-danger-from-islamic-state-militants-malaysian-police-say-idUSKBN14O0PX (accessed 10 September 2017).

Logan, W. (2010). 'Protecting the Tay Nguyen Gongs: Conflicting rights in Vietnam's central plateau', in M. Langfield, W. Logan and M. Nic Craith (eds), *Cultural Diversity, Heritage and Human Rights: Intersections in Theory and Practice*. London: Routledge.

Logan, W. (2012). 'States, governance and the politics of culture: World Heritage in Asia', in P. Daly and T. Winter (eds), *Routledge Handbook of Heritage in Asia*. London: Routledge.

Logan, W. (2017). 'UNESCO Heritage-speak: Words, syntax and rhetoric', in C. Antons and W. Logan (eds), *Intellectual Property, Cultural Property and Intangible Cultural Heritage*. London: Routledge.

Logan, W. (in press). 'Ethnicity, heritage, human rights and governance in the Union of Myanmar', in J. Rodenberg and P. Wagenaar (eds), *Cultural Contestation: Heritage, Identity and the Role of Government*. New York: Palgrave Macmillan.

Logan, W., Langfield, M. and Nic Craith, M. (2010). 'Intersecting Concepts and Practices', in M. Langfield, W. Logan and M. Nic Craith (eds), *Cultural Diversity, Heritage and Human Rights: Intersections in Theory and Practice*. Routledge, London.

Logan, W. and Reeves, K. (eds) (2009). *Places of Pain and Shame: Dealing with 'Difficult Heritage'*. London: Routledge.

Lostal Becceril, M. (2017). *International Cultural Heritage Law in Armed Conflict: Case-Studies of Syria, Libya, Mali, the Invasion of Iraq, and the Buddhas of Bamiyan*. Cambridge, UK: Cambridge University Press.

Manhart, C. (2016). 'The intentional destruction of heritage: Bamiyan and Timbuktu', in W. Logan, M. Nic Craith and U. Kockel (eds), *A Companion to Heritage Studies*. Chichester, UK: Wiley Blackwell.

Mason, R. and MacAskill, E. (2016). 'Saudi Arabia admits it used UK-made cluster bombs in Yemen', *The Guardian*, 20 December (online). Available at: www.theguardian.com/world/2016/dec/19/saudi-arabia-admits-use-uk-made-cluster-bombs-yemen (accessed 10 September 2017).

Mayor, F. (1995). *The New Page*. Paris: UNESCO Publications.

McNeill, S. (2017). Joint Exercise with Saudis during Yemen Blockade 'Taints' Australian Navy, Say Aid Groups. *ABC News*, 15 November (online). Available at: www.abc.net.au/news/2017-11-15/ran-exercise-with-saudis-criticised/9152438 (accessed 7 December 2017).

Menon, K. M. (2013). 'Lhasa's disappearing heritage', *The Diplomat*, 16 June (online). Available at: http://thediplomat.com/2013/06/lhasas-disappearing-heritage/ (accessed 23 August 2017).

Meskell, L. (2005). 'Sites of violence: Terrorism, tourism, and heritage in the archaeological present', in L. Meskell and P. Pels (eds), *Embedding Ethics: Shifting Boundaries of the Anthropological Profession*. Oxford: Berg.

Meskell, L. (2013). 'UNESCO's World Heritage Convention at 40: Challenging the economic and political order of international heritage conservation', *Current Anthropology*, 54(4), 483–494.

Meskell, L. (in press). *A Future in Ruins: UNESCO, World Heritage and the Dream of Peace*. New York: Oxford University Press.

Nasr, V. (2016). 'The war for Islam', *Foreign Policy*, 22 January (online). Available at: http://foreignpolicy.com/2016/01/22/the-war-for-islam-sunni-shiite-iraq-syria/ (accessed 10 September 2017).

NDTV (2015). *UNESCO Condemns 'Severe' Bombing Damage to Sanaa Old Town*, 13 May (online). Available at: www.ndtv.com/world-news/unesco-condemns-severe-bombing-damage-to-sanaa-old-town-762616 (accessed 11 September 2017).

Plets, G. (2017). 'Violins and trowels for Palmyra: Post-conflict heritage politics', *Anthropology Today*, 33(4), 18–22.

Reeves, K., Bird, G., James, L., Stichelbaut, B. and Bourgeois, J. (eds) (2016). *Battlefield Events: Landscape, Commemoration and Heritage*. Abingdon: Routledge.

Reiji, Y. (2015). 'Government downplays forced labor concession in winning UNESCO listing for industrial sites', *The Japan Times*, 6 July (online). Available at: www.japantimes.co.jp/news/2015/07/06/national/history/unesco-decides-to-add-meiji-industrial-sites-to-world-heritage-list/#.Wbjn6Y1ry00 (accessed 10 September 2017).

Reuters (2017). Indonesia to Bar Myanmar Protest at World's Biggest Buddhist Temple. *Reuters World News*, 5 September (online). Available at: www.reuters.com/article/us-myanmar-rohingya-indonesia/indonesia-to-bar-myanmar-protest-at-worlds-biggest-buddhist-temple-idUSKCN1BG0ZE (accessed 10 September 2014).

Rigg, J. (1991). 'Land settlement in Southeast Asia: The Indonesian transmigration program', in J. Rigg (ed), *Southeast Asia: A Region in Transition*. London: Unwin Hyman, pp. 80–108.

Sandwith, T., Shine, C., Hamilton, L. and Sheppard, D. (2001). *Transboundary Protected Areas for Peace and Cooperation*. Gland, Switzerland: World Commission on Protected Areas.

Shepherd, R. (2006). 'UNESCO and the politics of cultural heritage in Tibet', *Journal of Contemporary Asia*, 36(2), 243–257.

Stanton, J. (2015). 'ISIS show off their destruction of 2,000-year-old temple at Palmyra: Just single arch of ancient Temple of Bel is left standing', *The Daily Mail*, 11 September (online). Available at: www.dailymail.co.uk/news/article-3229268/Pictured-ISIS-destruction-2-000-year-old-temple-Palmyra-left-just-one-arch-standing.html (accessed 22 August 2017).

Techera, E. J. (2007). 'Protection of cultural heritage in times of armed conflict: The international legal framework revisited', *Macquarie Journal of International and Comparative Environmental Law 1*, 4(1) (online). Available at: www.austlii.edu.au/cgi-bin/viewdoc/au/journals/MqJlICEnvLaw/2007/1.html#fnB140 (accessed 29 August 2017).

The New York Times (1986). '7 killed and 38 hurt in Peru by bombing of train for tourists', 26 June (online). Available at: www.nytimes.com/1986/06/26/world/7-killed-and-38-hurt-in-peru-by-bombing-of-train-for-tourists.html (accessed 23 August 2017).

United Nations (UN) (1948). *Universal Declaration of Human Rights* (online). Available at: www.ohchr.org/EN/UDHR/Documents/UDHR_Translations/eng.pdf (accessed 5 September 2017).

United Nations (UN) (1954). *Convention for the Protection of Cultural Property in the Event of Armed Conflict with Regulations for the Execution of the Convention 1954* (Hague Convention) (online). Available at: http://unesdoc.unesco.org/images/0018/001875/187580e.pdf (accessed 5 September 2017).

United Nations (UN) (1966). *International Covenant on Civil and Political Rights* (online). Available at: https://treaties.un.org/doc/publication/unts/volume%20999/volume-999-i-14668-english.pdf (accessed 5 September 2017).

UNESCO (2007). *World Heritage: Challenges for the Millennium*. Paris: UNESCO World Heritage Centre.

UNESCO (2015). *Policy Document for the Integration of a Sustainable Development Perspective into the Processes of the World Heritage Convention* (online). Available at: http://whc.unesco.org/en/sustainabledevelopment/ (accessed 2 December 2017).

UNESCO (2016). *Operational Guidelines for the Implementation of the World Heritage Convention*. Document WHC.16/01 (online). Available at: http://whc.unesco.org/en/guidelines (accessed 27 August 2017).

United Nations Permanent Forum on Indigenous Affairs (UNPFII) (2007). *Declaration on the Rights of Indigenous Peoples* (online). Available at: www.un.org/esa/socdev/unpfii/documents/DRIPS_en.pdf (accessed 29 August 2017).

Vdoljak, A. F. (2016). 'Challenges for international cultural heritage law', in W. Logan, M. Nic Craith and U. Kockel (eds), *A Companion to Heritage Studies*. Chichester, UK: Wiley Blackwell.

Vileikis, O. (2016). 'Achieving dialogue through transnational World Heritage nomination: The Case of the Silk Roads', in W. Logan, M. Nic Craith and U. Kockel (eds), *A Companion to Heritage Studies*. Chichester, UK: Wiley Blackwell.

Wegener, M. (2011). 'Lessons from Preah Vihear: Thailand, Cambodia, and the nature of low-intensity border conflicts', *Journal of Contemporary Southeast Asian Affairs*, 3, 27–59 (online). Available at: www.martin-wagener.org/tl_files/Dokumente/Wagener-GIGA%20-LowIntensityBorderConflict-2011.pdf (accessed 24 August 2017).

Part III

Advisory Bodies' perspectives

Chapter 10

The role of World Heritage in achieving environmental sustainability

An IUCN perspective

Elena Osipova, Tim Badman and Peter Bille Larsen

This chapter attempts to analyse the environmental dimension of sustainable development in World Heritage management with a particular emphasis on natural sites. It analyses the current state of evidence and explores opportunities to both strengthen management and address the knowledge gaps that need to be filled.

The term 'sustainable development' was first introduced in 1980 in IUCN's *World Conservation Strategy: Living Resource Conservation for Sustainable Development* prepared by IUCN in cooperation with UN-Environment (formerly the United National Environment Programme) and the World Wide Fund for Nature (WWF) (IUCN et al. 1980). The aim of the Strategy was 'to advance the achievement of sustainable development through the conservation of living resources'. Later, in 1987, *Our Common Future* (the Brundtland Report) laid the foundation for mainstreaming the concept of sustainable development. It also coined the most commonly used definition of sustainable development; that is, development 'which meets the needs of the present without compromising the ability of future generations to meet their needs' (WCED 1987).

While the concept of sustainable development is not new, it has often been referred to in limited, challenging and imprecise ways in the field of heritage conservation. This raises particular challenges from the perspective of natural heritage especially given the sometimes problematic nature of development interventions for natural heritage conservation.

At the same time, the concepts of heritage and heritage conservation have often remained marginal in wider scientific and political discourses about sustainable development. At the international level, the 1992 Agenda 21 document makes a brief reference to the World Heritage Convention as one of the tools for conservation of important forest areas in its Chapter 11 on combatting deforestation (United Nations Conference on Environment and Development (UNCED) 1992). While the UN's *Transforming Our World: the 2030 Agenda for Sustainable Development*, in turn, specifically mentions protection of the world's cultural and natural heritage as one of its targets, it does so only in the relation to Goal 11: 'Make cities and human settlements inclusive, safe, resilient and sustainable'(UN 2015).

In the context of the World Heritage Convention, the adoption in 2015 of the *Policy for the Integration of a Sustainable Development Perspective into the*

Processes of the World Heritage Convention (referred to as the World Heritage and Sustainable Development Policy) (UNESCO 2015) has therefore marked an important milestone in linking heritage and sustainability. Its call for 'responsible interaction with the environment in both cultural and natural properties' as well as the push to avoid environmental degradation and ensure long-term environmental quality and resilience in the context of climate change sends a clear message.

However, the complex interlinkages between sustainable development and conservation of the world's cultural and natural heritage were already recognized in a number of earlier documents and meetings that led up to the development of the Policy. This includes the conclusions of the so-called Paraty Meeting on the Relationship between the World Heritage Convention, Conservation and Sustainable Development (29–31 March 2010), which recognized 'that securing sustainable development is – almost by definition – an essential condition to guarantee the conservation of the heritage' (UNESCO 2010).

The new policy consolidates the importance of this interlinkage. On the one hand, it positions the implementation of the protection and associated goals of the World Heritage Convention as contributing significantly to sustainable development and the wellbeing of people. On the other hand, it contends that strengthening the three dimensions of sustainable development, namely environmental sustainability, inclusive social development and inclusive economic development, as well as fostering peace and security may bring benefits to World Heritage properties and support the effective and equitable management of its Outstanding Universal Value. It also emphasizes the importance of building policy coherence with the other Multilateral Environmental Agreements. In this chapter, we focus on the implications of linking environmental sustainability and conservation of natural and cultural World Heritage.

Concepts and definitions

In 1969, IUCN adopted a mandate, which spoke to 'the perpetuation and enhancement of the living world – man's natural environment – and the natural resources on which all living things depend'. It also referred to the management of 'air, water, soils, minerals and living species including man, so as to achieve the highest sustainable quality of life' (Adams 2006). Since then, thinking about the sustainability concepts has appeared in global policy debates (such as the Stockholm Conference, 1972, processes linked to the World Conservation Strategy (1980) and the Rio outcomes (1992)). It has also led to a growing group of institutional actors (governments, business and social movements) readily engaging in both policy-level and operational definitions of sustainability.

What from one angle could be read as a conceptual victory from an IUCN perspective in terms of mainstreaming the sustainability concept also raises questions about engaging with the diversity of theoretical frameworks, policy directions and practical implications of different ideas and practices. Moldan et al. (2010), for example, link the concept of environmental sustainability with the concept of nature's services or ecosystem services by defining environmental sustainability as in relation to the need for maintaining nature's services. Building on the foundations laid by the Millennium Ecosystem Assessment (MA 2005), which provided a first assessment of the state of and trends in the condition of the world's ecosystems and the services they provide, the science of ecosystem services has developed extensively in the recent years with different frameworks, definitions and classifications now available.

The understanding of the importance of biodiversity and its central role in the provision of these services has also increased in recent years (Worm et al. 2006; Cardinale et al. 2012; Soliveres et al. 2016; Balvanera et al. 2006). This has led to new insights about the contributions of World Heritage conservation in terms of ecosystem services and benefits. The World Heritage and Sustainable Development policy specifically speaks to 'Protecting biological and cultural diversity and ecosystem services and benefits'. State Parties are encouraged to apply such principles in both the properties themselves and their buffer zones encouraging the integration of environmental, social and cultural impact assessment tools in planning processes (Article 15).

In operational terms, the devil is in the detail in terms of specific principles and environmental criteria. The OECD Environmental Strategy for the First Decade of the 21st Century (2001), for example, defines four criteria of environmental sustainability (OECD 2001):

- regeneration ('renewable resources shall be used efficiently and their use shall not be permitted to exceed their long-term rates of natural regeneration')
- substitutability ('non-renewable resources shall be used efficiently and their use limited to levels which can be offset by substitution by renewable resources or other forms of capital')
- assimilation ('releases of hazardous or polluting substances to the environment shall not exceed its assimilating capacity')
- avoiding irreversibility ('irreversible adverse effects of human activities on ecosystems and on biogeochemical and hydrological cycles shall be avoided').

Yet despite their apparent rationale, such criteria raise specific questions in the World Heritage context. Substitutability and off-sets, for example, suggest forms of action that may potentially authorize development threats to enter World Heritage sites through the back-door.

From an IUCN perspective, it is clearly the case that a World Heritage-listed forest area could not be clear-cut and, in the name of sustainability, replaced by a plantation or off-set by the protection of a neighbouring forest. There is a risk that damage to World Heritage Sites will seek justification based on such arguments that substitute, or balance, a concept of sustainability as equivalent to the protection of heritage. This points to the potentially treacherous nature of poorly defined sustainability concepts and calls for vigorous attention to ensuring that the fundamental protection of World Heritage Sites is not weakened in seeking to ensure they contribute actively and appropriately to sustainable development.

It is therefore important to highlight that preserving the world's most significant cultural and natural areas for the present and future generations represents a fundamental sustainability goal and requirement in itself, as well as a legal requirement of the World Heritage Convention. This is, indeed, underlined in the World Heritage and Sustainable Development Policy, in order to avoid any suggestion that the policy would water down the overall standards of protection that are required in the Convention. In this regard, it becomes clear that the 'avoiding irreversibility' criterion of environmental sustainability mentioned above is more aligned with the World Heritage Convention, which strives to preserve unique and irreplaceable cultural and natural assets of humanity. Careful and comprehensive attention is therefore needed to ensure that the ways in which sustainability criteria and indicators are employed adequately to reflect World Heritage standards. Of importance here is also the policy call that environmental sustainability should 'equally apply to cultural and mixed World Heritage properties, including cultural landscapes' (Article 14).

Contribution of natural and cultural World Heritage to achieving environmental sustainability

As part of the policy framing of World Heritage and Sustainable Development, a central question is how World Heritage sites contribute to the achievement of broader sustainable development goals and wider needs for environmental sustainability in particular. The remainder of this chapter addresses these questions with an emphasis on World Heritage sites listed for their natural values.

By conserving some of the most biodiverse and intact marine and terrestrial areas of the world, natural World Heritage sites contribute directly to achieving some of the Sustainable Development Goals, particularly Goal 14 (Conserve and sustainably use oceans, seas and marine resources for sustainable development) and Goal 15 (Protect, restore and promote sustainable use of terrestrial ecosystems, sustainably manage forests, combat desertification, and halt and reverse land degradation and halt biodiversity loss). By providing important ecosystem services to both local and global communities, such as water provision and carbon sequestration, these sites also potentially contribute to achieving Goal 6 (Ensure availability and sustainable management of water and sanitation for all) and Goal 13 (Take urgent action to combat climate change and its impacts).

This contribution is quite substantial considering that natural World Heritage Sites currently cover over eight per cent of the total area of the world's protected areas (IUCN 2017). These areas recognized for the primary purpose of nature conservation contribute in particular to the achievement of the Aichi Targets the Convention on Biological Diversity (UNEP 1992). Cultural World Heritage Sites, whilst outnumbering natural sites by a factor of four to one, are generally considerably smaller in size than natural World Heritage Sites, and not declared for their biodiversity values. Nevertheless, cultural World Heritage Sites do also include areas that are designated as protected areas and thus directly contribute to the Aichi targets. One particularly prominent group of sites in this regard is the World Heritage Cultural Landscapes. A recent assessment of the relationship to protected areas thus concluded that roughly two thirds of all World Heritage cultural landscapes coincide with protected areas (see Finke 2013). A wider analysis of cultural World Heritage sites is needed to reveal the full extent of this likely significant direct contribution to nature conservation by cultural World Heritage Sites.

Beyond these sites, there is also growing evidence of the importance of the contribution of sites recognized for their cultural and natural values through the recognition of large landscapes on the World Heritage List, not least in relation to the consideration of the customary territories and livelihoods of indigenous peoples (Kormos et al. 2017). As the World Heritage Convention improves its consideration of governance models for protection that involve alternatives to state-driven models alone (such as Indigenous and Community Conserved Areas) the significance of this interaction, and the ability of the Convention to respond to local needs and rights, is expected to increase.

However, it is also essential to understand how the potential contribution of natural and cultural World Heritage to all aspects of environmental sustainability can be better realized and understood by the wider public. This may allow for the strengthened integration of heritage conservation into political decision-making processes around sustainable development.

In 2014, recognizing the need to better understand the important contribution of natural World Heritage sites to the achievement of environmental sustainability, IUCN undertook an analysis of ecosystem services and benefits provided by natural World Heritage sites. The study entitled *The Benefits of Natural World Heritage: Identifying and Assessing Ecosystem Services and Benefits provided by the World's Most Iconic Natural Places* (Osipova et al. 2014) looked at a number of ecosystem services provided at global scale, such as carbon storage. Several case studies showcase the provision of different types of benefits and ecosystem services, such as water provision, natural hazards regulation, nature-based tourism as well as spiritual and cultural importance of many natural places of Outstanding Universal Value and their importance as natural laboratories for research and education. The study also looked at drivers of change, such as land use change, pollution, climate change, invasive species and overexploitation, affecting provision of these services. It highlighted that, in order to ensure the continuous provision of these important benefits, it is crucial to preserve the ecosystems that provide them in healthy and unimpaired condition, which again raises questions about applying the full range of environmental performance criteria in the context of social and economic processes.

The conclusions of the study showed that the contribution of World Heritage sites is extremely important. Collectively, the network supplies a wide range of benefits. The benefits most frequently identified at site level were 'recreation and tourism' (93 per cent of all sites), 'aesthetic values related to beauty and scenery'

(93 per cent), 'resources for building knowledge' (92 per cent), 'contribution to education' (84 per cent) and 'wilderness and iconic values' (84 per cent). Sixty-six per cent of the sites mentioned were considered important for the provision of water quantity and/or ensuring water quality. Soil stabilization and flood prevention were also identified as important ecosystem services provided by approximately half of all natural sites (48 and 45 per cent respectively). However, these ecosystem services also had high numbers of 'data deficient' responses (about 20 per cent) meaning that the figures could potentially be higher. The analysis also indicates that some benefits, such as for example provision of medicinal resources or the presence of sacred plants and animal species, are much harder to determine due to a lack of data or knowledge (Osipova et al. 2014).

The Convention is only recently starting to encourage more explicit attention to such local connections and nature-culture interlinkages. Furthermore, more works needs to be done on the distribution of costs and benefits associated with the protection and provision of such services. There were also notable regional differences detected in this analysis, further showing the importance of local and regional context to the contributions that sites make.

The IUCN World Heritage Outlook 2, a global assessment of conservation prospects of all natural World Heritage sites, was published in November 2017 (Osipova et al. 2017) and shows a concerning reduction in the reported management effectiveness of natural World Heritage Sites, as well as a growth in threats – notably in relation to climate change. This raises concern in terms of the effectiveness of the Convention in conserving the Outstanding Universal Value, but also prompts attention to the ecosystem services that are provided by well managed sites. It also points to the urgency of responding to climate change challenges.

While assessing benefits provided by natural sites through global analyses helps highlight the important contribution of these places to sustainable development, identifying, measuring and monitoring ecosystem services at site level can help inform better management decisions which would support both biodiversity conservation and provision of ecosystem services therefore contributing more to sustainable development and enhanced human well-being. Following the release of *The Benefits of Natural World Heritage* study, IUCN is currently working on evaluating existing tools for identifying, assessing and quantifying ecosystem services, including through testing some of these tools in a number of pilot sites, with the aim of developing guidance for planning and undertaking an assessment of ecosystem services in natural World Heritage sites.

As the analysis demonstrates, much work remains to be done. Not only are there major data gaps in terms of what is known about ecosystem services, knowledge about changes over time, distributional aspects in terms of costs and benefits arguably also remain limited. How is the provision of ecosystem services changing over time, and how are benefits distributed? Considering the importance of social inclusion in the World Heritage and Sustainable Development policy as well as the IUCN vision of 'just world that values and conserves nature', much more can be done to harness the social contribution of World Heritage conservation.

Such findings are equally relevant for cultural properties. As our understanding of multiple ecosystems services is broadened, this equally raises a range of questions about cultural properties not least in terms of productive landscapes and sacred sites (see also de Groot et al. 2004).

Sustainable development and climate change

In the face of climate change, it is particularly important to understand the importance of natural World Heritage sites for both mitigation and adaptation in general, but also to develop strategies for preserving heritage in the world of changing climate dynamics in specific.

Climate change adaptation and disaster risk reduction are issues that concern both natural and cultural World Heritage sites. While the specific impacts that climate change might have on natural and cultural sites will differ from site to site, World Heritage areas also face a number of similar challenges, such as the ways that climate change is affecting communities living in and around natural and cultural sites and dependent on them for their livelihoods and customary practices.

However, both natural and cultural World Heritage sites offer potential solutions to climate change challenges. In the case of natural areas, it is both their importance for climate change mitigation and adaptation, which need to be noted. *The Benefits of Natural World Heritage* study mentioned above found that an estimated 5.7 billion tons of forest biomass carbon is stored within natural World Heritage sites in the pan-tropical regions of the world alone (2014). While many protected areas are important as carbon stocks, the study also found that the terrestrial natural World Heritage sites on average contain higher forest biomass carbon density than the remaining protected areas network in pan-tropical biomes, which demonstrates the important contribution of natural World Heritage towards climate change mitigation (Osipova et al. 2014). At the local level, natural World Heritage sites also play an important role in reducing the exposure and vulnerability of local communities to climate change-related hazards, such as severe storms and floods. An example of such important regulation of natural hazards are the Sundarbans (Bangladesh) and the Sundarbans National Park (India), which are part of the largest expanse of contiguous mangrove forest in the world and inscribed on the World Heritage List.[1] These mangroves provide coastal protection to millions of people in this region, with a high incidence of cyclonic storms (UNESCO World Heritage Centre 2007; Giri et al. 2007).

In the case of some natural sites and many cultural landscapes, and potentially other cultural sites, the solutions offered include the preservation of traditional knowledge and cultural practices that may be crucial in relation to designing and implementing effective climate change adaptation strategies. Traditional agro-biodiversity, local breeds and varieties are critical resources in local adaptation approaches, just as traditional building techniques and cooperative practices (Tiwari, Shrestha and Bjønness 2018). The UNESCO *Hangzhou Declaration: Placing Culture at the Heart of Sustainable Development Policies* (UNESCO

2013) recognized that 'appropriate conservation of the historic environment, including cultural landscapes, and the safeguarding of relevant traditional knowledge, values and practices, in synergy with other scientific knowledge, enhances the resilience of communities to disasters and climate change'. Yet, there is need for a far more systematic approach to recognize and support traditional knowledge linked to cultivated plant varieties, local breeds and customary uses of the landscape in the World Heritage context. Two decades ago, FAO estimated that some 75 per cent of plant genetic diversity had been lost, and some 30 per cent of livestock breeds were in risk of extinction (FAO 1999). The expected impacts of climate change on food systems mainly reliant on some 12 plant and five animal species (FAO 2004) prompt urgent attention to interlinked natural and cultural diversity and the changing conditions in productive landscapes. Currently, most emphasis on biocultural diversity in the World Heritage Convention is in relation to cultural landscapes, yet it is widely recognized in several continents that a more systematic approach is required to address biocultural linkages in other types of properties as well (for Europe, see, e.g., Agnoletti and Emanueli 2016: 11).

The importance of cultural and natural World Heritage for climate change adaptation is today highlighted by the UNESCO World Heritage and Sustainable Development Policy which calls upon State Parties to 'recognise and promote the inherent potential of World Heritage properties for reducing disaster risks and adapting to climate change, through associated ecosystem services, traditional knowledge and practices and strengthened social cohesion' (UNESCO 2015). IUCN has adopted multiple resolutions on climate change over the last three decades (since its General Assembly in 1988), framing its policy recommendations around the promotion of nature-based solutions but equally stressing the importance of 'biodiversity protection, human rights safeguards, intergenerational equity, gender and other relevant IUCN general policy including on protected areas, biodiversity offsets and primary forests' (IUCN 2016). Such policy language, similar to the commitments of the World Heritage and Sustainable Development policy, stress the importance of a comprehensive approach to climate change.

Sustainability standards and best-practice examples

In addition to their direct contribution to sustainable development, natural and cultural World Heritage sites may play an important role in serving as best practice examples of the achievement of good standards of environmental sustainability and promoting such standards to broader sectors. In principle, for World Heritage Sites to demonstrate fully a leadership role in relation to environmental sustainability it would be essential to ensure that the management of both natural and cultural World Heritage sites adheres to the highest standards in relation to sustainability standards on a wide range of performance criteria, including energy and water consumption.

The parallel here could be drawn with work on environmental sustainability in the private sector, and World Heritage Sites could act in areas such as examining their procurement of goods and services, their use of water and energy, and their transport and waste management policies. Principles could include purchasing from suppliers who are recognized as providing materials from sustainable sources, prioritizing local produce or for sites to meet international accreditation for sustainability. Furthermore, site management could take a leadership role in encouraging such standards within their local communities and associated economic sectors. IUCN is currently launching a sustainability standard for protected areas, the IUCN Green List, and this could become a benchmark for wider performance of many World Heritage Areas.

Little has yet been done at the policy level to articulate how such broader sustainability standards could apply to World Heritage Site management. Nevertheless, there are notable examples of World Heritage sites that already showcase best practice examples in protected area management by striving to achieve effectiveness in their day-to-day operations in terms of energy use, transport and waste management. An example is the Joggins Fossil Cliffs in Canada, where a new visitor centre meets leading green building standards. A number of natural World Heritage sites have also formalized their commitment to sustainability through adoption of strategic plans and guidance documents. A notable example is the Yellowstone Strategic Plan for Sustainability. The plan includes goals at operational and infrastructure level aimed at minimizing impacts on the environment, while at the same time enhancing visitor experience, as well as living and working conditions of the park's employees. It also is focused around reduction of greenhouse emissions, as well as around energy, water and materials consumption and conducting day-to-day operations in an environmentally responsible manner (NPS 2012).

The concept of environmental sustainability is also starting to become more integrated in various aspects of cultural heritage preservation and management. Some recent examples include consideration of environmental performance of heritage buildings (Parks Canada 2008). A number of recent studies looked at energy efficiency considerations in the context of cultural World Heritage sites, such as for example the Historic Centre of Oporto, Luiz I Bridge and Monastery of Serra do Pilar in Portugal and Portovenere, Cinque Terre, and the islands of Palmaria, Tino and Tinetto in Italy (Flores 2016; Franco 2016). While discussing a number of possible energy efficiency improvement measures, these studies also highlight that in some case traditional buildings showed better thermal performance than predicted (Flores 2016), highlighting the importance of better understanding of their characteristics and conditions.

Establishing a fully developed approach to meet wider environmental sustainability standards for all World Heritage sites could be taken up by UNESCO, IUCN and the other Convention advisory bodies and partners, as a key leadership challenge where World Heritage Sites could implement and influence much stronger and more consistent results, beyond their 'core business' of heritage conservation.

Sustainable heritage is in this sense not only about sustaining heritage, but equally responding to wider social, environmental and economic challenges.

Conclusions

Only by maintaining healthy ecosystems can natural World Heritage sites continue to provide the numerous services and benefits they currently offer to both local and global communities. A similar situation exists for cultural sites which can only continue to play their important role in achieving sustainable development if their values are effectively conserved and managed. Protection of the Outstanding Universal Value of these unique places therefore ensures the continuous provision of the numerous benefits to local and global communities, even if we are only starting to comprehend the full nature and distribution and governance implications of such benefits.

Better understanding of the wider potential of World Heritage sites to contribute to different dimensions of sustainability also sheds light on the complex interlinkages between conservation and sustainable development. The concept of sustainable development underlines the importance of considering the different dimensions together and of integrating the natural environment, communities and economy on the path towards sustainability. The World Heritage Convention being the only international convention bringing together nature and culture is well placed to promote such holistic approaches, even if, at present, the World Heritage Convention is only recently embarking on a more integrative approach (Buckley, Larsen and Badman 2015; Larsen and Wijesuriya 2015). The World Heritage and Sustainable Development policy notes that 'sustainable development will necessarily have to take into consideration the interrelationship of biological diversity with the local cultural context' (UNESCO 2015: Article 8).

Environmental sustainability, as a whole, needs to be brought to the fore within this broadening of the World Heritage mission. The fundamental contribution of protecting and conserving World Heritage sites to sustainability is a foundation and statutory requirement of the Convention, and must be the first priority. But approaches need to go beyond this to recognise the contributions that sites potentially make to communities through the wider protection of vital ecosystem services and the aim to ensure equitable distribution of benefits that directly contribute to human wellbeing and help to provide for resilience. The contributions of all sites, and in particular cultural sites, need to be better understood.

Finally, World Heritage sites need to be challenged to go further and lead in demonstrating best practice in environmental sustainability in all of their direct work, and in the economies and communities that they support and influence. A more ambitious approach to building environmental sustainability into the core business of implementation World Heritage site management, and building on the Convention's unique influencing role is needed. The World Heritage and Sustainable Development policy offers an important window of opportunity to initiate the development of environmental standards for both the current 1,073 World Heritage sites and future ones in the making.

Note

1 See relevant World Heritage List documents at http://whc.unesco.org/en/list/798 and http://whc.unesco.org/en/list/452.

References

Adams, B. (2006). *The Future of Sustainability: Re-Thinking Environment and Development in the Twenty-First Century*. Report of the IUCN Renowned Thinkers Meeting, 29–31 January 2006 IUCN. Gland, IUCN.

Agnoletti, M. and F. Emanueli (eds) (2016). *Biocultural Diversity in Europe*. New York: Springer.

Balvanera, P. et al. (2006). 'Quantifying the evidence for biodiversity effects on ecosystem functioning and services', *Ecology Letters*, 9(10), 1146–1156. Available at: http://dx.doi.org/10.1111/j.1461-0248.2006.00963.x

Buckley, K., Larsen, P. B. and Badman, T. (2015). 'Crossing boundaries: Exploring biocultural concepts and practices in the World Heritage System', in M. di Stefano (ed), *ICOMOS Symposium 'Heritage and Landscape as Human Values', Conference Proceedings, Theme 5, Florence 2014*. Florence: ICOMOS.

Cardinale, B. J. et al. (2012). 'Biodiversity loss and its impact on humanity', *Nature*, 486(7401), 59–67 (online). Available at: www.nature.com/nature/journal/v486/n7401/full/nature11148.html?foxtrotcallback=true (accessed 1 October 2017).

de Groot, R., Ramakrishnan, P. S., van de Berg, A., Kulenthran, T., Muller, S., Pitt, D., Wascher, D., Wijesuriya, G. (2004). *Cultural and Amenity Services: Ecosystems and Human Well-Being: Current State and Trends*. MA.

Finke, G. (2013). *Landscape Interfaces: World Heritage Cultural Landscapes and IUCN Protected Areas: A Study Exploring the Relationships between World Heritage Cultural Landscapes and IUCN Protected Area Management Categories*. Gland, Switzerland: IUCN.

Flores, J. (2016). 'An investigation of the energy efficiency of traditional buildings in the Oporto World Heritage Site', in M. de Bouw et al. (eds), *Energy Efficiency and Comfort of Historic Buildings*, pp. 93–101. Flanders Heritage Agency (online). Available at: www.eechb.eu/wp-content/uploads/2016/12/Proceedings_EECHB.pdf (accessed 1 October 2017).

Food and Agricultural Organization (FAO) (1999). *Women: Users, Preservers and Managers of Agrobiodiversity*. Rome: Women in Development Service, Food and Agriculture Organization of the United Nations.

Food and Agricultural Organization (FAO) (2004). 'What is agrobiodiversity?', in *Building on Gender, Agrobiodiversity and Local Knowledge*. Rome: Gender and Development Service.

Franco, G. (2016). 'Eco-efficiency in a UNESCO World Heritage site: Safeguard, innovation and compatibility', in M. de Bouw et al. (eds), *Energy Efficiency and Comfort of Historic Buildings*. Flanders Heritage Agency (online). Available at: www.eechb.eu/wp-content/uploads/2016/12/Proceedings_EECHB.pdf (accessed 1 October 2017).

Giri, C. et al. (2007). 'Monitoring mangrove forest dynamics of the Sundarbans in Bangladesh and India using multi-temporal satellite data from 1973 to 2000', *Estuarine, Coastal and Shelf Science*, 73(1–2), 91–100 (online). Available at: http://pubs.er.usgs.gov/publication/70030176 (accessed 1 October 2017).

Goodland, R. (1995). 'The concept of environmental sustainability', *Annual Review of Ecology and Systematics*, 26, 1–24 (online). Available at: www2.econ.iastate.edu/classes/tsc220/hallam/goodland.pdf (accessed 1 October 2017).

IUCN (2016). IUCN Response to the Paris Climate Change Agreement. *World Conservation Congress Resolution 056*. Available at: https://portals.iucn.org/library/sites/library/files/resrecfiles/WCC_2016_RES_056_EN.pdf

IUCN, FAO, UNEP, UNESCO and WWF (1980). *World Conservation Strategy: Living Resource Conservation for Sustainable Development*. Gland, Switzerland: IUCN (online). Available at: https://portals.iucn.org/library/node/6424 (accessed 1 October 2017).

Kormos, C. F., Badman, T., Jaeger, T., Bertzky, B., van Merm, R., Osipova, E., Shi, Y. and Larsen, P. B. (2017). *World Heritage, Wilderness and Large Landscapes and Seascapes*. Gland, Switzerland: IUCN.

Larsen, P. B. and Wijesuriya, G. (2015). 'Nature: Culture interlinkages in World Heritage: Bridging the gap', *World Heritage*, 75.

Millennium Ecosystem Assessment (MA) (2005). *Ecosystems and Human Well-Being: Synthesis*. Washington, DC, USA: Island Press.

National Park Service (NPS) (2012). *The Greenstone: Sustainability Report 2012 Yellowstone National Park* (online). Available at: www.nps.gov/yell/learn/management/upload/2012-Greenstone-drafted-May-2013-small.pdf (accessed 1 October 2017).

OECD (2001). *OECD Environmental Strategy for the First Decade of the 21st Century* (online). Available at: www.oecd.org/environment/indicators-modelling-outlooks/1863539.pdf (accessed 1 October 2017).

Osipova, E. et al. (2014). *The Benefits of Natural World Heritage: Identifying and Assessing Ecosystem Services and Benefits provided by the World's Natural Wonders*. Gland, Switzerland: IUCN (online). Available at: www.iucn.org/theme/world-heritage/our-work/world-heritage-projects/benefits-natural-world-heritage (accessed 1 October 2017).

Osipova, E. et al. (2017). *IUCN World Heritage Outlook 2: A Conservation Assessment of All Natural World Heritage Sites*. Gland, Switzerland: IUCN.

Parks Canada (2008). *Sustainable Historic Places: A Background Paper for the Historic Places Branch, Parks Canada*. Ottawa: Parks Canada.

Soliveres, S. et al. (2016). 'Biodiversity at multiple trophic levels is needed for ecosystem multifunctionality', *Nature*, 536(7617), 456–59 (online). Available at: http://dx.doi.org/10.1038/nature19092 (accessed 1 October 2017).

Tiwari, S. R., Shrestha, P. and Bjønness, H. C. (2018). 'Local rights in World Heritage Sites: Learning from post-earthquake rehabilitation dynamics in the Kathmandu Valley', in P. B. Larsen (ed), *World Heritage and Human Rights: Lessons from the Asia-Pacific and Global Arena*. London: Earthscan Routledge.

UNESCO (2010). *World Heritage Convention and Sustainable Development*. Document WHC-10/34.COM/5D (online). Available at: http://whc.unesco.org/archive/2010/whc10-34com-5De.pdf (accessed 3 November 2017).

UNESCO (2015). *Policy Document for the Integration of a Sustainable Development Perspective into the Processes of the World Heritage Convention* (online). Available at: http://whc.unesco.org/en/sustainabledevelopment/ (accessed 2 December 2017).

UNESCO World Heritage Centre (2007). *Case Studies on Climate Change and World Heritage*. Paris: World Heritage Centre.

United Nations (UN) (2015). *Transforming Our World: The 2030 Agenda for Sustainable Development* (online). Available at: https://sustainabledevelopment.un.org/content/documents/21252030%20Agenda%20for%20Sustainable%20Development%20web.pdf (accessed 3 November 2017).

United Nations Conference on Environment and Development (UNCED) (1992). *Agenda 21: Programe of Action for Sustainable Development* (online). Available at: https://sustainabledevelopment.un.org/content/documents/Agenda21.pdf (accessed 3 November 2017).

United Nations Environmental Program (UNEP) (1992). *Convention on Biological Diversity (The Biodiversity Convention)* (Rio de Janeiro: UNEP) (online). Available at: www.cbd.int/convention/text/default.shtml (accessed 3 November 2017).

World Commission on Environment and Development (WCED) (1987). *Report of the World Commission on Environment and Development : Our Common Future Acronyms and Note on Terminology Chairman's Foreword.*

Worm, B. et al. (2006). 'Impacts of biodiversity loss on ocean ecosystem services', *Science*, 314(November), 787–791.

Chapter 11

'No past, no future?' An ICOMOS perspective on cultural heritage and the sustainability agenda

Luisa de Marco, Susan Denyer, Regina Durighello and Ege Yıldırım

Although the notion of sustainable development has only gained a high profile in the cultural heritage conservation realm relatively recently, concerns for resource depletion that form the basis of the sustainability concept have always been at the heart of the heritage conservation movement. The economic and energy crises of the early 1970s, along with the increasing expansion of the notion of cultural heritage, raised awareness that growth could not be indefinite and that resources are limited and need to be carefully used, as highlighted in the first report by the Club of Rome (Meadows et al. 1972). Even more recently, general concern has widened to embrace human resources, particularly traditional knowledge and practices which can and do have an enormous impact on our optimal use of resources.

This chapter aims to explore the evolution of thinking within ICOMOS on the role of cultural heritage in relation to the development agenda. It also considers the implications of the new United Nations Sustainable Development Goals (SDGs)[1] and the *Policy on the integration of a sustainable development perspective into the processes of the World Heritage Convention* (World Heritage and Sustainable Development Policy) (UNESCO 2015), all of which were adopted in 2015.

The SDGs refer to culture both explicitly and implicitly in several Goals and Targets, namely in relation to education, sustainable cities, food security, the environment, economic growth, sustainable consumption and production patterns, sustainable tourism and peaceful and inclusive societies. Culture has thus now attained a strengthened position within the international development agenda, most tangibly in the SDG Target 11.4 referring to cultural and natural heritage. This brings into focus the need to see culture and heritage in a new and dynamic way that acknowledges their role not only in shaping who we are and the places that we inhabit but also how they can act as enablers of sustainable development.

The World Heritage and Sustainable Development Policy, on its side, recognizes the need for the heritage sector to harness the reciprocal benefits for heritage and society that may be derived from a sustainable approach to development, to avoid ill-conceived forms of development and to ensure that World Heritage listing brings benefits to local communities. It aims thereby to persuade all stakeholders to act with social responsibility in pursuing World Heritage designations and in managing listed properties. The perspective of the Policy seems to suggest that sustainability is not necessarily inherent in World Heritage designations but needs to be made explicit and intentionally pursued through purposely conceived strategies. While at a first glance, this perspective may appear provocative, ICOMOS views it as offering valuable 'food for thought' and action.

Before 'sustainability': ICOMOS engagement in cultural heritage

Since the beginning of its activities, ICOMOS has focused on themes and issues that are today clearly linked to the sphere of sustainability, such as the importance of ongoing maintenance for heritage buildings; the need to avoid massive restoration projects; the need for conservation to be proportionate and use local resources; and the need to ensure that heritage meets the social needs of society. Indeed, ICOMOS has long advocated that heritage is seen as part of the past, present and future and that it contributes to social and economic viability.

The first ICOMOS Conference on the *Conservation, Restoration and Revival of Areas and Groups of Buildings of Historic Interest*, held in Caceres in 1967, offered an overview of the state of the art in Europe and a number of countries in other parts of the world with regard to the institutional frameworks and legal instruments that were needed and available for use (ICOMOS 1967). In particular, it identified those designed and tested to ensure that the conservation of cultural heritage involved not only physical fabric but also its 'revivification' in social terms. The final resolution of the conference suggested several topics for which studies were deemed necessary. These topics included strategies to integrate modern architecture into the historic urban fabric, preserve the scale and character of historic groups of buildings, manage vehicular traffic, provide 'protection against fire and natural calamities' and train specialists as well as to develop appropriate designs for street layout and urban furniture and to identify 'methods of revivification in connection with town and country planning schemes'.

In 1969, the ICOMOS Symposium on *Monuments and Society*, held in Leningrad, highlighted the role that monuments, broadly defined as in the Venice Charter,[2] could play as a 'powerful means of raising the standards of ethical and aesthetic education', thus clarifying what was perceived at the time as one of the key functions of monuments in society (ICOMOS 1971). The final resolution of the symposium underlined that 'the greater care modern society takes of the heritage of the past, the richer will be its culture and the wider its possibilities of development on a humanist level, the cultural heritage of mankind is both one of the essential factors enabling men to communicate with one another' (ICOMOS 1971: 45). It also stressed the need for inter-sectoral coordination among the different branches of the public administration, including those responsible for the protection of cultural heritage. It recommended that heritage protection bodies establish 'close cooperation with the town and area planning departments to ensure that provision is made within the framework of the development of contemporary living, for the protection of historical centres and monuments of cultural value' and that 'the greatest attention will be paid to the problem of efficient utilization of monuments in the service of culture' (ICOMOS 1971: 46).

It is worth noting how prophetic the preoccupations expressed by M.I. Sédei (Yugoslavia) were regarding threats from forms of tourism that considered monuments only as a way of attracting more tourists and economic returns – threats the sheer scale of which we experience at many World Heritage properties today. The approach taken in Finland was also interesting and forward-looking where, in the absence of a specialized institute for the protection of monuments, an interdisciplinary group was formed, including sociologists, economists, psychologists, architects, representatives of the administrations of cities and rural communities (ICOMOS 1971: 133).

Many of the ICOMOS participants in those conferences and meetings were actively engaged in the development of policies for the heritage sector heritage at the Council of Europe and reflections of this, both explicit and implicit, can be seen. For instance, it was perhaps not by chance that at a symposium in Rothenburg ob der Tauber ICOMOS again addressed the challenges related to the future of small historic towns from a socio-economic and heritage perspective (ICOMOS 1975). This was in the very same year as the European Year of Architectural Heritage, which officially inaugurated the notion of 'integrated conservation' (Council of Europe 1975). Three years later, ICOMOS went on to discuss further the complex and often dialectic relationship between cultural heritage and development at its 1978 ICOMOS Conference in Moscow and Suzdal on *Protection of Historic Cities and Quarters in Urban Development* (ICOMOS 1978). This explored several themes that continue to be relevant today, such as 'monuments and contemporary humanism', 'historic monuments and cultural identity', 'historic buildings, their role in economic and social development', 'monuments and youth', 'monuments and tourism' and 'public opinion and the safeguarding of monuments'.

These early ICOMOS documents already show a mature understanding of the crucial role of cultural heritage in relation to social and wider cultural issues. It can be said that at that time the theoretical background was already in place, the main challenges and issues were starting to be identified and so, too, was the overall agenda that later fed into the sustainability discourse. In the same decades, although with uneven commitment and results, these reflections began to inform legislation and, planning instruments. For instance, in France in 1962 the 'Loi Malraux' established the protection and safeguarding of historic urban sectors (*secteurs sauvegardés*). In Italy Law no. 765/1967, also known as 'Legge Ponte', and the related bylaws made it compulsory to define the boundaries of historic centres and develop detailed plans, subject to prior examination by the state offices for cultural heritage protection. A number of plans combining physical with socio-economic recovery were subsequently carried out in various Italian cities such as Gubbio, Assisi, Bologna and Taranto, some of which later became models of heritage-sensitive planning and urban recovery.

This early focus on sustainability-related themes, despite the fact that the word had not yet come into current use, continued at the ICOMOS scientific symposia on *No Past, No Future* (6th General Assembly, Naples, Italy (ICOMOS 1981)), *Economics of Conservation* (10th General Assembly, Colombo, Sri Lanka, 1993 (ICOMOS 1993)) and *The Wise Use of Heritage* (12th General Assembly, Mexico in 1999 (ICOMOS 1999)). The Sri Lankan symposium was particularly interesting because a range of methods for and experiences in assessing and measuring the economic impacts of built heritage conservation were shared and discussed among participants from around the globe. These highlighted the need for heritage conservation to be seen as an activity whose benefits were just as much social and economic as cultural and spiritual. The need to develop econometric models suitable for measuring quantitatively the direct and indirect economic benefits of cultural heritage for local economies and the need to acknowledge the importance of cultural heritage in stimulating human creativity were also expressed.

The intellectual ferment of the epoch in the heritage field, which was nurtured by the discussions held in these symposia, stimulated the development of a more detailed, operational and multidisciplinary research agenda. Both within and outside ICOMOS attempts were made to fill the gaps in knowledge on topics relevant for increasing the long-term effectiveness of conservation. ICOMOS research efforts in areas relevant to sustainable development are demonstrated by the establishment and research work of several of its International Scientific Committees (ISC) such as Historic Towns and Villages (CIVVIH), Economics of Conservation (ISCEC), Legal, Administrative and Financial Issues (ICLAFI), Cultural Tourism (ICTC), Energy and Sustainability (ISCES+CC), Interpretation and Presentation of Cultural Heritage Sites (ICIP), Risk Preparedness (ICORP) and Shared Built Heritage (ISCSBH). These have all directly contributed to increasing the body of knowledge and reflection topics related to the wide range of sustainability issues inherent in heritage conservation.[3]

The 'advent' of sustainable development on the international stage

Since 1987, when the notion of sustainable development was popularized thanks to the UN World Commission on the Environment and Development report 'Our Common Future' (also known as the Brundtland Report), the idea has been enriched by considerations of intra-generational solidarity, gender equality and inclusiveness and of the need for a model of economic growth that is environmentally sustainable and socially equitable (UN 1987). However, it has to be noted that in many early international documents discussing the environment, sustainability and development, the notion of environment did not explicitly include cultural heritage. This became a cause of misunderstandings; for example, when evaluating the impacts of projects on cultural property or on landscapes. Therefore, efforts have been progressively made to ensure that the concept of environment was not limited to its 'natural' dimensions but also addressed the human-made environment, particularly cultural heritage and landscape. For instance, the Council Directive 85/337/EEC – the first European directive on Environmental Impact Assessment – explicitly requested that

> environmental impact assessment will identify, describe and assess … the direct and indirect effects of a project on … human beings, fauna and flora, soil, water, air, climate and the landscape, the inter-action between the[se] factors … material assets and the cultural heritage.
>
> (European Union 1985)

Despite such efforts, the understanding that the notion of environment also encompasses landscape and cultural heritage is not firmly rooted in all countries. Acceptance of the notion depends on differing cultural and administrative traditions, and in some countries, protection of nature is given much prominence compared to that of cultural heritage.

The last decade of the twentieth century saw UNESCO launch the World Decade for Cultural Development (1988–1997), which was planned to be closely coordinated with the implementation of the International Development Strategy of the third United Nations Development Decade. In the early years of the twenty-first century, the United Nations also began a process to promote recognition of culture and cultural heritage as key factors in sustainable development. A milestone is represented by the Resolution adopted by the United Nations General Assembly in October 2010, 'keeping the promise: united to achieve the Millennium Development Goals' (UN 2010). Further reflections within the UN on culture and its role for sustainable development are expressed in the 2012 Thematic Think Piece by the UN Task Team on the Post-2015 UN Development Agenda, which is titled 'Culture: A Driver and Enabler of Sustainable Development" (UN Task Team 2012). The Thematic Think Piece underlines the importance of integrating culture into governance and into the conception, measurement and practice of development in a range of different ways.[4] In 2013, the International Congress 'Culture: Key to Sustainable Development' (UNESCO 2013) was held in Hangzhou and concluded by the adoption of the homonymous Declaration.

These documents and dialogue with key interlocutors aimed to prepare the ground for the inclusion of culture in the New Sustainable Development Agenda which replaces the Millennium Development Goals. The 2015 United Nations Resolution 'Transforming Our World: the 2030 Agenda for Sustainable Development' includes culture implicitly in several of the Sustainable Development Goals, but also explicitly in the specific Target 11.4 to 'strengthen efforts to protect and safeguard the world's cultural and natural heritage' and under Goal 11 to 'make our cities and human settlements inclusive, safe, resilient and sustainable' (UN 2015). Culture and cultural heritage are now, for the first time, part of the international agenda on sustainable development. This approach, which ICOMOS supports, implies a more dynamic way to look at cultures and human societies, their legacies and cultural creativity – a way that acknowledges their role and specific function in shaping who we are as individuals and as members of communities and society at large, as well as the places that we inhabit and how they have been and can continue to be enablers of sustainable development.

The above-mentioned UN documents have thus expanded the scope of the environment to include both the way it has been modified by people over time and the way in which they can recognize their engagement with it. These documents also set the ground for further research and creative thinking to turn the SDGs into reality. The UNESCO World Heritage and Sustainable Development policy, adopted in 2015 by the UNESCO General Assembly at its 20th Session, goes in the same direction. It highlights the need for compatible, sustainable, equitable, inclusive and participatory approaches when pursuing development through World Heritage properties and designations so as to ensure that World Heritage inscription truly manifests the principles of sustainability, inclusiveness and justice. Development must be compatible with sustaining Outstanding Universal Value, but it must also consider the other, no less important requirements of human cohabitation.

Recent ICOMOS steps in operationalizing sustainability within the cultural heritage realm

Exploration by ICOMOS of the interfaces between cultural heritage and socio-economic development continued into the twenty-first century with meetings, such as the 2011 ICOMOS scientific symposium on 'Heritage, Driver of Development', which advocated a collective reflection on the role of cultural heritage in the sustainable development agenda (ICOMOS 2011a). In the context of the applied research carried out over the last two decades, the symposium addressed the challenges of absorbing the relationship between heritage and sustainability into thematic operational objectives and that might make a more incisive and tangible contribution to 'environment-friendly' conservation.

The symposium concluded with the adoption of the Paris Declaration, which sets out the most updated collective position of ICOMOS members on this topic (ICOMOS 2011b). Building on the results of the Johannesburg World Summit on Sustainable Development (or Earth Summit) 2002, and on other important UNESCO and UN documents on the topic, the Paris Declaration stresses the need to develop approaches that take up the challenge of preserving and, at the same time, integrating heritage into the concept of sustainable development in order to reflect the crucial part heritage plays in social cohesion, wellbeing, creativity and economic appeal and in promoting understanding between communities. In some respects, the Paris Declaration was a forerunner of the UN SDGs and UNESCO's World Heritage and Sustainable Development policy.

Since 2011, ICOMOS has reinforced its engagement in strengthening the interlinkage between the heritage conservation and sustainable development agendas, establishing a Task Force that specifically deals with sustainable development and cultural heritage issues and mandating a Focal Point for the SDGs to coordinate

ICOMOS advocacy work towards this end. A fruitful result of these efforts was the ICOMOS participation at the UN Habitat III in Quito, Ecuador, in October 2016 and at the 22nd Session of the Conference of the Parties to the UN Convention on Climate Change (COP22) in Marrakech, Morocco, in November 2016.

As part of ICOMOS contributions to the New Urban Agenda,[5] which was adopted at Habitat III, an ICOMOS 'Concept Note' was released (Fusco Girard et al. 2016). It builds on the longstanding 'ICOMOS tradition' of care for cultural heritage, in all its forms, as well as on many key documents produced at the UN and EU levels. It also provides a thorough intellectual framework for different stakeholders in progressively integrating cultural heritage into their development plans, policies and programs. The paper also outlines the key challenges facing international, national and particularly local institutions in making sustainable development a reality and positions ICOMOS' work to apply sustainability considerations when dealing with cultural heritage conservation and revitalization.

ICOMOS has already begun to act upon the SDGs. In 2017, it developed an Action Plan that provides a foundation for its vision of cultural heritage as a driver and enabler of sustainable development (ICOMOS 2017). Its main objective is to advocate the implementation of the UN SDGs at the local level, with a particular focus on Target 11.4 related to the protection and safeguarding of the world's cultural and natural heritage as well as the UN-Habitat's New Urban Agenda. The Action Plan encompasses three major areas where action is envisaged:

1   Advocacy and organization: specific objectives include organization positioning, engaging with key UN Agenda themes, organizing research and content development, networking and fundraising;
2   Localizing the means of implementation: specific objectives include visibility building and awareness raising at national/local levels, liaising/partnering for local implementation, documenting case-studies and fundraising; and
3   Monitoring implementation: specific objectives include refining indicators for Target 11.4, developing further indicators, applying these indicators for reporting and review and fundraising.

All constituencies of ICOMOS are called to action, and the Action Plan suggests which could be the most appropriate responsible actors, according to their mandate within the organization. A key aspect of ICOMOS work in this regard will be strengthening cooperation with IUCN in order to further improve understanding of the interlinkages between natural and cultural heritage and to harness emerging synergies between the approaches of the two organizations and that of the United Cities and Local Governments (UCLG), notably its Committee on Culture. ICOMOS is also part of essential projects such as Our Common Dignity (Rights-based Approaches), the Connecting Practice and the Culture 2015 Goal, now updated to Culture 2030 Goal, which all contribute to inflect the notion of sustainability under differing, yet complementary perspectives. More specifically, in relation to its formal role as an Advisory Body to the UNESCO World Heritage

Committee, ICOMOS's Upstream work,[6] its evaluations of nominations for the World Heritage list and its advice on the State of Conservation of inscribed properties, all provide the opportunity to consider ways of strengthening the resilience of traditional social and other structures in relation to sustaining the value for which properties have been or might be inscribed.

ICOMOS and the World Heritage and Sustainable Development Policy

ICOMOS has long since seized the opportunity to rise to the challenges of ensuring the full integration of cultural heritage into the wider realm of human development. These challenges, nevertheless, require continuous renewal of the intellectual framework and the sharpening of analytical and implementation instruments. This holds particularly true for World Heritage properties. While there is no doubt that the World Heritage Convention is an international instrument conceived to foster the documentation, integrated protection, conservation, presentation and transmission to future generations of natural and cultural heritage, it runs the risk of being a victim of its own success: The success of the idea that heritage is an integral dimension that can improve the quality of human life and can also – and often does – lead to over-development (for instance, through insensitive tourism development) and inequitable distribution of resources (for instance, through the gentrification of heritage districts and houses).

The UNESCO World Heritage and Sustainable Development policy document aims to set out principles and mechanisms that support measures to address the development deficit, inequalities and lack of equitable opportunities. At the same time, these mechanisms should have the potential to reduce overexploitation of World Heritage inscription and the resulting commodification and reduction or unequitable distribution of the wealth and benefits.

Important steps are already being undertaken to begin to operationalize this policy such as the Vilm workshop on 'World Heritage and Sustainable development – From Policy to Action' (Isle of Vilm, Germany, 14–16 November 2016),[7] which produced an action plan that proposes sets of actions and related timeframes for the implementation of the policy. The results of the Vilm meeting are referred to in Decision 41COM 5C.11, adopted during the 41st Session of the World Heritage Committee at Krakow in July 2017. The Decision reads as follows:

> Commends the efforts undertaken by the State Party of Germany in collaboration with the World Heritage Centre and the Advisory Bodies concerning the operationalization of the World Heritage – Sustainable Development policy and calls for wider collaboration in consolidating these efforts.
>
> (UNESCO 2017)

However, the commitment by the participants that emerged in Vilm and other forums needs to be made operational through specific guidance on research and the development of relevant mechanisms, structures, actions and appropriate indicators. What has also been highlighted is the need to understand the complexity of social structures, what makes them resilient and how that resilience might be strengthened from within so that they are not overwhelmed by external forces. In this sense, what is emerging strongly is the similarity between natural and cultural heritage in the way they are both underpinned by complex systems that need to be understood, respected and, in many cases, strengthened and made more resilient.

This understanding of the interactions between cultural heritage and the resilience of the underlying social and other structures with which it is engaged lags far behind an understanding of the resilience of eco-systems. Human ecology needs to have a much higher profile in the discourse on engagement of cultural heritage within sustainable development. Overall, the notion of sustainability within World Heritage properties must be related to strengthening their resilience; that is, the capacity of their social and cultural processes to withstand natural and human-made disasters and to respond to incremental change through allowing adaptation and evolution that sustains their Outstanding Universal Value. This approach is important for all properties but particularly crucial for cultural landscapes, urban areas and mixed sites. Such an approach also highlights properties as positive resources for communities and encourages their active participation. All of this brings the need for more dynamic and precise management systems based on a firmer understanding of formal and informal structures and their complexity and resilience and for the development of adequate indicators that are able to show how approaches can strengthen resilience.

The Upstream process offers an innovative platform through which to explore how sustainability dimensions and objectives can be reflected throughout the whole World Heritage nomination process, beginning with the formation of Tentative Lists. The creation or updating of Tentative Lists is a time for reflection and beginning to understand better what might be the implications of World Heritage inscription for the properties, their immediate and wider setting and their associated communities. Tentative listing and World Heritage nomination provide a framework within which to consider the governance and management mechanisms needed to ensure that sustainability goals are linked to the specificities of properties and their potential Outstanding Universal Value and to extend the indirect benefits of World Heritage inscription to the territories in which the properties are located and to their communities.

The ability of World Heritage properties to become nodes for sustainable development fits with the ambition of the World Heritage Convention to promote the idea of World Heritage properties as the focus of multi-layered yet intertwined networks of inherited places, meanings, and processes. The Convention also stresses the importance of documenting, protecting and safeguarding cultural and natural heritage in general, well beyond the properties inscribed on the World Heritage List. Inscribed properties are thus seen as nodes of excellence within a much wider network of well cared-for heritage places at the national and local level. World Heritage properties, in this perspective, need to be seen as exemplars in relation to how sustainable development, in its widest sense in relation to strengthen the resilience of cultural and natural systems, can be embedded within management systems that are put in place to sustain their Outstanding Universal Value.

At the same time, it is essential that such sustainability practice within World Heritage properties does not stop at their boundaries. The cultural and natural systems that underpin these properties usually spread into the buffer zones and wider settings and sometimes into much wider regions. A crucial goal of strengthening the sustainability and resilience of World Heritage properties should be to optimize benefits across this wider context. Such an approach would allow sustainability principles and objectives to be related to communities of interest across wide geographical areas at a scale that could begin to have major impacts.

Notes

1 The Sustainable Development Goals declared in the official document known as *Transforming Our World: the 2030 Agenda for Sustainable Development* are a set of intergovernmental aspirational goals that form the 'Post- 2015 Development Agenda'. The goals are set out in paragraph 54 of the United Nations Resolution A/RES/70/1 of 25 September 2015. They replace the Millennium Development Goals.
2 The Venice Charter in art. 1 defines monuments as follows: 'The concept of a historic monument embraces not only the single architectural work but also the urban or rural setting in which is found the evidence of a particular civilization, a significant development or a historic event. This applies not only to great works of art but also to more modest works of the past which have acquired cultural significance with the passing of time'.
3 The results of this research activity can be found – partially – on the ICOMOS website www.icomos.org and of the International Scientific Committees and National Committees.
4 These include: capitalizing on the contribution of the culture sector to economic development and poverty reduction, supporting sustainable cultural tourism, promoting culture-based urban revitalization, integrating traditional knowledge and practices into sustainable development schemes, seeking synergies between traditional and innovative practices and technologies and promoting intercultural dialogue to achieve social cohesion and thereby establishing conditions favourable to development and creativity, particularly in post-conflict and post-disaster situations.
5 The New Urban Agenda outlines the key principles and commitments in pursuing 'a vision a vision of cities for all … seeking to promote inclusivity and ensure that all inhabitants, of present and future generations, without discrimination of any kind, are able to inhabit and produce just, safe, healthy, accessible, affordable, resilient, and sustainable cities and human settlements, to foster prosperity and quality of life for all' (Habitat III 2016: 2). The ICOMOS Action Plan of SDGs can be found at: www.icomos. org/en/what-we-do/focus/un-sustainable-development-goals/9329-icomos-action-for-the-sdgs-final-draft-now-online.
6 The Upstream process has now been defined in the *Operational Guidelines for the Implementation of the World Heritage Convention*, 2015, as follows:

> In relation to the nomination of sites for inscription on the World Heritage List, 'Upstream processes' include advice, consultation and analysis that occur prior to the submission of a nomination and are aimed at reducing the number of nominations

that experience significant problems during the evaluation process. The basic principle of the upstream processes is to enable the Advisory Bodies and the Secretariat to provide support directly to State Parties, throughout the whole process leading up to a possible World Heritage nomination. For the upstream support to be effective, it should ideally be undertaken from the earliest stage in the nomination process, at the moment of the preparation or revision of the State Parties' Tentative Lists.

7 Expert workshop organized by the German Federal Agency for Nature Conservation (BfN) in cooperation with IUCN World Heritage Program, ICOMOS International and ICCROM.

References

Council of Europe (1975). *European Charter of the Architectural Heritage 1975* (online). Available at: www.icomos.org/en/charters-and-texts/179-articles-en-francais/ressources/charters-and-standards/170-european-charter-of-the-architectural-heritage (accessed 10 October 2017).

European Union (1985). *Council Directive 85/337/EEC of 27 June 1985 on the Assessment of the Effects of Certain Public and Private Projects on the Environment* (online). Available at: http://eur-lex.europa.eu/legal-content/EN/TXT/?uri=CELEX:31985L0337 (accessed 2 November 2017).

Fusco Girard, L., Hosagrahar, J., Potts, A. and Soule, J. (2016). *Cultural Heritage, the UN Sustainable Development Goals, and the New Urban Agenda*. ICOMOS Concept Note for the UN Agenda 2030 and the 3rd UN Conference on Housing and Sustainable Urban Development (Habitat III), 2016 (online). Available at: www.icomos.org/en/what-we-do/focus/un-sustainable-development-goals/8778-cultural-heritage-and-sustainable-development (accessed 10 October 2017).

ICOMOS (1967). *Proceedings of the First Conference on the Conservation, Restoration and Revival of Areas and Groups of Buildings of Historic Interest, Caceres, 15–19 March 1967*. Paris: ICOMOS.

ICOMOS (1971). *Proceedings of the ICOMOS Symposium on Monuments and Society*, Leningrad, 2–8 September 1969 (online). Available at: www.icomos.org/en/what-we-do/disseminating-knowledge/publicationall/other-publications/157-articles-en-francais/ressources/publications/409-colloque-sur-les-monuments-et-la-societe–symposium-on-monuments-and-society (accessed 2 November 2017).

ICOMOS (1975). *Proceedings of the ICOMOS Symposium on Small Historic Towns, Rothenburg ob der Tauber, 29–30 May 1975*. Paris: ICOMOS.

ICOMOS (1978). *Proceedings of the ICOMOS Conference on Protection of Historic Cities and Quarters in Urban Development, held Moscow and Suzdal, 1978*. Paris: ICOMOS.

ICOMOS (1981). *Proceedings of Scientific Symposium of the 6th ICOMOS General Assembly 'No past No Future', Rome, 25–31 May 1981*. Paris: ICOMOS.

ICOMOS (1993). *Proceedings of the Scientific Symposium of the 10th ICOMOS General Assembly 'Economics of Conservation', Colombo, 1993*. Paris: ICOMOS.

ICOMOS (1999). *Proceedings of the Scientific Symposium of the 12th ICOMOS General Assembly 'The Wise Use of Heritage–Heritage and Development', Mexico City, 1999*. Paris: ICOMOS.

ICOMOS (2011a). *Heritage, Driver of Development Proceedings of the ICOMOS' 17th General Assembly Scientific Symposium*. Paris: ICOMOS.

ICOMOS (2011b). *The Paris Declaration on Heritage as a Driver of Development* (online). Available at: www.icomos.org/Paris2011/GA2011_Declaration_de_Paris_EN_20120109. pdf (accessed 10 October 2017).

ICOMOS (2017). *ICOMOS Action Plan: Cultural Heritage and Localizing the Sustainable Development Goals (SDGs)* (online). Available at:www.icomos.org/images/DOCUMENTS/ Secretariat/2017/ICOMOS_Action_Plan_Cult_Heritage_and_Localizing_SDGs_ 20170721.pdf (accessed 2 November 2017).

Meadows, D. H., Meadows, D. L., Randers, J. and Behrens, W. W. (1972). *The Limits to Growth: A Report for the Club of Rome's Project on the Predicament of Mankind.* New York: Universe Books.

UNESCO (2013). *The Huangzhou Declaration: Placing Culture at the Heart of Sustainable Development Policies* (online). Available at: www.unesco.org/fileadmin/MULTIMEDIA/ HQ/CLT/images/FinalHangzhouDeclaration20130517.pdf (accessed 5 October 2017).

UNESCO (2015). *Policy Document for the Integration of a Sustainable Development Perspective into the Processes of the World Heritage Convention* (online). Available at: http://whc.unesco.org/en/sustainabledevelopment/ (accessed 5 October 2017).

UNESCO (2017). *Reports of the World Heritage Centre and the Advisory Bodies 5C: World Heritage Convention and Sustainable Development* (online). Available at: http:// whc.unesco.org/archive/2017/whc17-41com-5C-en.pdf (accessed 2 November 2017).

United Nations (UN) (1987). *Our Common Future: Report of the World Commission on the Environment and Development* (online). Available at: www.un-documents.net/our-common-future.pdf (accessed 10 October 2017).

United Nations (UN) (2010). *Keeping the Promise: United to Achieve the Millennium Development Goals.* UN Resolution A/RES/65/1/2010 (online). Available at: www. un.org/en/mdg/summit2010/pdf/outcome_documentN1051260.pdf (accessed 5 October 2017).

United Nations (UN) (2015). *Transforming Our World: The 2030 Agenda for Sustainable Development.* UN Resolution A/RES/70/1/2015 (online). Available at: https://sustainable development.un.org/post2015/transformingourworldx (accessed 5 October 2017).

UN Task Team (2012). *Culture: A Driver and Enabler of Sustainable Development.* Post 2015 UN Development Agenda Report (online). Available at: www.un.org/millenniumgoals / pdf/Think%20Pieces/2_culture.pdf (accessed 5 October 2017).

Chapter 12

From 'Sustaining heritage' to 'Heritage sustaining broader societal wellbeing and benefits'

An ICCROM perspective

Jane Thompson and Gamini Wijesuriya

The new policy

As one of the three Advisory Bodies to the World Heritage Committee, ICCROM contributed to the drafting of the World Heritage and Sustainable Development policy adopted in November 2015 (UNESCO 2015). The policy sets out how the world's World Heritage properties can play an active role in enhancing all dimensions of sustainable development. How this will relate to managing heritage in practice is yet to be fully worked out, just as statutory amendments are still being considered. Nevertheless, progress is being made in the field and in capacity-building environments. Indeed, the policy is already a useful document for all interested parties working at a site level.

The principles of the World Heritage and Sustainable Development policy are sound, and this bodes well for guidance being translated into pragmatic tools for application at a site level within a couple of years. Even so, it may take longer for this more inter-sectoral and participatory way of working to become 'business as usual' for many heritage practitioners and institutional frameworks.

The big picture

Making people richer by promoting economic growth has been the assumption at the centre of economic priorities and international trade policy for a long time. Early modernist theory was built around the assumptions that if 'traditional' societies could be helped to develop in the same manner as more 'developed' countries there would be prosperity for everyone and that economic prosperity automatically equated with the collective wellbeing of communities. This mind-set continued to shape much international development, theory, aid and philanthropy throughout the second half of the twentieth century. According to Jennifer Lentfer, who worked for one of the NGOs active in the international development sphere for over 30 years, 'this ignored the colonial roots of the sector and the inequities that existed in so-called rich countries. Today, more and more people are recognising that neoliberal models of development belie the ecological realities of the earth's capacity, as well as basic human rights' (Lentfer 2017: 2).

The repercussions of applying international models indiscriminately triggered a variety of responses. A new emphasis on contextual knowledge and collective decision-making, on relocating decision making to those nearest the problems and holding powerful external actors accountable has emerged. Approaches in the cultural heritage sector have followed a very similar path with a wave of absolutes upheld by the few gradually being set aside in favour of multiple voices and more complex narratives. The World Heritage and Sustainable Development policy and the repercussions it will have on the ground mirror very closely what has already happened in other sectors.

This chapter describes developments in cultural heritage theory and practices over the last half century. Mainstreaming the sustainable development paradigm encourages institutions, practitioners, communities and networks to work with others and, differently, by working 'in context'. Parachuting-in 'expertise' is gradually giving way to building on local wisdom and create alternatives to top-down management. More and more recognition is also being given to the potential of heritage places to contribute to improving people's economic opportunities, working conditions, health, education, and overall wellbeing. For those places where heritage had become the realm of a restricted few, the so-called 'experts', and with management approaches distancing them from society, 'going local' (to borrow a slogan coined by the UK's National Trust) and promoting forms of inter-sectoral mobilization for the heritage cause are perhaps the biggest test for our generation of heritage practitioners.

Such reasoning is the basis for exploring progress in the sector, and in particular ICCROM's specific contribution. This is viewed not just with an eye to the role of heritage in improving wellbeing in society but also to lay claim to the numerous benefits that result in terms of greater equity and effectiveness of management models and governance of heritage places themselves. This is particularly significant for cultural heritage places whose less direct and obvious contribution to the future of the planet has remained marginal in mainstream sustainable development discourse. This is in sharp contrast to the higher profile of natural heritage in the sustainability agenda from the earliest global conversations in the 1980s and 1990s considering the contribution of protected areas to the environmental pillar. One of our most central challenges is overcoming the nature-culture divide. The very separation of nature and culture, a phenomenon most acute in Western post-industrial societies, has made us blind to the 'bio-cultural continuum' (Descola 2011) that perhaps obliges us to treat them as one and allows us to see heritage communities and society within that same equation (Larsen and Wijesuriya 2015).

Never has there been an era in which our heritage places need so much to draw on their full spectrum of heritage values and on *all* potential sources of support. Between the ever-expanding concept of what heritage is to the escalating array of threats and opportunities posed by a changing society and globalization, there is a pressing need to tap into civic society and grassroots initiatives capturing all the potential that is now widely recognized.

But how to go about it? Creating partnerships and alliances and building trust, particularly at a grassroots level, take considerable amounts of time. It is with this in mind that drawing often on progress in other sectors, the chapter concludes with a series of considerations regarding knowledge areas and strategic directions that could help those on the ground to build up existing capacities to give heritage a bright new future.

Global shifts in heritage issues

From heritage as islands to defend heritage as part of a biocultural continuum

Two recent anthologies outlining the current state of play in the heritage field – *Perceptions of Sustainability in Heritage Studies* (Albert 2015), and *A Companion to Heritage Studies* (Logan, Nic Craith and Kockel 2015) – pay homage to the fact that a generation of specialists in the cultural heritage sector are reeling from the changes being witnessed. These changes 'over the past 40 or so years' 'amount to a revolution' but have 'largely gone unnoticed', to borrow the words of Adrian Phillips, in relation to similar changes in the natural heritage sector (Phillips 2003).

In order to evaluate the implications for the future of the heritage sector of the shift from 'sustaining heritage' to 'heritage sustaining broader societal wellbeing and benefits' it is important to frame this change within the broader evolution of cultural heritage theory and practices over the last half century. As Table 12.1 shows, three key stages can be identified: 1964–1994, post-1994 (Araoz 2011) and the current time.

Two significant instances emerge from the table where a 'big picture' frame-work policy addressing the situation as a whole showcases new ways of working, both locally and internationally. The first is the 1972 World Heritage Convention itself (heritage for society and heritage as a stimulus for international coopera-tion), a rare piece of international legislation for those State Parties by whom it was ratified. Two decades passed before it became a springboard for new ways of working. The very ferment of policy work from the 1990s onwards culminated in the 2015 World Heritage and Sustainable Development Policy. This provides a much-needed, unifying platform to facilitate integration between the 1972 World Heritage Convention and the international conventions that followed. However, its positive repercussions do not finish there.

National or federal systems, which have sustainable development as a shared reference framework for sectoral goals and inter-sectoral coordination will find their heritage places becoming learning sites for others. An example is the cycle of 'Loch Lomond & The Trossachs' partnership plans, the high-level land use strategy for a Scottish National Park being specifically structured around a nation-wide sustainable development agenda (LLTNPA 2017) allowing inter-sectoral alignment. The World Heritage and Sustainable Development Policy is also a unifying framework encouraging natural and cultural heritage to be addressed together as a single ecosystem, a 'biocultural continuum' to quote Descola (2011). This nature-culture continuum allows for coordination across the nature-human

Table 12.1 Half a century of cultural heritage policy work

Defending monuments and sites One size fits all (1964–1994)	Use and significance Other voices, multiple horizons (1994 onwards)	Reciprocal benefits Beyond heritage (this decade)
Policy-work shaped by the reaction of post-industrial society to war. 1964 Venice Charter A watershed disseminating western conservation philosophy globally. Heritage as islands distinct from society. Defensive mind-set to preserve fabric. Conservation as an expert-led, scientific discipline. Assumption that European approaches can work globally. 1972 World Heritage Convention A response to increasing threats 'not only by the	Policy-work shaped by heritage principles emerging in other parts of the world and the applicability of European approaches. World Heritage 1992 Definitions of heritage expand vastly (e.g. 'cultural landscapes') and going beyond the preservation of the built environment. Processes shift from mere inscriptions to management and monitoring of properties. UNESCO, ICOMOS and ICCROM come together, as key trend setters.	1999 ICOMOS Australia Burra Charter (5th) Significance is 'embodied in the place itself, its setting, use, associations, meanings, records, related places and related objects'. People in the decision-making process, particularly those who have strong associations with a place. Standards for using cultural significance to manage and conserve.	2003 UNESCO Intangible Cultural Heritage Communities were officially brought in to define heritage within this Convention. Nara Plus 10 2004 Group advocating the intangible convention challenged the notion of authenticity and its validity for living heritage. 2005 Council of Europe Framework Faro Convention on the Value of Cultural Heritage for Society One of many regional responses to the need to focus on people.	Policy-work shaped by inter-sectoral alignment for a more dynamic role for heritage in broader sustainable development, and the resulting benefits for society and for heritage. 2012 World Heritage Committee 'only through strengthened relationships between people and heritage, based on respect for cultural and biological diversity as a whole, integrating both tangible and intangible aspects and geared toward sustainable development, will the "future we want" become attainable'. (Kyoto Vision).

(Continued)

Table 12.1 (Continued)

Defending monuments and sites *One size fits all (1964–1994)*	Use and significance *Other voices, multiple horizons (1994 onwards)*		Reciprocal benefits *Beyond heritage (this decade)*
traditional causes of decay, but also by changing social and economic conditions'. Emphasis on presentation and transmission to future generations (not on use). Pioneering (dealt with both natural and cultural heritage, sought to give heritage 'a function in the life of the community') but the first 20 years focused on inscriptions. 1979 ICOMOS Australia Burra Charter (1st) Cultural significance means having aesthetic, historical, scientific or social value for past, present or future generations	1994 Nara Document Attention to intangible attributes. Values and significance as foundation for assessing and managing heritage. Diversity: notion of authenticity as varying from culture to culture and depending on context.	2005 World Heritage SOUV required for all listed properties retrospectively. 2006 World Heritage Committee Engaging communities in all processes – 'Communities' as the 5th Strategic Objective.	2014 Nara Plus 20 Inadequacy of current approaches given the diversity of processes, the evolution of values, multiple stakeholders with conflicting claims and the role of heritage in sustainable development. International heritage guidance questioned given the evolving nature of conservation principles. 2015 World Heritage Sustainable Development Policy Conservation and management aligned to sustainable development objectives without compromising Outstanding Universal Value.
	2002 World Heritage Committee – Budapest Declaration 'an appropriate and equitable balance between conservation, sustainability and development, so that World Heritage ... can be protected through appropriate activities contributing to the social and economic development and the quality of life of our communities'.		

divide without heritage classification systems overly prejudicing how the world is known, how this knowledge is acted upon and how social and material relationships are remade in the process (van Bommel and Turnhout 2012).

ICCROM in context

Knowledge transfer to sustain heritage – the early years

Just 11 years after World War II, ICCROM was created by UNESCO as an intergovernmental organization to promote conservation of cultural heritage worldwide, primarily through research, contributions to policy work and training activities. In the 60-year period it has been actively capacity-building, ICCROM has reached generations of cultural heritage specialists and, in recent years, wider audiences. Understanding this journey is a useful lens through which to explore past and present trends also with a view to projecting future capacity-building needs for heritage.

Its training activities over the first 40 years focused primarily on conserving material traces of the past (monuments and sites). It focused on conservation as a scientific and technical discipline and depended heavily on the knowledge that had been developed in the Western world and in particular, the host country Italy. This reflected contributions of ICCROM's senior staff to the drafting of the 1964 Venice Charter and the creation of ICOMOS. ICOMOS then came forward as the most stringent guardian and promoter of the Venice Charter even when other organizations, ICCROM included, began to work in new directions.

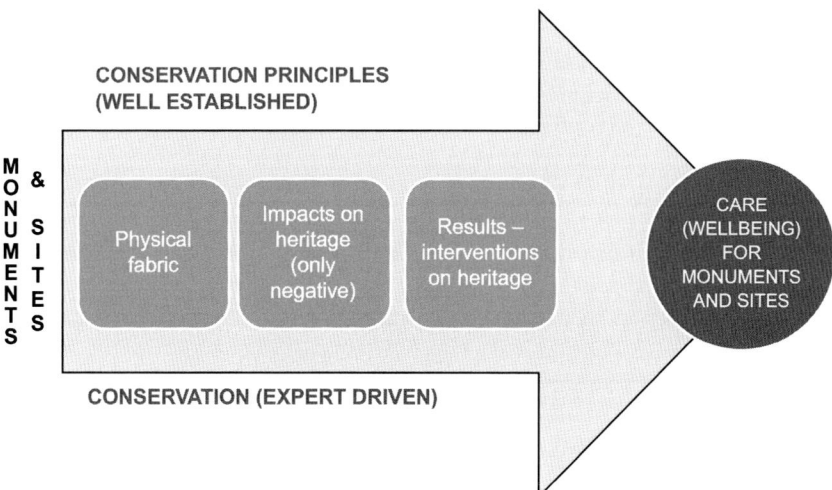

Figure 12.1 Conservation of 'monuments and sites' 1964–1994 – technical considerations predominate

Source: Wijesuriya 2016 modified by authors for this chapter

One of ICCROM's earliest activities was the development of an international training course on Architectural Conservation in 1966. This was to become a flagship program with global popularity. By the late 1980s, several modules on urban conservation were introduced in it, but the focus continued to be restricted to the material remains of the past through until the mid-1990s.

Knowledge acquisition by a variety of audiences – heritage sustaining broader societal wellbeing and drawing benefits

A major shift in approach from 'the conservation of monuments' to 'the management of heritage within which conservation is one component' and with increased emphasis on the role of heritage in society today took place in all areas of activities at ICCROM over recent decades. This was in addition to, not in substitution of emphasis on material preservation. From 1997, the Integrated Territorial and Urban Conservation (ITUC) program explored large regions and landscapes and their conservation, moving beyond the conventional 'monument' focus that had until then prevailed. Course curricula began to recognize landscapes and the dynamism that exists in heritage places, introducing sustainable development as a knowledge area for the first time in international courses. This is precisely the era in which cultural landscapes as a category of heritage began to play a significant role within the World Heritage context.

The Living Heritage Sites Programme, an offshoot of ITUC launched in 2003, further strengthened sustainable development as a theme (ICCROM 2005; Wijesuriya 2015). It recognized the importance of both the living aspects of heritage in terms of both continuity and change. Heritage components were considered as part of a living environment (Wijesuriya, Thompson and Court 2017). This came to the fore most strongly for those heritage places that continue to perform the function for which they were originally created. It concerned processes of continuity of connected community, the continuity of cultural expressions and the continuity of care often using traditional and established knowledge systems. Examples range from Buddhist temples to the London Underground. The program focused on people, the need for people to benefit from heritage, their right to engage in decisions and their role as the guardians of long-term care of heritage. This way of understanding heritage required new approaches to conservation and management. It opened up for new debates and began to address community and continuity as interlinked themes – both noticeable gaps in the ongoing heritage discourse (Wijesuriya 2010).

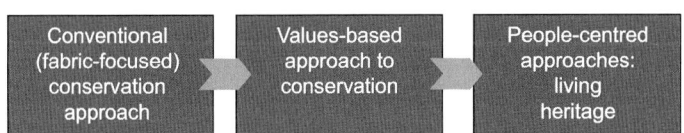

Figure 12.2 Evolving approaches to heritage conservation and management

Source: Wijesuriya, Thompson and Court (2017), © Wijesuriya

The new trend emerged in the urban conservation sector as well. The development of urban conservation is generally attributed to the second half of the 20th century (Bandarin and van Oers 2012) based on modern conservation principles with a focus on materiality. The Historic Urban Landscape (HUL) recommendations, adopted by UNESCO and in whose development ICCROM played a role, addressed some important gaps and finally went beyond material preservation. In essence, the HUL approach

> aims at preserving the quality of the human environment, enhancing the productive and sustainable use of urban spaces while recognizing their dynamic character, and promoting social and functional diversity. It integrates the goals of urban heritage conservation and those of social and economic development. It is rooted in a balanced and sustainable relationship between the urban and natural environment, between the needs of present and future generations and the legacy from the past.
>
> (UNESCO 2011)

This rethink was at the heart of the curriculum ICCROM developed from the outset for its courses on Heritage Impact Assessments for World Heritage. These built on guidelines prepared by ICOMOS (2011) and were conducted initially in Asia from 2012 and then more widely from 2014.

Sustainable development as a specific theme figured in the revised version of the Conservation of Built Heritage (CBH) course launched in 2007 with the introduction of a special module on 'World Heritage and sustainable development' in 2012. The first-ever training course of this nature tested the UK National Trust's 'Triple Bottom Line' (Lithgow 2011) to inform decision making in a variety of heritage conservation and management scenarios.

ICCROM research and policy work unfolding in parallel at the time demonstrated the broadening of perspectives. In coordination with the other Advisory Bodies, two UNESCO resource manuals were crafted: 'Managing Disaster Risks for World Heritage' (UNESCO et al 2010) and then 'Managing Cultural World Heritage' (UNESCO et al 2013). On one hand, there was the recognition that loss of heritage as a result of disasters was a major concern also because of the significant role that heritage plays in 'contributing to social cohesion and sustainable development, particularly at times of stress' (UNESCO et al 2010; UNISDR 2015). On the other hand, considerable attention was given to understanding, analysing and improving management systems currently in place at heritage places. The approach sought to place greater importance on building on current management strengths and on harnessing existing opportunities with a view to diversity, adaption and innovation being an alternative to mitigating threats and compromise for the heritage sector (UNESCO et al 2013).

In this period, ICCROM offered its first contributions and support to the first steps towards the World Heritage and Sustainable Development policy building on ICCROM's contribution to the World Heritage Capacity Building Strategy (UNESCO et al 2011). Management of change and continuity emerged at the heart of heritage management, building on the living heritage approach as relevant to all heritage. The overriding premise is that cultural heritage has been created by people as well as *for* people. These convictions led ICCROM to develop a follow-up program to Living Heritage entitled People-Centred Approaches to Conservation (PCA).

Capacity building initiatives within the PCA Programme from 2015 and onwards saw two significant shifts which essentially put the World Heritage Capacity Building Strategy (UNESCO et al 2011) into practice. On one hand, there were increasing numbers of participants from civil society in annual courses in the form of representatives of local associations and other NGOs operating near or with heritage issues. On the other, the involvement of specialists from both the natural and cultural heritage sector as both participants and resource people in these courses became the norm instead of isolated experiments, as did a strong curriculum emphasis on nature-culture linkages (Larsen and Wijesuriya 2015). The success of this approach was a further stimulus to ICCROM and IUCN's work on nature-culture inter-linkages that translated into a dedicated joint course in 2017 Linking Nature and Culture in World Heritage Site Management and the broader World Heritage Leadership Programme.

By this time, the shift of focus in ICCROM's capacity-building approaches from 'conservation of monuments' to 'management of heritage within which conservation is one component' had gone one step further in a move a move to pursuing 'the wellbeing of both heritage and society as a whole'. This ultimate goal of the sustainable development paradigm has profound implications for the way we

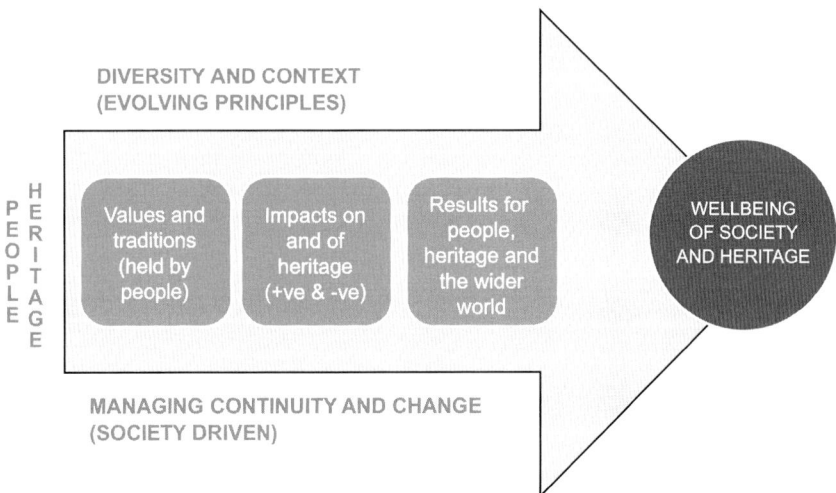

Figure 12.3 'Heritage management' 1994 onwards – greater recognition of people-centred approaches

Source: Wijesuriya 2016 modified by authors for this chapter

manage heritage. The diagram above attempts to capture this shift (in contrast to the earlier diagram encapsulating approaches in the previous two decades).

The unprecedented growth of World Heritage processes and requirements to be fulfilled by State Parties had made effective capacity building for the care and enjoyment of heritage a real priority both for civil society and state authorities. A new generation of participants in ICCROM courses today are often more abreast of this tide of change compared to earlier 'experts'. It has meant that the need to filter heritage management actions through sustainable development dimensions is already relatively widely accepted, even if translating it into practice is naturally not without its challenges.

Beyond heritage, for heritage – the future

The heritage sector has experienced somewhat of an awakening in recent decades. This involved the gradual recognition of what was already discernible but had perhaps been obscured by the tunnel vision so typical of the disciplinary silos and knowledge fragmentation of our times. The following diagram uses the legend of the glass half empty/half full in an attempt to capture the paradigm shift in the heritage sector as three distinct but overlapping phase, and with the last still very much incomplete, where context and thinking outside the box allow a fuller story to be told.

In the last two decades, the opportunities provided by evolving World Heritage processes have triggered ICCROM to augment its focus on communities

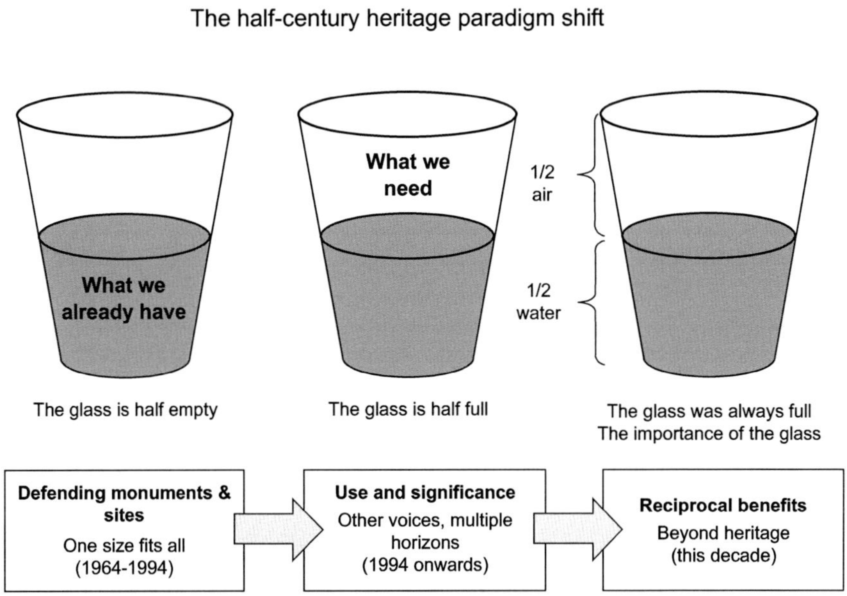

The half-century heritage paradigm shift

Figure 12.4 A half-century heritage paradigm shift in a glass

and managing continuity and change in and around heritage. Sustainable development is the most recent expression of these themes and is at the heart of ICCROM's 2018–2024 strategic programming. However, many challenges remain.

One such challenge concerns the mandate of heritage agencies and practitioners in this new approach since responsibilities are no longer limited to certain designated spots but extend in a capillary fashion over entire territories with the aim of 'representing one among other legitimate societal interests, all deeply connected within the bio-cultural continuum' (Boccardi 2015: 94). Safeguarding connections, not just nodes, becomes one of the most central challenges transforming the heritage sector quest. This entails a shift from traditional heritage inventories to mapping heritage values, mapping who perceives them as well as their interdependencies with the other values associated with the dimensions of sustainable development. For those working at any level in the sector, the shift translates on a day-to-day level into more expectations, more obligations and more results. This essentially creates a state of perpetual 'start-up' in a sector that was already often struggling to have sufficient capacity for conservation alone.

Another challenge is that of changing the mind-sets of a generation of heritage practitioners strongly entrenched in the conventional approaches, while also meeting the needs of a new generation coming through already thinking 'outside the box'. There is still resistance and a need to 'digest' the ideas of managing change and sustainable development (Wijesuriya, Thompson and Court 2017). This is perhaps a result of the sector remaining relatively self-referential and insular for too long. Diverse views and evolving ideas were not forthcoming for a long time. There were few opportunities for heritage practitioners in the field to think differently and training activities remained top-down knowledge transferal in nature, hampering debate and creativity.

The mind-set of the new generation of heritage practitioners coming through in the last two to three years is already significantly different, with a tangible shift from individual practitioners to a coalition of like-minded altruists. Table 12.2 summarizes the paradigm shifts as well as the evolving knowledge areas and skill sets in the cultural heritage field.

The kinds of changes encapsulated in the table challenge organizations like ICCROM to adapt and build capacity to turn the World Heritage and Sustainable Development Policy into action. Today, the best experiences in the heritage sector remain embryonic compared to approaches matured in other sectors. There is a need to secure progress in all three areas where heritage capacities reside (UNESCO et al 2011) and look *outside* the heritage arena for ways to approach sustainable development considerations more effectively. Needs on the ground must be the basis for identifying capacity-building priorities as our sector moves further towards considering the wellbeing of society (today and in the future) as inseparable from the wellbeing of heritage.

Table 12.2 'Summary of People-Nature Problematics in International Conservation (1960–1999)' (Jeanrenaud 2002: 21), revisited for cultural heritage in 2017

	1964–1994	1994–2014	Current
Perception of heritage	Defending monuments and sites Inward looking sector Heritage as islands Historic city centres – museum-like	Safeguarding values through managing physical attributes of cultural/urban landscapes Heritage as the combined work of man and nature Historic city centres – healthy, lively and creative with heritage as one source of solutions to the challenges of our time. Quantity and quality as the race to World Heritage inscription	Heritage and communities as a biocultural continuum Outward looking sector Heritage as an ecosystem A role in building resilience in communities 'Place making' instead of public spaces as a paradigm for heritage management Quantity, quality and diversity of heritage as a driver of democratic consensus
Management and conservation approach	Limited to conservation Set standards, compile content One size fits all Conservation as mitigation/reducing harm	Management recognized Enabling others Management as a sum of diverse contributions also from outside the sector Recognition of diversity Go local Managing continuity and change	Managing connections not just nodes, empowerment Nature-culture linkages Customize solutions Foster secure environments for co-management Incremental, small steps and capillary action Management as adaption and responsiveness
Governance	Disciplinary silos 'Top down', mindful of jurisdictions beneath Expert-led Rational	Interdisciplinary voices New heritage typologies, new management hybrids Multi-stakeholder approaches	Inter-sectoral voices 'Bottom up', self-organizing Peer to peer Fluid, messy Words into action

(Continued)

Table 12.2 (Continued)

	1964–1994	1994–2014	Current
Knowledge	Intelligence concentrated in centre Scientific emphasis	Participants are wired up Information and knowledge fed to all players	Intelligence is pervasive Inverted hierarchies All players offer knowledge Recognition of traditional knowledge systems
Cultural heritage values	History and aesthetic based Timeless Only identifiable by experts	Ascribed by a variety of interest groups, timeless Non-heritage values matter (religious values, pillars of sustainable development)	People are part of the values ('living heritage') Values change
Diagnosis of cultural heritage problems	Threats to heritage, not only the traditional causes of decay, but also changing social and economic conditions (WH Convention) People are a threat	As heritage broadens as a concept the need to define it in terms of cultural significance ascribed (values and attributes, also qualified in terms authenticity and integrity) and by whom Impact assessments to identify one-off identity threats	Society as a source of opportunities not just threats Ensuring cultural heritage is a catalyst rather than a victim of sustainable development Impact assessments to identify and manage routine threats and opportunities
Representation of communities	People as a threat People as consumers	People cannot be ignored People are a resource	Alignment with local communities and indigenous peoples People as drivers
Solutions and technologies	Materials sciences to defend physical fabric Defining boundaries and zones to 'buffer' heritage from society	The idea of setting and integrated conservation and development programs Sustainable use; community-based conservation No magic 'cure-all' to the complexity involved	Transformative power of heritage Link biological diversity and local cultures Alternative management models: adaption instead of mitigation, people-centred approaches People, their democratic consensus and diversities as part of heritage values Human rights

	1964–1994	1994–2014	Current
Power relations	Alliances with elites	Technocratic alliances	Alliances with grassroots
Key influences	Colonial conservation; elitist interests	Sustainable development debate; growing concern for livelihoods Harnessing heritage benefits Gain a greater democratic consensus for heritage	Democracy/human rights movement; participatory development; post-modern influence on natural and social sciences
Capacity-building approaches	Knowledge transfer to heritage practitioners Training	Capacity-building of organizations, including NGOs Interdisciplinary learning environments Recognition of all three areas where heritage capacities reside Capacity-building for World Heritage	Endogenous approach drawing on and strengthening all heritage capacities for lasting change Knowledge acquisition by diverse audiences Diverse learning environments Inter-sectoral learning environments Capacity-building relevant to all heritage, and not simply World Heritage
Capacity building knowledge areas	Technical and scientific knowledge Monitoring management outputs Disaster responses for heritage	Management as a new knowledge area for heritage Heritage impact assessments Monitoring and evaluating management processes and results (efficiency and effectiveness) Disaster preparedness for heritage General skills: project management, networks, consensus building, consultation etc.	People-centred approaches Nature culture linkages Governance Human rights The role of heritage in peace and reconciliation Heritage as a source of resilience for communities to face disaster Monitoring and evaluating all outcomes (overall effectiveness) Peer learning Drawing from the experience of other sectors

References

Albert, M.-T. (ed) (2015). *Perceptions of Sustainability in Heritage Studies*. Berlin and Boston: De Gruyter.

Araoz, G. (2011). 'Preserving heritage places under a new paradigm', *Journal of Cultural Heritage Management and Sustainable Development*, 1(1), 55–60.

Bandarin, F. and van Oers, R. (2012). *The Historic Urban Landscape: Managing Heritage in an Urban Century*. Chichester, UK: Wiley-Blackwell.

Boccardi, G. (2015). 'From mitigation to adaptation: A new heritage paradigm for the anthropocene', in M.-T. Albert (ed), *Perceptions of Sustainability in Heritage Studies*. Berlin and Boston: De Gruyter.

Descola, P. (2011). *L'écologie des autres: L'anthropologie et la question de la nature*. Paris: Éditions Quae.

ICCROM (2005). *Report on Living Heritage Sites Programme, First Strategy Meeting of 2003* (Internal Report). Rome: ICCROM.

ICOMOS (2011). *Guidance on Heritage Impact Assessments for Cultural World Heritage Properties*. Paris: ICOMOS (online). Available at: www.icomos.org/world_heritage/ HIA_20110201.pdf (accessed 10 December 2017).

Jeanrenaud, S. (2002). *People-Oriented Approaches to Global Conservation: Is the Leopard Changing Its Spots?* London: International Institute for Environment and Development.

Larsen, P. B. and Wijesuriya, G. (2015). 'Nature: Culture interlinkages in World Heritage: Bridging the gap', *World Heritage*, 75, 4–15.

Lentfer, J. (2017). 'International development is a loaded term: It's time for a rethink', *The Guardian*, 3 May (online). Available at: www.theguardian.com/global-development-professionals-network/2017/may/03/international-development-is-a-loaded-term-its-time-for-a-rethink (accessed 10 December 2017).

Lithgow, K. (2011). 'Sustainable decision making: Change in National Trust collections conservation', *Journal of the Institute of Conservation*, 34(1), 130–144.

Loch Lomond and the Trossachs National Park Authority (LLTNPA) (2017). *Loch Lomond & the Trossachs Draft National Park Partnership Plan 2018–2023* (online). Available at: www.lochlomond-trossachs.org/park-authority/get-involved/consultations/ nppp/ (accessed 10 December 2017).

Logan, W., Nic Craith, M. and Kockel, U. (eds) (2015). *A Companion to Heritage Studies*. Chichester, UK: Wiley-Blackwell.

Phillips, A. (2003). 'A new paradigm for protected areas', *World Conservation*, 2, 6–7.

UNESCO (2011). *Recommendation on the Historic Urban Landscape* (online). Available at: http://portal.unesco.org/en/ev.php-URL_ID=48857&URL_DO=DO_TOPIC&URL_ SECTION=201.html (accessed 28 June 2017).

UNESCO (2012). *Kyoto Vision* (online). Available at: http://whc.unesco.org/en/news/953 (accessed 28 June 2017).

UNESCO (2015). *Policy Document for the Integration of a Sustainable Development Perspective into the Processes of the World Heritage Convention* (online). Available at: http://whc.unesco.org/en/sustainabledevelopment/ (accessed 2 December 2017).

UNESCO, ICCROM, ICOMOS and IUCN (2010). Managing Disaster Risks for World Heritage. Paris: UNESCO World Heritage Centre. (World Heritage Resource Manual) (online). Available at: http://whc.unesco.org/uploads/activities/documents/activity-630-1. pdf (accessed 2 December 2017).

UNESCO, ICCROM, ICOMOS and IUCN (2011). Presentation and Adoption of the World Heritage Strategy for Capacity Building. Paris: UNESCO World Heritage Centre (Document WHC-11/35.COM/9B) (online). Available at: http://whc.unesco.org/archive/2011/whc11-35com-9Be.pdf (accessed 10 December 2017).

UNESCO, ICCROM, ICOMOS and IUCN (2013). Manual on Managing Cultural World Heritage. Paris: UNESCO (online). Available at: http://whc.unesco.org/en/managing-cultural-world-heritage/ (accessed 2 December 2017)

UNISDR (2015). *Sendai Framework for Disaster Risk Reduction 2015–2030* (online). Available at: www.unisdr.org/we/coordinate/sendai-framework (accessed 10 December 2017).

van Bommel, S. and Turnhout, E. (2012). 'The (onto)politics of classifying biocultural diversity: A tale of chaos, order and control', in B. Arts, S. van Bommel, M. Ros-Tonen and G. Verschoor (eds), *Forest-People Interfaces*. Wageningen, Netherlands: Wageningen Academic Publishers.

Wijesuriya, G. (2010). 'Conservation in context', in M. S. Falser, W. Lipp and A. Tomaszewski (eds), *Proceedings of the International Conference on 'Conservation and Preservation-Interaction between Theory and Practice, in memoriam Alois Riegl (1858–1905)*. Florence: Edizioni Polistampa.

Wijesuriya, G. (2015). *Living Heritage: A Summary* (online). Available at: www.iccrom.org/wp-content/uploads/PCA_Annexe-1.pdf (accessed 10 December 2017).

Wijesuriya, G. (2016). *Global Trends in Human Resources Development in Protection of Cultural Heritage*. Paper presented at International Conference on Human Resources Development, Nara, Japan.

Wijesuriya, G., Thompson, J. and Court, S. (2017). 'People-centred approaches: Engaging communities and developing capacities for managing heritage', in G. Chitty (ed), *Heritage, Conservation and Communities: Engagement, Participation and Capacity Building*. London: Routledge.

Part IV

World Heritage site case studies

Chapter 13

Implementing the World Heritage Sustainable Development Policy in Egypt

An opportunity for collective engagement in heritage conservation

Dina Ishak Bakhoum

Egypt, a country with serious socio-economic issues, is also a country rich in cultural and natural heritage. For centuries, the sites that represent Egypt's Ancient Egyptian, Greco-Roman, Christian and Islamic cultures have been and still are attractive destinations for travellers, explorers and, nowadays, domestic visitors, international tourists, and scholars. Seven Egyptian sites are inscribed on the World Heritage List. These and other sites in Egypt are major tourist destinations and thus significantly contribute to the country's economic growth and development. As elsewhere, each of these heritage sites is significant to different stakeholders, whose interests sometimes coincide and sometimes differ; they often co-exist but seldom work in partnership. Within this context, the chapter aims to demonstrate, through examples drawn from the author's personal experience, that heritage-related projects, such as research, archaeology, restoration, conservation and management, and not only tourism development, are crucial for achieving sustainable development goals.

Examples from Historic Cairo, a World Heritage Site since 1979, will be used throughout the chapter to discuss the processes of some of these projects in order to illustrate the strong interconnection between heritage and development and how such projects are opportunities for positive change especially in a developing country like Egypt where historic and archaeological sites stand, both within and in close proximity to urban centres with numerous socio-economic challenges and diverse values. During the decades of the late twentieth and early twenty-first centuries, numerous international and national, governmental and non-governmental institutions, bodies and donors have been involved with restoring and protecting Cairo's heritage. Their efforts will not be discussed here as they have been summarized in numerous other publications (see, for example, Bacharach ed. 1995; Sedky 2009) and, most recently, in UNESCO's Urban Regeneration Project for Historic Cairo (UNESCO-WHC 2012). This chapter will rather trace some of the changes that have occurred in recent decades in order to show how it has become apparent that conservation must contribute much more to the sustainable development of Cairo.

The discussion is set in the wider heritage conservation framework resulting from a shift away from focusing chiefly on the artistic, scientific and historic values of heritage to respecting and incorporating the social and spiritual values attached to heritage by communities. This worldwide shift is very significant as it repositions heritage as a right for everyone and not merely a luxury. In the past, heritage professionals and government bodies have often ignored communities and even considered them as a threat to heritage, while in fact they have long been important custodians of heritage and they could and should be its main protectors. The long experience of numerous professionals on the ground working on heritage sites has demonstrated, however, that the protection and safeguarding of these places can only be achieved by respecting the complex matrix of values encapsulated in them. This wider concept has been reflected in numerous documents and recommendations, such as the Getty Conservation Institute's *Research on the Values of Heritage (1998–2000)*,[1] the Strategic Objectives of the World Heritage Committee, especially the addition of the fifth 'C' for Communities in 2007 complementing the four 'C's of the Budapest Declaration (UNESCO 2002), and in the Recommendation on the Historic Urban Landscape (2011) and the Australia ICOMOS Burra Charter (1979, 1999, 2013), to mention only a few. The concepts and standards expressed in these documents, together with the *Policy for the integration of a sustainable development perspective in to the processes of the World Heritage Convention* (UNESCO 2015) are important tools for governments, non-governmental institutions, practitioners and funding agencies working in the field of cultural heritage.

Historic Cairo and sustainable development

Historic Cairo faces, like many historic cities around the world, severe pressure affecting its conservation, maintenance and protection.[2] It is a complex site in need of constant and regular management, conservation and maintenance. The *waqf* (endowment) system supported maintenance and was considered by scholars as a traditional maintenance system (Jokilehto 2011: 12–13). The *waqf* ensured that revenue-generating properties provided the money needed for the maintenance of endowed properties (El-Habashi 2001: 11–58; Bakhoum 2004: 11–62; 2011, 2014b). While this system is a good model for sustainability, it failed over time and for numerous political and economic reasons to provide the required maintenance. Consequently, by the mid-nineteenth century, Cairo's monuments were in a bad state of conservation. Pressure by foreign and Egyptian art connoisseurs led in December 1881 to the establishment of a committee under the Ministry of *Awqāf* (Endowments), the *Comité de conservation des monuments de l'art arabe* (hereafter *Comité*) or *Lajnit hifz al-athar al-'arabiyya*.[3] Its mandate was to work on conserving Arab/Islamic art and, later, Coptic art and architecture in Egypt. The efforts of the *Comité* were responsible for saving much of Cairo's architectural heritage and returned many heritage buildings to practical use. In 1971, the Egyptian Antiquities Organization (EAO) was established under the

Ministry of Culture, taking the responsibility of all heritage sites in Egypt. In 1994, it became the Supreme Council of Antiquities (SCA). In 2011, the Ministry of Antiquities was established, and the SCA was transferred from the Ministry of Culture to the Ministry of Antiquities.

In the early years around and after the inscription of Cairo on the World Heritage List in 1979 and after the 1992 earthquake that damaged many of Cairo's monuments, a number of restoration and conservation projects were initiated, predominately, but not exclusively, by foreign institutions. The focus was on the physical fabric of the buildings, which was either in a poor state of conservation or seriously damaged, requiring considerable restoration. These projects were technically complicated and required skilled personnel. Therefore, many of these projects created job opportunities and encouraged in situ training, developing the skills of conservators, technicians and craftsmen.[4] Some projects also combined practical training with theoretical lessons, such as that of the *Centro-Italo Egiziano per il Restauro e l'archaeologia*, which ran a *cantiere-scuola* or a work-site school (Fanfoni 2006: 78).

The late 1990s and early 2000s saw more projects and more government and non-governmental funding directed towards Historic Cairo. Many of the government-funded and managed monument conservation projects under the aegis of the Historic Cairo Restoration Project (HCRP) were mainly located in the vicinity of the Khan al-Khalili market, a popular tourist destination (Figure 13.1). The HCRP project followed an urban area conservation approach and achieved the restoration of a great number of historic buildings in dire need of intervention including the replacement of dilapidated infrastructure and work on renovating facades of buildings and the street paving as well as the reuse of the *sabil* (drinking fountain building) of Muhammad 'Ali as a textile museum. In 2010, some of the restored houses were used as temporary showroom spaces for designers to display their work.[5] However, the HCRP project was sometimes criticized for creating an 'open air museum' for the tourists to enjoy, while ignoring the communities' needs, especially in an area equally in need of projects targeting socio-economic development (Williams 2006: 275–287; Aslan 2006; Tadamun 2017).

Other projects and institutions have focused on areas that are 'off the beaten track' with even greater socio-economic problems but where important historic buildings and markets are located, thus offering potential attractions for visitation and development (Figure 13.2). For example, the American Research Center in Egypt (ARCE 2014a, 2014b) and the Aga Khan Trust for Culture (AKTC), one of the agencies of the Aga Khan Development Network (AKDN 2016a), managed restoration projects of monuments located in the southern part of al-Mu'izz Street and in al-Darb al-Ahmar district (Figure 13.1) for 15 to 20 years from the mid-1990s.[6] Funding for ARCE's projects came mainly from the United States Agency for International Development (USAID). AKTC's restoration projects were mainly funded by the Aga Khan Development Network and the World Monuments Fund. The projects were carried out in collaboration with the Supreme Council of Antiquities (initially under the Ministry of Culture and later moved to

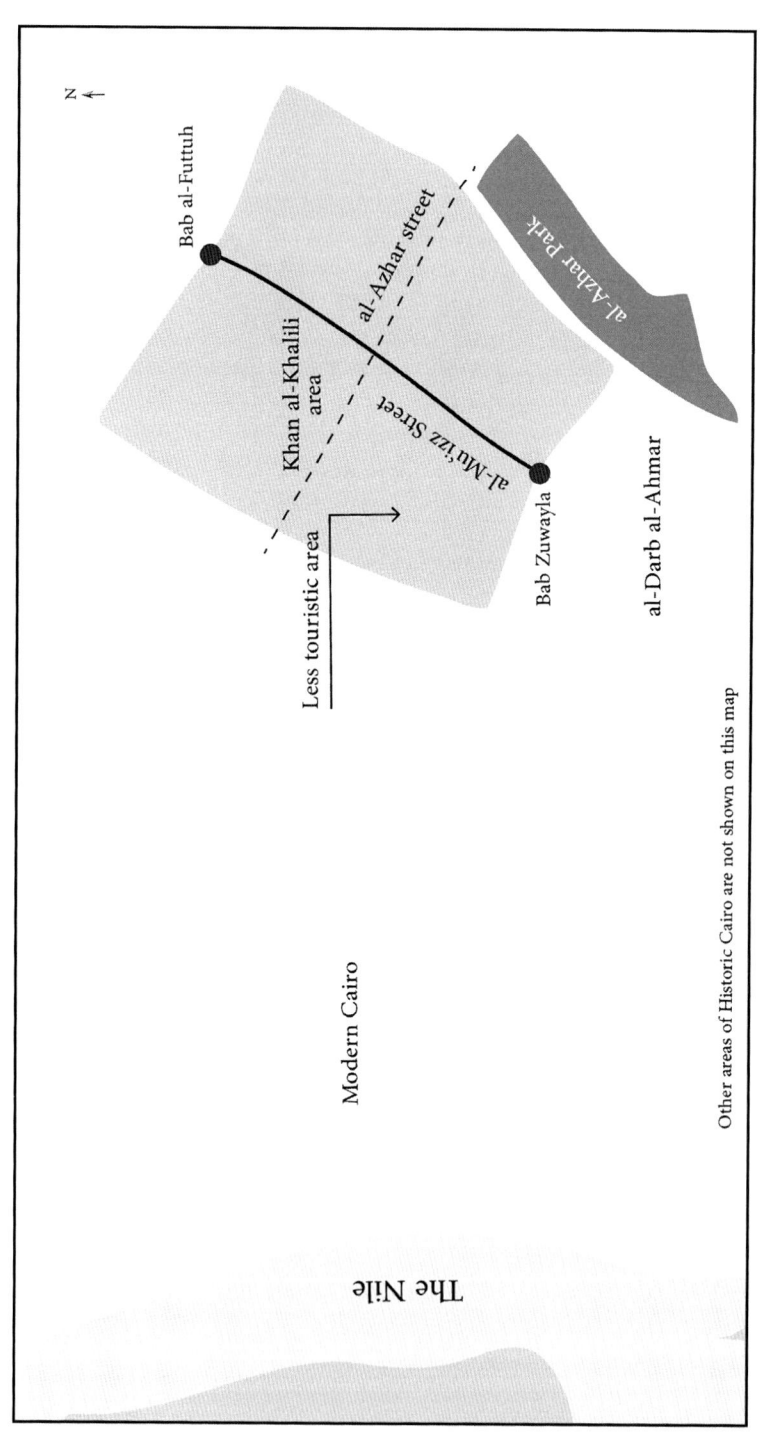

Figure 13.1 Map of Historic Cairo showing the location of Khan al-Khalili, al-Darb al-Ahmar and the Azhar Park

Figure 13.2 Historic Cairo, a living heritage site. View of the less touristic part of al-Mu'izz
street with the local market and medieval architecture, April 2013

Photo: © Matjaž Kačičnik

the newly created Ministry of Antiquities in 2011), the Cairo Governorate, and the Ministry of *Awqāf* (religious endowments) when applicable.

The Aga Khan Development Network (AKDN) has for decades been promoting the notion that culture is an important tool for development.[7] Accordingly, its projects in Cairo were a turning point for how heritage related projects were implemented in this historic city. The intervention started with the creation of al-Azhar Park, transforming a waste dump site close to the historic area of al-Darb al-Ahmar into a garden, providing Cairo's inhabitants and visitors with a 'green lung' in the overcrowded urban landscape. The Azhar Park was a catalyst for a number of socio-economic and cultural activities in the neighbourhood. The socio-economic interventions included access to credit, employment and access to basic social services including health, education, vocational training and solid waste disposal. Following an urban area conservation approach and understanding the communities' needs, an important component of the project dealt with improving infrastructure, upgrading open spaces and housing rehabilitation, enterprises very much in line with the essence of the newly issued World Heritage Sustainable Development Policy.

The AKTC monuments conservation program was part of this wider approach to development and followed and respected sustainable development concepts to ensure that the process of conserving monuments was not carried out in isolation from the complex socio-economic problems affecting the community using and living around them. The projects created numerous job opportunities; hence through training and transfer of knowledge, the projects ensured the revitalization of crafts and skills related to the conservation field. Men and women conservators from a variety of backgrounds worked together restoring the same object and interaction between team members from widely different circumstances was a regular initiative (Figure 13.3).

In effect, heritage conservation projects are characteristic for allowing teamwork among architects, craftsmen, conservators, researchers, planners and labourers, often drawn from different social and religious backgrounds, creating interdependency and engendering professional collaboration on a daily basis. Often, international team members are also involved and therefore such projects allow not only for exchange of knowledge and information but, more significantly, offer important opportunities for cultural exchange and understanding between the individuals involved, who, with time, grow more comfortable with one another. In the process, the common workplace becomes a social space.

Project team members also interact daily with community members both at formal consultations and in regular informal encounters and in discussions seeking to understanding and connect with their needs. Throughout, it was important to convey the message that the purpose of the restoration of this precious inheritance is to protect their historic, artistic and also social and religious values. All the restored religious buildings, namely mosques, are now used by worshippers and are open to the public to visit and enjoy.

For buildings whose original functions had ceased the story was different. While the reuse of historic buildings for a 'socially useful purpose' (Venice

Figure 13.3 Conservation project of Aslam al-Silahdar mosque: team members from different social and religious backgrounds working together on the restoration of 14th-century Mamluk woodwork, November 2009.

Photo: Matjaž Kačičnik, © AKTC and ARCE, archive ASL_307

Charter 1964: Article 5) has long been internationally encouraged, it has not been very common in Egypt. Non-governmental institutions working in Egypt have, however, demonstrated how the reuse of a historic building guarantees its maintenance and accessibility so that now this is an accepted practice of the Ministry of Antiquities. AKTC has used one of its restored houses for cultural activities in the neighbourhood. This is the al-Darb al-Ahmar art school established in partnership with a local NGO, *al-Mawred al-Thaqafi* (AKDN 2016c; Al Mawred Al Thaqafy 2012). In the restored house, children from the neighbourhood are trained in circus arts and music, providing them with skills for future employment and raising their awareness of the values of art and culture. ARCE's restored Sabil of Muhammad Ali-Tusun Pasha was transformed into a museum displaying the objects found in situ, providing information on the history and restoration of the building and also allowing visitors to enter and explore its underground cistern (ARCE 2014b).

Other cultural activities were organized for both children and adults with the purpose of cultivating appreciation for the historic and artistic values of the heritage in their midst and reinforcing residents' pride in their heritage and encouraging responsibility for maintenance and protection. The AKTC also launched initiatives to train young community members to become local guides for visitors and for local residents keen to learn about their neighbourhood's history, architecture and culture. ARCE produced a small guidebook for a selection of buildings in al-Darb al-Ahmar area that can be downloaded for free in Arabic and English for residents interested in exploring their own district and for visitors to this less frequented area (ARCE 2014b). In recent years, the number of Cairenes visiting sectors beyond the usual tourist routes around Khan al-Khalili and al-Darb al-Ahmar has increased. They enjoy visiting recently restored monuments, and many also pray in the historic mosques or sit in a local coffee shop and relish the street's hustle and bustle. Access to Cairo's green lung, the Azhar Park, is also possible from al-Darb al-Ahmar area, through a small gate next to Bab al-Mahruq, one of the twelfth-century gates in the historic Ayyubid wall.

During implementation of the conservation projects mentioned above, their direct socio-economic benefits were apparent through increased employment opportunities and the greater purchasing capacity of local vendors. While it may seem that the benefits ended with the completion of the projects,[8] this chapter argues that their positive impacts go beyond the life-span of the projects and can still be observed in other parts of the country, since they have encouraged a shift in how future heritage-related projects are being planned and managed.

The practical experiences of numerous architects, urban planners and conservators working with institutions in Historic Cairo have led many other practitioners to reach similar conclusions; namely that the conservation of a historic building and the upgrade of a neighbourhood is not simply a highly technical project but also one that has great potential in ensuring inclusive socio-economic development as well as peace and security. In recent years, many of these experienced practitioners have established their own companies, architectural offices and NGOs running cultural-heritage-related projects. They often have predominantly sustainable socio-economic development activities and objectives[9] and work in close collaboration with government entities and other heritage and development institutions and donors. Their projects are in areas both within and areas outside the capital, frequently at locations that are less touristic but with many socio-economic challenges, and most of them follow an urban conservation approach.

For example, 'Megawra: Built Environment Collective' is a local NGO, founded in 2011. Most of its activities take place in Historic Cairo in areas 'off the beaten track' with lots of cultural initiatives for community members, especially children, encouraging them to realize that the 'Monument is Ours', or 'al-Athar Lina', as one of their initiatives is called. Megawra's diverse activities, varying from heritage conservation to organizing public lectures, make it especially important, as it has an 'equal focus on the craft, science, public use and lyricism in restoration' (El-Gibaly 2017).

As elsewhere in Historic Cairo, one of the areas where Megawra is working, al-Khalifa, has faced serious drainage problems. Through the efforts of Megawra with government bodies, the responsible ministries have started to take action to deal with the problem (El-Gibaly 2017). In this way, Megawra is cooperating with the government agencies, drawing their attention to the community's needs, while encouraging each ministry to carry out its mandate and responsibilities. It is essential that different governmental institutions become leading partners in the overall management system of the historic city, providing support to those implementing heritage-related projects while playing a serious and leading role in tackling major problems that affect not only the monuments but the people living around them.

Although Historic Cairo with its areas 'off the beaten track' have great potential for regular visitation and projects with a high socio-economic impact, many areas still face numerous urban problems and lack services and facilities such as cultural centres, restaurants, guesthouses or shops selling local crafts that would encourage more visitors and development. Improvements are constrained by abundant administrative issues, among which the lack of communication and collaboration between different governmental sectors is particularly obstructive. The evolution of a more visitor-caring environment requires involvement by different interest groups and stakeholders who support economically viable initiatives that balance business motives with economically, socially and culturally inclusive benefits. Such concepts and ideas need to be implemented in the overall policies of the government's plans and management systems, encouraging a change in how heritage conservation, restoration and rehabilitation projects are planned and implemented.

The role played by qualified and experienced practitioners in this process is essential. They share a great responsibility to transmit their knowledge to future generations to ensure the means for sustaining conservation interventions and encourage the shift towards implementing projects respecting sustainable development goals. It is therefore necessary that young government employees become aware of contemporary changes. In recent years, UNESCO and its Cairo office have launched a number of capacity building courses in collaboration with governmental bodies. For example, in April 2013, the Urban Regeneration Project for Historic Cairo (URHC) brought together young representatives from the Ministry of Antiquities, the Ministry of *Awqāf*, the National Organization of Urban Harmony, the Cairo Governorate and the Central Agency for Public Mobilization and Statistics for training over a period of one year. The participants in the course joined in the project activities, including socio-economic and architectural surveys and GIS data organization. Lectures by URHC team consultants on various topics related to urban conservation and management issues were also part of the training (URHC second report: 17).

Another capacity-building course on the implementation of the World Heritage Convention was carried out in four modules by the UNESCO Cairo office in collaboration with the Ministry of Antiquities between 2013 and 2014. This course targeted managers from all seven Egyptian World Heritage sites as well as sites on Egypt's Tentative List. Two modules took place in Cairo, one module in Luxor and another in Aswan, allowing the participants to familiarize themselves with Egypt's World Heritage sites and discuss their common and different management issues (Bakhoum 2014a). Building on the outcomes of this course, another capacity-building course was organized in 2016 to assist in training a group of new team members of the Department of International Organizations for Cultural Heritage and International Cooperation in the Ministry of Antiquities. Both courses drew attention to the importance of considering the socio-economic concerns of communities living around and within the World Heritage sites and discussed how heritage and culture could and should contribute to sustainable development through being culturally, socially, economically and also environmentally inclusive.

The impact of these and other courses is starting to become noticeable as site managers undertake initiatives that ensure the involvement and support of local communities in ways that they would probably not have considered necessary in the past. The Ministry of Antiquities has recently established two new units, one of which is the Training Unit that conducts courses for its personnel while the other is the Heritage Awareness Unit with branches throughout Egypt. The latter unit works with community members, school children, local NGOs and other organizations in raising their knowledge and appreciation of their cultural heritage.

Donors play a crucial role in encouraging heritage-related projects that are in line with sustainable development goals by helping steer how such projects are planned and carried out. To list some examples: The United States Agency for International Development, in collaboration with the Government of Egypt, has a bilateral agreement entitled Sustainable Investment Tourism in Egypt (January 2015–September 2018) that is funding a variety of conservation and preservation activities that are 'generating economic benefits for those living in and around the project sites' (USAID 2017) Similarly, the European Union, in collaboration with the Government of Egypt, is launching a project in Egypt entitled Cultural Heritage for Social and Economic Development' as part of its Inclusive Economic Growth Programme. As noted in the Guidelines for grant applicants, the grant 'aims to finance initiatives demonstrating the link between heritage and socio-economic development' (EC 2017).

These initiatives reflect a local and global change in how cultural heritage conservation and management projects are being planned and implemented, shifting the focus towards sustainable development goals. The process is a long one requiring collaboration and commitment from a great number of stakeholders and interest groups. Projects need to be designed in ways that ensure their sustainability beyond the lifespan of the implementation and funding phase. Governments need to ensure that their overall policies provide solid support for such projects and for the sustainable development goals. The issuing of the World Heritage Sustainable Development Policy is therefore highly beneficial and its implementation with the full engagement of community members, heritage institutions, donors and government bodies will be crucial.

Final remarks

The author is involved with the American Research Center in Egypt in outreach and capacity building activities related to the ongoing conservation and restoration project at the Red Monastery Church in Sohag, Upper Egypt.[10] Numerous stakeholders are involved including the clergy, community members, employees of the Ministry of Antiquities and others. A theoretical and practical training course on conservation is among the recent activities carried out for local conservators working for the Ministry of Antiquities in Sohag. As part of this course, site visits with the conservators were organized to nearby areas allowing them to critique and discuss the state of conservation of these sites and the management issues they face. One of the visits was to Akhmim, where many of the trainees are working. Akhmim contains excavated remains of Ancient Egyptian, Christian and Islamic heritage (Figures 13.4 and 13.5). A large part of the archaeological site is still un-excavated, and the residents have great fear that they might be removed so that the ancient city can be uncovered. Some employees of the Ministry of Antiquities consider the community a threat to preservation and to furthering archaeological discoveries and scholarly research.

During this visit, discussions took place with the conservators and other employees of the Ministry of Antiquities in order to draw their attention to the importance of working with the community to reduce the tension between them and those involved with the archaeological and heritage aspects of the site. During the discussion, the concepts in the World Heritage Sustainable Development Policy were explained, and the importance of having the support of the Egyptian Government for this policy was emphasized as vital to guaranteeing that the community members do not feel alienated from their heritage but rather partners in

Figure 13.4 The archaeological site of Akhmim in Upper Egypt, a partially excavated site within the village, 2017.

Photo: Dina Bakhoum

Figure 13.5 The archaeological site of Akhmim in Upper Egypt, a partially excavated site within the village, 2017.

Photo: Dina Bakhoum

its protection. The policy, if seriously considered and implemented by official government agencies in a way that ensures the active participation and empowerment of all stakeholders, is a great opportunity to manage heritage sites in a more inclusive manner, leading to achieving sustainable development goals.

Notes

1 For a list of publications, see GCI (no date).
2 For more information on these pressures, see Tung (2001: Ch. 5).
3 The author of this article is currently writing her PhD on the Comité. For more on the Comité and its members, see (Reid 1992; Speiser 2001; El-Habashi 2001; Volait 2002; Ormos 2009).
4 For projects from the 1970s until the 1990s, see Bacharach 1995. For projects by the German Archaeological Institute Cairo between 1973 and 2004, see Mayer and Speiser (2007).
5 This was part of the '+20 Egypt design' initiative. For more, see EFEC (no date). Most of the houses were restored by the HCRP; Bayt al-Suhaymi was restored by 'Nadim'.
6 ARCE restored the sabil of Muhammad Ali-Tussun Pasha, the sabil and wikala of Nafisa al-Baida, the Bab Zuwayla with the upper minarets of the mosque of al-Mu'ayyad Shaykh, the Zawiyya of Farag ibn Barquq and Bayt al-Razzaz. AKTC restored the Madrasa-Mosque of Umm al-Sultan Sha'ban, the Khayer Bek Complex, the Tarabay al-Sharifi Mausoleum, the Aqsunqr Mosque (the Blue Mosque) and a large section of

the Historic Ayyubid city wall. ARCE and AKTC collaborated on the restoration of Aslam al-Silahdar mosque. For more on ARCE's project in Historic Cairo and all over Egypt between 1995 and 2005, see Danforth ed. (2010). For maps on the monuments of Historic Cairo see Warner (2005); an ARCE supported project.

7 For more on the Aga Khan Trust for Culture's Historic Cities Program around the world, see Jodidio ed. (2011). On AKTC's work in Cairo, see Bianaca and Jodidio ed. (2004). Other publications can be found in AKDN 2016b.

8 AKTC completed most of the conservation projects in 2012 and handed over the buildings to the MoA and the Ministry of *Awqāf*. AKDN remains present in the area however through the Azhar Park and other socio-economic and cultural activities.

9 Examples are many, but to mention a few: Built Environment Collective 'Megawra', Takween Integrated Community Development, Archinos Architecture, Turath Conservation Group, Egyptian Heritage Rescue Foundation and Nadim for Heritage and Development-Nawal Messiri and Asaad Nadim Foundation, among others.

10 The project is directed by Michael Jones. For more information on the first phase of the project, see Bolman ed. (2016) and Jones (2016).

References

Aga Khan Development Network (AKDN) (2016a). *Organisation Information* (online). Available at: www.akdn.org/about-us/organisation-information (accessed 4 June 2017).

Aga Khan Development Network (AKDN) (2016b). *Publications* (online). Available at: www.akdn.org/press-centre/publications (accessed 19 May 2017).

Aga Khan Development Network (AKDN) (2016c). *Egypt: Cultural Development* (online). Available at: www.akdn.org/where-we-work/middle-east/egypt/cultural-development (accessed 16 May 2017).

Al Mawred Al Thaqafy (2012). *Darb Al Ahmar Arts School* (online). Available at: http://mawred.org/programs-and-activities/darb-al-ahmar-arts-school/ (accessed 16 May 2017).

American Research Center in Egypt (ARCE) (2014a). *Walking Tour for Historic Cairo* (online). Available at: www.arce.org/conservation/historic-cairo-guides (accessed 16 May 2017).

American Research Center in Egypt (ARCE) (2014b). *The Monuments of al-Darb al-Ahmar, Cairo* (online). Available at: www.arce.org/files/user/page332/EN_Drb_Leafl_PrintA4.pdf (accessed 16 May 2017).

Aslan, R. (2006). *Rescuing Cairo's Lost Heritage* (online). Available at: www.worldpress.org/Mideast/2343.cfm (accessed 15 March 2017).

Australia ICOMOS (1979, 1999, 2013). *The Burra Charter: The Australia ICOMOS Charter for Places of Cultural Significance*. Burwood, Victoria: Australia ICOMOS.

Bacharach, J. L. (ed) (1995). *Restoration and Conservation of Islamic Monuments in Egypt*. Cairo: The American University in Cairo Press.

Bakhoum, D. (2004). *The Waqf in Relation to Maintenance and Repair: The Medieval Sources and Their Uses for Contemporary Practices*. Unpublished M.A. thesis, the American University in Cairo.

Bakhoum, D. (2011). 'The Waqf system: Maintenance, repair and upkeep', in P. Ghazaleh (ed), *Held in Trust, Waqf in the Islamic World*. Cairo, New York: The American University in Cairo Press, pp. 179–196.

Bakhoum, D. (2014a). 'Increasing World Heritage Capacity in Egypt', in L. Leitão (ed), *World Heritage Capacity Building Newsletter 4*, pp. 30–32 (online). Available at: www.unesco.org/fileadmin/MULTIMEDIA/FIELD/Cairo/images/whcapacitybuilding_eg.pdf (accessed 4 June 2017).

Bakhoum, D. (2014b). *Awqaf Properties Maintenance and Management' Report Produced in the Framework of the Urban Regeneration Project for Historic Cairo UNESCO, World Heritage Centre* (online). Available at: www.urhcproject.org/Content/studies/20_bakhoum.pdf (accessed 4 June 2017).

Bianaca, S. and Jodidio, P. (eds) (2004). *Cairo Revitalising a Historic Metropolis.* Turin: Umberto Allemandi & C. for the Aga Khan Trust for Culture.

Bolman, E. S. (ed) (2016). *The Red Monastery Church: Beauty and Asceticism in Upper Egypt.* Yale: Yale University Press.

Danforth, R. (ed) (2010). *Preserving Egypt's Cultural Heritage.* Cairo: The American Research Center in Egypt and the American University in Cairo Press.

Egyptian Furniture Export Council (EFEC) (no date). *+20 Egypt Design, 3–7 June 2010* (online). Available at: http://20egyptdesign.net/Default.aspx (accessed 16 May 2017).

El-Habashi, A. (2001). *Athar to Monuments, the Intervention of the Comité de Conservation des Monuments de l'Art Arabe.* Unpublished Ph.D. dissertation, University of Pennsylvania.

Fanfoni, G. (2006). *Il restauro della Sama'Khana dei dervisci mevlevi al Cairo.* 2nd ed. Cairo: Centro italo-egiziano per il restauro e l'archeologia.

El-Gibaly, L. (2017). *Making Sure Heritage Is a Resource Not a Burden* (online). Available at: www.madamasr.com/en/2017/03/07/feature/culture/megawra-making-sure-heritage-is-a-resource-not-a-burden/ (accessed 19 March 2017).

European Commission (EC) and International Cooperation and Development (2017). *Call for Tenders: Cultural Heritage for Social and Economic Development–Egypt* (online). Available at: https://webgate.ec.europa.eu/europeaid/online-services/index.cfm?ADSS Chck=1491520920797&do=publi.detPUB&aoref=154927&orderbyad=Desc&searchty pe=AS&debpub=&orderby=upd&nbPubliList=25&zgeo=35582&aoet=36538&ccnt=7 573876,7573877&page=1&userlanguage=en (accessed 4 June 2017).

The Getty Conservation Institute (GCI) (no date). *Research on the Values of Heritage (1998–2005)* (online). Available at: www.getty.edu/conservation/our_projects/field_projects/values/values_publications.html (accessed 16 May 2017).

International Council on Monuments and Sites (ICOMOS) (1964). *The International Charter for the Conservation and Restoration of Monuments and Sites* (The Venice Charter).

Jodidio, P. (ed) (2011). *The Aga Khan Historic Cities Programme: Strategies for Urban Regeneration.* Munich: Prestel.

Jokilehto, J. (2011). *A History of Architectural Conservation.* New York: Routledge.

Jones, M. (2016). 'Rehabilitating a late antique mural painting at the red monastery, sohag', in M. Ayad (ed), *Studies in Coptic Culture: Transmission and Interaction.* Cairo: The American University in Cairo Press, pp. 173–184.

Mayer, W. and Speiser, P. (eds) (2007). *A Future for the Past: Restorations in Islamic Cairo 1973–2004.* Mainz am Rhein: Verlag Philipp von Zabern.

Ormos, I. (2009). *Max Herz Pasha 1859–1919: His Life and Career.* Cairo: Institut français d'archéologie orientale.

Reid, D. M. (1992). 'Cultural imperialism and nationalism: The struggle to define and control the Heritage of Arab Art in Egypt', *International Journal of Middle East Studies,* 24, 57–76.

Sedky, A. (2009). *Living with Heritage in Cairo.* Cairo: The American University in Cairo Press.

Speiser, P. (2001). *Die Geschichte der Erhaltung arabischer Baudenkmäler in Ägypten. Die Restaurierung der Madrasa Tatar al-Ḥiǧāzīya und des Sabīl Kuttāb 'Abd ar-Raḥmān Katḫudā im Rahmen des Darb-al-Qirmiz-Projektes in Kairo (Abhandlungen des Deutschen Archäologischen Instituts Kairo, Islamische Reihe 8).* Heidelberg: Heidelberger Orientverlag.

Tadamun (2017). *Mashrū' taṭūir shari' al-mu'iz li-dīn Allāh al-fāṭimī (al-mathaf al-maftūh), the rehabilitation project of al-mu'iz street (the open air museum)* (online). Available at: www.tadamun.co/?post_type=initiative&p=9048#.WOZEuRhh0ci (accessed 30 March 2017).

Tung, A. (2001). *Preserving the World's Great Cities*. New York: Three Rivers Press.

UNESCO (2002). *The Budapest Declaration on World Heritage*. Paris: UNESCO.

UNESCO (2011). *Recommendation on the Conservation of Historic Urban Landscapes*. Paris: UNESCO.

UNESCO (2015). *Policy Document for the Integration of a Sustainable Development Perspective into the Processes of the World Heritage Convention* (online). Available at: http://whc.unesco.org/en/sustainabledevelopment/ (accessed 2 December 2017).

UNESCO-World Heritage Centre (UNESCO-WHC), Special Projects Unit (2012). *Urban Regeneration Project for Historic Cairo* (online). Available at: www.urhcproject.org (accessed 15 May 2017).

USAID (2017). *Economic Growth and Tourism* (online). Available at: www.usaid.gov/egypt/economic-growth-and-tourism (accessed 18 May 2017).

Volait, M. (2002). 'Amateurs français et dynamique patrimoniale: aux origines du Comité de conservation des monuments de l'art arabe', in D. Panzac and A. Raymond (eds), *La France et l'Égypte à l'époque des vice-rois 1805–1882*. Cairo: IFAO, pp. 311–325.

Warner, N. (2005). *The Monuments of Historic Cairo: A Map and Descriptive Catalogue*. Cairo: The American Research Center in Egypt and the American University in Cairo Press.

Williams, C. (2006). 'Reconstructing Historic Cairo: Forces at Work', in D. Singerman and P. Amar (eds), *Cairo Cosmopolitan*. Cairo: The American University in Cairo Press, pp. 267–294.

Chapter 14

Applying a sustainable development approach to the World Heritage 'Town of Bamberg' site

Challenges met, opportunities seized

Patricia Alberth

The concept of sustainability is already found in the UNESCO *Convention Concerning the Protection of the World Cultural and Natural Heritage*, which refers to the 'duty of ensuring the identification, protection, conservation, presentation and transmission to future generations of the cultural and natural heritage' (UNESCO 1972: Article 4). In the management of its World Heritage site, the City of Bamberg seeks to follow the Convention and meet the needs of the present without compromising the ability of future generations. In order to accomplish this, it addresses the different dimensions of sustainable development as defined in the 2015 World Heritage and Sustainable Development policy: environmental sustainability, social sustainability, economic sustainability and peace and security (UNESCO 2015).

This chapter introducing the case of Bamberg offers a local perspective on the relevance of the policy and explores some of the emerging issues and challenges. The 'Town of Bamberg' was inscribed in the UNESCO World Heritage List in 1993 due to its exemplary nature as a central European town with a basically early medieval plan and numerous well preserved ecclesiastical and secular buildings of the medieval and Baroque periods.

Bamberg, which is located in Northern Bavaria, Germany, has 73,331 inhabitants (Goller 2017) and 1,347 registered monuments (as of December 2015). The World Heritage site encompasses 142 hectares including the so-called Market Gardeners' District (Figure 14.1), the City on the Hills with its ecclesiastical architecture and the Island District. The street layout of the three historic core areas retains the medieval features. When Henry II, Duke of Bavaria, became King of Germany in 1007, he made Bamberg the seat of a bishopric. With its four towers, the imperial cathedral of St. Peter and St. George is the city's most prominent building. Inside are the Bamberg Horseman, a life-size stone equestrian statue by an anonymous medieval sculptor; the tomb of Pope Clement II, the only papal grave in Germany; and the tomb of Emperor Henry II and his wife Cunigunde. The Cathedral Square is lined by the medieval Old Palace and the Baroque New Palace. Another landmark is the Old Town Hall that is located in the river Regnitz and accessible by two bridges.

Figure 14.1 Market Gardeners' District
Source: © City of Bamberg/Jürgen Schraudner

This chapter is structured around four sections. The first explores how Bamberg not only addresses it Outstanding Universal Value (OUV) in isolation, but how this is equally connected to important intangible cultural heritage connected to the urban gardening tradition. The second section addresses the question of environmental sustainability, whereas the third and fourth sections concern, respectively, the issues of social inclusion and peace and security.

World Heritage meets intangible cultural heritage

Ever since the Middle Ages, urban gardening has been playing an important economic and cultural role in Bamberg. Europe-wide trade in seeds and liquorice root once formed a significant part of the local economy (Scheinost 2009: 27). In 2016, Bamberg's gardening tradition was included in the national list of intangible cultural heritage following its inclusion in the Bavarian list in 2014. However, over the past decades the gardening tradition in the inner-city area has been facing development pressure and demographic change (Wußmann 2002: 16). Where once there were more than 500 gardening businesses, only about 40 are active today.

The Market Gardeners' District, an integral part of the World Heritage site, emerged along the former 'Steinweg' (now 'Königstraße'), an important medieval trade route. The settlement is characterized by urban areas of cultivable land which are accessible exclusively through the houses of the gardeners. The cultivable land is part of the conservation area and therefore protected from building developments – much to the chagrin of the owners who often feel discriminated against by the municipality in the light of this restriction.

Yet, the visible link between agriculture in the form of market gardens and vineyards and the urban distribution centre makes Bamberg unique. Without this particular feature, Bamberg's OUV would be at risk. Several cities have already sacrificed their historical market gardens, among them World Heritage cities such as Bath in England and to an extent Istanbul in Turkey. However, the cases can only be compared to a limited extent. The City of Bath, which was inscribed on the World Heritage List in 1987, had lost its urban agricultural land long before its inscription. Accordingly, the market gardens are not related to the site's OUV. In Istanbul, on the other hand, the Yedikule gardens on the historic Sultanahmet peninsula along the Byzantine-era ramparts provided a livelihood for more than 200 people until very recently. In 2016, however, the municipality started to demolish the farmers' sheds, display tables, and the temporary walls that protected the gardens. The future of the market gardens that stem from the Middle Ages is uncertain. At the same time, the Historic Areas of Istanbul, whose World Heritage inscription dates back to 1985 and whose OUV 'resides in its unique integration of architectural masterpieces that reflect the meeting of Europe and Asia over many centuries, and in its incomparable skyline formed by the creative genius of Byzantine and Ottoman architects', currently faces several major development projects that seem to be a far more serious conservation concern than the disappearance of the Yedikule gardens.

In contrast, Bamberg's Market Gardeners' District forms a crucial part of the World Heritage property's OUV. Building on the city's urban agricultural land, a common practice before the site's inscription on the UNESCO List, would clearly jeopardize the UNESCO title. Correspondingly, to counteract the further loss of gardening tradition and land, the municipality started embracing and cultivating this district. Due to its relatively poor infrastructure – narrow footpaths, scarce gastronomical outlets and lack of toilets – and the seemingly ordinary architecture, this district has been neglected for a long time. But the new approach empowers the gardeners and promotes economic opportunity and quality jobs for community residents. Key elements of this initiative were an information campaign targeting locals and visitors alike, the promotion of local produce and the legal protection of the gardening areas. As a concrete result of this campaign, the number of gardeners sitting on the City Council has increased from one in 2005 to five by 2017. The presence of gardeners on the City Council is a key to the interests of this particular group being considering in municipal decisions.

Petrus Zweidler's city map of 1602 (Figure 14.2) illustrates how the urban fields characterize the city's historic structure and therefore contribute to the site's

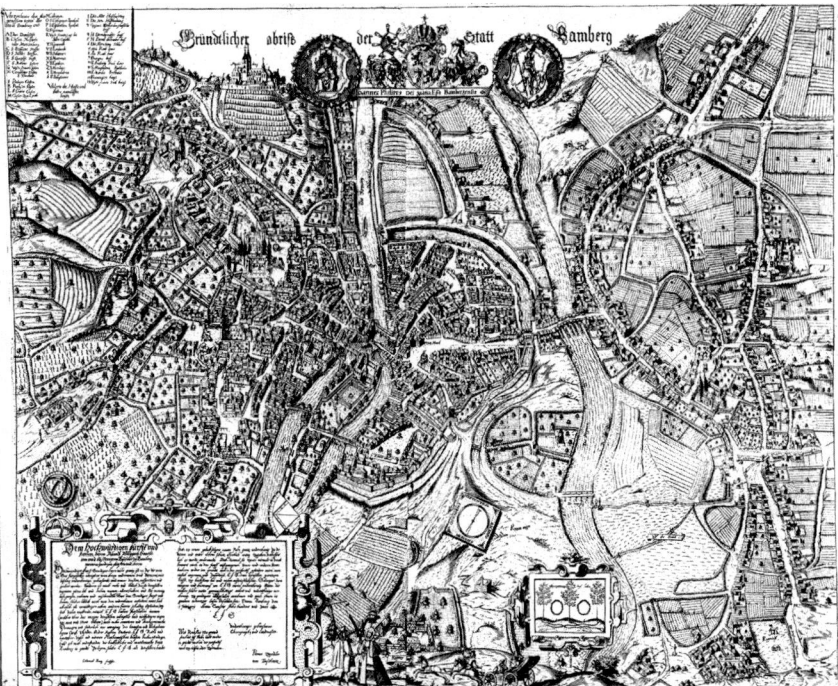

Figure 14.2 City map of 1602 by Petrus Zweidler

OUV. The best way to protect those fields from construction development is continued cultivation. Consequently, the City of Bamberg supports local produce, which – at least partly – is cultivated on historic urban fields in Bamberg. An interest group of 19 market gardeners coordinates joint actions such as the annual 'Day of Open Market Gardens' or the publication of a buyer's guide for local produce. This consortium of gardeners has its own logo, which reads '*Gutes aus der Gärtnerstadt*' (Good produce from the Market Gardeners' District; Figure 14.3).

Environmental sustainability

The goal of environmental sustainability is to conserve natural resources while reducing pollution and harm to the environment. Bamberg's sustainable development approach to the environment has particularly helped to achieve the reduction of carbon emissions and the recycling of resources.

Even though transport might not be the major component of the total carbon emissions from agriculture, the fact that Bamberg's consumers are supplied by local gardening fields and do not have to rely on vegetables brought by motor vehicles from further afield is a key sustainability benefit. The short freight distances keep

Figure 14.3 Produce from the Market Gardeners' District
Source: © City of Bamberg/Diana Büttner

fuel use and emissions down and serve to protect the climate. In addition, local suppliers and service providers are promoting local collaboration and contribute to the preservation of the historic garden areas as part of the World Heritage site. The strengthening of local structures constitutes one of the most important strategies for fostering sustainable development: In economic terms, new value chains can emerge, in social terms social disadvantages can be absorbed and in ecological terms transport routes and resources can be saved. Bamberg's moderate size proves conducive to a well-connected network of local stakeholders. As a result, gardeners, supermarkets, media and activists have established numerous joint projects aiming at locally selling produce from the Market Gardeners' District.

Consequently, Bamberg was invited by UNESCO in 2015 to present the horticultural heritage of the city as a good practice example for food sustainability within the framework of EXPO 2015 in Italy themed 'Feeding the Planet – Energy for Life'. With photos from the Market Gardeners' District and movie screenings from Bamberg's Market Gardeners' and Winegrowers' Museum, the exhibition presented the skills and the knowledge of the Bamberg gardeners to an international audience.

Moreover, Bamberg's World Heritage Office introduced a product locally that referres to Bamberg's gardening tradition and at the same time applies sustainable consumption and production patterns. In collaboration with the fashion workshop

'*Mode macht Mut*' (Fashion gives Courage), where migrant women learn to sew with donated textile materials, gardening aprons from recycled materials have been produced. They can be purchased as unique souvenirs at the Market Gardeners' and Vintners' Museum and other tourist locations in Bamberg and contribute to raising awareness of the connection between World Heritage and sustainable development.

In order to promote the initiative and communicate the connection a photo exhibition was launched featuring well-known Bamberg citizens wearing the gardening aprons and commenting on the significance of Bamberg's gardening tradition. Bamberg's Lord Mayor – together with representatives of the Bavarian State Conservation Office and the German National Commission for UNESCO – helped the publicity (Figure 14.4).

Figure 14.4 Lord Mayor Andreas Starke wearing a gardening apron from the recycling project
Source: © City of Bamberg/Jürgen Schraudner

In terms of environmental sustainability, Germany is known for its comprehensive recycling system. The country's waste management success really comes down to two things: firm government policy and strong citizen support. Since 1991, manufacturers have been obliged to take responsibility for the recycling of their product packaging after consumption. Moreover, in 2016 Germany's government signed an agreement with the retail industry to curb the use of plastic bags by stopping them from being given to shoppers for free. Those principles also apply in Bamberg. Reusable shopping bags are widely used – not only when buying vegetables.

Furthermore, in an attempt to reduce car emissions a national framework of low emission zones exists in Germany. This affects all motor vehicles except motorcycles. A number of cities also have transit bans on heavy duty vehicle through-traffic. Supplementary bans for diesel vehicles are currently under discussion for cities suffering from heavy air pollution. So far, Bamberg is not affected by the bans. This is despite the car being the most popular means of transport with 41 per cent of distances travelled in Bamberg being by car, according to a recent municipal survey. Travel by bicycle follows with 30 per cent. The bike's popularity cannot be attributed to good cycling infrastructure but is due to the narrow medieval city grid that makes driving a car both challenging and time-consuming. Finally, 19 per cent of the distances are covered walking and ten per cent by public transport.

Inclusive social development

The key aspects of inclusive social development in connection with Bamberg's World Heritage site refer to social cohesion and making the site accessible to a wide range of people. In Bamberg, as probably in many other World Heritage cities, too, it is mostly elderly residents from an academic background who show interest in heritage conservation matters. As an episcopal see and university town, the place is historically characterized by a well-educated middle and upper class that perceives the city's World Heritage in the same vein as attending a concert of the Bamberg Symphony. Many people from more remote and less privileged parts of the city only vaguely identify with the World Heritage site as working group discussions in connection with the development of the new World Heritage management plan have revealed.

Therefore, and in consideration of Article 5 of the World Heritage Convention which calls upon State Parties to 'adopt a general policy which aims to give the cultural and natural heritage a function in the life of the community', the City of Bamberg tries to involve a larger audience in its World Heritage-related activities. It is against this backdrop that, in 2017, the City of Bamberg launched its first brochure on World Heritage in 'Simple German' (a national language standard). The brochure uses a limited vocabulary and simple grammar. World Heritage as a topic is unfamiliar to many and complex in its ideas. Using 'Simple German' to explain World Heritage makes it easier for people with different needs, such as children, people with learning difficulties and people who are trying to learn German, to comprehend the concept.

Another intervention aims at reconciling the tensions between the local population and Bamberg's tourists. Bamberg is a popular travel destination, with an estimated 6.5 million visitors per year. While some inhabitants benefit greatly from this fact, others feel rather disturbed by congested alleys and rising prices. They perceive tourists as intruders. The increasing number of river cruises is of particular concern in this context because the tourist passengers appear suddenly and in large groups and are generally little sensitive to their environment, being equipped with earphones and tablets. Occasional free guided tours for local residents entitled 'Unser Bamberg – Da schau her!' (Look, our Bamberg!), organized by Bamberg's Tourism Department, enable a change of perspective and foster tolerance towards visitors who, after all, contribute to the prosperity of the city. The World Heritage Office takes an active approach in bringing heritage matters to less privileged schools in the city. Members of the team, upon request, provide teaching material for a number of teaching levels. However, most importantly, the World Heritage Office applies participatory methods whenever the occasion occurs. Those methods range from mere information provision to consultation and partnership. Especially during the current development of a new World Heritage management plan there is a high degree of participation within the different thematic groups.

Bamberg's first World Heritage management plan dates back to 2004. While this plan was rather compact, advanced international standards and recent developments in the city called for a new planning document that considers local regulations and bodies. Correspondingly, the World Heritage Office launched a new planning process in November 2015. The new management plan identifies the core values of the site, recognizes challenges and threats and sets out policies and measures to preserve and enhance the site. In order to prepare the plan, working groups were established covering heritage conservation and urban development; education and research; urban gardening; World Heritage and tourism; and World Heritage and economic development.

The groups met over a span of eight months to discuss current challenges and effective ways of to handle them. Stakeholders from educational institutions, civic associations, religious institutions, museums, conservation services and the tourism industry contributed to the results. The process was accompanied by a scientific advisory council, while a board of trustees consisting of representatives from the City of Bamberg, the District of Bamberg, the City Council and the regional government of Upper Franconia supported the development of the management plan on a political level.

Moreover, a World Heritage visitor centre is currently being built. The new house will open in Spring 2018. The exhibition will explain why Bamberg is a World Heritage site and embed the city in the global UNESCO context. The conceptualization process entailed several workshops that included stakeholders from different sectors. On a more playful level, the municipality used the annual World Heritage day in June 2016 to invite the local population to present their views in a World Heritage-themed pop-up centre. A temporary space was converted into an exhibition with photographic and stage activities as well as some elements for young guests.

Inclusive economic development

Each year, the German National Tourist Board undertakes an online survey to identify the 100 most popular destinations in Germany. Most of the German World Heritage sites are on this list. Bamberg held position 32 in 2016. According to the local Tourism Department, Bamberg's economy earns an estimated 253.5 million EUR per year from tourism. Besides those figures, the municipality continuously points out the positive side effects, such as a very rich cultural infrastructure that could not be maintained exclusively on the basis of the local audience.

Very few economic activities have such a strong local impact on the creation of jobs, the increase in household income and the demand created in other industries as the rehabilitation of historic buildings (Rypkema 2014: 2). The municipality's investments in heritage conservation can, therefore, be seen as a key element in the inclusive economic development of Bamberg. In the face of the high number of historical buildings in the city several small and medium-sized enterprises have specialized in their conservation. Correspondingly, those businesses benefit from such investments. With decades of experience some of those businesses are also in high demand at a national level.

Within the framework of the *National Investment Programme for UNESCO World Heritage Sites* the German Federal Ministry for the Environment, Nature Conservation, Construction and Reactor Safety provided from 2009 to 2014 a total of EUR 8.1 million of federal funding for heritage conservation projects in Bamberg. Several local firms were involved in the implementation of the projects. After the program ended, the Ministry adopted an investment program for urban development and provided an additional EUR 12.5 million of federal funding for heritage conservation projects in Bamberg. These federal funds resulted in considerable subsequent investments from the private sector within the municipality.

Of course, the conservation of historic building in Bamberg is a responsibility of the city council as stipulated in the *Bavarian Law for the Protection and Preservation of Buildings*. The city's conservation team provides free advice on conservation matters. Apart from the fact that many buildings in Bamberg are listed and therefore protected, from a sustainability point of view the maintenance of existing buildings should be preferred to using raw materials for new structures (Zanger 2009: 198). Moreover, the council seeks to revitalize neighbourhoods and make communities better places in which to live (Rypkema 2014: 100).

In tandem with these local efforts, the interest group also sought to integrate Bamberg's gardening culture into the framework of regional tourism, food and lifestyle initiatives that had similar goals. These include Slow Food Deutschland (the German branch of the 'Slow Food' movement), *Metropolregion Nürnberg*

(Nuremberg metropolitan region), *Genussregion Oberfranken* (Upper Franconia: Culinary Region) as well as the campaign '*Region Bamberg – weil's mich überzeugt!*' (Bamberg region – because it convinces me!). These collaborations resulted in local educational and capacity-building programs such as a workshop in marketing and product presentation fostering local entrepreneurship. As a result, more people in Bamberg are now aware of the availability of local produce. In addition, national media learned about this historically rooted particularity in Bamberg and reported about it, which, in return, brought new visitors to Bamberg who were extremely interested in the place's gardening tradition.

The above catalogue of activities demonstrates that World Heritage is an economic factor far beyond the tourism sector. Regrettably, the benefits from World Heritage cannot always be quantified. Reliable figures are extremely helpful when advocating World Heritage and gathering them represents a wide opportunity for cooperation with research institutions.

Fostering peace and security

Bamberg generally is a peaceful and safe place with a high degree of social cohesion. Additionally, the municipality encourages moral courage with an award program entitled 'Acting instead of looking the other way' is running. This recognizes exemplary civil engagement against violence, xenophobia or discrimination, as well as unselfish civilian engagement for a peaceful resolution of conflicts between sections of the population, for the equality and integration of minorities and for intercultural dialogue.

Gardens are places of cooperative human interaction. Working the soil together can create opportunities for socializing and learning. Having this in mind the City of Bamberg supported the establishment of an 'Intercultural Garden' in the wake of the State Garden Show in Bamberg in 2012. The project aims to unite people of different origins, ethnicity and religion through gardening and promote social exchange between them. According to the local Immigrant and Integration Council, 20 per cent of Bamberg's inhabitants have a multicultural background. Both migrants and locals are addressed by the project, which is designed to be a joint effort and rather than emphasizing cultural differences, aims to help overcome prejudices.

While the Intercultural Garden is located outside of the World Heritage site, a 'Heritage Garden' lies at the heart of it next to the Gardeners' and Vintners' Museum. The Heritage Garden preserves the biodiversity of Bamberg's crops and at the same time makes history and environmental education come alive. It makes an important contribution to safeguarding the intangible heritage associated with the World Heritage site. During winter, the harvested vegetables are used for cooking workshops in which old local recipes are adapted for modern use. The initiative is also open to refugees. In 2015, Bamberg opened a major registration centre for asylum seekers. Hence, there is a special need in Bamberg for initiatives that enable interaction between different cultures.

In line with UNESCO's guiding principle of peaceful coexistence as well as with Bamberg's international significance as a World Heritage site, the World Heritage Office regularly participates in the Intercultural Weeks of the City of Bamberg. For this purpose, international experts are invited to lecture on current heritage issues in one of the working languages of UNESCO. The University of Bamberg has proven a reliable partner in this endeavour.

Conclusion

In summary, it can be seen that all four principal dimensions of sustainable development apply to the 'Town of Bamberg' World Heritage site. However, none of the initiatives outlined above were systemically planned in consideration of the Operational Guidelines (UNESCO 2016). Instead, they responded to the need for action in certain areas as well as the availability of human and financial resources. For the long term, by contrast, systematically applying a sustainable development approach is indispensable and, in collaboration with a wide range of stakeholders, a number of projects fostering sustainability have been implemented. They range from capacity building initiatives for market gardeners to extensive investments in heritage conservation. Generally, the World Heritage Office places great importance on a participatory approach as elaborated above.

The challenge in applying a sustainable development approach at a site level lies in the very limited funds and human resources available for this purpose. While the responsibilities of World Heritage sites keep expanding, budgets develop in the opposite direction. Those responsibilities grow with each revision of the Operational Guidelines and include conducting heritage impact assessments, developing risk preparedness plans as well as working in concert with other UNESCO programs and conventions. On the positive side, collaborative efforts can lead to an increased impact. Consequently, the identification of the site's stakeholders is indispensable together with the application of suitable participation strategies. Against this background, unusual collaborations are also worth trying. They can lead to unique projects such as the development of gardening aprons from recycled fabric, as described above.

Generally, as World Heritage is a rather popular topic, it has been relatively easy in most cases to find partners to work with regarding the different dimensions of sustainability. The same counts for funding. The Bamberg experience shows that national funds can help to tackle issues of sustainability as it was the case with *the National Investment Programme for UNESCO World Heritage Sites*. Against this background, special emphasis should be placed on sharing good practice among World Heritage sites globally in order to spread effective approaches in sustainable development and integrate this abstract topic better into workaday life. Existing networks such as the Organization of World Heritage Cities might provide a suitable platform for such an exchange of good practice ideas.

References

Goller, T. (2017). *Bamberg in Zahlen 2016: Statistisches Jahrbuch der Stadt Bamberg.* Bamberg: City of Bamberg.

Rypkema, D. (2014). *The Economics of Historic Preservation: A Community Leader's Guide.* Washington, DC: PlaceEconomics.

Scheinost, M. (2009). *Vom Wirtschaftsfaktor zum Welterbe. Bambergs Gärtner und Häcker. Begleitband zur Ausstellung des Lehrstuhls für Europäische Ethnologie der Otto-Friedrich-Universität Bamberg im Historischen Museum Bamberg vom 18.07.2009 bis zum 01.11. 2009.* Bamberg: Stadtarchiv Bamberg.

UNESCO (1972). *Convention Concerning the Protection of the World Cultural and Natural Heritage.* Paris: UNESCO.

UNESCO (2015). *Policy Document for the Integration of a Sustainable Development Perspective into the Processes of the World Heritage Convention* (online). Available at: http://whc.unesco.org/en/sustainabledevelopment/ (accessed 2 December 2017).

UNESCO (2016). *Operational Guidelines for the Implementation of the World Heritage Convention.* Paris: UNESCO World Heritage Centre.

Wußmann, W. (2002). *Ein Zwiebeltreter bin ich gern. Bamberg und seine Gärtner* [I Enjoy Being an Onion Trimmer: Bamberg and Its Gardeners]. Gundelsheim: Genniges.

Zanger, O. (2009). *Vom Nutzen des Umnutzens: Umnutzung von denkmalgeschützten Gebäuden* [On the Benefits of Adaptive Re-Use: Adaptive Re-Use of Listed Buildings]. Düsseldorf: StadtBauKultur NRW.

Chapter 15

Sustainable development and nature-culture linkages in the Coffee Cultural Landscape of Colombia

Juan Luis Isaza Londoño and César Augusto Velandia Silva

The Coffee Cultural Landscape of Colombia (CCLC) is an exceptional example of a living, continuous and productive agricultural landscape. It reflects a centennial tradition of small-scale coffee production and adaptation at mountain altitudes under difficult conditions. It also embodies a distinctive culture based on collective work in coffee production and evolving associative processes passed down through generations. These collective efforts are fundamental to the continued use of land and have generated innovative management practices for natural resources under extremely challenging geographic conditions.

Sustainable development challenges faced include the economic and social well-being of the coffee farmers and other inhabitants of the site, their appropriation of the cultural heritage and the environmental sustainability of coffee production in the living cultural landscape. The case of the CCLC illustrates how conservation and sustainable development are mutually interdependent and cannot be planned in isolation. Likewise, the understanding of the nature-culture linkages illustrates how deep this relationship is and how these may be related to the cultural landscape management model.

Complexity in the Coffee Cultural Landscape of Colombia

The CCLC illustrates the deep connection between conservation and sustainability. This includes geographical and biological heritage (the natural environment), the cultural expression of its inhabitants over time (including both material and immaterial heritage) as well as the centrality of nature-culture linkages.

From another perspective, the cultural landscape reflects a distinct process of 'territorialization' not least through the social transformation of the particular agricultural production space. An understanding of this process requires an epistemology that allows the cultural landscape to be interpreted as a territorial space transformed by man and affected by climate change and other factors. In this regard, it is important to point out that the social and cultural factors of a territory have a strong and fundamental influence on its geography. Heritage studies have progressively recognized the interdependence between culture, nature and people for both heritage and

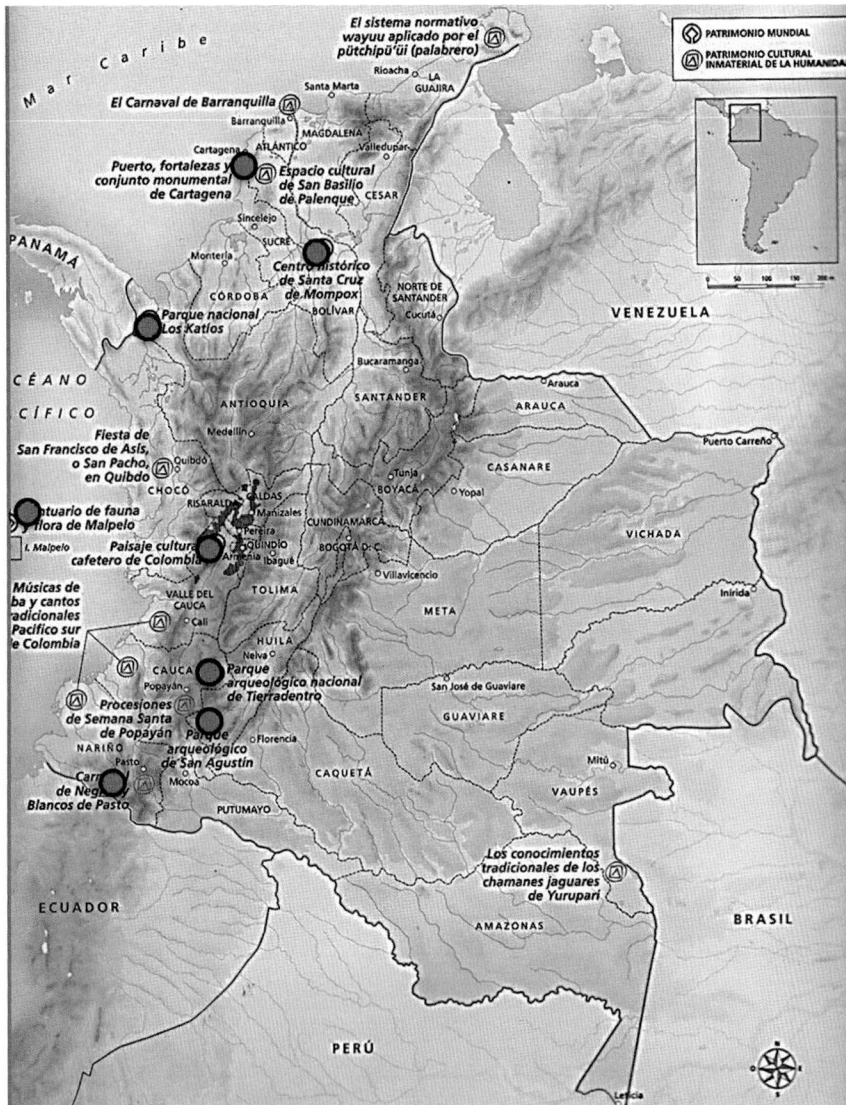

Figure 15.1 Properties in Colombia inscribed on the World Heritage List

Source: World Heritage in Colombia, Bogotá: Ministry of Culture 2013

sustainability. Nature-culture links are seen as among the deepest values of heritage sites, especially symbolic traditions and biocultural diversity. This recognizes that cultural identities have been 'forged in specific environments ... and the apprehension of heritage both in the natural field and in the cultural field has evolved ... as dynamic, interrelated and complex' (Larsen and Wijesuriya 2015: 6).

Figure 15.2 One of the main physical and visual characteristics of the CCLC is the way in which coffee crops have adapted to the difficult mountainous conditions of the region

Photo: Juan Luis Isaza Londoño 2010

The CCLC exemplifies the second category of cultural landscape established by the Operational Guidelines for the Implementation of the World Heritage Convention – one that has evolved organically as a result of an original social, economic, administrative and/or religious requirements and has reached its present form by association with and in response to its natural environment (UNESCO 2016). These landscapes reflect an evolutionary process in their form and composition and present clear material evidence of evolution over time. At the same time, they are part of the sub-category defined as a 'living landscape', one that retains an active social function in contemporary society, closely linked to the traditional way of life and in which the evolutionary process continues.

The CCLC site, located in the foothills of the Andes, is made up of six main zones, with a total area of 141,120 hectares located in 47 different municipal jurisdictions. It contains 14 urban areas and an estimated human population of 301,882 inhabitants, of whom 221,862 are urban (73.49 per cent) and the remaining 79,960 are rural (26.51 per cent). The buffer zone, in turn, has a physical extension of 207,000 hectares located in 51 different municipal jurisdictions and has 17 urban areas and an estimated human population of 294,062 inhabitants, of whom 223,145 are urban (75.88 per cent) and the remaining 70,917 are rural (24.12 per cent).

The area is considered an exceptional example of a symbolically important productive cultural landscape. In fact, it comprises six coffee landscapes that reflect a centuries-old tradition of cultivating coffee on small plots in high forest country.

Justification of the Outstanding Universal Value (OUV)

On 25 June 2011, during its 35th Session in Paris, the World Heritage Committee inscribed the CCLC on the World Heritage List based on criteria (v) and (vi). In accordance with criterion (v) it was determined that continuity of land-use, collective efforts and innovation reflected a strong coffee community with an 'unparalleled cultural identity' expressed through cultural patterns, materials and settlement practices.[1] In accordance with criterion (vi), it was determined that the coffee tradition was a symbol of national culture recognized globally constituting a legacy manifested in, among other things, the harmonious integration of the productive process into social organization and local traditions, the typology of houses and costumes such as the *aguadeño* hat[2] and the *carriel*[3] (López and Samper 2013: 111).[4]

The region is characterized by rich soil and slopes located between 1,200 and 2,000 metres above sea level. The climate, typical of the tropical Andes, has average temperatures of around 22°C and an average rainfall ranging from 1,200 to 3,000 millilitres. The rainfall is well distributed throughout the year, which is one of the most important natural conditions for the optimum production of a type of *Coffea Arabica*, known as Mild Colombian.[5]

The inscribed area is considered particularly representative of the cultural landscape.

A total of 16 variables that express the OUV involved were selected by technical teams led by eight of the region's universities (Table 15.1).

Table 15.1 CCLC attributes

1. Mountain-grown coffee*	10. Concentrated settlement and fragmented property structure
2. Coffee institution and related networks*	11. Influence of modernization
3. Coffee predominance*	12. Urban heritage
4. Slope coffee growing*	13. Coffee production historical tradition
5. Age*	14. Smallholding as a landownership system
6. Natural heritage*	15. Multiple crops
7. Water source availability*	16. Sustainable production and technologies in the coffee productive chain
8. Architectural heritage	
9. Archaeological heritage	

*Higher-valued attributes

Source: UNESCO 2017

The area is considered a living landscape, inhabited by industrious people with an exceptional social fabric and physical environment based on the production of superior coffee (Ministry of Culture – Colombian CGF 2013: 24). The compositional pattern of the coffee landscape and the century-old predominance of small and medium-sized landholdings are characteristic and very distinctive. An extraordinary archaeological, architectural and urban heritage also exists. The urban settlements mostly located on the hilltops present the orthogonal grid characteristic of the Hispanic-American city (Figure 15.3) and have a distinctive architectural style created by settlers from the Spanish-influenced region of Antioquia (Figure 15.4).

This architecture reflects the Hispanic heritage through, for example, the use of ceramic tiles, but it also uses regional materials extensively such as bamboo, specifically *Guadua angustifolia*, and *tapia* (*Crateva tapia*). Elements of indigenous cultures are incorporated, such as walls made of *tapia* and *bahareque* (braided reeds) and roofs of clay tiles, giving rise to *mestizo* constructive techniques known for the high quality of their ornamental carvings and their characteristic

Figure 15.3 Aerial view of El Cairo, municipality of the department of Valle del Cauca. Urban settlements are often situated on mountain peaks and are accessible by winding roads. There is a close relationship with the surrounding landscape where the streets, rectilinear and orthogonal – in spite of the slopes – having as visual endings the coffee plantations or the views on the Andes mountain range

Photo: Juan Luis Isaza Londoño 2010

Figure 15.4 Rural dwellings are a fundamental part of the CCLC; they are distinguished by their perimetric corridors, walls of *tapia* and *bahareque* and ceramic tile roofs. They have adjoining constructions for the '*beneficiaderos*', dryers and other spaces related to the cultivation and processing of the coffee. There are also 'barracks' that allow temporary harvesters to be housed, as well as stables, poultry houses and other agricultural units

Photo: Juan Luis Isaza Londoño 2010

use of colour. Some of these materials still persist in parts of the World Heritage property (UNESCO 2017).

In terms of social capital, the Colombian Coffee Growers Federation (CGF) and its departmental and municipal committees form an important institutional axis. It was formed in 1927 to represent Colombian coffee growers nationally and internationally and to work for the improvement of their quality of life. The CGF is today considered one of the largest independent rural organizations in the world representing more than 500,000 coffee families. Based on a democratic and representative structure, coffee producers and their families are regularly consulted and reach the necessary consensus to define programs and actions for their common benefit. The CGF is also involved in research, extension services to improve quality. In the market place, it seeks to optimize prices and establish beneficial trade arrangements (CGF n.d.).

The CCLC region is considered to be a biodiversity hot spot of conservation. Its natural wealth is of local and global importance, as there are less than seven eco-regions with the same type of habitat in the world (Ministry of Culture–Colombian

CGF 2013: 80–82). The balance between the productive landscape and the conservation of biodiversity and the environment is, however, not easy to reach and requires constant work and dedication.

The management approach

There are two main instruments for the management of the area. First, there is the legal framework related to the protection of the site. This includes a regulatory, administrative and legal body that has provisions of a general nature in the cultural, natural and coffee fields as well as more specific ones, such as land use management and the instruments for denomination of origin of the Coffee of Colombia.

Secondly, institutional arrangements designed to support the Management Plan include an alliance between the national government, the regional authorities, the CGF, environmental authorities and universities. The three overall management principles for sustainability concern:

- Economic and social well-being: The Management Plan seeks satisfactory living standards for the population, as well as an articulation of tradition with new productive technologies.
- Social appropriation of cultural heritage: It aims to conserve and strengthen the coffee culture as an element of identity and social cohesion.
- Environmental sustainability: It seeks to increase awareness of the importance of the environment and designs policies and incentives that promote environmental sustainability.

The Management Plan is structured around the four values that contribute to the OUV, with the goals, strategies and main threats defined for each of them as shown in Table 15.2.

The institutional setup for implementing the Management Plan has four hierarchical levels. The *National Steering Committee* is the most important level for the formulation of policies focused on management and conservation. It is made up of the Ministry of Culture, the CGF and the Governors of the Departments of Caldas, Quindio, Risaralda and Valle del Cauca or their delegates, in whose jurisdictions the CCLC is located. The National Steering Committee is articulated with national ministries and the Planning Department. The *Regional Technical Committee* is a space for sharing information and coordination between the different regional institutions.[6] The four *Departmental Technical Committees* engage with other departments such as the Chambers of Commerce. Finally, some 51 *Municipal Technical Committees* are active at the local government level.

Sustainable development challenges

Between 2010 and 2014, the so-called Prosperity Agreements took place. These were periodic dialogue exercises in a region of the country, led by the ministry or other entities in charge and chaired by the President. Their objective was to

Table 15.2 CCLC management plan

Value	Goal	Strategies	Led by
1.1.1.1 Human, family, generational and historical effort put into producing excellent quality coffee	1.1.1.3 Foment the coffee industry's competitiveness	1.1.1.4 Achieve a young, productive and profitable coffee industry	1.1.1.5 Colombian Coffee Growers Federation
	1.1.1.6 Encourage the development of the coffee community and its environment	1.1.1.7 Improve the education and training processes in the coffee community	1.1.1.8 Colombian Coffee Growers Federation and local governments of Caldas, Quindío, Risaralda and Valle
		1.1.1.9 Implement projects that improve the community's infrastructure	1.1.1.10 Colombian Coffee Growers Federation and local governments of Caldas, Quindío, Risaralda and Valle
1.1.1.2			1.1.1.11
		1.1.1.12 Encourage the development of tourism and productive projects that generate value for the rural population	1.1.1.13 Ministry of Commerce, Industry and Tourism; Colombian Coffee Growers Federation; and local governments of Caldas, Quindío, Risaralda and Valle
1.1.1.14 Coffee culture for the world	1.1.1.15 Preserve, revitalize and promote cultural heritage while linking it to regional development	1.1.1.17 Foment research, evaluation and conservation of the cultural heritage	1.1.1.18 Ministry of Culture, local governments, Mayoralties and Universities of the CCLC
	1.1.1.16	1.1.1.20 Promote social participation in the evaluation, communication and diffusion of the cultural heritage and social values of the Colombian Coffee Cultural Landscape	1.1.1.19

(Continued)

Table 15.2 (Continued)

Value	Goal	Strategies	Led by
1.1.1.21 Strategic social capital built upon an institution	1.1.1.22 Strengthen strategic social capital	1.1.1.23 Foment the coffee grower population's leadership and participation	1.1.1.24 Colombian Coffee Growers Federation
	1.1.1.25 Promote integration and regional development	1.1.1.26 Integrate the Colombian Coffee Cultural Landscape's conservation goals to the regional, national and international policy	1.1.1.28 Colombian Coffee Growers Federation and Ministry of Culture
		1.1.1.27	
1.1.1.29 Relationship between tradition and technology to guarantee product quality and sustainability	1.1.1.31 Support the CCLC's productive and environmental sustainability	1.1.1.32 Develop initiatives that generate a positive impact in the environment	1.1.1.33 Colombian Coffee Growers Federation, Cenicafé and Regional Environment Agencies (CAR)
		1.1.1.34 Provide scientific and technological developments that encourage the sustainable use of the CCLC	1.1.1.36 Colombian Coffee Growers Federation and Cenicafé
1.1.1.30		1.1.1.35	

Source: UNESCO 2017

achieve social cohesion, better governance and streamlined development of the different sectors in each region. Two months after the CCLC was inscribed on the World Heritage List, in August 2011 Agreement for Prosperity No. 43 mandated the inclusion of the CCLC in the national Land Use Management Plan, a long-term technical and policy planning instrument comprising a set of administrative and physical planning actions and policies to guide the development of municipal areas, both urban and rural. The Agreement also called for the definition of zones of mining exclusion and approved the development of a National Council for Economic and Social Policy (CONPES) policy document for the CCLC by the National Planning Department. This document was published in February 2014 under the title *Conpes 3803: Policy for the Preservation of the Cultural Coffee Landscape of Colombia* (NPD 2014).

According to Conpes 3803, the chief factors threatening the CCLC are:

a) Deterioration, loss and lack of social appropriation of the cultural heritage of the CCLC;
b) Decreased acreage dedicated to coffee by the increased profitability of alternative uses of land and buildings;
c) Low profitability of coffee growing;
d) Little resilience to the effects of climate change and environmental pollution;
e) Reduction in ease of access and movement for the performance of activities associated with tourism and coffee trade;
f) Vulnerability of the OUV of the CCLC to changes caused by extractive activities and large infrastructure projects; and
g) Negative effects of risk and disaster threats.
                                            (National Planning Department 2014: 48)

The document aims to provide a policy that will protect the property's OUV and improve conditions for environmental, cultural, social and economic sustainability. It defines the strategies, programs, actions and funding required to ensure the sustainability of the CCLC and proclaims these are as commitments for the Colombian government. Specific objectives of this policy include:

a) To strengthen the understanding and appreciation (social appropriation) of cultural heritage by local communities and to articulate the social and economic development of the region;
b) To develop strategies to promote and protect employment generation in the region;
c) To design and implement the necessary mechanisms to develop risk management plans in that recognize and counter the CCLC's threats, vulnerabilities and risks, including a strategy for environmental management of mining that is consistent with the preservation and sustainability of the landscape;
d) To promote the sustainability of coffee production by encouraging competitiveness, profitability and balanced coexistence with other productive activities in the territory; and

e) To improve accessibility and mobility to strengthen coffee production and related activities such as sustainable tourism.

Regional committees have recently undertaken the task of updating the management plan and instigated a long process to increase the number of local and regional organizations involved in CCLC management. A recent work by Rincón (2016) presents a balance sheet of the achievements of these committees. He notes that, although progress has been made in bringing ministries together to integrate national and regional policies, local and regional actors demand a greater participation by the national government and they call for a major international project to assure the sustainability of the CCLC (p. 223). There has also been considerable coordination of environmental institutions led by the CGF (p. 224). Rincón comments that the strategies 'Developing initiatives that have a positive impact on the environment' and 'Providing timely and relevant scientific and technological developments that promote the sustainable use of CCLC' fit well with the trade union interest and are highly developed. One great achievement, among others, has been to decipher the most important aspects of the coffee genome. Rincón adds, however, that it is important to the cultural heritage areas and to all the strategies of the Management Plan to promote timely and relevant scientific and technological developments that promote the sustainable use of the CCLC (p. 224).

Conclusion

As a general rule, sustainability challenges are mainly addressed through the management system and often, as in Colombia's CCLC, using the cultural landscape model. The strategies and objectives of landscape management instruments such as the Management Plan are relevant as long as they are directed towards 'maintaining living models of sustainable land use and natural resources' (Rössler 2003: 21). Current practice tends to focus on integrated and population-centred approaches to heritage management and conservation, as recommended by the 2013 Hangzhou International Congress on 'Culture: the key to sustainable development'. For an effective and complementary integration of heritage and sustainable development, it is necessary to explore systematically the complexity of the nature-culture linkages in order to establish a creative dialogue between the past, the present and the future. Such linkages are commonly expressed in agricultural cultural landscapes.

Today, however, heritage efforts must go beyond the preservation and safeguarding of tangible and intangible expressions and effectively commit to incorporating goals that promote inclusive and equitable societies. The benefits accruing from heritage can contribute to the reduction of poverty and improving social welfare and can also take into account environmental sustainability considerations, including the improving community resilience and combating climate change. New approaches should take advantage of culture to foster innovative models of cooperation, participation and empowerment that effectively connect all dimensions of sustainability discourse.

First, it is fundamental to improve actions that strengthen the social sustainability dimensions of the landscape. Many youths do not want to work as coffee farmers. This 'generational change' is a common feature in agricultural landscapes around the world and including the CCLC. Early childhood and youth education enables the learning of heritage values and financial and technical training is offered to young coffee growers to make it more attractive to stay on the farm. It has been necessary to diversify economic practices, even participating in the production of specialty coffees and the promotion of coffee with denomination of origin. Business programs such as trade promotion and the sale of future crops have been developed, which stimulates the permanence of coffee production. Connectivity plans and faster internet access allow young people to be connected with the world without having to migrate to urban areas. A program has also been established to convert young landless farmers with low economic resources into profitable and innovative coffee companies. In response to environmental concerns, sustainability practices such as wastewater management, crops renovation and plant control are actively promoted.

Second, to improve productive and environmental sustainability the CGF is implementing a Sustainability 2027 Strategy (CGF 2017: 10), supported by four fundamental pillars: economic profitability, social welfare, environmental sustainability and organizational governance and leadership. The first pillar aims for improved economic profitability based on increased farm productivity, improved product quality, more efficient use of inputs, more innovative harvesting processes and stronger market penetration in emerging economies. The objective of the social welfare pillar is to achieve the formalization of the labour force of the coffee farmers and collectors so as to ensure equitable access to social security, to improve living conditions and to strengthen the skills base through wider and better training provisions. The environmental sustainability pillar aims to improve agricultural practices for the conservation of ecosystems, including the development of new varieties of coffee adapted to the agro-ecological supply and climate change in collaboration with Cenicafé and global research centres.

The pillar of the CGF organization is aimed at maintaining and strengthening leadership and governance through a consultation process with the coffee farmer membership. But this is confronted by a great challenge in that the agents of the global coffee value chain have the co-responsibility to co-finance, to find mechanisms to reduce the risk associated with the high volatility of coffee prices and to search for technological and genetic solutions to the need for the crop to adapt to climate change.

Finally, with regard to risk-related changes of agricultural land use in the CCLC, the conservation of agriculture is supported as part of a national food security policy linked to the wide-ranging CONPES policy. There is also a defined territorial capacity for cropping and food security is improving articulation with land management. Likewise, tourism activities are being directed to ecotourism, agro-tourism and ethno-tourism practices and to the certification of high-quality services, all in the quest for sustainable use of the potential of the natural and cultural landscape.

Lastly, when the CCLC was instituted there were no antecedents, or even similar cases, in Colombia – or South America, for that matter – in areas related to the articulation, management, regulation, authorization and control of a cultural landscape and its heritage. All the instruments and mechanisms that, theoretically, should work, were devised and put into action: human and technical teams that did not exist were set up and procedures that only existed on paper were implemented. To everyone's surprise, things have gone well so far, despite some difficulties, which have been solved favourably and positively. In general, the balance is more than good: the heritage significance of the site has been recognized globally through its World Heritage listing, the site's OUV has been protected, and, above all, there has been a constant, daily and positive impact on the quality of life of the coffee growers who inhabit, exploit, conserve and live in the CCLC, giving them sustenance, identity and contributing to the construction of a better, more just and inclusive world.

Notes

1 Criterion (v): The CCLC is an outstanding example of continuing land use, in which the collective effort of several generations of *campesino* families generated innovative management practices of natural resources in extraordinarily challenging geographical conditions. The strong community focus on coffee production in all aspects of life produced an unparalleled cultural identity, which finds its physical expression in the cultural patterns and materials used for coffee farming as well as the urban settlements (UNESCO 2017).
2 The aguadeño hat comes from the municipality of Aguadas, in the department of Caldas. It is woven with fibres obtained from the Iraca *Carludovica palmata Ruiz and Pav*, a terrestrial plant that resembles a palm tree. Corresponds to the well-known Panamanian hat.
3 The *carriel* is a typical leather handbag for men. It is traditional in this region of Colombia.
4 Criterion (vi): The coffee tradition is the most representative symbol of national culture in Colombia, for which Colombia has gained worldwide recognition. In the CCLC, this coffee culture has led to rich tangible and intangible manifestations in the territory, with a unique legacy, included in, but not limited to, the harmonious integration of the productive process in the social organization and housing typology, and communicated through associated local traditions and costumes, such as the sombrero *aguadeño* – a traditional type of hat – and the rawhide shoulder bag, still used by the coffee producers (UNESCO 2017).
5 Produced exclusively in Colombia, Kenya and Tanzania.
6 The Regional Autonomous Corporations of Colombia are the highest environmental authorities at the regional level. They are corporate public entities, created by law and integrated to constitute a geographic ecosystem or geopolitical, biogeographic and hydrogeographic unit. They are endowed with administrative and financial autonomy and are in charge of administering within their areas of jurisdiction the environment and renewable natural resources and promoting their sustainable development, in accordance with the legal provisions and policies of the Ministry of Environment and Sustainable Development Wikipedia 2017).

References

Colombian Coffee Growers Federation (CGF). (2017). 'The CGF strategy of 2017: Sustainability and co-responsibility', *Coffee Tolima*, July–August, 261(28), p. 10. Available at: https://issuu.com/tolimacafetero/docs/perio__dico_tolima_cafetero_edicio__92cc635db04250 (accessed 30 October 2017).

Colombian Coffee Growers Federation (CGF) (n.d.). *Quiénes somos?* [Who Are We?] (online). Available at: www.federaciondecafeteros.org/particulares/es/quienes_somos (accessed 8 May 2016).

Larsen, P. and Wijesuriya, G. (2015). Interrelations between Nature and Culture in World Heritage. *Links Nature Culture*, April, no. 75. Paris: World Heritage Centre. Available at: http://whc.UNESCO.org/en/review/75 (accessed 3 August 2016).

López, S. M. and Samper, G. L. (2013). 'Coffee cultural landscape of Colombia', in J. O. Melo (ed), *World Heritage in Colombia*. Bogotá: Ministry of Culture (online). Available at: www.banrepcultural.org/blaavirtual/historia/colhoy/colo9.html (accessed 3 August 2016).

Ministry of Culture–Colombian Coffee Growers Federation (2013). *Coffee Cultural Landscape: Exceptional Fusion between Nature, Culture and Collective Work*. Bogota: Ministry of Culture-CGF.

National Planning Department (NPD) (2014). *Conpes 3803: Policy for the Preservation of the Cultural Coffee Landscape of Colombia*. Bogota: DNP (online). Available at: www.researchgate.net/publication/273766211_POLICY_FOR_THE_PRESERVATION_OF_THE_COFFEE_CULTURAL_LANDSCAPE_OF_COLOMBIA_CONPES_DOCUMENT_N_3803_ENGLISH_TRANSLATION_CREDITS_MINISTRY_OF_CULTURE_OF_COLOMBIA_2015?_iepl%5BviewId%5D=GTCQ1s5XWRCD6p2RNfA2871Q&_iepl%5BprofilePublicationItemVariant%5D=default&_iepl%5Bcontexts%5D%5B0%5D=prfpi&_iepl%5BtargetEntityId%5D=PB%3A273766211&_iepl%5BinteractionType%5D=publicationTitle (accessed 5 August 2017).

Rincón Cardona, F. (ed) (2016). *Coffee as a Cultural, Social and Productive Heritage: Cultural Landscape Cafetero de Colombia: Five Years as World Heritage Site: Interinstitutional Management within the Framework of the Management Plan of the Coffee Culture Landscape between 2011 and December 2015*. Manizales, Colombia: Ministry of Culture and Colombian Coffee Growers Federation.

Rössler, M. (2003). 'Linking nature and culture: World Heritage cultural landscapes', *World Heritage Papers*, 7, 10–15 (online). Available at: http://whc.UNESCO.org/documents/publi_wh_papers_07_en.pdf (accessed 30 September 2017).

UNESCO (2016). *Operational Guidelines for Implementation of the World Heritage Convention* (online). Available at: http://whc.unesco.org/en/guidelines (accessed 27 August 2017).

UNESCO (2017). *World Heritage List: Colombia: Coffee Cultural Landscape of Colombia* (online). Available at: http://whc.unesco.org/en/list/1121 (accessed 28 September 2017).

Wikipedia (2017). *Corporaciones Autónomas Regionales* (online). Available at: https://es.wikipedia.org/wiki/Corporaciones_Aut%C3%B3nomas_Regionales (accessed 17 October 2017).

World Heritage and sustainable development in Viet Nam

Duong Bich Hanh, Tran Thi Thu Thuy, Pham Thi Thanh Huong and Nguyen Viet Cuong

Since the inscription of the country's first site in 1993, the number of World Heritage sites in Viet Nam has grown to eight – five Cultural, two Natural and one Mixed (Table 16.1). Covering a total of 280,000 hectares in the northern half of the country and are home to 1.2 million people, the sites are diverse in attributes, characteristics and management mechanisms. They are also a source of national pride and concrete evidence of the country's engagement in international cooperation and globalization.

For Viet Nam's heritage managers, officials and policy makers from other sectors, and the public at large, there are two terms that are regularly associated with heritage in general and World Heritage in particular: conservation (*bảo tồn*) and development (*phát triển*). The dynamic relationship between these two terms captures the widely accepted perception about the importance that the heritage has in itself for current and future generations (the reason for it to be conserved) and, at the same time, the potential benefits that it can bring for the economic and social development of neighbouring communities and the country as a whole. A commonly heard motto in heritage management circles is 'conservation for development, development for conservation' (*bảo tồn để phát triển, phát triển để bảo tồn*). The mandate that the government assigns to the relevant heritage agencies – Ministry of Culture, Sports and Tourism (MoCST), local governments and management boards of each of the World Heritage sites – focuses on site protection (*bảo vệ*), which is closely linked to conservation, and promotion (*phát huy*), capitalizing on the values of heritage for development outcomes. While the discussion on the protection of the heritage values is quite well versed in Viet Nam, the discussion on sustainable development aspect is less well elaborated except for the commonly acknowledged direct impact of heritage on tourism development. To date, the potential to deepen and perhaps challenge the relationship between conservation and development has not yet been fully explored.

In the latest periodic reporting cycle for the Asia Pacific in 2012, where each of the State Parties to the 1972 Convention (UNESCO 1972) in the region self-assessed its level of protection and management of World Heritage sites, Viet Nam ranked itself 4 on a scale of 4 for all of the pre-described benefits of World Heritage status. These include i) to strengthen both legal and practical aspects of

Table 16.1 World Heritage sites in Viet Nam

Year of inscription	Site	Type	Criteria	Area of core and buffer zone	Resident population
1993	Complex of Hué Monuments	C	iv	Core: 315.47ha BZ: 71.93ha	741,629
1994, 2000	Ha Long Bay	N	vii, viii	Core: 150,000ha	c. 215,000 (Ha Long City)
1999	Hoi An Ancient Town	C	ii, v	Core: 30ha BZ: 280ha	91,993
1999	My Son Sanctuary	C	ii, iii	Core: 142ha BZ: 920ha	c. 5000 (Duy Phu Commune)
2003, 2015	Phong Nha-Ke Bang National Park	N	viii, ix, x	Core: 123,326ha BZ: 220,055ha	c. 15,000
2010	The Central Sector of the Imperial Citadel of Thang Long – Ha Noi	C	ii, iii, vi	Core: 18.395ha BZ: 108ha	c. 4,500 (Quan Thanh ward)
2011	Citadel of the Ho Dynasty	C	ii, iv	Core: 155.5ha BZ: 5,078.5ha	54,405
2014	Trang An Landscape Complex	M	v, vii, viii	Core: 6,226ha BZ: 6,026ha	c. 35,000

heritage conservation; ii) to encourage the public's appreciation for heritage and awareness of the need for heritage protection; iii) to improve heritage interpretation; iv) to increase prestige and pride; v) to enlarge the revenue and strengthen collaboration; and vi) to increase the economic development of communities living around the heritage sites. Despite the government fully acknowledging in the periodic reporting the benefits that the country receives from the World Heritage recognition, it is still not completely clear how these benefits are expressed in concrete terms and who in reality receives them.

In the context of the recently adopted Policy for Integration of Sustainable Development Perspective into the Processes of the World Heritage Convention (UNESCO 2015), it is an opportune moment to review how the current World Heritage conservation and management efforts in Viet Nam are contributing to sustainable development and the well-being of the people, and in return, how strengthening the implementation of sustainable development may bring benefits to World Heritage properties and support their OUV (Policy, para 3).

This chapter seeks to examine how the legal framework and the practices currently being carried out as part of the World Heritage processes in Viet Nam contribute to addressing the emerging challenges of 'changing demographics and climate, growing inequalities, diminishing resources, and growing threats to heritage' to ensure the country's sustainable development. The chapter attempts to offer some recommendations on measures that can be taken place to advance the discussion on development thereby strengthening the conservation–development relationship.

The chapter uses the information gathered from a desk study including official documents submitted to the World Heritage Committee, Viet Nam's policy documents as well as reports submitted by the World Heritage management boards. This analysis is supplemented by information gathered by the authors from discussions and interviews with various stakeholders during the past few years, including management staff of the sites and local communities.

Protection and management of Viet Nam's World Heritage sites

The Government of Viet Nam places an important emphasis on the protection of heritage sites, even before they are inscribed in the World Heritage List. The overall legal framework governing the management of World Heritage sites in Viet Nam is the Law on Cultural Heritage,[1] which was approved in 2001 and amended in 2009 to reflect the evolution of the international cultural heritage instruments to which Viet Nam is a signatory, especially the World Heritage Convention and its Operational Guidelines. The World Natural Heritage sites are also governed by a series of other laws and sub-laws such as Law on Environmental Protection and its decrees, Law on Forest Protection and Development (to be amended into Law on Forestry), Law on Biodiversity, Law on Construction etc. The implementation of the law is further detailed by a series of decisions and guidelines focusing on specific topics and covering a wide spectrum of aspects concerning heritage management.[2]

In its self-assessment for the 2012 periodic report, the Vietnamese legal heritage system is considered to i) recognize different types of ownership of cultural heritage; ii) clearly identify rights and obligations of institutions and individuals; iii) clearly identify restricted behaviours and develops the legal framework to secure participation of the society in heritage preservation; iv) define the management structure and responsibilities of different levels of management in safeguarding and promoting values of cultural heritage; v) define comprehensive criteria for identifying items to be protected; vi) preserve and promote the most outstanding values of cultural heritage; and vii) encourage different economic sectors, especially heritage owners to contribute to preserving and promoting the values of cultural heritage. However, there has recently been strong advocacy, primarily led by MoCST and the World Heritage site managers, for the World Heritage properties to be placed under a special category within the national legal framework to ensure its strongest protection. This has led to the development of a separate decree on World Heritage, which was approved in September 2017. The decree specifies the requirements for the protection of World Heritage sites, including the need to develop a management plan and management guidelines, as well as responsibilities of the concerned stakeholders in managing the sites. For the first time in relation to Viet Nam's heritage, the decree directly touches upon a series of sustainable development issues, such as engaging local communities as both heritage guardians and beneficiaries.

At a more practical level, as per the instruction set out in the current legal framework, there are three management documents that are required as part of the site management system – a master plan for protection, management and promotion, a management plan and a set of regulations concerning protection and management. These management documents, if prepared properly, may contribute to sustainable development in a number of ways, such as outlining in a concrete way the potential negative impacts and proposing measures to overcome them. In many cases, the management plans also include auxiliary plans such as visitor management plans or disaster risk reduction plans, which contribute to addressing specific development issues that might not be fully dealt with otherwise.

The management entities for the eight World Heritage sites are officially recognized as 'management boards' in the country's administrative system and come under the technical supervision of the Department of Cultural Heritage in MoCST. All the management boards are financed through the government budget and from the revenue gained from tourism and other related services. In theory, this condition should allow for an adequate site protection. However, the decentralized nature of Viet Nam's government system has resulted in the boards having different positions in the country's administrative hierarchy, which affects the boards' authority and their abilities in dealing with stakeholders in their efforts to protect and manage the heritage. Further, the enactment of 2010 Law on Government Officials has categorized World Heritage sites' management boards as 'government public services agencies', which means the salaries of all staff except for a few top officials are to be financed through the public services provided. This means the management boards have to generate enough income to maintain the workforce. This situation not only potentially means a reduction of time and energy spent on site protection, but it might also lead to an over-emphasis on the tourism focus of World Heritage, as the sites' revenue at the moment mainly comes from ticket sales and tourism-related services.

While there have clearly been great efforts to protect and manage the heritage by MoCST and other relevant agencies such as the culture departments at the provincial levels or the management boards of heritage sites, it is also widely acknowledged that managing World Heritage is a complex task and further improvements are to be made. Firstly, it is evident that heritage management should not be solely the responsibility of the culture sector. Much will need to be done to engage stakeholders outside of the culture sector for them to appreciate the importance of heritage protection and contribute effectively to it, and to streamline coordination mechanisms in order to avoid overlapping and confusion. Secondly, while there is a relatively adequate legal framework concerning the protection of World Heritage in the making, the implementation at the practical level still reveals some gaps. To improve this situation, further legal adjustments and enforcement will be needed both within the culture sector and beyond. Thirdly, as the chapter argues, the strengthening of the protection of the heritage can materialize fully only when conservation discussions are situated within the sustainable development context.

The common motto needs to be changed to 'conservation for sustainable development, sustainable development for conservation'.

In the remainder of the chapter, the analysis will turn to the current development discourse by reviewing the contribution the World Heritage in Viet Nam is making to the country's sustainable development and suggesting ways to strengthen this contribution. The analysis will follow the four sustainable development dimensions that have structured the new Policy on World Heritage and Sustainable Development, namely environmental sustainability, inclusion social development, inclusive economic development and fostering peace and security.

Viet Nam's World Heritage's contribution to economic development

The Law on Cultural Heritage specifies that the heritage should be used to benefit society (Article 12) and that the Government needs to have adequate policies to protect and promote the heritage values in order to enrich the spiritual life of the citizens as well as to contribute to the country's socio-economic development (Article 9). While the nomination of sites to the World Heritage List is often done with the best intention to gain international recognition and to ensure a proper protection framework, it is undeniable that the economic development is an important rationale behind this lengthy and costly nomination process.

In Viet Nam, the contribution of heritage to tourism is well recognized by heritage managers, government authorities and the public. Statistics demonstrate that this recognition has a concrete basis. Viet Nam's World Heritage sites have seen a steady increase in both the number of visitors and the revenue gained from ticket sales. Although it is not clear to what extent the growth results from the inscription itself or is due to other factors, such as economic reform and the growth in domestic tourism reflecting the improved living standards, there is a clear difference between the number of visitors to the World Heritage sites before and after their inscription.

One of the benefits from the increasing number of visitors has been the revenue gained from entrance ticket sales, a policy area which is currently enforced in all Viet Nam's World Heritage sites. A part of the revenue is returned for regular maintenance of the sites or paying salaries for staff. Additional funds can be requested for specific conservation projects through an approval process. The remaining amount is invested by the local government into other development areas such as healthcare, education, social services or infrastructure. For instance, Ha Long Bay, which is the top among eight World Heritage sites in Viet Nam in terms of generating the revenues from visitors, contributed USD25.3 million, accounting for 15.2 per cent of the total Ha Long city's government budget in 2016. One can safely say that tourism development is an area where the 'conservation for development and development for conservation' debate is most tangibly expressed.

Furthermore, it is clear that tourism development in World Heritage sites not only benefits the government budget. A multitude of other stakeholders in the

Table 16.2 Number of visitors and ticket sales revenues at World Heritage sites in Viet Nam

Site	2006		2016	
	Number of visitors	Revenue (USD)	Number of visitors	Revenue (USD)
Hue	1.45 million (630,500 foreign)	3.6 million	2.5 million (1.35 million foreign)	11.7 million
Ha Long Bay	1.4 million (728,000 foreign)	2.64 million	2.8 million (968,000 foreign)	30.5 million
Hoi An	878,700 (423,500 foreign)	28,000	1.6 million (1.2 million foreign)	7.8 million
My Son	130,000 (89,500 foreign)	245,000	314,000	2 million
PN-KB	250,488 (7,158 foreign)	620,000	705,000 (82,400 foreign)	5.22 million
Thang Long	No record	Free entrance	400,000	237,700
Ho Citadel	No record	Free entrance	113,000 (1,500 foreign)	19,700
Trang An	No record	No record	4 million (600,000 foreign)	14 million from ticket sales (total 42 million for all tourism services including ticket sales)

Notes: Statistics collected from WH Management Boards and in VND. Exchange rate: 1USD = 15,900VND in 2006 and 1USD = 22,000 in 2016.

tourism sector also gain a share. Few data exist on this aspect, but it is obvious that the distribution of gains from the tourism development is not shared equally by any means, and this inequality varies among different sites. The structure of some sites, such as Thang Long, Ho Citadel or My Son, does not allow for an extensive involvement of external stakeholders in the tourism services, except for some travel companies bringing visitors to the sites. In My Son, there have been efforts to expand and spread the benefits from tourism through homestays and small restaurants to the local villagers, who primarily depend on farming and operating small businesses for their living. In Hue and Hoi An, due to their characteristics as living cities with integrated communities, more benefits flow to the communities through the operation of tourism-related businesses. For example, the homestay businesses in Hoi An, most of which are owned by local communities, provide 10 per cent of all accommodation available in Quang Nam province, generating revenue of over 1.5 million USD and jobs for over 500 people.

Quang Binh Province, home to the Phong Nha – Ke Bang natural World Heritage site, also reported the generation of 4,000 jobs thanks to the tourism development, which contributes greatly to improving the livelihoods of local communities. In Trang An, tourism business within the boundary of the site creates 7,000 jobs for local people, which accounts for 50 per cent of the total tourism-related jobs in the province (Figure 16.1). Ninety per cent of the jobs are held by women, which helped increase the average individual income ten-fold between 2006 and 2016 (Bui Van Manh 2016). However, the concession scheme currently implemented in both Phong Nha – Ke Bang and Trang An also means that local communities can only work as employees for the concession companies rather than have opportunities to establish and run their own businesses. Similarly, in Ha Long, where 21.2 per cent of 476 cruises in Ha Long are operated by ten companies,[3] the benefits primarily go to larger and more established businesses.

The strong interest in the tourism development has been further emphasized by the 2017 decision to re-establish the Department of Tourism as a separate entity from the Department of Culture and Sports in a number of provinces that have World Heritage sites or other sites of national significance. The tourism sector is considered a spearheading sector for the provincial economies and contributes at

Figure 16.1 Tourist boats in Trang An, Viet Nam's first mixed property, inscribed in 2015

Source: W. Logan

least 10 per cent to the provincial GDP.[4] The rational for this decision is both to support the full tourism development in these provinces and at the same time to provide this fast growing sector with adequate staffing capacity and more effective and better enforced regulations. The decision to place the management board of the World Heritage sites (e.g. Trang An) under the newly established Departments of Tourism may be seen as acknowledging a need to manage the industry better, but also raises concern about the emphasis on the 'promotion' aspect of a World Heritage site as against the 'conservation' aspect. Further, once the management board no longer has access to the income generated by tourism services, there might be a risk of not having sufficient human resources to protect the site.

Tourism development has for a long time been recognized as a double-edged sword (Salazar 2014). It was identified as a concern by most of World Heritage sites in Viet Nam, both through their latest periodic reports and in recent State of Conservation reports of some of the sites. The growing crowds of visitors, while bringing in higher revenue, can negatively impact on the conservation status of the site, especially as most World Heritage sites are in fragile states. The increasing number of tourists consequently requires more infrastructure and facilities, the construction of which is often in conflict with maintaining the authenticity and integrity of the sites.

Hoi An's experience points to some concrete ways to develop and promote inclusive and equitable economic investments in and around World Heritage properties. For most of the last decade, the city of Hoi An has been committed to expanding tourism well beyond the World Heritage-listed ancient town. This measure has been implemented both to reduce the heavy and potentially negative impacts of tourism on the World Heritage property and to extend the tourism benefits for the populations who live in the vicinity of the heritage area. Official policies and regulations have led to active participation by the private sector which is today the main driver of the process. The result has been the diversification of the tourism services and products and increasing income for both local businesses and communities.

Apart from tourism, the restoration and documentation work at World Heritage sites can create opportunities for local people to learn and equip themselves with new skills which later can help them to get jobs with improved incomes. In My Son, over 50 local farmers who were engaged in the restoration projects of group G monuments[5] over a ten-year period have become skilled workers often sought after for restoration and construction projects elsewhere in the province (Figure 16.2). Following this on-the-job training within the tripartite cooperation of Viet Nam, Italy and UNESCO, a vocational school in restoration of brick structures was established in Quang Nam in 2016. Similarly, the 130 restoration projects conducted in Hue Complex of Monuments between 1996 and 2016 employed thousands of local skilled labourers and national professionals. Among the positive impacts has been the revival of traditional craftsmanship in making enamel and the regeneration of several local craft villages as specialized producers and suppliers of restoration materials. In Hoi An, the restoration projects as well as adaptation of the local architecture in surrounding areas helped to revive the production of traditional bricks and tiles and to increase the demand for woodcarving

Figure 16.2 Local workers trained for pilaster restoration in My Son
Source: UNESCO Ha Noi

skills. This has led to the revival of the two traditional craft villages – Thanh Ha
for pottery and Kim Bong for wood carving.

The economic benefits from World Heritage sites with forest coverage also
come through the payment policy for forest environment services (Decree
99/2010/NĐ-CP since 2010). Phong Nha – Ke Bang, with 126,236 hectares core
zone and 220,055 hectares buffer zone, 83.74 per cent of which is natural forest,
is a case in point. The management board receives 1–1.5 per cent of annual revenue from the Paradise cave concession company, as well as 15 per cent of the
revenue from the Son Doong cave concession company in the form of environment services. This has contributed to a budget close to USD 800,000 during the
first nine months of 2016, a part of which has been returned to the site for its own
activities and to subsidize some of the promotion activities directly implemented
and covered by the provincial authorities.

Contribution of Viet Nam's World Heritage sites
to inclusive social development

While the contribution to economic development of World Heritage sites can tangibly be expressed through concrete figures, the contribution to inclusive social

development is more abstract and harder to measure. There are various aspects through which the contribution to social development can be captured, such as the participation of local communities, the empowerment of marginalized groups or the improvement of the wellbeing of local residents. This section will examine some of these key aspects in which Viet Nam's World Heritage sites currently make their strongest contribution and identify areas where this contribution can further be enhanced to maximize the World Heritage's potential.

As outlined in the previous section, communities living around the World Heritage sites may benefit from local economic development leading to the enhancement of their quality of life and wellbeing. In many cases, local communities gain their economic benefits in a proactive way, rather than simply being employed in tourism sector at the end of the supply chain. Hoi An ancient town has been mentioned many times elsewhere mainly because its impressive tourism and economic growth radically changed the quality of life and wellbeing of local people (Pham Thi Thanh Huong 2016: 278). Community-based tourism initiatives have emerged in several villages near Hoi An and Hue where local residents have actively set up their own tourism cooperatives in order to strengthen their own business status as well as providing a benefit-sharing mechanism with other stakeholders.

That World Heritage inscription impacts on the local quality of life and wellbeing can also be seen in areas other than direct impacts of incomes from tourism and related economic activities, such as the priority and requirement of fire-fighting and prevention system. Hoi An's Disaster Risks Management Plan pointed out that fire is the top risk in the ancient town, not only because of the prevalence of the ancient wooden buildings but also the local residents' professions of running tailoring and textile shops. In this context, the regulations which were developed and monitored initially for the purpose of preventing risks to the heritage properties, also contribute to improve the wellbeing, security and sustainability of the entire community.

An important aspect of the contribution of World Heritage to inclusive social development lies in the greater accessibility local communities are given to their own heritage as well as opportunities to participate in World Heritage processes. The free entrance policy for local school students all year round or local residents on special occasions that is implemented by the management boards of most sites undoubtedly gives local communities an incentive to visit the sites for their cultural enjoyment. Since its opening to the public, for instance, Thang Long Citadel in central Ha Noi has become a popular photo shoot location for groups of school students for their final yearbook. Some sites, such as Hoi An, have made efforts to ensure accessibility to people with disabilities through the refurbishing of their ticket booths, information centres and public restrooms. In the area of participation, a good practice found in Hoi An involves the inviting local people, heritage building owners and tour operators a year to a consultation workshop to voice their concerns. Their position is strong and no important decision on site management can be made without prior consultation with them. Similarly, in Hue, some members of local clans serve on scientific committee under the management board (Phan Thanh Hai 2015), and regulations have given 3,000 households the power to negotiate a full compensation package in case of relocation (Nghiem Kim Hoa 2017).

However, scratching beneath the surface reveals that the participation of local communities is a complex issue because neither the concepts of local communities nor participation have been clearly defined. This makes passive participation and/or information-sharing more of a norm (Larsen 2017). At the policy level, it has also recently been pointed out that specific mechanisms to engage local communities are also absent in heritage management regulations (Nguyen Linh Giang 2017). Involvement of communities often happens on an ad-hoc basis because of the particular site managers' willingness rather than as a systematic, rights-based approach. Therefore, sometimes, the local communities are kept out of the making of decisions that are very important to their lives, such as the relocation of 450 households from the floating village on Ha Long Bay as per Decision no. 2178/QD-UBND/2012 by the Quang Ninh Provincial People's Committee, which was made without in-depth research into potential social and cultural impacts or proper community consultation processes. In negotiation involving business companies, the power of communities is generally weak and there has not yet been developed any mechanism for them to protect themselves as a vulnerable group or to enable them to counterbalance the companies' business motivation (Nghiem Kim Hoa 2017).

There is in general much more potential for the management boards of World Heritage sites in Viet Nam to enable other types of participation such as delegated power, citizen control or co-management. This can be done through the development of appropriate policies and regulations, the strengthening of community groups and non-government organizations and awareness-raising among the site managers about the role and the rights of the local communities, particularly in the context of new requirements to integrate heritage management into sustainable development. With the adoption of the global sustainable development policy in World Heritage process as well as the recent development of the new Decree on World Heritage management, one can expect that new reflection will take place on the ground. In fact, some reflection has already begun taking place at the site level in Viet Nam. For example, in Hue, two among four management objectives are sustainable development oriented, with one specifically highlighting the connection between heritage property and local residents and sustainable socio-economic development (Hue Monuments Conservation Centre 2015). The My Son Management Board has put considerable effort into seeking approval for a revised management plan that creates more opportunities for community partnership, a matter that was not mentioned in the version adopted in 2008 (UNESCO 2008, 2016).

Contribution to environmental sustainability

Among the World Heritage sites, there have been some initial efforts made to strengthen the sites' preparedness to meet natural disaster risks, particularly at Thang Long Citadel, Hue Complex of Monuments and Hoi An Ancient Town.

Considering the increasing intensity and impacts of natural disasters, these efforts present a concrete step forward in the maintaining of environmental sustainability. For instance, in its Disaster Risks Management Plan for the Hue site, the Hue Monuments Conservation Centre implements regular checks of the drainage system and river embankments around the relics, working in coordination with the Provincial Steering Committee of Flood and Storm Prevention and Control. The risks are more serious in the mountainous and rural areas such as in the upstream Perfume River where several royal tombs and other heritage elements are located. Here, regular investigation of vulnerable spots, planting forests and consolidation of river banks against floods are undertaken where affordable and given priority by the local people and governments.

World Heritage sites in Viet Nam also benefit from a number of environmental policies and practice. Circular ordinance 31/2016/TT-BTNMT dated 14 October 2016 regulates environmental protection in industrial and commercial sites, including craft villages. This includes the requirement for the craft villages to submit Environmental Impacts Assessment (EIA) reports and put in practice measures to effectively deal with liquid and solid waste and be assessed on the level of negative impacts that they place on the environment. As there are many craft villages in and around the World Heritage sites, and there is a strong interest in reviving the craft sector to provide better local services and products to visitors, there is a strong need to ensure that the development of the craft villages adhere to the environmental protection requirements to avoid potential negative impacts. The national laws also make the EIA compulsory for all new development projects, regardless whether they are in World Heritage sites or not. However, it will be important however for management boards to build the capacity of their professional staff so that they can properly understand what EIA might entail and how to ensure the quality of the EIA reports.

Overall, a common environmental sustainability pathway shared among the World Heritage sites in Viet Nam has two paradoxical trends. On the one hand, the nomination process often triggers a heightened sense of the need for protection, which overall has resulted in very positive outcomes. An excellent example has been the reorientation of the development targets of Ninh Binh Province. Here, policies and regulations now seek to reduce the operation of the cement industry that was over-exploiting a wide tract of the karst mountain with its rich geological and biodiversity values and scenic landscape. Strict regulations on levels of dust and noises applied for all cement factories in the buffer zone of the property are helping to reduce air and land pollution of the area. A survey conducted by Trang An World Heritage Management Board (Bui Van Manh 2016) indicated that over 90 per cent of surveyed local residents expressed their satisfaction with the lower levels of dust and air pollution in their living environment since the site's inscription. Similarly, Quang Ninh Province, which hosts the Ha Long Bay property, has adopted the long-term development objective of converting from 'grey industry' to 'green industry'. It aims to shift from heavy industries (coal mine, maritime transportation) on which the province has been long dependent, to 'smokeless' industries (tourism and commercial services), taking Ha Long Bay World Heritage site as a key driver and example for this changed direction. On the other hand, however, the over-emphasis on tourism as discussed above has caused a series of other social and environmental pressures – such as ever-increasing numbers of tourist arrivals and the consequential high-level energy consumption, population increase and rapid conversion of land use from agricultural to commercial.

This dilemma is by no means unique to the World Heritage sites in Viet Nam. One can only hope that World Heritage status does help to strengthen the arguments against large-scale investment in insensitive development projects and instead favour the safeguarding heritage assets. Indeed, the majority of site managers confirm this point, which can be illustrated by recent proposals to construct cable cars leading to the top of Phan Si Pan, the highest mountain in Viet Nam, and in Phong Nha – Ke Bang National Park (Figure 16.3). These proposed investments by the same company sparked controversy and while the former opened in 2016, the Phong Nha Ke Bang project has not materialized precisely because of the legal protection framework imposed on this World Heritage site – at least, not yet (Hoang Tao 2017).

Figure 16.3 A cable car project has been proposed in Phong Nha Ke Bang

Source: Phong Nha Ke Bang Management Board

Contribution to peace and security

With the motto 'unity in diversity', the Government of Viet Nam has made moderate efforts in recognizing the cultural richness of the country's minority ethnic groups (Logan 2010). The World Heritage List and the Representative List of Intangible Cultural Heritage of Humanity recognize that My Son Sanctuary as the vestige of a religious centre of Champa Kingdom and still related to today's Cham ethnic group, Hue's royal court music and dance belonging to the last feudal dynasty and the Space of Gong culture of the Central Highlands' ethnic groups. These listings reflect the depoliticized practices of heritage preservation and tourist promotion (Long 2003) and the softening policy towards ethnic minorities which brings the Vietnamese government more closely in line with the various international statements on minority rights (Logan 2012).

The programs to safeguard and promote these heritage elements after their inscription have significant support to reconciliation and intercultural dialogues in a post-conflict society. For instance, the inscription of My Son sanctuary has contributed considerably to the visibility of the Cham civilization which reached its peak in the ninth and tenth centuries. This is to be applauded given the context in which the history taught in schools remains very limited with regard to ethnic minorities. The involvement of Cham descendants, who nowadays live in the southern part of the country, has become normalized, both in their traditional cultural practices such as pilgrimage to and festival celebration at the site as well as in the consultation that now occurs between site managers and senior Cham community representatives. Both MoCST and Ministry of Education and Training have made a significant effort to promote heritage education which no doubt will contribute to raising students' awareness of the culture and heritage of others, thus promoting a more diverse and respectful society.

While the issue of human rights, particularly the rights of the ethnic groups, remains sensitive in the Viet Nam context, it deserves mention that the issue has been opened to public discussion in the field of heritage management with a two-day seminar entitled 'Understanding Community Participation and Rights-Based Approaches in World Heritage' in Ha Noi in November 2015. Starting from the search for ways to manage sustainably Viet Nam's globally recognized heritage, the importance of community custodianship and the transmission of intangible heritage between generations, the officials and site managers discussed rights-based approaches that would enable the participation of ethnic groups and local communities. A further stepping stone was made in June 2017 with formulation of the Hoi An Declaration on Urban Heritage Conservation and Development in Asia (UNESCO 2017), which states:

> Clear heritage policies and mechanisms are needed that adopt a rights-based approach to ensure active community participation in design, management and equitable benefit sharing. This will help to reconcile the conservation goals with social equity and the living standards of local residents and the traditional owners and custodians of the urban heritage elements.

Conclusion

As the chapter shows, there is clear evidence of the contribution that the World Heritage sites in Viet Nam have made to the country's development, whether this is inclusive economic or social development, environmental protection or peace and security. The economic contributions have been made tangibly in the form of increased revenue, primarily if not exclusively, from tourism development. There have also been concrete efforts, albeit unbalanced among the provinces, to ensure that the economic gains would reach beyond the government budget to other sectors such as private sector or the communities. The current policies also ensure that there is some revenue returned for site conservation. Contributions to the remaining areas, although not as visible, have been expressed, through the inclusion of communities to some World Heritage processes, through the better recognition of the diversity of heritage sites and elements or through ensuring that the environmental protection is integrated into the management of the sites.

While there is also a positive sign that the officials and site managers recognize the dynamic relationship between development and culture in general and heritage in particular, there is a continuing need to stress and further elaborate upon the sustainability aspect within the development discourse. Specifically, the contribution to the economic dimension might be further diversified to reduce the dependence on tourism development that presents some risk to the sustainability of the sites themselves. Similarly, the sustainable development aspects can also be further emphasized through the stronger emphasis on sustainability aspect of the tourism development and through ensuring that the communities are a more integral part of the site management and protection. There are equally a number of social and environmental concerns, which merit further attention.

While the legal and institutional environments can be considered relatively adequate for the physical heritage conservation, there is still a need to reinforce the regulations as well as strengthen the authority and capacity of the site managers who deal with broader, complex situations on a daily basis. An awareness among the World Heritage site managers of sustainable development issues has been raised, but still lacking are the concrete targets, tools and good models of effective management practices that would ensure a rights-based approach, effective community participation, public-private partnerships, stakeholder engagement and conflict resolution are put into practice.

Notes

1 The Law on Cultural Heritage also has effect over natural heritage sites, as, by its definition, 'cultural heritage' also includes the category of of *danh lam thắng cảnh* – scenic areas, which are natural sites or sites combining both natural aspects and architecture of historical, aesthetic and scientific values.
2 Research report 'Preliminary Results on World Heritage and Human Rights in Viet Nam: A Legal Review' under the framework of UNESCO 'World Heritage Sites and Rights in Viet Nam: Understanding the Issue and Looking Forward' project, which focuses on the

human rights aspect of heritage-related rights, is a useful reference for the range of legal documents that are currently available to serve the protection of the country's World Heritage sites.

3 Ha Long Bay Management Board in 2017.

4 Draft Decree on the regulations for establishment of professional entities under the People's Committees of the provinces and central cities (version 5, dated 6 February 2017).

5 The complex of Cham monuments in My Son sanctuary was classified by Henri Parmentier, a French archaeologist who inventoried the site in 1903–1904. He assigned a letter to each of ten principal groups of monuments, namely A, A', C, D, E, F, G, H, K and L. Group G monuments is made up of five buildings dating from the second half of the twelfth century.

References

Breglia, L. (2006). *Monumental Ambivalence: The Politics of Heritage*. Austin: University of Texas Press.

Bui Van Manh (2016). *Involving Local Communities in Managing Conserving the World Cultural and Natural Heritage*. Unpublished paper, Trang An Landscape Complex Management Board, Ninh Binh.

Cornwall, A. (2008). 'Unpacking "participation": Models, meanings and practices', *Community Development Journal*, 43(3), 269–283.

Hoang Tao (2017). 'Vietnam's PM endorses cable car plan to world famous cave system', *VN Express*, 26 August (online). Available at: https://e.vnexpress.net/news/travel-life/travel/vietnam-s-pm-endorses-cable-car-plan-to-world-famous-cave-system-3633015.html (accessed 22 September 2017).

ICCROM (2015). *People-Centred Approaches to the Conservation of Cultural Heritage: Living Heritage*. Rome: ICCROM. Available at: www.iccrom.org/wp-content/uploads/PCA_Annexe-2.pdf (accessed 10 August 2017).

Larsen, P. (2017). 'Case study: Ethnic minorities and World Heritage sites in Vietnam: The case of Phong Nha Ke Bang', in *World Heritage Sites and Rights in Vietnam: Understanding the Issues and Looking Forward*. Hanoi: Vietnam Academy of Social Sciences.

Logan, W. (2010). 'Protecting the Tay Nguyen gongs: Conflicting rights in Vietnam's central plateau', in M. Langfield, W. S. Logan and M. Nic Craith (eds), *Cultural Diversity, Heritage and Human Rights: Intersections in Theory and Practice*. London: Routledge.

Logan, W. (2012). 'Culture diversity, cultural heritage and human rights: Towards heritage management as human rights-based cultural practice', *International Journal of Heritage Studies*, 18(3), 231–244.

Long, C. (2003). 'Feudalism in the service of the revolution: Reclaiming heritage in Hue', *Journal of Critical Asian Studies*, 35(4), 535–558.

Nghiem Kim Hoa (2017). 'Balancing rights and responsibilities of the local people in the World Heritage process in Vietnam: Summary of a rapid assessment', in *World Heritage Sites and Rights in Vietnam: Understanding the Issues and Looking Forward*. Hanoi: Vietnam Academy of Social Sciences.

Nguyen Linh Giang (2017). 'World Heritage and human rights policy in Vietnam: A legal review', in P. B. Larsen (ed), *World Heritage and Human Rights: Lessons from the Asia-Pacific and Global Arena*. London: Routledge.

Pham Thi Thanh Huong (2016). 'Living heritage, community participation and sustainability: Redefining development strategies in the Hoi An Ancient Town World Heritage property, Vietnam', in S. Labadi and W. Logan (eds), *Urban Heritage, Development and Sustainability: International Framework, National and Local Governance*. London: Routledge.

Phan Thanh Hai (2015). *Community Participation in the Conservation and Promotion of Hue Cultural Heritage: Practical Experience (Sự tham gia của cộng đồng trong hoạt động bảo vệ và phát huy giá trị di sản văn hóa Huê: Những kinh nghiệm thực tiễn)*. Hue: Hue Monuments Conservation Centre.

Salazar, N. B. (2014). '1972–2012: Forty years of World Heritage Convention: Time to take tourism seriously?', in M. Gravaris-Barbas and S. Jacquot (eds), *Patrimoine mondial et dévelopment au défi du tourism durable*. Quebec: Presses de l'Université du Quebec.

UNESCO (1972). *Convention Concerning the Protection of the World Natural and Cultural Heritage*. Paris: UNESCO.

UNESCO (2008). *The Effects of Tourism on Culture and the Environment in Asia and the Pacific–Impact*. Bangkok: UNESCO Bangkok.

UNESCO (2015). *Policy Document for the Integration of a Sustainable Development Perspective into the Processes of the World Heritage Convention* (online). Available at: http://whc.unesco.org/en/sustainabledevelopment/ (accessed 2 December 2017).

UNESCO (2016). *Research Report on World Heritage Management Practices in Viet Nam*. Hanoi: UNESCO.

UNESCO (2017). *The Hoi An Declaration on Urban Heritage Conservation and Development in Asia*. Hanoi: UNESCO (online). Available at: www.unesco.org/new/fileadmin/MULTIMEDIA/FIELD/Hanoi/Hoi_An_Declaration_2017_01.pdf (accessed 22 September 2017).

UNESCO, ICCROM, ICOMOS and IUCN (2013). *Managing Cultural World Heritage Resource Manual*. Paris: UNESCO.

UNESCO, World Heritage Centre (2015). *World Heritage and Sustainable Development*. WHC-15/39.COM/5D.

Vietnam National Administration of Tourism and Spanish Agency for International Development Coorperation (AECID) (2009). *Management and Tourism Development Orientation in World Heritage Areas in Vietnam*. Hanoi: AECID.

World Heritage Centre (2015). *Management Plan of the Complex of Hue Monuments*. Available at: http://whc.unesco.org/en/list/678/documents/ (accessed 22 September 2017).

Chapter 17

Ng'ambo Tuitakayo, the buffer zone we want

Articulating heritage values in urban planning of Zanzibar town

Muhammad Juma

The Stone Town of Zanzibar, listed as a World Heritage site in 2000, is an excellent case for demonstrating the evolving understanding and practices of urban conservation and heritage management in an African context. It is also a good example for showing how, through the application of the Historic Urban Landscape (HUL) approach, local authorities shaped a new thinking on spatial planning in Zanzibar. Today, by linking spatial growth and cultural development, the local authorities not only raise awareness in inclusive economic growth but also enhance inclusive social development and promote environmental sustainability as part of their sustainable development approach. Such experiences of planning in the buffer zone offer important insights into the relevance of key aspects of the World Heritage and Sustainable Development policy.

Since 2007, the majority of the world's population can be said to live in urban areas. By 2050, Africa is estimated to become 56 per cent urban (UN-Habitat 2014). Zanzibar is a different case compared to the rest of Africa. With 1.5 million inhabitants (GoZ 2017) and an area of 2,654 km², the Islands of Zanzibar have an urban population of more than 46.3 per cent. To fully harness the transformative power of the growing levels of urbanization, the authorities opted for a new vision for the role of urban growth as an opportunity for fostering economic and social progress in Zanzibar. In 2015, the Government of Zanzibar adopted the National Spatial Development Strategy (NSDS) to underline the new vision of urbanization of the Islands with a focus on using culture as a driver and enabler to ensure its sustainable development (GoZ 2015a).

There are examples of a strong relation between urbanization and the prosperity of a country (World Bank 2009). Yet, unmanaged growth and uncontrolled urbanization are equally sources of social disaffection and environment degradation. The growth of Zanzibar Stone Town's buffer zone, known locally as Ng'ambo, started to reveal some challenges related to the sustainability of the World Heritage site. The population who lived in the area were not happy about the way the status of World Heritage site was interpreted by the local authorities. The context of Stone Town's buffer zone exemplifies the situation of many historic cities in Africa where buffer zones face challenges related to their image, management and development. Situated between Stone Town and the inner city,

Ng'ambo has always been considered as a 'secondary' zone, despite containing older and more diverse structures than Stone Town itself. Ng'ambo was also less valued by national and international heritage circles.

The lack of a deeper perspective for the area affected the population's inspiration for social development and economic opportunities. Uncontrolled development also threatened environmental sustainability. The challenges of Ng'ambo were directly linked to the way the local authorities managed the area by erroneously interpreting the role of the buffer as of minor importance compared to the core zone. In fact, for a long time, Ng'ambo played only one role, which was to protect the World Heritage site. Covering a larger area, and having a bigger population and more buildings than the World Heritage site, the economic dynamism of Ng'ambo was always second to that of Stone Town. Its management was also problematic as it was sandwiched between Stone Town Conservation and Development Authority (STCDA), which manages the buffer zone and the Zanzibar Municipal Council, which administrates all social, economic and environmental sectors inside the area. This polarization created a challenging situation for the sustainability of both Ng'ambo and the World Heritage site.

Being at the centre of the fast-growing city of Zanzibar, and putting in perspective the idea of transforming Ng'ambo into a new Central Business District (CBD) of the city, the area crystalizes the challenges of integrating conservation and development. This is jeopardized by both its own heritage values as well as the Oustanding Universal Value (OUV) of the UNESCO site. It is impossible to imagine the UNESCO site managed integrally without the larger urban context. Hence the importance of the sustainability perspective, which recognizes that both parties depend on each other. In 2011, UNESCO and the Government of Zanzibar (GoZ) organized a workshop to discuss the application of the Historical Urban Landscape (HUL) Recommendation in Africa (UNESCO 2011). The specific challenges of Ng'ambo were also discussed. As an outcome of the meeting, in 2014, local authorities together with international stakeholders conceived a project specifically targeting Ng'ambo to have a closer look at the link between culture and urban planning. It sought to better integrate heritage management of the UNESCO site with inclusive economic growth, inclusive social development and environmental protection. The parallel process of developing the Zanzibar Structural Plan Zans-Plan (GoZ 2015b) was already beginning to highlight Ng'ambo as a new centre of urban Zanzibar, so the bridging of the gap between urban planning, living culture and heritage promotion became even more urgent.

In a continuation of the Zans-Plan, the Department of Urban and Rural Planning approached the complex process of developing the Local Area Plan (LAP) of Ng'ambo as the future city centre of the town of Zanzibar. The plan was entitled *Ng'ambo Tuitakayo* (the buffer zone we want). It included ideas about heritage promotion and urban growth for sustainable development. It even proposed a new vision of urban conservation and heritage management, using a range of participatory processes to include people and their living cultures in the planning process.

This chapter will show how all these sometimes conflicting approaches and ideas were brought into one unified discussion about the future of Ng'ambo. Alongside the process of preparing the plan for Ng'ambo, discussions on the World Heritage and Sustainable Development policy (UNESCO 2015) were also intensified and the idea of a buffer zone was also clarified. The local authorities took the opportunity to exploit the idea of heritage for sustainable development to re-link conservation and urbanization. Four measures were agreed upon to achieve the articulation between heritage management and the new development plan for the buffer zone in order to promote social, economic and environmental sustainability. Today, 'N'gambo Tuitakayo' is a laboratory for the preparation of a National Urban Policy (NUP) in the Islands, placing culture, resilience and inclusiveness at the centre of development, a new step in the implementation of the New Urban Agenda and the Sustainable Development Goals.

Urban management and conservation in Zanzibar town

In 1927, the Islands of Zanzibar passed its first legislation concerning the protection of ancient monuments: *The Ancient Monuments Preservation Act, Cap 23 of 1927*. This piece of legislation was also enacted in other British colonial territories of East Africa. As the name indicates, the legislation focused mainly on monuments, which were defined as 'any edifice, which has historic, artistic and archaeological values' (GoZ 1927). When it comes to urban conservation and heritage management in Zanzibar, this legislation was a milestone, and served until the late 1980s. The next significant step in the domain of urban conservation in East Africa took place in the early 1970s.

This time the process was initiated in Lamu, a small coastal town in Kenya, where the authorities commissioned a preliminary survey on urban heritage and started planning for its conservation (Ghaidan 1976). This project not only pioneered new practices that were later adopted in many Swahili towns along the East African coast, but also laid down a foundation and introduced tools that are still used today across Eastern Africa. The approach to conservation was what we today might call a 'monumental approach', which mainly consisted of codified typologies of buildings and prescribed standards for their conservation (Heathcott 2013). Yet, the work in Lamu was a true catalyst for the progress of urban conservation and heritage management in the region. In Kenya, for example, the Government passed a new Antiquity and Monument Act in 1983, and in 1986 a plan for the conservation of the town of Lamu was realized (Siravo and Pulver 1986).

Following the example of Lamu, two new institutions were established in Zanzibar during the same period. Recommended by the United Nation Centre for Human Settlement (UNCHS 1983), a Stone Town Conservation and Development Authority (STCDA) was established in 1985 to deal with all issues related to urban conservation in the Stone Town area. In addition, a Department of Archives, Museums and Antiquities (DAMA) was established in 1986 to further enhance the heritage management system of Zanzibar. Yet, the biggest influence of the Lamu work on Zanzibar was in the preparation of the conservation Master Plan of Stone Town itself. This conservation Master Plan introduced the idea of a 'conservation area', derived from the 1964 Venice Charter and the 1976 UNESCO Recommendation concerning the Safeguarding and Contemporary Role of Historic Areas (Siravo 1996; LaNier and McQuillan 1983).

In fact, most Swahili towns appear to have a 'division' between the stones and the mud constructed areas. Yet, this was simply a division between the rich and the poor (Myers 1995). Over time, the construction materials manifested the social status of a community. In the case of Zanzibar, the 'division' line used to be a creek between Stone Town and the Ng'ambo area. Nevertheless, such divisions were temporary and fluctuated as a result of the economic and social transformations of a town (Sheriff 1995). With time, one area of Ng'ambo could be transformed and integrated into the core zone of Stone Town. This was based on the idea that 'Stone Town is a foetus and not a fossil' (Yahya 1995). However, in 1996, when the Conservation Master Plan of the Stone Town of Zanzibar was officially adopted, the division was structured, and Stone Town became the core conservation area. In 2000, when Stone Town was inscribed on the World Heritage sites list, the conservation area became the heritage zone and Ng'ambo its buffer zone.

Fixed heritage boundaries and 'conservation areas' hinder continuity between Stone Town and Ng'ambo and deter their management and development. This also relates closely to the way the local authorities interpret the idea of buffer zone. With this approach, social and cultural divisions were accentuated and legitimized, ultimately discouraging urban dynamism in the N'gambo area. In addition, as the mandate to manage the buffer zone is shared between the STCDA and the Zanzibar Municipality Council (ZMC), the buffer zone became a zone of conflicts around the management of heritage values. It also became a space symbolizing the difference in terms of the approach to urban conservation and management. Where the STCDA emphasized conservation and heritage management of the buffer zone and the historic city, ZMC highlighted planning, development and the transformation of the Ng'ambo area in order to cope with social and cultural dynamism. The tension has become even more noticeable since 2000, following the World Heritage inscription. The main issue became how the obligation to protect and manage the OUV of Stone Town could be achieved within a context of ever-increasing demands of the densifying urban context of Ng'ambo. With urban growth, the management of the buffer zone became more problematic. The dynamism of the social and economic growth of Ng'ambo stood in contrast with the attempt to conserve the heritage values of Stone Town.

The poor state of conservation of the Ng'ambo area, the threat of its rapid transformation and the conflicts between the institutions responsible for conservation management have been a concern of the World Heritage Committee since 2006,

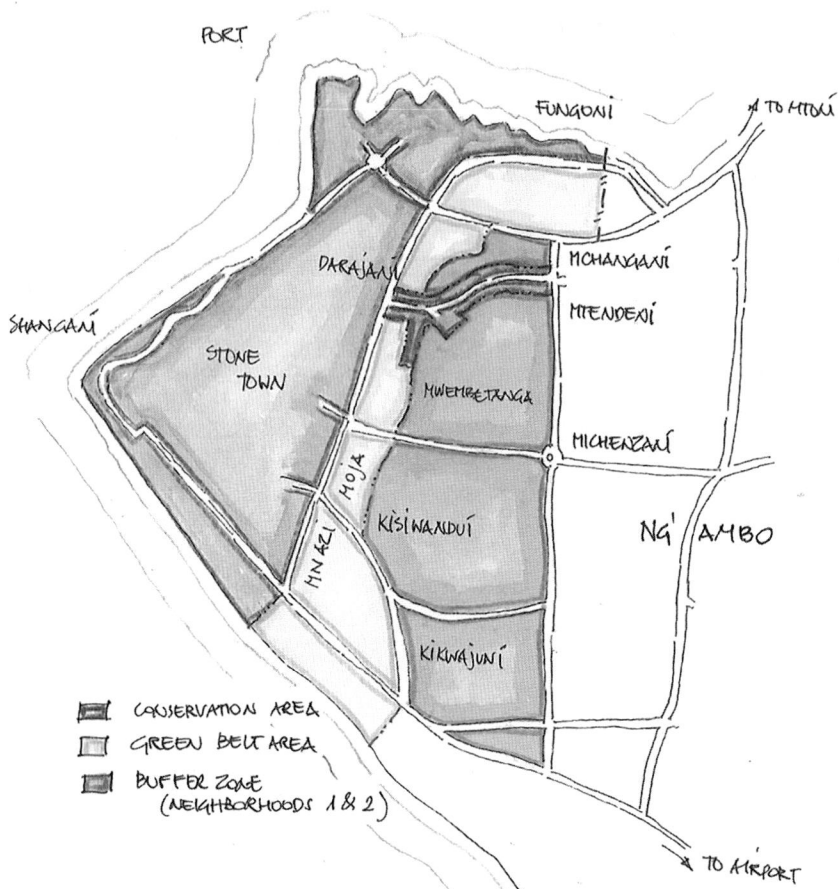

PORT

FUNGONI

A TO MTONI

MCHANGANI

MTENDENI

DARAJANI

SHANGANI

STONE
TOWN

MWEMBETANGA

MICHENZANI

MNAZI MOJA

KISIWANDUI

NG'AMBO

KIKWAJUNI

CONSERVATION AREA

GREEN BELT AREA

BUFFER ZONE
(NEIGHBORHOODS 1 & 2)

A TO AIRPORT

Figure 17.1 The sketch shows the spatial relation between Stone Town and Ng'ambo
Courtesy of the Department of Urban Planning, Zanzibar

during the first Reactive Monitoring Mission. For that reason, the local authorities reacted and manifested their intention to resolve issues related to the management of the Ng'ambo area. In this context, the discussions on the application of the HUL became an inspiration and common ground for both camps to find a new way for the development of the buffer zone as well as for the sustainability of a World Heritage site. It thereby became an opportunity to test the latest ideas and processes on 'how the management and conservation of World Heritage properties should contribute to fostering inclusive economic and social development, to improving environmental protection and to enhancing livelihoods, compatibly with the protection of their OUV' (UNESCO 2015).

Spatial planning and development of the Ng'ambo area

Historically, the Islands of Zanzibar share similar trends of development with other islands and towns along the coast of Eastern Africa, such as Shanga, Pate and Lamu (Middleton 1992). Chronicles of Arab travellers in the 10th century, and Portuguese conquerors in the 15th century offer testimonies about Swahili people, their islands and towns (Strandes 1971). Yet, the growth of the Islands of Zanzibar particularly accelerated in the 19th century, when the Sultan of Oman, Sayyid bin Said, shifted his court from Muscat to Zanzibar (Freeman-Greenville 1988). To solidify his power and increase his influence, Sayyid Said invited the British and Indian populations to be trading partners in a lucrative commerce of ivory, spices and slaves (Sheriff 1987, Pearce 1920). Until the beginning of the 20th century, the history and the character of Zanzibar Town was primarily the history of its centre: the Stone Town of Zanzibar.

With the Zanzibar Revolution of 1964, the situation changed. The new Revolutionary Council, in reaction to the previous regime, shifted the centre of Zanzibar town from Stone Town to Ng'ambo: the 'other side' of the creek. In 1968, the third Master Plan proposed an important upgrading scheme for the area. At the core of this national urban flagship program was a modern multi-level housing scheme. This so-called Michenzani scheme not only provided modern amenities but also introduced a new spatial order that accentuated the idea of Ng'ambo being different and divided from Stone Town (Sheriff 2010).

Figure 17.2 New urban landscape under the Michenzani Scheme
Courtesy of the Department of Urban Planning, Zanzibar

The fourth Master Plan in 1982, drafted by Chinese partners, did not attempt to bridge and harmonise the spatial gap between the two urban realities found in Stone Town and Ng'ambo (GoZ 1982). The growth of the Ng'ambo area accentuated the need to make it the centre of the Zanzibar town. Ng'ambo expanded from 208,571 inhabitants in 1985 to 611,000 inhabitants in 2015. Bearing in mind that by the year 2035, the total area of Zanzibar town is projected to have 1.5 million inhabitants (GoZ 2015b), one can better imagine the role of the Ng'ambo area in a broader urban context. With such growth, the pressures of densification and built development are ever-mounting. It is with this pressure of urban growth that the role, value and management of Ng'ambo must change: it is a question of protection and enhancement (Turner 2009). It can continue to be considered a buffer zone, a protective layer, but also with a different role, to add a layer of social and economic dynamism to enhance the value of the core zone.

The idea of a 'conservation area', as it has long been practiced in the management system, does not, however, encourage a new perspective for the buffer zone. Nor has it enhanced the urban continuity between two urban areas to create the overlapping space. Today, as a buffer zone, Ng'ambo remains a secondary zone of Stone Town, although social and economic dynamism requires a new understanding to integrate all aspects of the fast-growing urban development pressures.

For Ng'ambo, a different approach could be considered, which would respect the values of this historically and socially important part of town, while also accommodating the forces of change. The slogan of 'Ng'ambo Tuitakayo', 'the buffer we want', evokes that new thinking and interpretation of the buffer zone is in the making.

This idea is in line with a new vision of spatial planning in Zanzibar crafted in NSDS (GoZ 2015a), to harness both historic and social qualities and tap into the transformative forces of urbanization. This includes uniting around the target of making Zanzibar one of the most sustainable countries in Africa by 2030. Such discussions recall one of the main challenges faced by the historic city: namely the division and polarization between the core and the buffer zone. As the discussion from the HUL approach reveals, in a context where the complex relationship of a city is compromised, it is the sustainability of the historic city that suffers the most.

UNESCO recommendation on Historic Urban Landscape and sustainable development perspectives

The idea of the HUL approach was first introduced in Zanzibar in 2009, during a workshop organized by UNESCO and the Government of Zanzibar, to look at the application of the concept in an African context. The key word during this workshop was 'continuity'. The experts worried about the current practices of urban conservation that threaten the continuity of the historic towns, which is an essential element for their development and sustainability (Choay 1999). The relationship between the Stone Town of Zanzibar and its buffer zone Ng'ambo exemplified such challenges. The 2009 workshop led to other meetings and workshops in

Zanzibar, Lamu and Island of Mozambique and the publication of a report entitled *Swahili: Historic Urban Landscape* (van Oers 2013).

In 2013, the GoZ initiated a process to prepare the fifth Master Plan for the Zanzibar town, also called the Zanzibar Structural Plan or Zans-Plan 2015 (GoZ 2015b). During the same period, the United Nations was in an advanced stage of discussion about a shift from Millennium Goals to Sustainable Development Goals, and the UN-Habitat was preparing a New Urban Agenda. In Zanzibar, the preparation of the new Spatial Framework (NSDS-2015a) drew from these international processes and laid the ground for the debate taking place during the development of the Zans-Plan. NSDS has four pillars, but two of them, growth and environment, have a direct link to this issue. As such, the new Spatial Framework laid down principles that oriented the vision of the Zans-Plan by underlining two objectives: to harness the growth of Zanzibar town while maintaining the position of Stone Town, and to enhance the role of culture in urban planning and development in Zanzibar.

Again, capitalizing on the debate about Sustainable Development Goals and HUL, the department of Urban and Rural Planning (DoURP) initiated a new dynamism that envisaged making culture a central element for the urban development of Zanzibar town to achieve sustainability in all dimensions. This was grounded in a sustainable development perspective (SD) that advocated the promotion of values of a site to contribute to all dimensions of sustainable development where conservation and management strategies are aligned with broader sustainable development objectives. Again, from a sustainability perspective the issue of the buffer zone was further expanded to be considered as a 'planning tool' to enhance the benefit of the local communities as well as the heritage itself. To paraphrase words from the sustainability framework, the aim of the policy is to 'integrate conservation and management approaches for World Heritage properties within their larger regional planning frameworks, giving consideration in particular to the integrity of socio-ecological systems' (UNESCO 2015). Following wide discussions, it was quite logical for Zans-Plan to rethink the idea of a buffer zone and propose for Ng'ambo to be the new centre of the Zanzibar town. As the World Heritage and Sustainable Development policy proposes, 'the potential of buffer zones (and other similar tools) should be fully harnessed'. The proposal to make Ng'ambo the city centre was ultimately approved by the Government in 2017.

Ng'ambo Tuitakayo (the buffer zone we want) and inclusive social and economic development

The project of *Ng'ambo Tuitakayo* (the buffer zone we want), offered a new vision of Ng'ambo by shifting the current approach of heritage management. It changed its role from the buffer zone at the periphery, only there to protect Stone Town, 'as added layers of protection', to the centre that enhances and promotes culture for sustainable development. The process itself was very participatory with local communities, local stakeholders and multiple national and international partners, most notably UNESCO and the city of Amsterdam.[1] This initiative helped to combine the legitimate aspiration of the inhabitants of Ng'ambo to engage in the transformation of their urban space, while also safeguarding heritage values – both local and global. This involved a value-based approach associated with pluralistic meanings and human values about their living environment (Bandarin and van Oers 2015). Also, it was a test of how the HUL Recommendation could be applied in Zanzibar together with all dimensions of sustainability.

Intensive research, and the mapping of both tangible and intangible values of Ng'ambo together with several inventories, was then undertaken. Thematic workshops were organized with experts and local inhabitants along with two vision-formulating workshops for the whole town, in February 2013 and April 2015. On both occasions, the meetings were convened with inhabitants to explain the HUL approach, its target and procedures. In both thematic and vision workshops, inhabitants were keen to discuss the idea and to participate in the planning process having realized that the novel approach makes room for a transformation of their spaces and for promotion of their heritage values.

With different stakeholders and partners,[2] four steps were essential for overcoming the challenges of discontinuity between Stone Town and Ng'ambo. By integrating social and economic dynamics in urban conservation, the process sought to articulate heritage values in the context of promoting inclusive economic and social development of the buffer zone. The first step of the process was the preparation of a Local Area Plan for the Ng'ambo area (Ng'ambo-LAP). It introduces the idea

Figure 17.3 The visionary meeting with the community to discuss the Ng'ambo Project

Courtesy of the Department of Urban Planning, Zanzibar

of 'continuity' and the necessity of integrating the management system in the broader urban context. The new plan has changed the understanding of the meaning and the role of the buffer zone. The buffer zone of the Stone Town of Zanzibar has now become a planning tool to 'enhance mutual benefits for local and other concerned communities and for the heritage itself' (UNESCO 2015). Hence, with the new Local Area Plan, Ng'ambo has become both the buffer of the UNESCO Heritage site and the centre of the Zanzibar town.

The new approach also touches upon ideas of good governance and social justice. One of the issues that was discussed during the discussion of HUL was a need to reform the current system of urban management. The control mechanism in the institutional framework for the development of the Ng'ambo area lacked transparency. In response, a new institution, the Development Control Unit (DCU) was established to facilitate the new management system of the Ng'ambo area, by allowing both the STCDA and the ZMC to discuss together the future development of Ng'ambo. Hence, the second step was thus the establishment of DCU to allow for broader consultation and participation of the community. This would also enhance questions of social cohesion, a key factor for inclusive social development.

The third step was the creation of a forum to enhance inclusiveness and involvement of local inhabitants and communities. The involvement of the local communities, stakeholders and partners in decision making has not only given credibility to the Ng'ambo plan itself, but also offered room to 'recognise, respect, and include the values as well as cultural and environmental place-knowledge of local communities' in the planning process (UNESCO 2015). It has allowed the local institutions to learn how consultation and participation can be used as positive tools for integration and ownership. This has led to an emphasis on inclusive and participatory approaches for all proposed development projects to make local inhabitants willing to participate in the future development of their town and to promote their own wellbeing.

In addition, by underlining connectivity, vibrancy and inclusiveness the pilot project of Ng'ambo Tuitakayo has already helped local authorities to better understand and respect the social and cultural values of Stone Town and its buffer zone. This was essential for the government to practically realize that the respect and integration of local cultural and heritage aspects in a value-based methodology is worthwhile and can be used in other places as well. It potentially allows for the emergence of civic conscience for the inhabitants of the town through a process of 'planning by the people'. This is a novel approach, which may very well enhance sustainability and resilience. It notably allows the inhabitants of Ng'ambo to see, understand and believe in a possible equilibrium between conservation and development. It also forges the potential of strong partnerships for sustainable development by encouraging partners to work together.

Finally, the presence of partners both local and international allows for the harnessing of best practice and encourages the exchange of experiences and lessons learnt. This is the fourth step which was instrumental in the creation of projects. Current projects in Ng'ambo, such as the Green Corridor, the development of mixed-used centres and the construction of new bus terminal have benefited from these experiences. They not only seek to create employment, but also enhance the vibrancy of Ng'ambo as well as Stone Town. They can be considered activities that contribute towards enabling 'enduring, inclusive, equitable and sustainable economic development, as well as full, productive and decent employment for local communities, including marginalized populations' (UNESCO 2015).

Conclusion

This chapter shows how the pilot project of Ng'ambo Tuitakayo attempted to better implement the 1972 Convention in the spirit of promoting inclusive economic and social development and environmental protection in order to integrate a Sustainable Development Perspective. Like many towns in Africa, Zanzibar Town is now facing rapid urban growth and needs an innovative approach to accommodate the different parameters of urban development. Research and inventory efforts realized in Ng'ambo have shown that all dimensions of sustainability of this area could be enhanced through a new comprehensive Spatial Framework that emphasises the link between spatial development and culture promotion. However, with an out-dated interpretation of the status of the buffer zone, Ng'ambo was isolated and only considered as a protective layer. Its fabric was considered insignificant, and its values were marginalized. By adopting new perspectives promoted by the historical urban landscape and sustainable development approaches, a new planning process was initiated to change this understanding.

With the new Local Area Plan (Ng'ambo Tuitakayo), Ng'ambo is becoming a place of enhancement that enables the articulation between heritage values in the context of inclusive economic and social development.

The UNESCO Recommendation on HUL and discussions on sustainable development have been instrumental in shifting the ways in which the heritage, culture and development of Zanzibar town are being articulated. This allowed for a new understanding of the buffer zone to emerge, which links it to the different dimensions of sustainability. This new framework has also offered possibilities for the local authorities to face the challenge of addressing development by linking Stone Town with its larger territory. In fact, the classical approach that codifies typologies and limits the understanding of heritage, conservation and management hindered a more unifying effort to deal with the issues of a buffer zone of the Stone Town of Zanzibar. The HUL approach showed a new direction where the question of links between culture and development could be discussed, allowing for a new perspective of sustainable development to emerge.

Notes

1 An NGO from Amsterdam called African Architecture Matters (AAMatters) has also been an important partner since the inception of the first initiatives regarding Ng'ambo in 2013.

2 Zanzibar Social Security Fund (ZSSF); the People's Bank of Zanzibar (PBZ); UN-Habitat; Shelter Africa; the city of Amsterdam; African Architecture Matters (AA Matters) and Stadsherstel from Amsterdam.

References

Bandarin, F. and van Oers, R. (2015). *The Historic Urban Landscape: Managing Heritage in an Urban Century*. Chichester, UK: Wiley-Blackwell.

Choay, F. (1999). *L'allégorie du patrimoine*. Paris: Seuil.

Freeman-Greenville, G. S. P. (1988). *The Swahili Coast, 2nd to 19th Centuries: Islam, Christianity and Commerce in Eastern Africa*. Oxford: Variorum Collected Studies.

Ghaidan, U. (1976). *Lamu: A Study in Conservation*. Nairobi: The East African Literature Bureau.

Government of Zanzibar (GoZ) (1927). *The Ancient Monuments Preservation Act, Cap 23 of 1927*. Zanzibar. Governement Press.

Government of Zanzibar (GoZ) (1982). *Zanzibar Master Plan, 1982*. Zanzibar. Governement Press.

Government of Zanzibar (GoZ) (2015a). *National Spatial Development Strategy*. Zanzibar. Government Press.

Government of Zanzibar (GoZ) (2015b). *Zanzibar Master Plan* (ZansPlan). Zanzibar. Government Press.

Government of Zanzibar (GoZ) (2017). Socio-Economic Survey 2016, The Office of the Chief Government Statistician, Zanzibar.

Heathcott, J. (2013). 'Historic urban landscape: The Swahili Coast: New framework for conservation', in R. van Oers and S. Haraguchi (eds), *Swahili: Historic Urban Landscape: Report on the Historic Urban Landscape and Field Activities in the Swahili Coast in East Africa*. Paris: UNESCO, pp. 20–39.

LaNier, R. and McQuillan, D. A. (1983). *The Stone Town of Zanzibar: A Strategy for Integrated Development*. Unpublished Working Document commissioned by the United Nations Centre for Human Settlements (UNCHS). Nairobi.

Middleton, J. (1992). *The World of the Swahili: African Mercantile Civilization*. New Haven: Yale University Press.

Myers, G. A. (1995). 'The early history of the "other side" of Zanzibar Town', in A. Sheriff (ed), *The History and Conservation of Zanzibar Stone Town*. London: Eastern Africa Studies, pp. 30–45.

Pearce, F. B. (1920). *Zanzibar: The Island Metropolis of East Africa*. London: Unwin.

Sheriff, A. (1987). *Slave, Spices and Ivory in Zanzibar*. London: James Currey.

Sheriff, A. (ed) (1995). *The History and Conservation of Zanzibar Stone Town*. London: Eastern Africa Studies.

Sheriff, A. (2010). *Dhow Cultures of the Indian Ocean: Cosmopolitanism, Commerce and Islam*. London: C. Hurst & Co.

Siravo, F. (1996). *Zanzibar: A Plan for the Historic Stone Town*. Geneva: The Aga Khan Trust for Culture.

Siravo, F. and Pulver, A. (1986). *Planning Lamu: Conservation of an East African Sea Port*. Nairobi: National Museums of Kenya.

Strandes, J. (1971). *The Portuguese Period in East Africa*. Nairobi: East African Literature Bureau.

Turner, M. (2009). 'Introduction', in O. Martin and G. Piatti (eds), *World Heritage and Buffer Zones* [World Heritage Papers No. 25]. Paris: UNESCO, pp. 15–18.

UNESCO (2011). *Recommendation on the Historic Urban Landscape* (online). Available at: http://whc.unesco.org/en/hul/ (accessed 16 November 2017).

UNESCO (2015). *Policy Document for the Integration of a Sustainable Development Perspective into the Processes of the World Heritage Convention* (online). Available at: http://whc.unesco.org/en/sustainabledevelopment/ (accessed 16 November 2017).

UN-Habitat (2014). *World Urbanisation Prospects* (online). Available at: https://esa.un.org/unpd/wup/publications/files/wup2014-highlights.pdf (accessed 16 November 2017).

van Oers, R. (2013). 'Applying HUL in East Africa', in R. van Oers and S. Haraguchi (eds), *Swahili: Historic Urban Landscape: Report on the Historic Urban Landscape and Field Activities in the Swahili Coast in East Africa*. Paris: UNESCO.

World Bank (2009), *Reshaping Economic Geography*, World Development Report 2009, Washington, DC, World Bank.

Yahya, S. (1995). 'Zanzibar Stone Town: Fossil or foetus', in A. Sheriff (ed), *The History and Conservation of Zanzibar Stone Town*. London: Eastern Africa Studies, pp. 116–120.

Chapter 18

Cooperative post-disaster reconstruction of Xijie historic quarter, China

Directing conservation practice towards inclusive social and economic development

Zhou Jian

The Xijie historic quarter is located in the buffer zone of the 'Dujiangyan Irrigation System' World Heritage site, covers an area of 4.03 hectares and comes under the administration of Dujiangyan city. On 12 May 2008, China's Sichuan province experienced one of its most devastating earthquakes measuring 8 M_s,[1] during which the Xijie historic quarter was severely damaged. Eighty per cent of the buildings in the historic quarter could not continue functioning. A reconstruction project started in 2009 and was completed in 2013 (Figures 18.1 and 18.2).

Within the current policy framework in China, the conservation of historic quarters is generally implemented in a 'top-down' approach. Governments and/or markets are the main actors for investments and implementation. Due to the special background of post-disaster reconstruction and considerations concerning the sustainable development of the region, the Xijie reconstruction project adopted an innovative policy design and a cooperative working approach in response to local residents' requests for housing improvement and employment security (Dujiangyan People's Government 2009). It actively involved the key stakeholders, especially house owners, in the whole process of the reconstruction and broke through some policy restrictions on the use and transaction of houses. The Xijie project tried to explore a practical way to synergize physical heritage conservation with community development in an urban context. Upon completion of the project, Xijie historic quarter has been transformed from a declining area to a prosperous tourism district, which indicates clearly the contribution of cultural heritage to sustainable urban development (Tongji Urban and Social Science Research Centre 2016). In line with the UNESCO policy on World Heritage and Sustainable Development (2015), this chapter describes the reconstruction process of Xijie historic quarter and the role of conservation practices in promoting social and economic inclusion of the heritage community (Shanghai Tongji Urban Design and Research Institute 2009).

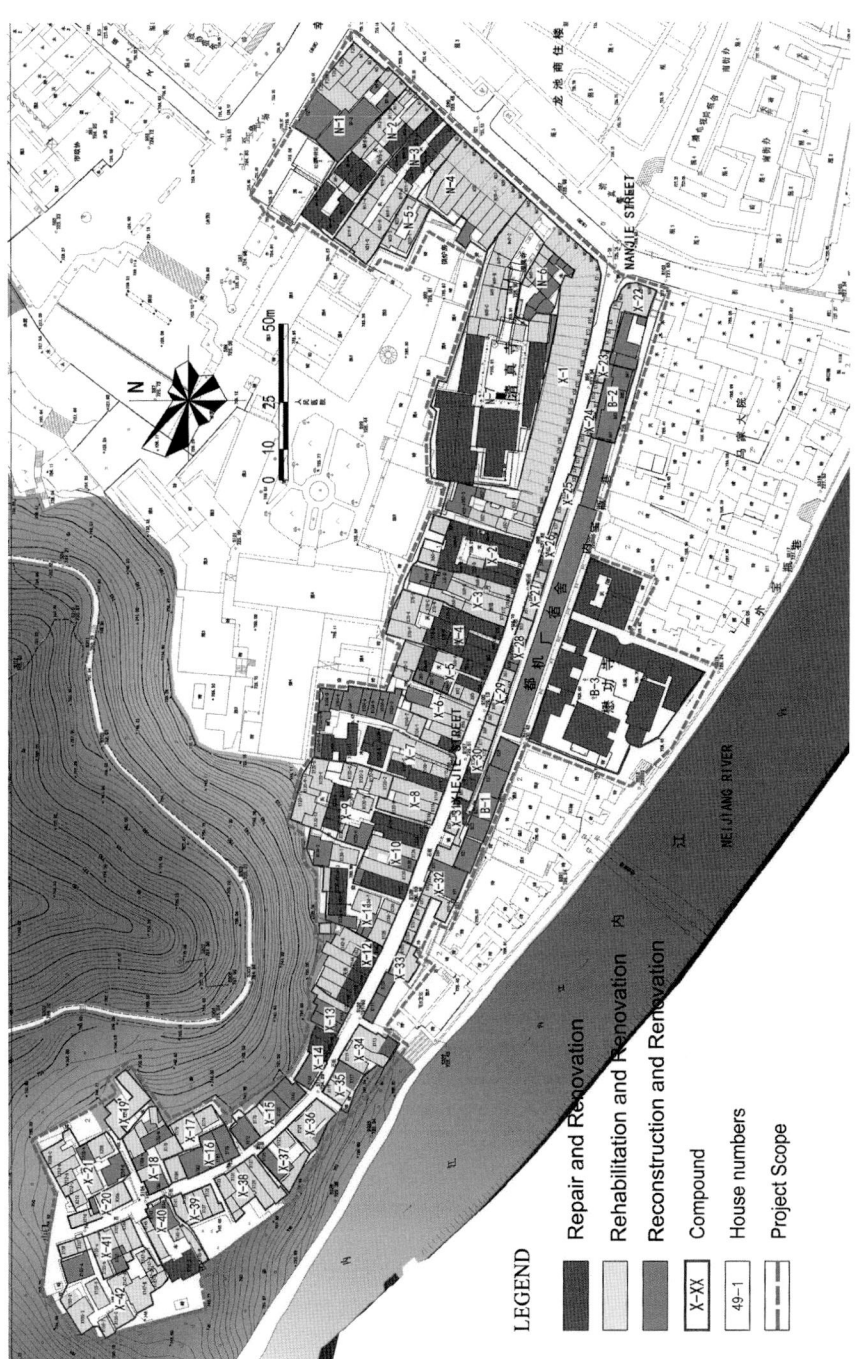

Figure 18.1 Geographic scope of the Xijie reconstruction project and building classifications on conservation interventions

Source: Zhou Jian

Figure 18.2 Comparison of streetscapes before and after the Xijie reconstruction project
Photos: Zhou Jian

Policy design for multiple objectives

Heritage

The Xijie historic quarter was first constructed during the years of Jiajing in the Ming Dynasty (1522–1566 CE). It is the starting point of the Song Mao ancient route and the strategic pass from the Tibet Plateau to Chengdu Plain. More than 70 per cent of the buildings in the Xijie historic quarter have been standing for over 100 years, one of which is a major historical and cultural site protected at the provincial level, while two others are protected at the city level.

Community

Before the Wenchuan Earthquake in 2008, the infrastructure and residential buildings in the Xijie historic quarter had not been upgraded for over 20 years. Since the 1990s, Xiejie people have slowly migrated out to new urban districts that are better equipped with infrastructure and where residences are more spacious. The Xijie historic quarter has been one of the areas in Dujiangyan city where underprivileged groups were most concentrated, making heritage buildings and local communities very vulnerable to external forces. The Xijie historic quarter was characterized as a district with many seniors and underprivileged people. According to the survey prepared for the reconstruction project, there were 391 households in the Xijie historic quarter, and almost every household had at least one senior (that is, over 65 years old) in the family. There were around 100 seniors aged over 70, and more than 40 seniors were over 80. Forty-two households were identified by the government as low-income families. Seventy-six per cent of the households were living in homes smaller than 30 square meters, and more than 90 per cent of the households had no sanitary facilities in their houses.

Objectives

The destructive impact of the Wenchuan Earthquake brought a major reconstruction project onto the local government agenda. Based on the general post-disaster reconstruction policy – that is, housing reconstruction and urban transformation – the city of Dujiangyan included the conservation of cultural heritage in its post-disaster reconstruction policy, with the four-fold aim of regenerating old districts through the re-use of cultural heritage, developing cultural tourism, increasing job opportunities and benefiting local communities as well as individuals. These were refined down to three objectives when the local government developed the policy design for the Xijie reconstruction project: heritage conservation, housing improvement and tourism development.

Policy design

The Xijie reconstruction project put emphasis on cooperation in its policy design. First of all, it offered ample choices for individual housing improvement. Local residents could exchange their private properties for residences newly constructed by the government in new urban districts. The lowest standard for the replaced residences was 16 square metres per person or 70 square metres per household without charge. Alternatively, they could take monetary compensation offered through the governmental requisition, or they could stay in Xijie and repair/reconstruct their properties with a fixed subsidy (1200 RMB per square metre) from the government. For historic buildings identified in the conservation plan, the government took on the full repair cost. Second, it allowed the transition of residential buildings to tourism usages or cultural services, without charge, whereas according to the regulation a land transition fee normally applies to landowners when the use of land changes. Third, the Xijie historic quarter was identified in the zoning scheme as an 'opening tourism' district, which indicated further investment and infrastructure improvement from the government.

This policy was designed to relieve the financial burdens of local residents in the process of their housing improvement. Due to the profitable prospect thus provided by the project, local residents were more willing to participate in the conservation and reconstruction of the historic quarter, and this also encouraged more active involvement of other partners, such as local entrepreneurs and tourism practitioners. The policy design reflected clearly the intention of local government to develop heritage tourism and to actively involve local residents in the reconstruction project.

Cooperative implementation

Public-private partnerships

The project was designed and implemented through close cooperation among concerned governmental agencies, state-owned enterprises, local communities/residents and universities (Figure 18.3). The governmental agencies were

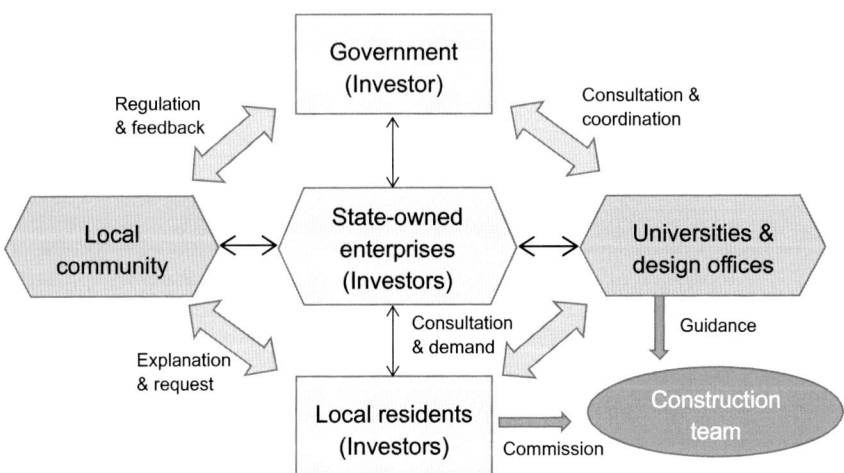

Figure 18.3 Partnerships in cooperative implementation

Source: Zhou Jian

responsible for managing and providing subsidies/funds for the reconstruction project, for organizing relevant community participation activities as well as for investing in municipal facilities and public space. The state-owned enterprises were in charge of the reconstruction and re-use of emptied residential properties, which were replaced with new residences in new urban districts. Local residents took care of their own housing reconstruction. The universities offered their expertise to compile a conservation plan and provide technical support to design schemes in consultation with local residents; they also took on responsibilities in public consultation, policy advice and community advocacy. Table 18.1 below shows the project items and funding resources.

Table 18.1 Project items and funding resources in partnerships

Items	Sub-items and scale	Funding resources in partnerships	Amount (US$10,000)
Reconstruction of municipal facilities	Road network, pipelines, electric power cables, public toilets, the city wall, and public signage	Post-earthquake Reconstruction Fund from the Central Government	2,812.5
		Dujiangyan Municipal Government	134.6
		Chengtou Co.	96.8
Restoration and repair of the Mosque	3430 m^2	Owner's self-finance (the Mosque)	63.5
		Post-earthquake Reconstruction Fund from the Central Government	43.6
		State Religious Affairs Fund	16.6
Restoration of Maogong Temple	2815.15 m^2	Owner's self-finance (Xingyan Co.)	274.3
Compensation to residents (owners/ renters)	3200 m^2	Post-earthquake Reconstruction Fund from the Central Government	417.2
Restoration/ reconstruction of public properties	3500 m^2	Owner's self-finance (Xingyan Co.)	174.7
Repair/ reconstruction of private properties	12173.57 m^2	Owner's self-finance (residents)	294.6
		Post-earthquake Reconstruction Fund from the Central Government	167.3
		Dujiangyan Municipal Government	68.2
Total			**4563.9**

Community participation

Within the policy framework, the government introduced an effective community-participation procedure in order to enable local residents to make their own decisions on their properties and participate in relevant design process throughout the Xijie reconstruction project. At the community level, local residents were organized around residential courtyards. Between three and ten households were grouped together to establish a homeowners' committee to pursue their best interests in discussions with government agencies, planners, architects and construction teams during the process of the project implementation. The community participation was designed in five steps:

1   introduction to the conservation plan;
2   public advocacy of community participation;
3   establishment of homeowners' committees;
4   survey on demands and feedbacks;
5   decision-making by homeowners about their private properties, including putting forward design requests, confirming design schemes, choosing construction teams with the technical support from community planners and supervising the implementation and quality of their own projects.

IMPORTANT ACTIONS AND CHALLENGES

Community planners

The Xijie project had employed a brand-new policy design. Therefore, the first challenge lay in the difficulties experienced by local residents in understanding the policy and its implementation mechanism. A group of experts, including urban planners, architects and social workers, worked on-site on a daily basis. They played an important role in coordinating various interests of stakeholders, in relation to policy design and technical support. They were responsible for introducing the conservation plan, explaining policy design and technical requests on the preservation and reconstruction of residential buildings and clarifying the development visions for Xijie historic quarter. They were in frequent contact with local homeowners, listening to homeowner requests and adopting in a fair manner reasonable homeowner proposals. They were also in charge of examining the design schemes proposed jointly by architects and homeowners and making necessary revisions in consultation with homeowners. Meanwhile, during the implementation, they were also responsible for supervising the progress of construction and giving technical guidance on-site.

The second challenge was associated with conflicts between the demands of local residents and the current regulations on land-use right and title to a housing property. For example, local residents demanded strongly that they be allowed to keep their illegally constructed toilets. Due to the lack of sanitary facilities before the reconstruction project, it was quite common to find that local residents had built toilets in their courtyards without government permission. By simply dismantling those illegal constructions and integrating their functions into the residence, the living areas for other functions would be reduced, which would create difficulties in the daily use of their residences, particularly for those living in rather small residences. The community planner had conducted a survey for households with such problems and adjusted the district plan in consultation with government agencies. By this means, the traditional courtyards were restored by removing the illegal constructions and an additional 2.5 square metres for each household was approved in order to integrate a new toilet into their redesigned residences.

Demonstration project

The third challenge was encountered at the beginning, when most people were very hesitant to participate in the reconstruction project. Homeowners did not have a clear idea about the requirements of the conservation plan, the method of housing reconstruction and relevant costs (according to the policy, homeowners should cover repair costs over and above the government subsidy). Therefore, most of them tended to stay on the sidelines. In response to this situation, in April 2010, a demonstration project was launched at a public-owned housing property. The demonstration project adopted a traditional timber structure with traditional building materials and techniques. It employed waterproofing and insulating materials and added a separate kitchen and toilet for a better living quality. The demonstration project enabled local residents to understand the conservation requirements and the quality of the reconstructed housing in a direct way. Meanwhile, the costs for the reconstruction and repair were made public in order to serve as a practical reference for local residents when they considered the agreement with the government.

Signing agreements

Following the demonstration project, the voluntary application period for participating in the reconstruction project started in July 2010. Within three months, 60 per cent of the households had signed the agreement with the government for their participation and within eight months, 99 per cent of the households had signed. The reconstruction project proceeded in the sequence set out in the signed individual agreements and was carried out by four construction teams, one household after another. In this way, the earlier repaired houses became the prototypes and encouraged their neighbours to participate in the project.

Customized housing design scheme

Another challenge was the diverse and individual demands of homeowners regarding the reconstruction, repair or improvement of their houses. In order to respect these requests and to preserve the diversity of heritage assets, architects were employed by the government to provide a customized housing design scheme for each household. In total, more than ten architects from five different firms were involved in this reconstruction project. Through continuous discussion with homeowners, they provided individual solutions and design schemes according to the specific situation of each household, satisfying both the requirements of the conservation plan and the functional requests of homeowners (Figure 18.4).

Improving public facilities and environment

The reconstruction project went beyond individual housing repair, such as updating kitchens and sanitary facilities. It also repaved the streets, separated storm water and sewerage, designed new underground pipeline systems with added natural gas pipelines, established a circuit route for firefighting trucks, updated fire hydrants and installed an all-weather monitoring system.

Figure 18.4 Examples of interior after repairs

Photos: Zhou Jian

Re-use of replaced properties

Some local residents substituted their properties in Xijie with new residences in new urban districts. Those properties left in the Xijie historic quarter were handled by the state-owned enterprises in three main ways:

1   Some were demolished to make way for a new circuit route for firefighting trucks or for the exhibition of city wall ruins.
2   Others were repaired and/or reconstructed as public cultural or community facilities;
3   Yet others were repaired and/or reconstructed as tourism service facilities.

Conclusions

Improvement of community capacity and social inclusion

The capacity of local communities to play a key role in the conservation and the sustainable development of heritage sites has been strengthened as a result of the Xijie reconstruction policy. Through participating in the reconstruction project, local residents improved their capacity to re-use their heritage and reconfirmed the asset value of their heritage by putting it to a viable use (Zhong and Kou 2015). At the same time, they gained fair and significant development opportunities and the social status of the Xijie historic quarter has been greatly improved.

Through agreement between private homeowners and the government, public funds were invested in the repair of private properties, heritage conservation and the improvement of the local living environment. The policy design of the Xijie reconstruction project paid special attention to the low-income families and helped private homeowners to deal with their financial shortage in housing repair. In line with the conservation plan, community participation throughout the project enabled full respect to be paid to the decision-making power of local residents in the design and construction of their housing. The policy encouraged heritage properties to accommodate new functions through adapting to the specific requirements of individual homeowners. It also allowed greater autonomy of homeowners in dealing with their properties. After the repair or reconstruction, some homeowners chose to live in or manage the properties themselves; some decided to partially or fully rent them out on a commercial basis; while some ended up selling their properties. The newcomers, whether they were new residents or new merchants, integrated well with the original residents in this process, which prevented the heritage site from becoming an 'isolated island' within the wider city. Meanwhile, it improved the social resilience of local communities.

Upon completion of the reconstruction project in 2015, a social survey with local residents was conducted. The data showed that only one household was not satisfied with the project policies. Ninety per cent of households were satisfied with their housing condition after repair or reconstruction. More than 80 per cent of households were satisfied with the improvement of the infrastructure. More than 70 per cent of households were satisfied with the neighbourhood relationships and none said they were unsatisfied. Local residents expressed a higher level of trust in their communities and local organizations. In general, after the reconstruction project, local residents are more satisfied with and proud of the Xijie historic quarter (Figure 18.5).

Win-win cooperation towards a continuous economic growth

The established public-private partnerships and the creative policies on heritage conservation with respect to multiple stakeholders' interests made it possible to achieve more than the three objectives defined at the beginning; that is, heritage conservation, housing improvement and tourism development. The successful implementation of the Xijie project has driven the regeneration and development

Figure 18.5 Comparison before and after the Xijie reconstruction project
Photos: Zhou Jian

of a wider area. Effective re-use of heritage properties enabled heritage conservation as a valuable resource to generate further wealth for the civil society.

People who replaced their properties in the Xijie historic quarter with newly constructed housing in new urban districts have resettled with better living conditions, while local residents who remained in the historic quarter enjoyed the subsidies from the government and the professional support from community planners/architects for their housing repairs or reconstruction. The repaired or reconstructed residences offered more safety, comfort and functionality to local residents. The whole public environment and urban infrastructure have been updated. Through the Xijie reconstruction project, not only were the physical fabrics much improved, building heritage restored and spatial quality of the streets enhanced, but the district also became more attractive and economically more vibrant through newly introduced functions, such as tourism services supported by the government and small-scale businesses and services initiated by the local residents. The real estate price and rentals have increased four to five times since the completion of the project. Both homeowners and local enterprises had considerable financial gains. On weekends and public holidays, daily tourists in the historic quarter number over 20,000. This means that the district is generating more tax income for the local government, and the tourism development of the whole Dujiangyan city is further boosted.

Experience and lessons learned for future implementation

In order to meet the multiple objectives set out at the beginning of the Xijie reconstruction project; that is, heritage conservation, housing improvement and tourism development, a cooperative implementation, including active community participation, has been employed during the policy design. Accordingly, a number of concrete measures and innovative actions have been developed in response to various challenges encountered in the process, such as hesitation in participating, conflicts with current regulations on land-use right and individual demands of homeowners on housing improvement. The project has delivered satisfactory results in dealing with the complicated and difficult situation of post-disaster reconstruction. The achievements of the project have also been acknowledged among peer reviewers. However, due to the constraints of current national policies on land use and housing and the prevailing top-down approach of urban conservation, there are still many obstacles along the way to promote the policy design and the approach adopted in this project.

Following the completion of the Xijie reconstruction project in 2013, local residents gradually left the historic quarter by renting out or selling their properties. The follow-up social survey indicated that it was not their original intention to leave the Xijie historic quarter. After the reconstruction, rental and real estate prices of the historic quarter have increased to a much higher level than other areas in the city. For example, the rental price in the historic quarter was more than twice as expensive as other urban districts in average. Therefore, local residents were more willing to leave the quarter so that they could afford bigger housing in other areas. During the return visit in 2015, ten per cent of the surveyed residents in the Xijie historic quarter were not very satisfied with their repaired or reconstructed housing, mainly due to the construction quality. The survey also indicated a perceived lack of public space in the historic quarter. The return visit also found out that a number of homeowners and business owners had made unauthorized modifications to the façades of traditional buildings.

These negative outcomes were not expected during the project planning, and therefore counter measures were not well prepared. There are a few lessons that can be learned from this project for future implementation. First, although community participation procedures ensured the proper rights of homeowners, the duties and obligations of beneficiaries were not well defined in the policy design. For instance, maintaining the traditional façades of heritage buildings should be the obligation of homeowners who received government subsidies. Second, contractual provisions should include pre-arranged plans to deal with conflicts of interests, particularly when multiple stakeholders are involved. For example, the complaints about the construction quality of repaired/reconstructed housing as previously mentioned could be easily solved if such provisions were defined in advance. Third, information and/or materials for community consultation should be well prepared and explained to ensure that local stakeholders share a common understanding and acquire enough information for decision-making. The perceived lack of public space reflected in the survey is related to the lack of effort in explaining maps and figures to local residents in the planning process. Last but not least, the speed and impact of gentrification should not be underestimated or overlooked, in particular for practices aimed at safeguarding living heritage.

Note

1 Surface wave magnitude is one of the magnitude scales in seismology to categorize earthquakes.

References

Dujiangyan People's Government (2009). *Implementation Scheme for Housing Improvement and Protective Re-Use of Xijie Historic Quarter in Dujiangyan City*. Internal DPG Report. Unpublished.

Shanghai Tongji Urban Design and Research Institute (2009). *Conservation Plan of Xijie Historic Quarter in Dujiangyan City*. Internal STUDRI Report. Unpublished.

Tongji Urban and Social Science Research Centre (2016). *Evaluation Report on the Implementation of the Xijie Reconstruction Project*. Internal TUSSRC Report. Unpublished.

UNESCO (2015). *Policy Document for the Integration of a Sustainable Development Perspective into the Processes of the World Heritage Convention* (online). Available at: http://whc.unesco.org/en/sustainabledevelopment/ (accessed 2 December 2017).

Zhong, Xiaohua and Kou, Huaiyun (2015). 'Influence of community participation on the historic block conservation: A case study on the post-disaster reconstruction of Xijie historic block, Dujiangyan city', *Journal of City Planning Review*, 39(337), 87–94. Beijing: City Planning Review.

Index

Page numbers in italic indicate a figure and page numbers in bold indicate a table.